A GLAC
REPORT

A GLACKIN REPORT

My Life of Luck and Law

John Glackin

First published in 2022 by
John Glackin, Dublin, Ireland

Library of Congress Cataloguing-in-Publication Data are available for this book.

A CIP catalogue record for this book is available from the British Library.

ISBN: 978-1-9993234-9-3 (Paperback)

Copyediting: Myles McCionnaith
Cover design and layout: Carrowmore.ie
Printed in Ireland by Sprint Print

CONTENTS

FOREWORD

This book is the culmination of a process that probably commenced when I first made some entries in a diary while in my early teens. I cannot say that I diligently kept a diary since then but in every year since then, almost sixty years ago, I made some entries in a diary. As I got older, I became more diligent, perhaps as my memory capacity reduced. In my late sixties, after I had ceased involvement in my profession and in sports administration, I started to research my ancestors and put together a family tree but then tried to find out more about the lives of those ancestors. I found that interesting but frustrating, as there was no easy manner to do so and no single source for any one of them. By the time that I developed my new interest, my parents were long dead and records were scarce.

My wife, Mary, suggested that I record my own life story so that my descendants, if they ever developed a similar interest, would have some basis to work from and not end up as frustrated as I sometimes did. After some subtle prompting over a couple of years, I did eventually commence to do so in February 2020. Little did I realise that, within a couple of weeks, the country would enter lockdown because of Covid 19 and that senior citizens like me would be expected to 'cocoon'. What started as a fairly simple project developed in ambition over the next few months and I found myself enjoying the process as I reminisced about relations who had died, friends and acquaintances, some of who I had forgotten about and had not seen for many years, and occasions and events both happy and sad. I read through those diaries and records that I had retained and looked back at old photographs and newspapers – and, of course, in some instances used Google and Wikipedia to help my memory.

I often became distracted or lost momentum, not making progress for weeks at a time, but gradually the story took shape and I saw that it might have an interest beyond my immediate descendants. At a certain stage, perhaps twelve months after I started, it occurred to me that I should consider publication, at least to the extent of having my writing printed. I read about and then contacted Ronan Colgan of Carrowmore Publishing and this moved my project to a different level by his advice and professionalism. He also introduced me to Myles Mac Cionnaith who edited and proof read my drafts and was of significant assistance to me.

There is no doubt that it requires some level of egotism to write about yourself and hope that others might want to read about it but, having admitted that, I believe that history should be the story of ordinary individuals and not limited to the story of wars, famines, kings, queens and despots. I hope that more people like me take the effort to record their own life story as I believe that history is your story, my story, his story, her story, and it is the combination of all these stories that will give future generations a reasonably clear picture of life in our times. This is not intended as an academic treatise, rather it is a collection of facts, impressions, opinions and recollections and I trust that the reader will recognise the distinction.

Before signing off on the book, I want to acknowledge the encouragement, patience and assistance that I have received from my wife, Mary, my son Shane and my daughters, Louisa and Sinead, and to thank them sincerely for that. Not only have they been a major part of my life story but they have contributed immensely to my sense of happiness and pride and their love has been a great source of inspiration to me from the beginning.

Other friends have helped in different ways; some by reading extracts of early drafts for me and making helpful suggestions, others by helping my reminiscing and others by simple encouragement. I won't mention individuals by name but I do very much appreciate their contribution.

However, they are not responsible for all errors that might remain, and any such are my responsibility. To those who do read the book, I hope that you enjoy it, that it helps to bring back some good memories for you and that it encourages you to follow suit.

INTRODUCTION

Known as John, Seán, Tubby, Jack, Johnny, Glackin and Glacko at various times during my life – and, indeed, interchangeably – I never really had a preference. But if asked at any stage what my name was, I invariably answered John. I'm sure I was called other names at different times, but not to my face. I was christened John; I was sometimes dubbed Jack by my father; I was called Seán in primary school (where the Irish language was regularly used). From the age of about 10, I was nicknamed Tubby – some old schoolmates who I've not met in years might still call me by the nickname. More recently, and to most friends, I am Johnny. But I'm still John to family and those who know me best. Some teachers called me Glackin, as teachers were wont to do, and some of the younger members of the Leinster Rugby squad called me Glacko when I was branch president. I don't think in either case there was a lack of respect; I prefer to think it was more a case of familiarity without the contempt. I don't think the variety of names has adversely affected me, but others can judge that.

Born on 7 September 1948 in the National Maternity Hospital, Holles Street, Dublin, I experienced the narrow dividing line between good and bad luck very early in life – the first of a number of such occasions. Within two days of my birth, I was unlucky to develop double pneumonia. I was at serious risk of not getting to enjoy the life I have but was very lucky that there was an excellent young doctor on duty at the time, Dr Kieran O'Driscoll, who later became the master of the maternity hospital. Dr O'Driscoll was training in obstetrics but had to perform some paediatric medicine as well when he was on call. It was my mother who relayed this information to me many years later, and I know that she had a very high regard for Dr O'Driscoll and the hospital. I survived; indeed, at a later stage in my life, I became the legal adviser to that hospital and met and advised a number of subsequent masters of the hospital in my professional capacity.

It was nearly ten years later when I experienced this narrow dividing line again. I had broken my leg when cycling out of the lane adjoining Belgrove Boys' National School, in Clontarf, onto Seafield Road one Saturday afternoon during rehearsals for the school concert. I collided with a car being driven by the mother of one of my school colleagues. I was thrown up onto the bonnet and then onto the ground. I was taken to Temple Street Children's Hospital and diagnosed with nothing worse than a broken leg—in fact, two fractures: the tibia and the fibula. A few days later, I was lying in bed at home with my leg up on a support wrapped in plaster of Paris. A neighbour, Mrs Evans, called to visit, and in the course of chatting to me, she told me that I was very lucky to be alive. That surprised me, as I had thought that I was very unlucky that the car happened to be passing at the very moment that I came racing out of the laneway.

A little more than twenty-two years later, I had an unusual accident in the Royal Dublin Golf Club. After playing a round of golf at a school past pupils outing, I went into the bar. In leaning across a glass table to hear something that someone was saying to me, I slipped and fell through the glass table. It cracked and broke but didn't shatter as a car windscreen might. Two large shards of glass became embedded in my back, one almost piercing my lungs and the second almost piercing my kidneys. My spurting blood ruined the newly decorated Christy O'Connor room of the bar; someone remembered that Frank O'Driscoll, a doctor (but no relation of Dr Kieran), had been playing a few holes behind us, so someone went looking for him.

Frank was rushed urgently from the shower to the bar upstairs, and although only half-dressed, he tended to me as best he could by effectively closing the wounds with gauze strips (or so it seemed to me) and then applying very tight bandages. He called for an ambulance, but some friends decided to drive me to Jervis Street Hospital without awaiting the ambulance. I was operated on that night. I was told on a number of occasions by the nurses and surgeon that I was very lucky to be alive – a few more millimetres of either laceration would have pierced my lung or kidney – and maybe I was, but I thought that I was very unlucky to have suffered such a freak accident.

In any event, I consider myself to have been lucky in life and lucky in love. But luck can apply in many different ways. One can win raffle prizes, which I have often done, or non- or minimal-skill prizes in newspapers, like those I've won in spot-the-ball competitions – particularly when much younger. One can be in the right place at the right time without any skill being involved. My luckiest break was the night I met my wife, Mary.

It was the Monday of the June bank holiday in 1975. Some friends and I had been out for the day, probably at a beach, and then went for a drink before deciding to finish the night by going to a disco in the Dublin Sports Hotel in Kilternan. We drove out there, taking some time and maybe stopping for another drink, but when we got there after 11 pm, we discovered that there was no disco – it had been on the previous night. Most of the group wanted to go home, but I was the driver and suggested that we try somewhere else.

Someone suggested a disco in Killiney Court Hotel just off Killiney Beach, so we made the relatively long drive there, bearing in mind that we all lived in Clontarf. When we went to the door, one of my friends was refused entry, as he was wearing denim jeans. The others decided that we would give up and go home. At the instant that we were leaving, Mary walked past the entrance on her way from the cloakroom to the disco itself. I saw her and immediately told the others that I was going in regardless of what they wanted to do.

I did go in. The others followed me soon afterwards, and the friend in denims went back to the car and changed into different trousers. I saw Mary again in the hall, plucked up all my courage and asked her to dance. I was smitten and realised immediately that she was someone special without even having spoken to her. I didn't realise that we would still be together more than forty-six years later; that I had started the most significant part of my life that evening. It nearly didn't happen – partly because I very nearly didn't go in, and partly because Mary very nearly didn't go either. She was studying all weekend for exams later that week for her Higher Diploma in Education; her flatmate dragged her out for a break, which had not been planned in advance. That was definitely the apex of my luck, but not the end of it.

But I have been most consistently lucky on the various occasions during my life when I had two options that I could choose. As Robert Frost put it in 'The Road Not Taken':

> Two roads diverged in a yellow wood,
> And sorry I could not travel both
> And be one traveler, long I stood
> And looked down one as far as I could
> To where it bent in the undergrowth;
> Then took the other [...]

Or as Shakespeare put it in Julius Caesar, 'There is a tide in the affairs of men which, taken at the flood leads on to fortune; Omitted, all the voyage of their life is bound in shallows and in miseries.'

On reflection, there were many occasions when I could look at two diverging roads or pathways of life but could only choose one. I have to presume that I was lucky enough to always choose the correct one. For me, at this stage, I can truthfully say in the words of Edith Piaf, 'Je ne regrette rien'. I believe that I have taken the tide at its flood; that it has led to the fortune of happiness; that my life has not been bound 'in shallows and miseries'.

However, there were many other occasions later in life, in my practice as a solicitor, when I thought myself lucky. In some instances, I remembered a previously overlooked deadline – an important one – with just enough time to get it done. Indeed, there were a few times when I was shaving in the morning and remembered something to be done or someone to meet, or thought of a new argument or approach in negotiating a deal. On other occasions I decided at the last minute to re-review a document or draft agreement that was about to be signed, and with which I was satisfied, before noting an important amendment that was needed to achieve exactly what I wanted.

I could never understand why I rechecked the document on such occasions and could only assume that once again I was very lucky. On reflection, it may be that in all these instances what was occurring was a concentration on the relevant issue at the appropriate time – that it was as much my subsconscious mind getting the timing right as it was simple luck. Nevertheless, at the time, I always felt lucky and grateful for the last-minute change or addition.

After my first bout of luck – surviving the double pneumonia – I was brought home to 35 Nottingham Street, North Strand, which my parents had bought in 1947, before they got married. I was soon followed by a sister, Bernadette, and a brother, Joe, who were born in January 1950 and November 1951 respectively. I started school in 1953 in North William Street National School, which was run by the Sisters of Charity. The only thing that I can remember of fifteen months at that school was the large bonnets that the nun teachers wore.

Nottingham Street lies off North Strand Road, which was one of the main arteries into the city centre from the north-east suburbs of Dublin and probably about a mile and a half from Nelson's Pillar. For much if not all of our time there, my parents had lodgers in the house. There were four members of a family from Valleymount in County Wicklow – initially two sisters and then two brothers. The two sisters were working in Dublin city and the two brothers were university students, but I don't think that there were ever more than two living in our house at any one time. My mother stayed very friendly with the two sisters and continued to meet them long after they left Nottingham Street and had married; indeed, in my early days as a solicitor, many years later, I advised one of the brothers in the purchase of a property.

Between Nottingham Street and the city centre, there was a large area of vacant ground that seemed to contain only rubble. Large blocks of Corporation flats were built subsequently, but when I was going to school at the convent in North William Street in 1953 and 1954, that ground was still vacant. This was the site that was bombed by the German Luftwaffe on 31 May 1941. At that time, it consisted of small houses and large tenement houses; twenty-eight innocent residents were killed, ninety injured, and three houses were damaged or destroyed by the bombing. Four bombs were dropped that night: three on the North Strand and the fourth in the Phoenix Park.

There were various explanations for the bombing of Dublin despite the fact that Ireland was neutral during the war. One was that the bombers thought that they were over Belfast – in a 'legitimate' mission to destroy the shipyards there, which were building warships for the British navy. Another was that it was revenge after the Dublin fire brigade had gone to Belfast a short time beforehand to help their colleagues in the North in dealing with the blitz they were facing; this would most certainly not have been grounds for a legitimate attack, even under the so-called rules of aerial bombardment. Another more bizarre explanation was that the British radar defence somehow tricked the Luftwaffe, who had thought they were bombing Liverpool.

The Second World War had ended in 1945 without further bombing of civilian targets in Dublin but to the extent that the world war meant anything to me as a young boy, it was just that bomb site. I had no knowledge of the bombing of London and other parts of England or of the other horrors of the war. Even though there was still food rationing to some limited extent up to the time that I was born, I don't think that I was adversely affected by it and I certainly don't ever remember seeing a photograph of me where I looked undernourished.

North Strand, like many other suburbs within a couple of miles of the city centre, such as Sandymount, Drumcondra, Ballsbridge, Donnybrook, Rathmines and Ranelagh, was built at a time when England governed Ireland and when Dublin was quite anglicised. Accordingly, many street names in these suburbs were based on English names, including Shrewsbury Road, Ailesbury Road, Northumberland Road, Dorset Street, Chelmsford Avenue, Whitworth Road, Nottingham Street, Buckingham Street, Waterloo Road, Waterloo Avenue, Richmond Road and Windsor Avenue. Nottingham Street did not seem particularly anglicised, but it was probably similar to suburbs of London or Manchester with short rows of terraced houses and laneways behind them for access to their rear – and which were likely intended at first for carts or carriages and horses.

North Strand Road was a fairly busy road, with lots of buses, cars and lorries passing regularly, although it was relatively quiet by today's traffic levels. On one occasion, obviously feeling a little peckish and adventurous, I ventured on my own up to a sweet shop on North Strand Road. It didn't involve crossing the main road, as the shop was close to the top of Nottingham Street. I'm sure that I thought I was old enough and fully entitled to go and get sweets whenever and wherever I wanted, and that I didn't need to ask or tell my mother.

There was consternation when my mother discovered that I had wandered off from outside our home and that no one knew where I was. I was tracked down in the shop trying to persuade the shopkeeper that I wanted sweets and to give them to me even though I didn't have enough money. I think that a neighbour recognised me, knew of my mother's search and let her know where I was. I don't remember whether I got any sweets, but I do remember my mother being torn between relief and anger. Maybe there was also a little admiration at my 4-year-old independence and negotiation attempts, but I was given a strict warning not to leave the street on my own again. I used my capacity to disappear as a threat some time later when refusing to go to the local doctor for an injection, but I don't remember the threat being successful.

At that time, my father was a law clerk in Irish Life Assurance Company; shortly after I was born, he became apprenticed to the company solicitor there and commenced his legal studies. Life was very busy for him then – and for the next few years – as he continued his full-time job, looked after a growing and demanding family, attended law lectures in the Incorporated Law Society offices, which were then at the Four Courts, and studied for his law examinations. He qualified as a solicitor at Michaelmas (autumn 1953) with eleven other students (he was probably the eldest and certainly the only one with three children already). At that time, there were only a few hundred solicitors in Ireland, and only between fifteen and twenty qualified each year, so it was a tremendous achievement.

I was impressed by his study efforts and can still vaguely remember finding a college scarf belonging to one of our lodgers, putting it around my neck, taking my father's briefcase and going into the room where he studied; I refused to allow my sister, Bernie, into the room because I was 'a scollege boy', she wasn't and I had to study. I'm sure she didn't know what I meant, and she ran off crying to our mother.

Our mother came to the door and insisted that I wasn't allowed to stay there and study any more than Bernie was – she wasn't yet 3 years old and I wasn't yet 4. At that time I didn't know that I would eventually become a 'scollege boy', but I clearly liked the image from an early age; when I started university many years later, one of my early purchases was a law faculty scarf. I think it lasted three weeks before I mislaid it and had to wait for a birthday or Xmas to get a replacement. I now sometimes wonder if my grandsons will become 'scollege boys' like me.

When I was 4 or 5 years old, I went to Holyhead in Wales with my sister Bernie, our mother and granny Sharkey to visit our aunt Teresa, who was a novice nun in Barnsley but was on vacation in Holyhead in a convent there. I don't actually remember being there, but I remember seeing a group photograph and my mother telling me that Bernie had done something to annoy or provoke me – probably trying to boss me, which never went down well with me, and still doesn't, and that the nuns, including our aunt, were quite annoyed with her behaviour. I was rewarded with extra sweets for being a good boy, but I can't say whether Bernie's behaviour towards me improved afterwards.

I don't have many memories of my time in Nottingham Street, but I do remember one occasion when I was standing on the back of a homemade chariot or go-kart. It was comprised of pieces of timber nailed together, old pram wheels and a piece of rope – the latter was held by the driver and attached to the front wheels to facilitate rudimentary steering. The braking system was even more rudimentary and didn't allow for gradual slowing.

It wasn't my go-kart, but I was the pusher. When it got moving, I jumped on the back, holding on to the shoulders of the driver (the owner), who was a couple of years older than me, as he raced down the street. It reminds me now of a bobsleigh in the Winter Olympics. It was relatively safe until my mother emerged from the house, saw what was happening and called for me to stop and get off. The driver got a fright, braked suddenly, and I was catapulted over his shoulders, head first onto the road; I suffered a number of lacerations but no fractures. When I state that it was relatively safe, I should add that there was no safety equipment, and helmets, shoulder pads and knee pads were unheard of. My mother's fright caused the very result that she was trying to prevent, as sometimes happens – but as on many other occasions throughout life, I was very lucky.

On another occasion, I was getting a lift with a pal and his father, who had recently bought a secondhand car and was learning to drive. We passed the Five Lamps on the North Strand, and as we were approaching Newcomen Bridge, the steering wheel came out of its socket – without the ability to navigate, the car skewed into the footpath and then back across the road. The driver eventually remembered to apply the brakes and stopped the car. It was a slalom ride until he stopped. We had to walk home, which wasn't very far, and I presume my pal's father got a mechanic to repair the car, as it soon reappeared on our road. I don't think I was a passenger in that car again, however.

Probably the most significant event that occurred during my life in Nottingham Street – besides being joined by two younger siblings – was just before we moved to our new home in Clontarf. The River Tolka burst its banks on 8 December 1954, resulting in widespread flooding in Fairview and North Strand, with the river flowing down the main road and adjoining streets, including our own. I don't know whether my father went to work the next morning, but I guess it was unlikely as he may have had to go by boat, such was the level of the flooding.

His father, my grandfather, who lived in Marino – which was on higher ground than Fairview and North Strand – ventured out and walked down to our house with emergency provisions and to check that we were safe. He was in his mid-seventies then; in one of the evening newspapers on the following day, there was a photograph of him wading through the floods at Edges Corner in Fairview as he came to help us. We were taken to his house on Brian Road in Marino and treated royally by him and our grandmother, Sarah Anne, for a few days. We then made the move to Clontarf, never going back to the house in Nottingham Street.

I have only lived in five different homes throughout my life, all of them on the north side of Dublin: North Strand, Clontarf, Malahide, Sutton and Baily. Even though I only lived in Clontarf for twenty years, they were the formative years – when I grew up, was educated and developed my love for sport. If asked where I'm from, I still answer Clontarf, even though I moved from the neighborhood more than forty-five years ago. I recently went back to Nottingham Street and walked past the house where I first lived, but I have no clear recollection of what the house was like on the inside save that there was a downstairs toilet. Perhaps I'll remember more as I get older, but my memories of childhood really only date from 1954, when we moved to Clontarf.

I have lived in my present home in Baily for much longer than any of my previous homes, and I still feel privileged to live in such a magnificent area. I have often said that there are probably very few capital cities anywhere in the world that are as close to such a beautiful area as Howth, and particularly the Baily side of the hill. As I did when I was first shown the site by an estate agent in 1981, I experience the wow factor every time I look across Dublin Bay to the Dublin and Wicklow mountains.

The story of how I got to here in Baily, and why I stay here, is the story of my life to date.

CLONTARF

My parents had been looking for a new house for some months; many of our Saturday afternoons in the late summer and early autumn of 1954 were spent house hunting with them. Most, if not all, of the houses they looked at were in Clontarf, which is a large suburb of Dublin; it is by the sea and a couple of miles further away from the city centre than Nottingham Street. The only thing that I can remember about the search for a house was looking at one that had a flat roof. I suppose the memory sticks with me because even at that early age I was aware that a flat-roofed house was unconventional – and as later life proved, I was attracted to unconventional house design. It was only a few years later when I realised that it was one of the flat-roofed houses on Kincora Road, near Clontarf Castle. Anyway, that was not the house that my parents bought. They purchased 10 Seafield Avenue, the house name on the gate being 'Thomond', presumably as the original owners were from Limerick. I wasn't yet familiar with Thomond Park, the famous rugby ground in Limerick, as it wasn't famous in 1954 – but as life transpired, I became quite familiar with the name in later years.

The house on Seafield Avenue was to be my home for the next twenty-one years. In fact, although I moved out in 1975, when I bought my first house, my mother lived there until her death in 2006, and until then I saw it as my 'home from home'. The house on Seafield Avenue was sold in 2007, my father having died in 1982 and all my siblings having moved out and got married. Nevertheless, it served us very well for more than fifty years. I can't remember exactly what my parents paid for the house in 1954, but when it sold in 2007, it achieved a multiple of more than five hundred. I'm sure that my parents did not consider it as a mere investment when they stretched their financial resources and bought it in 1954, but they would have been delighted to know how shrewd their purchase transpired to be.

It was not the financial shrewdness that was most important. What they bought was a comfortable, spacious house that they turned into a fantastic home in a fabulous area. They reared seven children there – six younger than me – all of whom had a very happy childhood and upbringing. In April 1955, not long after we moved to Clontarf, my sister Mary was born; in January 1958, Thérèse was born; and in July 1959, to the great shock of my father (who had only learned shortly beforehand), the twins, Angela and Gerard, appeared. I have always considered myself privileged to grow up in Clontarf; although I moved from Clontarf in 1975, I didn't move far and retained close connections with the area – connections that continue to the present time.

The house was a three-bedroom semi-detached and some years later an extension was added bringing it to four bedrooms with a new modern kitchen. Originally there was a large sitting room, with folding doors to a separate dining room – this space, in turn, led to a garden patio through French doors. There was a breakfast room and a relatively small kitchen, but the rear garden was quite large and the front garden had a lawn and concreted parking area and was populated by a number of nice trees. The rear garden had apple trees, a plum tree and a pear tree, a lilac bush, a vegetable patch that was gradually extended by my father over the years, and a large area of lawn that was ideal for playing games. The garden backed on to the playing field of Greenlanes National School, which was managed by the Church of Ireland – or the 'Protestants', as we called them. This playing field was big enough for a full-size football pitch, so there was a sense of open space that did not apply to our previous home in Nottingham Street.

At that time the other half of the semi-detached, number 12, was owned by a Welsh couple, Mr and Mrs Hywel Evans, who did not have any children. Our other next-door neighbours in number 8 were the Coakleys, who had three children – Pat, Kay and Denise – who were in their mid to late teens at that time. I am still in contact with Pat, who is about twelve years older than me; he is a fellow sports fan and a good friend. Denis Coakley, their father, who was the buyer in the furniture department of Clerys store on O'Connell Street, brought home the *Financial Times* every day – the only time I saw a pink newspaper until I was finished secondary school and became interested in the business world.

Beside them, in number 6, were the Predys; in number 4 were the Kellys; and in number 2 were Mr and Mrs Cox. Further up on our side of the road, in number 20, were the Langans, where there was one boy, Mick, who was about seven or eight years older than me; he had four sisters, three of whom were older than me. Mick became a priest, and one of the girls became a nun and lived in Chile. She is mentioned in a book titled *To Tierra del Fuego and Back*, which I read before visiting Tierra del Fuego in 2019.

There were lots of children of our age living close by, as well as some others who were a little older. Even though all the gardens were relatively large and a 44A bus travelled up the road every twenty minutes or so, much of our play was out on the avenue. Some of our neighbours had motor cars, but my father did not get one until 1961, so the fact that we were on a bus route was an advantage – despite the interruptions to play.

On the other side of the avenue were the odd numbered houses. Almost all of the residences on the avenue were similar but numbers 1 and 3, across the road from us, were detached and a little different in design. They were occupied by the Twohigs and the McCarthys, and the next house, number 5 – which was opposite ours – was occupied by the Killens. The Twohigs didn't have any children, but they had two Scottish terriers, Robbie and Rastus, who were very diligent guards of their patch and probably responsible for my early aversion to dogs. Robbie and Rastus sometimes thought they were entitled to guard the entire lower part of the avenue, keeping young children like me at bay with lots of barking and a little nipping. The Killens had a beautiful boxer dog named Dopey – scary-looking but in fact a very indolent and playful pet, and well named.

The O'Connells lived in number 9, the O'Boyles in 11, the Moylans in 15, the Walshes in 17 and the Enrights in 19; when taking into account the Malleys, who lived on Seafield Road just around the corner, I had plenty of boys to play with. My best friends for many years, and probably until the age of fifteen or sixteen, were Donie O'Connell and Frank O'Boyle. We were all born within eight or nine months of each other. They both took an extra year in the senior cycle of secondary school for different reasons, and we drifted apart over the next year or so, going our separate ways and acquiring new friends. Both Donie and Frank have died since – Donie in the USA (where he practised as an architect) a few years ago; Frank in Dublin more recently, in 2021.

The Rev. Melville lived in number 13 with his wife and two children, who were slightly older than me. Rev. Melville was a preacher of the Plymouth Brethren, but he was never referred to as reverend. None of us knew what the Plymouth Brethren was at the time, but we knew it was different. Rev. Melville – or as we knew him, Mr Melville – was a courteous, quiet man; it was hard to imagine, as I subsequently learned, that he preached fire and brimstone on O'Connell Street and in his church in Fairview. We did get his son, Philip, out to play football with us on the road on two occasions. Philip could not have been described as an elegant footballer, but he seemed to like it and had a kick like a mule. The second time we played with him, he kicked the ball very hard but very wide and broke the window in our front door. It didn't unduly bother my father, as he knew that I had broken at least one neighbour's window before that, but Philip's father heard about it and was very upset. Philip wasn't allowed to play with us again. He himself became a clergyman, but we lost contact many years ago.

Further up the avenue, in number 25, were two single ladies who were sisters, the Stuart Watts. They seemed elderly to me at the time, but in retrospect they were probably not very old – and certainly younger than I am now. I guess that my parents considered them a little eccentric, but to me they were exotic. They had lived in Africa for many years and had a beautiful garden with unusual plants; they had similarly unusual artifacts in their house. We were always welcome when we visited, and I believe that my interest in geography and foreign places was influenced at least to some extent by these two women and their stories of life in Africa. I was an avid stamp collector at the time, and they were very generous in giving me some unusual stamps from faraway places such as Tanganyika, Zambia, Rhodesia, Nyasaland, Ethiopia and the West Indies.

In the garden of a house across the road from the sisters, there was a monkey puzzle tree; the only other place that I had seen such a tree was in the zoo. Many other gardens had beautiful trees and bushes, and our own garden had a few beautiful bushes, one of which was a lilac bush – and another produced lovely blue flowers. Mr and Mrs Evans had prize-winning roses in their garden; probably for that reason, they resented stray footballs and chasers coming in and trampling on them. There was a horticultural society in Clontarf, which seemed very active and had at least one horticultural show every year; I suppose the fact that there were some gardening enthusiasts on the avenue induced others to improve their own gardens.

Besides the usual games of hopscotch, skipping, marbles, hide and seek, cowboys and Indians, and football, hurling and rounders, we had a unique game of tag on Seafield Avenue involving the gates and railings at the entrance to Greenlanes National School. There were two high gates for vehicle access and egress; beside them, two high gates for pedestrian access. There were four sets of railings, two splayed at an angle and two facing the avenue. Most of these did not seem to have any purpose other than to provide a play area for us – they constituted a network of safe zones, which we raced to and jumped up on, avoiding the tagger. It was not particularly exciting, but it was different and very often whiled away an hour or so when there seemed nothing more exciting to do.

During the twenty years that I lived on Seafield Avenue, there were changes as some people died and others moved to other parts of Dublin or further afield. The Wards, Taddeis, Currans, Ryans, Cuddihys, Donnellys, Weirs, Stanleys, Seán Dublin Bay Loftus and Miss Bell (who bought the Evans house next door to us) came and joined the Langans, Shields, Smyths, Harringtons, McLoughlins, McDonnells, O'Tooles and McMahons, in addition to those I mentioned earlier. Other than the disagreements about playing football on the avenue, it was always a harmonious neighbourhood, and I was never aware of any major disputes between any of our neighbours.

As our family grew with the arrival of Thérèse and the twins, Gerry and Angela, bedroom space became more limited and the configuration changed a few times; at the time I wasn't conscious of any sense of overcrowding, though it may have been different in my subconscious mind. The difficulty, if there was any, was when we were studying. There would be three or four of us trying to learn poetry at the same time or concentrating on a mathematics problem while someone else was practising a song they had to know for the following day. That may be the explanation for why I was never able to remember a poem, no matter how many times I repeated it, and still cannot; I remember one or two lines of half a dozen poems, but that is the limit. I still have that difficulty in trying to remember the words of a song, and while I love to sing, I have often come up stuck in public – so when possible, Mary sits beside me and prompts me when I volunteer.

When the family first moved to Clontarf, my mother initially shopped on Vernon Avenue in Maddens, which later changed to Nolans when bought by P.J. Nolan. Maddens was an old-style shop, and Mr Madden and his assistants wore brown or beige jackets, which looked as if they were covered in flour. I liked going to Maddens and later Nolans with my mother, as we had to pass McCulloughs, a sweet shop, and there was always the possibility of a treat. Vegetables were delivered to us by Paddy Cullen, milk by Woodpark Dairies (a local farm and dairy) and bread by Kennedys. The milk and perhaps some other deliveries were conveyed by horse-drawn cart, which meant that there was manure on the road. My father used to collect it and bring it into the back garden as feed for his vegetables and rhubarb; before long, that became my job.

After 1957, when shops were built opposite the new St Gabriel's church, my mother often went there. She particularly liked Eglintons butchers; it was owned by international footballer Tommy Eglinton, but as he was playing professionally in England, it was run by his brother, Brendan. My mother also liked Cronin's pharmacy, operated by Brendan Cronin, and sometimes used Jimmy Harrisons, a newsagent beside Cronins, when she went to Mass in St Gabriel's. Other shops that she sometimes used on Vernon Avenue were Whelans Vernon Stores, Furlongs, Doyles Pharmacy, McCluskeys Pharmacy, the Nook (a small sweet shop) and Penders (a drapery store that was just around the corner, on Clontarf Road). Sixty years later, most of these shops are gone or have at least changed ownership, but Doyles Pharmacy and Nolans have stayed in the family – albeit Nolans is now a much larger supermarket and hardware store.

Clontarf is a very old part of Dublin, probably most famous for the Battle of Clontarf in 1014, which resulted in the defeat of the Vikings by the native Irish forces under the leadership of Brian Boru. It is situated along the north shore of Dublin Bay and includes the Bull Island and Dollymount Strand on its southern boundary; on the north boundary is St Anne's Park and the old road from the city centre to the fishing village of Howth. St Anne's was acquired by Dublin Corporation from some members of the Guinness family, who had lived in a large mansion there. Unfortunately, this mansion was burned down in 1943. Clontarf stretches, on the city side, from the railway bridge on the Dublin–Belfast line near Fairview Park to where St Anne's Park meets the coast road on James Larkin Road, which is a more recent route from Dublin to Howth and Sutton.

For centuries, fishing and farming were the main occupations in Clontarf, and it was a trading port from the late fourteenth century. A manorial house, the precursor of Clontarf Castle, had been there since the late thirteenth century, but it was destroyed in 1641 after the rebellion of that year. The invasion by the Cromwellian army followed, and in 1656, Captain John Vernon, a quartermaster of that army, acquired the estate of nearly six hundred acres. That family built a new manorial house, which became what is now Clontarf Castle. The Vernon family stayed in Clontarf into the twentieth century.

Clontarf Castle is now a very successful hotel and hospitality venue close to the centre of Clontarf itself, and also to the main sports clubhouses – rugby, cricket, Gaelic football, hurling and tennis – all of which are on lands that were originally part of the castle estate. One of the Vernons who lived in Clontarf Castle in the eighteenth century was Dorothy Vernon, better known as Dolly. Dolly was friendly with the great composer George Frideric Handel, who stayed in Clontarf Castle during the premiere performance in Dublin of his famous work *Messiah*. This Dolly is remembered in the area of Clontarf known as Dollymount, which is close to the sea and is also the name often given to the beach on the Bull Island.

In the nineteenth century, as Dublin developed and grew, its population moved outside the old city between the canals to the new suburbs such as Blackrock, Kingstown, Kilmainham, Drumcondra and Clontarf; they absorbed what had been small villages or hamlets, which soon became self-governing townships. Clontarf was such a township from 1869 until it was brought within the city municipal boundaries in 1900. Among the town commissioners of Clontarf between 1869 and 1900 were John Vernon, who was the chairman; Sir Arthur Guinness, who later became Lord Ardilaun; Graham Lemon of the Lemon's Sweets business; and William Prescott of the laundry and dye-works business.

One of the principal changes to the Clontarf area arose when the Bull Wall was built in 1819. It was designed by Captain William Bligh of 'Mutiny on the *Bounty*' fame to eradicate the sand bar at the entry to the Liffey estuary, which made Dublin a dangerous port for entry and egress. This resulted in the formation of the Bull Island, with Dollymount Strand, just off the eastern half of Clontarf; it also helped develop Clontarf in becoming one of the main recreation areas of the city, with two golf links and multiple water-based sports on the island, as well as the usual field sports onshore. The Bull Island is now a bird sanctuary and has been for many years.

The Guinness family built St Anne's mansion in the eastern part of Clontarf on lands originally leased from the Vernons. Throughout the nineteenth century, the Guinness family acquired more land by buying existing Vernon estate houses and lodges with attached lands; by the 1880s, the family had an estate of five hundred acres in Clontarf and the adjoining parish of Raheny. They laid out their lands in beautiful landscaped gardens and tree-lined walks, but later generations of the family, who had inherited the estate, were not in a position to maintain the large house and lands.

In 1938, St Anne's estate was acquired by Dublin Corporation, which used it for cultivation, helping to alleviate food shortages in the city during the Second World War. In December 1943, there were two successive fires within a few days; they destroyed the large mansion house, leaving only the walls standing. The shell of the house was eventually demolished in 1968 and a large mound was left behind.

After the war, Dublin Corporation allocated land from the estate to playing fields for various sports, including tennis courts and a Par 3 course, and added the renowned rose garden in 1975, which is still there today. Most of the features of the original gardens, such as ornamental bridges, lakes and ponds, miniature temples and shelters, mounds and glorious trees, also remain even today, but in the 1950s and 1960s, they were the makings of an adventure land for the young people of Clontarf and Raheny. As I describe later, it was also the location of another of my lucky episodes. At one stage it was thought that St Anne's was acquired by Dublin Corporation for a massive housing development, but thankfully that has not transpired; St Anne's Park remains as a superb amenity for the local residents and, indeed, for other Dubliners.

From the beginning of the twentieth century, Clontarf was served by trams, buses and trains, and from the 1920s it became very popular as a residential area for the increasing middle class. Housing development took place rapidly in the grounds of the big houses that had been built in the previous century, and in the early 1930s Seafield Avenue was developed. The builder of most of Seafield Avenue, including number 10, was Joseph

McGonagle. By a coincidence, his son, Liam, was a neighbour of mine in Baily many years later and his nephew J.C. Savage was a good friend and client.

When we moved to Clontarf, there were three national schools: Belgrove boys' and Belgrove girls' schools on Seafield Road, which were controlled by the Roman Catholic authorities, and Greenlanes National School on Seafield Avenue, which was controlled by the Church of Ireland authorities. There were also four secondary schools: the Holy Faith Convent school for girls on Belgrove Road, comprising junior and secondary sections; St Paul's College for boys on Sybil Hill, which also comprised junior and secondary sections (and which had just opened a few years before we moved to Clontarf and was operated by the Vincentian Fathers); Kostka College for boys on the corner of Seafield Road and Vernon Avenue, which was a lay school but catered for Catholic boys; and Royal Hibernian Marine School for boys, situated on Seafield Road near where St Gabriel's Road was subsequently built and which catered for non-Catholic boys, both boarders and day pupils. Mountjoy School, a boys' boarding and day school, also for non-Catholics, was quite close; it had an entrance on the Howth Road, and it merged some years later with the Royal Hibernian Marine School to become Mount Temple.

In 1954 there were five churches: St John's Roman Catholic on the coast road near the end of Vernon Avenue, which is still there; St Anthony's Roman Catholic, also on the coast road but closer to the city at the end of St Laurence Road, and which has since been replaced by a newer church beside it; and St John's Church of Ireland on Seafield Road near Castle Avenue, which is still there. There were Presbyterian and Methodist churches at the city end of Clontarf, which are also still in existence. In 1956, a new and much bigger Roman Catholic church, St Gabriel's, was opened on the then new St Gabriel's Road in the eastern half of the suburb; it catered for the expanding population and the anticipated development of St Anne's estate for residential purposes. The church is still there, although its massive size is no longer required and many of the pews have been removed.

Clontarf was to some extent divided between east and west, with Castle Avenue providing a somewhat curved dividing line. In 1954 there were effectively two villages: one on the coast road, near St Anthony's church and the Garda station (to the west, closer to the city centre), the other on

Vernon Avenue (to the east). After St Gabriel's church opened in 1956, a smaller village – or at least a cluster of shops – was developed at St Gabriel's Road. When growing up, I had very little involvement with the western part of Clontarf and, other than boys that I met in school, would not have known many residents of that part of the suburb.

One effect of this was that, unlike boys who grew up on the western or city side of Castle Avenue who watched rugby and cricket and started to play those games at Clontarf rugby and cricket grounds between Castle Avenue and the Stiles Road, I don't remember watching a rugby or cricket game there until I was 11 or 12 years old. We were closer to the Gaelic football and hurling pitches in St Anne's Park; that was where we went to watch those games being played, and played ourselves, as there were goalposts there that we were able to use.

These were the games played in Belgrove National School – or Scoil Eoin Baiste, as it was sometimes called – so until I went to secondary school in St Paul's College, I hadn't played any rugby and my sporting passions were Gaelic games. Where I lived had an influence on what games I played, but perhaps that is not unusual. Nevertheless, a greater influence on my early sporting passions was undoubtedly my father and his interests and background.

PARENTS AND ANCESTORS

So who were my parents, where did they come from and how did they get to Seafield Avenue together?

My father, Joe, was born in March 1913 in Dungannon, County Tyrone. He went to the national school, called a public elementary school, in Edendork, which was a small village between Dungannon and Coalisland. He then went to St Patrick's Academy in Dungannon, which was a secondary school catering for Roman Catholic boys of the area; he finished his senior certificate there in 1932, having completed his junior certificate in 1929. He was the first of his family, and indeed among his cousins, to finish secondary school – and when he was later admitted as a solicitor, he was probably the first to qualify as a professional. Austin Currie, in his autobiography *All Hell Will Break Loose*, refers to Edendork National School, where he and his father before him went to school. He refers to the teacher Master Molloy, who retired around the time that Austin started school but who had taught his father (and would have also taught my father – a friend of Austin's father, albeit a couple of years younger). He describes Master Molloy as 'a teacher of the old school' and added, 'My father would recount stories of the pretty brutal corporal punishment inflicted on him and his schoolmates, which he averred never did any of them any harm.'

I don't remember my father referring to Master Molloy by name, but I do remember his telling me of getting whacked a few times in school, and he was never surprised or upset if I came home from school and told him that I had received some corporal punishment. It mightn't have happened too often, but he had the same attitude to it as Austin Currie's father, and he was probably right.

Although I am not certain of it, I am fairly sure that my father was awarded a scholarship to attend secondary school. His father, John, was a carpenter and joiner, as were John's two brothers and his own father, Patrick; indeed, my father's brother, another John Glackin, was also a carpenter. My great grandfather Patrick, as well as being a carpenter, was also a farmer with a small landholding. These Glackins were all from the Coalisland area near Lough Neagh in County Tyrone, although it is estimated by genealogists that the genetic homeland of the native distinct Glackin clan, with one founding ancestor, was the Donegal–Tyrone borderland, which is northwest of the Lough Neagh area.

My maternal grandmother, Sarah Ann (née Marlow), and her family were also from the Coalisland area. Sarah Ann's father, John, was a miner for part of his life, as indeed were many of the population around Coalisland; he also had a small landholding. Sarah Ann had five brothers, two of whom went to the USA, and three sisters. Most of these had families, and I have met some of their descendants – second cousins who grew up and lived in the Coalisland and Edendork areas of County Tyrone.

My grandfather Glackin and his two brothers had a carpentry business in Dungannon in the early years of the twentieth century, but apparently a dispute arose between his two brothers over the excessive drinking of the elder one. Shortly after that, the younger brother, Edward, who was a non-drinker, tragically died from pneumonia; he left behind a widow and three small children, as well as an unborn son. His widow, who I never knew – and I'm not sure that my father knew her either – moved to Scotland after her youngest son was born and stayed there, rearing a young family in the Motherwell area. They were Elizabeth, Edward, John and Patrick Glackin. Some of these stayed in Scotland and some went to Corby in Northamptonshire, England. In recent years I have traced and met some of their offspring, second cousins of mine.

One of that clan is Eddie Linden, a second cousin of mine, who was born Edward Seán Glackin but was later adopted and had his name changed. Eddie achieved some fame in Irish and English literary circles for his poetry writing and publishing; his poetry periodical, *Aquarius*, published new poems by the likes of Seamus Heaney, Brendan Kennelly, Paul Durcan, Derek Mahon, John Montague and Margaret Attwood. He was one of the founders of the Simon Community in London and of the Campaign for Nuclear Disarmament with Bruce Kent; he was generally more bohemian than any of my other cousins or ancestors. Eddie's most famous poem was probably 'City of Razors', which was about life in Glasgow, where he grew up.

The older brother of my grandfather, James, stayed in Coalisland, as did some of his family; one son, Randal, emigrated to the USA. My grandfather also had a few sisters, one of whom died young, and the others went to Scotland; one of them married a Cullen and two married O'Neills, but I never knew anything about them until I started genealogical research in recent years.

My grandfather, who had previously worked as a tradesman in England and other parts of the north of Ireland, went back to work in Belfast, in the shipyards, after the business with his brothers collapsed; for many years, he only saw his young family, at best, at weekends. He was caught up in the pogroms in the Belfast shipyards, and although a friend of his – who was near him at the time – was murdered and he himself was attacked and wounded, he managed to survive and ultimately left Belfast. He eventually came to Dublin, where he worked as a carpenter with his eldest son, my uncle John.

His youngest daughter, Nan, who would have been my aunt, tragically died on 19 March 1936, having suffered a serious head injury in a camogie match on St Patrick's Day. My father's eldest sister, Bridget, got married later that year to Patrick Donnelly from County Armagh, who had bought a farm in Kilsallaghan in north Dublin and had established a fruit farm there called Colmcille Fruit Farm. Bridget moved there upon her marriage, and lived at Colmcille until her death many years later, rearing five children, Marita, Patricia, Aidan, Kierie and Brede.

In 1937 my grandmother, my father and another sister, Alice, moved to Dublin, after my grandfather bought a house on Brian Road – number 64 – in Marino, where he and my grandmother lived until their respective deaths. I can remember my grandfather, who died in 1963, but I have very little memory of my grandmother, who died in 1956. Any memories I do have of her are revived by photographs. It was to this house on Brian Road that my siblings and I were brought after we were rescued from our old home in 1954 during the North Strand flood.

Marino is probably one of the best planned suburbs in the greater Dublin area, with a mixture of houses, all well designed – at least for the 1930s – and still looking well; a mixture of curved avenues and a few straight ones, like spines; and lots of parks and open green areas, the principal park being Marino Green, from which a series of avenues spread out like the spokes in a bicycle wheel. I still see Marino fairly regularly, as I tend to park my car in the area when attending a game in Croke Park. On those occasions, I walk to and from the neighborhood and sometimes reminisce about my grandfather when I walk close to his former home.

My grandfather Glackin worked as a carpenter in Dublin for many years, but he fell from the roof of a building on which he was working while in his sixties and broke his neck. After my grandfather died, my father told me that he had had to lie on his back for six months while recuperating. He did recover, and walked again, but he did not go back up on a roof again after that fall. I remember as a young child being brought down the Bull Wall in a buggy to Dollymount beach; as we passed it, my father pointed out the Royal Dublin Golf clubhouse and told me that granddad had worked on the roofing of the building – which was being rebuilt, having been burned down in 1943. I haven't been able to ascertain if his fall was from the roof of Royal Dublin, but I sometimes think of him when I see the clubhouse from the golf course – and it would be coincidental if it was, considering that I had my own serious accident there in 1981.

My father, who had been a good footballer in school and had been selected for the Tyrone minor football team in 1931, became a founder member of the Edendork GAA Club – also in 1931. He had also achieved high grades in his senior certificate, but a university education was not feasible for him and his family. He commenced work as a law clerk in a solicitor's office in Dungannon, John Hoy Son & Murphy. Becoming a solicitor's apprentice and qualifying as a solicitor was not an immediate option for him at that time in Northern Ireland, although he had the ambition to do so. This was not least because it required a significant capital sum or premium to be paid to the solicitor master, and neither he nor my grandfather had the capacity to pay that when he left school. Nevertheless, he was still considering it with J.P. Murphy, his boss at the time, six years later when the family moved to Dublin.

After my father moved to Dublin, he obtained a position as a law clerk in Messrs M.S. Bergin, a solicitor's office on Dawson Street; after a few years, he moved to Irish Assurance Company, the forerunner of Irish Life Assurance Company, as managing clerk to the chief solicitor, William

Healy. He sat and passed his first few insurance institute examinations but retained the ambition to qualify as a solicitor. In May 1943, Mr Healy promised that if my father got exemption from the Preliminary Examination of the Incorporated Law Society, he would be pleased to have him as an apprentice.

He had met my mother in Dublin in the early 1940s, and their developing relationship probably helped to sustain his ambition to progress. After a lot of petitioning, appealing and arm twisting – which involved continued pressure on the Incorporated Law Society to be exempted from the Preliminary Examination on the grounds that he had attained a standard of education equal to that required by the examination – he succeeded and ultimately completed all his examinations and was admitted as a solicitor. He was apprenticed to an 'in house' solicitor, Mr Healy, the chief solicitor of Irish Life, although he was originally told that this was not allowed by the regulations.

The arm twisting was done by Gerry Boland, the then Minister for Justice and a TD for Roscommon – my mother's home constituency and where some of her family were sufficiently well known to the minister to persuade him to intervene with the law society. Gerry was a brother of Harry Boland, who was killed in the civil war and is referred to later in the context of my mother's aunts. My mother and father were not married at the time of the minister's intervention, but my father's stubborn northern ambition must have impressed his future in-laws enough for them to call in a favour.

I guess that the persuader was my mother's paternal uncle Fr Paddy Sharkey, a well-known local parish priest and historian. My father spent a few days in 1945 or 1946 – around the time of the All-Ireland football finals, which featured the Roscommon team – selling tickets on O'Connell Street in Dublin for a car draw. It was a fundraising venture for Fr Paddy, who wanted to develop a football pitch and community centre in Ballinameen, a small parish in Roscommon where he also revived a sports festival for children. I don't think my father was too enamoured of this ticket-selling task, but it was a small price for the political intervention that got his legal career off the ground.

Some time after he arrived in Dublin to live and work, my father joined Ard Craobh, which was a sports club under the general aegis of Conradh na Gaeilge, the Irish cultural and language revival movement founded in 1893 by Eoin MacNeill; it had been revitalised in the late 1930s and early 1940s after the 1937 Bunreacht na hEireann (Constitution of Ireland) had declared Irish to be the first language of the state. I don't remember my father speaking the Irish language, but he was supportive of Irish culture and sports. He won a Dublin Junior Football Championship medal with Ard Craobh in 1941, and many of his friends in Dublin came from his time in that club. Being from county Tyrone in the North of Ireland and having suffered discrimination and disadvantage from the partition of Ireland in 1921, he retained a dislike and mistrust of England and its politicians, but he did not openly express or display that dislike except at the time of the Hunger Strikes in 1981, shortly before he died.

My mother's parents and grandparents were all from County Roscommon and, indeed, all came from within a relatively small radius. Her father was from the townland of Drinane between Strokestown, Tulsk and Elphin. Her paternal grandfather was from the townland of Mantua. Her paternal grandmother was from the townland of Brackloon, which was fairly close. My mother's mother was from Carrownagleragh in Aughrim parish, which was a little further away. Her maternal grandmother was from the same. Her maternal grandfather, Patrick Beirne, was from the townland of Lisgarve – again, not far away, but it would have taken longer to travel the distance at the time.

My mother, Isabel Sharkey, was born in 1918 in Strokestown, County Roscommon, and was christened Veronica Elizabeth. I never heard any explanation of how her name changed, but she was always known as Isabel and told us that as a young girl she was teased about her name by her friends asking, 'Is a bell necessary on a bike?' I know from my recent genealogy studies that there was nobody else among her ancestors with that name, although many of the Christian names in the family were – as was normal at the time – handed down from one generation to another.

It was only in March 2019 that I found a possible answer. I visited Buenos Aires province in Argentina trying to find traces of Patrick Beirne, my great grandfather, who lived and worked as a peon with gauchos on an estancia near Monsalvo, now Maipu, between 1863 and 1873. We were brought to see the nearest pulperia – a local bar, grocery store and social meeting place (now long closed and derelict) – and to my surprise noted that it had been named Pulperia Santa Isabel. I concluded without much more evidence that my mother was named after her grandfather's favourite bar. I don't think she ever knew that, and although she liked her name, I don't think she would have been impressed with my explanation.

She had most of her secondary education as a boarder in St Joseph's Convent School in Lincoln, England. I never learned exactly why she was educated there, but I do know that one of her younger sisters, Teenie, also spent at least one year there. As far as I know, my mother enjoyed her time there, although she missed home in Strokestown and only got home once or twice a year.

Her home in Strokestown was on Church Street, which was reputedly the widest street in Europe and was built by the Mahon family in the mid-eighteenth century; it was based on the design and span of the Ringstrasse in Vienna and acted as the avenue from Strokestown House, which they owned, to their church at the top of the town.

The Mahon family had gained international notoriety for their mass evictions and assisted emigration of those evicted to Canada during the famine of the 1840s. The ships arranged by the Mahons, the *Virginius*, *Erins Queen* and the *Naomi*, were substandard and led to a high level of deaths when transporting the emigrants from the townlands surrounding Strokestown; or if they didn't die during the journey, there was every chance the emigrants' lives would be cut short upon their arrival at the quarantine station on Grosse Île near Quebec. This operation also led to the murder, in 1847, of the then owner of the house and estate, Major Denis Mahon. Nevertheless, despite these tragedies, Strokestown became a busy market town in the second half of the nineteenth century and up to the second half of the twentieth century.

My grandfather, John Sharkey, owned a business on Church Street, Sharkey Bros, comprising a bar, grocery shop, ironmongers and hardware store, and at one time an undertaking business. The undertaking business resulted in his nickname 'Deadman', although I didn't know that until nearly sixty years after he died. He also owned a small farm on which cows were grazed a little way outside the town, and the family lived over and beside the shop in a very comfortable home, where the older few of my siblings and I had some great holidays. I don't know if my grandfather always had sweets for sale in the shop, but there were lots of them when we were there.

There was also a Sharkey and Son shop on Elphin Street in Strokestown, originally operated by his brother Thomas, and a Sharkey Sisters shop and business, also on Church Street, operated by two of his sisters, Una and Lena. Those two sisters were remarkable ladies; they operated a very successful business under the name American Novelty Stores, where they sold a wide range of haberdashery goods, books and stationery, and carried on a book-lending service (the Éire Óg library), a jewellery and tobacconist business, an Irish-made goods depot, all while still in their early and mid-twenties, one having been born in 1888 and the other in 1894. They had also commenced a craft knitting business, with a view to providing local employment

They both became very nationalistic after the Easter Rising of 1916. Una, the elder of the two, who had been christened Winifred, changed her name to the Irish version later in 1916. In autumn 1916, the sisters' shop was raided by the local RIC, and material that was considered seditious was confiscated. Among the seized materials were printed sheets of a poem titled 'Easter Week', which they had for sale. What may have drawn the attention of the RIC to the shop was the new tricolour flying from the building, along with the Stars and Stripes that they had been using since opening their business in 1914. They flew this flag to reflect the name of the shop, the fact that some of their stock was sourced in the USA and perhaps also that they had received their retail training there. The tricolour was not new, but it was new in Strokestown, which was a strong garrison town for the British army.

The sisters started a campaign of passive resistance, which lasted for the next few years. They took an active part in the short by-election campaign in February 1917, which saw Count George Noble Plunkett elected to the vacant Westminster seat for North Roscommon and was the first parliamentary victory for Sinn Féin (although Plunkett ran as an independent and didn't join Sinn Féin until a few months later). Plunkett had promised that if elected he would not attend the House of Commons in Westminster. The sisters had placed an advertisement in the local newspaper, the *Strokestown Democrat* edition of 13 January 1917, which was purportedly for their business but was headed in bold print 'Another Rising'.

Following the successful election of Count Plunkett – who was the father of Joseph Mary Plunkett, one of the leaders of the rising and a signatory of the Proclamation of the Irish Republic who was executed by the British after the rebellion was suppressed – the sisters were further harassed by the RIC. On 15 March 1917, their shop was again raided and more 'seditious' material was removed – they had a copy of 'The Ballad of Easter Week'. They were brought before the court and bound over to the peace for twelve months. The knitting machine that they had had installed in their premises caused concern for the local police sergeant, who assumed it was some kind of gun or bullet-making apparatus. He did not believe the explanation given him by the sisters and called in a military engineer to inspect it and advise him. The military engineer enjoyed the joke as much as the owners of the knitting machine, but it only incensed the policeman, who shortly afterwards was given charge of the Black and Tans when they appeared in Strokestown; with them, he continued to harass the two sisters – as well, of course, as the other inhabitants of the town and its surrounds.

On 14 September 1918, the police raided their shop once more. This time they seized some Sinn Féin songs and publications, including a framed copy of the Proclamation. They subsequently returned the frame and glass, but retained all the seized documents. A month later, the premises was raided again and police carried off a number of poems, ballads, newspapers and books; they also took a poem by Thomas Ashe and mortuary cards in tribute to him.

The *Strokestown Democrat*, in reporting on this, commented that 'these premises have been raided on several occasions since May 1916 and the action of the authorities is annoying two defenceless young girls who are only trying to earn a living and is severely criticised and condemned by the general public.' That did not prevent the authorities taking the matter further, and within a few days the sisters were charged with 'exposing seditious literature for sale thus exciting discontent in the minds of the people' at the Strokestown Petty Sessions. The sisters didn't appear in court, however, as they didn't recognise its authority.

The case was adjourned for two weeks, but when they again ignored it, the case was withdrawn by the police. Instead, a few weeks later, a military motor van drew up in front of the shop with about twenty police. Some of them entered the shop. It was a fair day in the town, and when the two sisters emerged after half an hour and were put in the military van, the crowd cheered and shouted 'Up the Rebels'. They were forcibly taken to court and sentenced to one month's imprisonment for failing to recognise the court and abide by its ruling that they desist from selling seditious material.

They were released on 17 December 1918 and returned to Strokestown to a hero's welcome. Despite threats from the police not to demonstrate, people lit candles in their windows and displayed tricolours in support of Una and Lena. A bonfire was ignited and a crowd of hundreds gathered to welcome them. On the following day, Fr Michael O'Flanagan, vice president of Sinn Féin, and Harry Boland, then right-hand man of Michael Collins, called to their shop to welcome home the two sisters. The sisters had been imprisoned in Sligo jail, and on the day before their release, the police sought and were granted an order under the Defence of the Realm Act to have their shop closed.

The order included the following wording: 'the shop portion of the premises occupied by Winifred and Lena Sharkey is being used in a manner prejudicial to the public safety by the said Winifred and Lena Sharkey who are persons suspected of attempting to cause sedition and disaffection among the civil population.' It was served to Una on 18 December, but the sisters ignored it and continued their business; however, the Christmas trade was now severely affected.

On 13 January 1919, an order was served requiring that no goods be stored on the premises. In mid-January the sisters were arrested and brought before the court, where the resident magistrate decided that they would have to give security to keep the peace or, in default, go to jail for two months. Neither of the sisters replied to the charge and they were removed to Sligo jail. While in jail, their business was continued by their brothers, and an advertisement appeared in the *Strokestown Democrat* reading:

> Sale Sale Sale
> Sharkey Sisters In prison for being true to their country
> Wish to announce to their Friends and Patrons that
> Great Cash Sale continues in their Absence.

They were released on 19 March and returned home. Trouble was expected by the police, who had called in reinforcements, but it passed off quietly.

Nevertheless, in the *Strokestown Democrat* of 29 March, the sisters published the following advertisement:

> The Dangerous Sisters
> Bargain Sale For Nine Days commencing 4th April
> 'Seditious' Goods must be sold.
> We want the cash and must sell even at a sacrifice.
> This is a unique opportunity for the purchaser.
> MISS IT NOT
> Drapery, hosiery, skirts, underclothing Various Novelty Goods--- Pictures, photoframes, brushes, razors, pipes, sticks, stationery, wall-papers, rugs, mats and several other 'Seditious' goods.
> It's Your Chance We offer it
> Sharkey Sisters, Strokestown

On 22 May, police under the control of the district inspector raided the premises again, cleared the shop – taking goods to the value of £3,450 – and closed it up. The sisters then took an appeal by way of judicial review to the King's Bench Division of the High Court in Dublin. They sought to quash the order from January – the cause of the recent confiscation and jail time – and were ultimately successful in the court appeal. In the meantime, however, the sisters were forced into bankruptcy.

Subsequently, on 11 October, a military wagon guarded by police armed with revolvers conveyed back to the sisters what they maintained were the goods seized in May, which had been stored in Boyle Military Barracks. In response to a report critical of their reactions, the sisters wrote a letter to the editor of the *Irish Independent*, published in November 1919, in which they set out their description of events:

> After five and a half months a half lorry load of filthy, broken and heterogeneous goods were flung to us as our goods. This pile of rubbish in no way resembled the heavily laden lorries of merchandise which had been taken from us and we refused to receive them back as reparation. The fact that we had been forced into bankruptcy took the matter out of our hands and the Receivers had the dilapidated fraction that had been flung back at us auctioned off. The proceeds of the auction amounted to £85. Of this £85, about

> £30 went for auctioneers and advisory expenses so that the net proceeds of the £3450 worth of goods was £55.

As it transpired, friends and family arranged a testimonial for the sisters, subscriptions came from all over the country, they got a discharge from bankruptcy and they resumed business. But their days of passive resistance were finished: from then on – having joined Cumann na mBan, the republican women's paramilitary organisation founded in Dublin in 1914 – they took a very active part in the War of Independence. In fact, Una became the first secretary of the Roscommon branch and a Connacht representative of the GHQ in Dublin. At the same time, she was elected chairman of Strokestown District Council, chairman of the local poor law guardians and a Roscommon county councillor. Lena became captain of the local Cumann na mBan and later married the local commander of the IRA, Liam O Doherty from Donegal. Liam and Lena later set up another business together in Elphin, a nearby town in Roscommon, while Una continued the business in Strokestown until her death in 1943.

Their brother Thomas was arrested by the Black and Tans (recruits mostly made up of unemployed former British soldiers that reinforced the Royal Irish Constabulary during the War of Independence) and severely tortured in Strokestown House, probably arising from the sisters' activities. He never fully recovered from the torturing and died at a young age, leaving four young children.

My grandfather also became involved in the by-election for North Roscommon in early 1917 and was a supporter of – and platform speaker for – Count George Plunkett. As Sinn Féin's first parliamentary victory, it was the beginning of the end of the previously dominant Irish Parliamentary Party, or Redmondites, who were wiped out in the full election in 1918. That first 1917 by-election success in North Roscommon had been followed by a few more by-election successes that year, including that of de Valera. Each of these candidates also promised not to attend the parliament at Westminster; it was the start of Sinn Féin's abstentionist policy, which still continues even though the world and the entire political scenario have changed since then.

My Sharkey grandfather was not militant in any form, but he knew many of those who became so from 1919 onwards, including his siblings.

On one occasion he was persuaded to allow some IRA members to hide guns in a loft in an outhouse behind his house. Somebody obviously informed the police, and the house and gardens were raided by the Black and Tans. The outhouse was searched, but they decided not to check the loft above it. If they had found the guns, my grandfather would certainly have been shot on the spot – and maybe the rest of the family, too.

My grandmother and her children, including my then 3-year-old mother, were on their knees in the house saying the rosary and other prayers while the raiders searched. My grandmother always maintained afterwards that the prayers worked and that it was God who stopped the Black and Tans from finding the firearms. I don't know how religious my grandmother was before this incident, but her faith was certainly strong after it – and until her death in 1989, shortly after her ninety-ninth birthday. My grandfather did not allow himself to be compromised again, and although his sisters were actively involved in the War of Independence and the Irish Civil War, he stayed out of it.

He had a brother, Michael, who had emigrated in his mid-twenties to Massachusetts and stayed there, becoming a successful insurance and real estate broker. Another brother, Paddy, had been ordained as a priest and then emigrated to the USA, where he ministered as a curate in New York state. He also became very involved in the Irish political support movement, which had commenced before 1916 but which grew rapidly afterwards. He appeared before the committee on foreign affairs at the House of Representatives on Capitol Hill in Washington, DC in December 1918, which was holding hearings on 'the Irish Question'. It would seem that Fr Paddy played a significant role in de Valera's stay in the USA, when the latter – as president of Dáil Éireann – went to rally support and funds for the fledging Irish state. One of Fr Paddy's parishioners was a close relative of de Valera's; he had never met him before Fr Paddy introduced them privately.

When Fr Paddy returned to Ireland and sought a curateship in his own diocese of Elphin, he was refused by the bishop on the grounds of his political activities in the USA. He was offered a position by Bishop Fogarty of Killaloe, who shared his political sympathies, and he served as a curate in Liscannor, west Clare. Nonetheless, he appealed to the Pope in Rome against the discrimination he previously encountered. He was successful, and the Bishop of Elphin was forced to offer him a position. He served as a curate in a few parishes and eventually became a parish priest in Ballinameen. He wrote a number of books, the first of which, *The Heart of Ireland*, he self-published with the assistance of what is now known as crowd funding. Another of his books had the title *The Moytura Record*. This included an account of a part of ancient Irish history: the second battle of Moytura between the Tuatha Dé Danann and the invading Fomorians.

According to a report in the *Irish Independent* of 6 September 1920 – and in other newspapers that week – Fr Paddy had an altercation with the British military in Liscannor. Uniformed men interrupted a sports meeting and ordered him, the priest in charge, to remove the republican flag, the tricolour, which he had hoisted at the sports pitch. He refused when told to do so by the officer in charge; the officer withdrew, returning later with a large force. Fr Paddy told the officer that if he fired on the flag, he would be accountable for his life if he was shot, too. Machine guns were planted on the hill over the sports park, but the uniformed men withdrew in half an hour and the flag was still there. A few days later, an officer along with military in full equipment raided St Macrechy's House, the residence of the Liscannor priests, and searched the rooms of Fr Paddy and his colleague Fr O'Fagan. Although not recognised as such at the time, this was a premonition of the murders by the British military on Bloody Sunday, which took place two months later in Croke Park.

The four brothers and two sisters were all successful in a variety of businesses and professions. It is interesting to realise that they grew up on a small landholding in Drinane outside Strokestown, and Fr Paddy, Una, Lena and another sister, Bridget, were all educated in boarding schools in Sligo and Dublin. As far as I have ascertained, my Sharkey grandfather also had two other sisters; one became a nun, the other married another business owner in Strokestown.

My maternal grandmother, Josephine, also came from County Roscommon, having been born and reared in Carrownagleragh in Aughrim parish. Her father, Patrick Beirne, having returned from his adventures in South America, bought a farm, married into another holding and became relatively prosperous – a success that was further bolstered by some capital he brought back with him from Argentina. He later bought another two farms and became a member of the Irish National League and one of the nationalist poor law guardians in north Roscommon. The poor law guardians oversaw the running of the local workhouses, which had been established by the Poor Law Act of 1834. The guardians were initially drawn from the landed gentry and unionist class, who were levied with the cost of the workhouses. Gradually, however, nationalists and nationalist landowners became involved.

Patrick, who was known as Patricio in Argentina, became known locally as Bony Pat, 'Bony' being a shortened Roscommon version of Buenos Aires. He died in 1905; my mother never knew him, as she was born in 1918. Nevertheless, I think he influenced her in ways she wasn't conscious of. After his death, his widow, Catherine, changed the family name to O'Beirne, in keeping with the nationalist movement and increasing gaelicisation of the time.

Patrick and Catherine had three sons and five daughters, all of whom had families. I have met many of them, either first cousins once removed or second cousins. I'm not aware of any of my Sharkey grandmother's siblings having emigrated to the USA, but two of her sisters did move to and live in Wallasey on Merseyside.

My mother had five sisters and three brothers. Two of her brothers, Patrick Pearse and John Joseph, died as infants, and two of her sisters, Marian and Bernadette, died as young women. I only knew her brother Tommy and three sisters, Margaret, Teenie and Teresa, the last of whom became Sister Mary Catherine.

My mother played hockey and tennis when she was younger, but from the period when I was born she didn't have the time for sport. Even still, she was always very encouraging of me and my siblings' involvement in all forms of such activity. In later years, from the late sixties onwards, she regularly watched *Match of the Day* on BBC One on Saturday nights; later still, she became a great fan of Jack Charlton and Mick McCarthy, liking in particular their north of England accents, which probably reminded her of her schooldays in Lincoln. When she came to live in Dublin, she resided in a flat with some of her sisters on Morehampton Road on the south side of Dublin, near where an uncle and aunt lived. She and her sisters rented a house in Howth each summer, beside where the summit car park is now situated, and commuted to work using the Howth tram (to get up and down Howth Hill).

A few years after my Sharkey grandfather died in 1961, the business of Sharkey Bros in Strokestown was sold and my grandmother came to live in Dublin until her death in 1989, so she spent at least her last twenty years there. My father's brother John had married my mother's sister Teenie in 1953, and they lived in the house on Brian Road with my Glackin grandparents until those grandparents died in 1956 and 1963. It was to that house that my Sharkey grandmother moved in the mid-1960s, thus continuing my connection with that house even though my uncle John died in 1974.

That is a brief story of my most immediate ancestors. As is clear, their influences – brought to bear on me through the medium of my parents – were exceedingly varied.

Looking back now, there are some characteristics that I recognise, but many that have not survived through a couple of generations. While I may be a small landowner (owning a large garden), I certainly could not claim to be a farmer like many of my ancestors. Nor could I claim to have any ability as a carpenter, but I still love the smell of sawdust, which I remember from my paternal grandfather's workshop on Brian Road.

I certainly could not see myself surviving as a coalminer, but I recognise that my father's maternal grandfather, John Marlow, was probably not very enamoured of that job either – it's unlikely he had an option if he wanted to stay living near his County Tyrone home and land.

I have possibly inherited my maternal grandfather Sharkey's interest in business, although probably not his acumen. While I may have inherited my maternal grandmother's love of singing and music, I have not maintained her belief in God and the power of prayer.

Like my Sharkey grandaunts, I didn't hesitate to resort to the High Court when I needed to during my career – though I was not a litigator, and generally tried to avoid courts if I could find a way to resolve a dispute without them.

Like my mother's maternal grandfather, Patrick Beirne, I like to travel. But I'm not sure that I would have had the courage or patience to travel to Argentina on a six-week sea journey in a ship that didn't at least have a nice luxurious cabin for me above deck.

Although not quite as delayed as my father's entry to the legal profession, like him I didn't take a direct path to qualification – it was only after trying something else for a couple of years that I followed in his footsteps and became a solicitor. The story of how I got there, what I did on the way and what happened after that form my life story so far.

Compared to what I know of the life of my ancestors, my life has been very easy and comfortable so far. In that regard, I have also been lucky. It will be many years before it is known whether my descendants – Shane, Louisa, Sinéad, Josh, Lexi, Cody, Charlie and Éabha – have had as happy a life as I, but it is all that one can hope for one's children and grandchildren.

PRIMARY EDUCATION AND PRE-TEEN YEARS

I started in Belgrove National School, or Scoil Eoin Baiste, in senior infants' class in January 1955, having completed junior infants and the first term of senior infants in North William Street National School. The junior and senior infants and first class were mixed boys and girls and held in the girls' school building. My first teacher was Miss Heade; when I moved up to first class at the end of that academic year, the teacher changed and I was then in Mrs O'Boyles class.

Mrs O'Boyle also lived on Seafield Avenue, opposite our house. Her younger son and daughter, Frank and Aideen, were friends of ours, and Mrs O'Boyle was a very nice and courteous lady, and a good teacher, so that was a pleasant school year. My main memory from the time was making my First Confession and Communion in St John's church, where the parish priest was Fr Carton.

Fr Carton was quite deaf. I remember going to confession one time, maybe my first confession, to have him reply to my shy description of my sins with the words 'You did what?' in a very loud voice; when I left the confession box, I was highly embarrassed, not realising that it was his deafness and not his shock that caused his reaction.

Apparently I had been worried about my First Confession, and when my mother asked what was worrying me, I told her that it was all my sins: I was disobedient, told lies and when I was 4 years old I used to swear and curse. She laughed and told me that the swearing and cursing wasn't my fault – in fact she had forgotten about it, but that I was only copying words that I had heard out playing in Nottingham Street.

The school yard where we played at break times was largely concrete, so there were often cuts and bruises from falls or trips. The outdoor toilets did not have a roof, and the boys' and girls' toilets adjoined each other. One of the competitions played by the boys was to try to pee over the wall onto the girls. I don't remember anyone succeeding; we were 7 years old at most, so the wall was a little too high for us.

The principal of the girls' school was Áine Ní Cheanainn, a formidable woman but well recognised and respected as an educator, Irish language enthusiast and administrator. She subsequently spent some time on the board of Teilifís Éireann, when it opened in 1961.

When we moved to Clontarf in December 1954, there was no difficulty in enrolling me into the school from January 1955, after the Christmas break, as I had already been in school for fifteen months and this had been arranged in advance. However, my parents wanted to have my sister Bernadette enrolled in junior infants, as she was to be 5 years old at the end of the month. That caused some difficulty, as she should have been 5 years old in September, when the school year commenced. She was initially refused enrolment, but my parents were not happy with that. They learned of Miss Ní Cheanainn's home address on Castle Avenue from Mrs O'Boyle and had a pleading personal letter delivered to her home during the holiday break. I guess that Mrs O'Boyle might have had a word with her colleague as well: Bernadette was accepted to start school, as my parents wanted.

After finishing first class in June 1956, my friends and I graduated to the boys' school in the building next to the girls'. Entering second class, we were taught by Fergus O'Kennedy, who was a real man's man, and we started to grow up quickly. Fergus was an excellent teacher, as were all the teachers that I encountered in my five years in that school, but notably, his pet interests were sport and drama. Although drama would not have been my forte, and I still have limited interest in it, I did participate in a few school plays in national school and some operettas in secondary school. This is despite a bit of a fiasco on what was supposed to be my stage debut.

Mr O'Kennedy had devised a small play, or sketch, for his class, with singing, dancing, speaking and some unimportant story – which gave background to the performance – and entered this in a school drama festival in the Damer Hall. The sketch was built around his star performer, Alan O'Duffy – the son of Michael O'Duffy, a well-known professional singer and entertainer. Alan had joined our class at the beginning of the school year, when his father had come back to Ireland from London. He was taller than most in the class and spoke with an English accent, so he stood out in more ways than one. He was a good singer and seemed to have a stage presence.

I cannot remember what the story behind the sketch was, but what I do remember was that Alan had to sing a song with three verses. In the second verse there was a reference to 'the wild west'; I was a Native American warrior who, at the mention of the words 'wild west', was to rush out on stage, do a war dance, wave a tomahawk and run off. To me as an 8-year-old, this was exciting. I hadn't heard of the Damer Hall – or Halla Damer, as it was known in Irish – but it was in the city centre and therefore had to be important in my thinking. We had a number of rehearsals in the school in the weeks beforehand, but none of these were 'dress rehearsals', so I didn't realise what exactly was involved.

The day of our big performance arrived; we went into the city on a special bus and arrived into the dressing room behind the stage, where we dressed and undressed. I was stripped to the waist and given long suede trousers to put on. On my head, I had a bandana – to the bandana was attached a strip of feathers, which were then glued to my head. This was the makings of an Indian chief's headdress. The mothers of two of my classmates, who were assisting the teacher, painted my upper torso with red stripes and designs of different colours. I was completely covered in paint, feathers and makeup.

Unfortunately Alan O'Duffy, having sung the first verse really well, forgot the second and went straight to the third verse, where there was no reference to the 'wild west' and therefore no cue to send a young Indian warrior onto the stage to do his war dance. Having spent half an hour or so being painted, plastered and feathered, I didn't even get to go on stage. I think it took my mother two days of scrubbing to clean me up.

Some of these trivia that stick in the memory are surprising. Perhaps I wouldn't have remembered this incident if Alan O'Duffy hadn't later achieved some considerable fame in the entertainment business.

Alan left Dublin at the end of that school year, going back to London with his father and family. He resurfaced more than fifteen years later as a record producer for the Rolling Stones and many other famous rock 'n' roll groups. It amused me to see the guy who had screwed up my nascent theatrical and dancing career cavorting with Mick Jagger, the late Charlie Watts and their pals on TV and in newspapers and magazines. He had a very successful career in the music industry, also working with Eric Clapton, Paul McCartney, Andrew Lloyd Webber and Tim Rice, among many others. I suppose he has totally forgotten the fact that back in 1957 he forgot the second verse of a song in what was probably his first stage appearance, leaving me with my career in tatters before it began.

Luckily, Mr O'Kennedy, without acknowledging the error of his young protégé, and probably recognising that my talents lay elsewhere, compensated by taking a greater interest in my sporting development. At that time he was the coach of the school under twelves (junior team) and under fourteens (senior team) hurling and Gaelic football teams, and of the athletics team. I can remember his sitting on top of a desk in class, down among the boys, chatting to us about some football match that had taken place over the previous weekend; he engaged with us as if he was one of us, rather than our teacher.

There was a field behind the school, and we used to play football there; however, being only 8-year-olds, we didn't get much space from the older boys except when we got to play during PE class. I don't know how widespread PE class was in other national schools at that time, but it was a feature of our school; we also had football practice with Mr O'Kennedy and drill practice with Sergeant Ryan. There was a school sports day in June each year, and one feature of the activities was the drill display by the boys in each class. We dressed up in whites, used small flags, marched in unison, performed exercises and twirled our flags like real soldiers – or as we subsequently learned, like American high school girl cheerleaders.

In any event, Mr O'Kennedy encouraged me, and at the end of the year he made me the captain of a team in an interclass league for 8 and 9 year olds, even though I was one of the youngest playing. Before this league commenced, my father brought me into Boylans shoe shop in Talbot Street to buy me a pair of football boots. A friend of his, Seamus Mooney, was the manager there, and I presume that he got a good deal. At any rate, I now felt unbeatable in my new studded boots and could discard the old hobnailed pair that I had been using.

We had a series of games in St Anne's Park, and I guess the purpose of the tournament was twofold: competition for the sake of competition and exercise, but also trials for the school teams for the following year. My team won, and we were awarded medals. As winning captain, I received a shield trophy – the first of many medals and trophies that I have been fortunate to win during my life. I hope to continue to do so, albeit now only for golf.

I can remember the members of that team. There were ten of them – including Mick Gaffney, with whom I won lots of finals over the next few years. The one that sticks out most in my memory, even after sixty years, is Dermot Pierce. Piercey, as we knew him, turned out to be a brilliant Gaelic football, soccer and rugby player. He was always a very amusing character, with a very witty turn of phrase. He later became a successful chartered surveyor and property developer and was largely responsible for the development of the East Point Business Park and Earlsfort Plaza developments in Dublin. Unfortunately, Dermot died too young, when only in his early fifties, but I still remember his war cry, 'Have no fear, Piercey's here.' In those early days, he was always off doing something else and frequently late – which gave him plenty of opportunities to yell those memorable words.

Sometime around then, I had an unusual experience when my mother sent me on an errand to the shops on Vernon Avenue. I bought whatever I was to get, which was quite small, and was walking home along Seafield Road, three hundred yards from home. A youth who was in his late teens, maybe nine or ten years older than me, was cycling by and stopped to ask me the way to St Anne's Park. I was very proud to be able to give him directions. He then offered to give me a lift home on the crossbar of his bicycle. I was flattered to be asked by a boy that much my senior and agreed. As we passed the bottom of Seafield Avenue, he suggested that I continue with him to show him the way, and I agreed without recognising any danger. He told me that he would give me a lift home later.

We went up Seapark Road, along Mount Prospect Avenue and into St Anne's Park. He then continued through the park, which was almost empty, and further than I had ever been – off the roads and paths, and into trees. There was a shed there, which was open but unoccupied. He told me to go in and followed me. I cannot remember what he said afterwards, but I do remember his producing a knife at some stage. He was flicking the knife, telling me how sharp it was, and at one stage he put it up to my neck. I cannot remember being scared, but I did urge him to take me home, as I was now worried that I was late and would get into trouble. He eventually did so, giving me a lift and dropping me off at the top of my road. I walked down the avenue and into my home.

I didn't know how long I was away, but my father had returned home from work and was worried sick when I wasn't there; my mother couldn't explain where I was. There was initially a mixture of relief and anger at my being so late. My mother hugged me and then stayed outside the sitting room while my father asked me to explain where I had been. When I relayed the story to him, he broke down and cried. That was dramatic for me, as I had never seen my father cry. He asked me to describe the person who had given me the lift; I did, explaining that he was tall and that I thought I had seen him at Mass in St John's church sometime previously.

My mother wanted my father to call the police, but he said he wouldn't, as the person didn't seem to have done anything wrong. I didn't realise at the time that my father was questioning me to ascertain if I had been sexually assaulted, but he was clearly satisfied from my answers that nothing of that nature had occurred. Nevertheless, he wanted to find out who the person was. On the following Sunday, my mother and father and I stood on Vernon Avenue after Mass, and I pointed out the actual person to them. He was with a friend of his, and I also recognised the bicycle involved. My father sent us home and he followed them further up Vernon Avenue. I never heard if my father confronted him, but I remember overhearing him tell my mother that the person lived on Blackheath Park.

I forgot this entire incident for decades, but it did come back to me a few years ago, even to the extent of seeing in my mind's eye the person and his friend on Vernon Avenue that Sunday morning. I realised then that eventually, after I left secondary school, I grew to know both of them quite well – one from playing basketball with the St Paul's College past pupils' team, and the other from the past pupils' committee, to which I had been elected as the representative of my class. When I remembered the incident, I realised that I did not recall the fraught episode or their involvement during the period when I was meeting them fairly regularly – and when the memory did come back, I initially couldn't remember which of the two was the guy actually involved. By the time that I had forced my memory to dredge that up, the person had died.

His friend is still alive, and I used to meet him fairly often at various sports events; however, I never raised the subject with him. I did raise the matter recently with a friend, Cormac Hughes, who lived near the guy who had given me a lift through St Anne's that day. He confirmed to me that that person had been suspected on other occasions of deviant behaviour but that no charges were ever made.

I also remembered that, a couple of years after the incident, I was playing for the school team against Raheny National School on the Raheny end of St Anne's Park, and we were brought to a shed to change into our football gear. I recalled that I recognised the shed from the earlier incident but didn't say anything to anyone about it – and I then forgot about the entire experience for nearly fifty years. To me the whole affair was another example of my good luck, and I know that I was never as naive again in my life. I do not know whether the older boy had intended to molest me or cut my throat, but he did neither; it was my poor mother and father who suffered most from the incident.

One of the images that I saw on BBC News on television in 1956, when visiting my uncle Patrick and aunt Bridget's home in Kilsallaghan, was the Russian tanks rolling through the streets of Budapest to put down the Hungarian Uprising, which had started in late October and was crushed by the second week in November. I'm not sure of the reason that it made such an impression on me, but it was probably the first occasion that I saw live footage of a war, and it caused me some lost sleep. I had heard a little about the Second World War and knew about the Luftwaffe bombing of the North Strand in 1941, but that seemed remote in history and this seemed very real and near. We didn't yet have a television set at home, so the novelty of the BBC News probably added to the impact.

When I moved to third class, the teacher changed; alhough I still had a lot of contact with Mr O'Kennedy through sports, my teacher for the next year was Mr Joyce. When we moved to fourth class, we then had Mr Motherway; in fifth class, Mr Clery. Each of them was likewise a great educator. At some stage during those years, John McGahern, who subsequently became renowned as a writer, joined the teaching staff of the school. He was never my teacher directly, but occasionally, if my teacher was absent, some of the class would be moved temporarily to another classroom; I was moved on a couple of occasions to Mr McGahern's classroom.

My recollection of him from that limited experience was that he lived in a different world. I can still envisage him standing at the top of the classroom, looking absentmindedly out of the window as if in a dream, with his hands in his pockets. I guess he might have been writing his novels in his head during those reveries.

I cannot comment on whether he was a good teacher or not, as I couldn't judge from my limited experience. He was removed from his teaching job some years later by my old acquaintance Fr Carton, who was the school patron, but by that time I had left Belgrove and was in secondary school in St Paul's College. One of Mr McGahern's novels, *The Leavetaking*, dealt with his time in Dublin, including his time teaching in Belgrove, and it was interesting to get the description of the school and some of the other teachers from his perspective.

Belgrove had a well-earned reputation at that time for its top-grade teachers, good students and satisfactory results in the primary certificate examinations and the entrance and scholarship examinations for entry to secondary school. It also had a number of innovations: there was the option to take Latin and French lessons (for fifth and sixth class students), to join a choir, to compete in drama festivals and feiseanna ceoil, and to attend film shows in the school hall. Also, each year in May or June there was a very comprehensive concert, with each class putting on a show and a multi class operetta, and boys of any age could audition.

As well as competing in inter-school competitions in hurling and Gaelic football, athletics was coached and promoted, and there was an annual sports day. All of this was led by the principal of the school, Micheal O'Ceilleachair, or Kelleher, who was recognised as one of the leading educators of that generation in Ireland.

Sometime between 1961 and 1967, Belgrove boys' school took over the infant boys' education from the girls' school and was divided into a junior boys' school (5–8 years old) and a senior boys' school (9–12 years old). Mr Motherway became principal of the junior boys' school and Mr O'Ceilleachair, principal of the senior boys'. Coincidentally, my wife, Mary, was a teacher in the junior boys' school between 1967 and 1971, before she left to go as a volunteer teacher to British Honduras, known as Belize since independence. I didn't know her at that time, but she shares good memories of the school from the perspective of a young teacher, and even though Mr O 'Ceilleachair was not her direct boss, she knew him and held him in high regard. Her boss was Seán O'Boyle, who had succeeded Mr Motherway as principal – Mr O'Boyle being my former neighbour and the husband of Mrs O'Boyle, my teacher in first class.

I'm conscious that I could be prone to over-romanticising the school, but I do know that I enjoyed my time there; I believe that it had a beneficial effect on the rest of my life. Nevertheless, I am equally conscious that it was not all sweetness and roses, particularly for those boys who came from a poor or dysfunctional background, with no education tradition in their families; those who had little encouragement from home to study and keep up with the homework that we were expected to complete each night.

The school had an ethos of work and study – doing homework and expecting its pupils to want to learn and advance themselves. This ethos was great for those solid middle-class boys whose parents were high achievers or who recognised the advantages of being such and were ambitious for their boys. Those who didn't have that encouragement and ambition from their home environment were initially encouraged in school, and most teachers seemed to be patient and supportive of these boys, but if there wasn't an appropriate response to this initial patience, the punishment that followed was often harsh.

We all suffered some level of physical or corporal punishment in school, but some of those boys that I described got more than their fair share. I don't think that it was ever sadistic, but it was often painful. It would constitute criminal behaviour now, but at that time it was accepted as normal disciplining for perceived or actual bad behaviour. This, together with the lack of encouragement from home, often resulted in some boys staying away from school, or 'mitching', which was the start of a cycle that soon involved school attendance officers and ended up with some boys being sent to 'reformatory schools'. I remember hearing of Daingean and Letterfrack, which later became infamous. Although we were conscious that these were places to be avoided, I'm sure that we were not aware – nor, I'm sure, were the teachers – of how terrible and depraved these so-called 'reformatory schools' were.

It was only many years later, when some survivors went public about these institutions, that the horrors were revealed. Paddy Doyle wrote a book, *The God Squad*, and another survivor, Mannix Flynn, wrote a play; both works were about their time in one of these establishments, and were eventually followed by some investigations by newspaper and TV journalists. Ultimately the government instigated formal inquiries into their operations, which showed the hell of deprivation and sadism to which these unfortunate boys were subjected. We know now how barbaric these institutions were. Even though most people had no idea, there were some persons in authority who did. Those individuals, and the religious institutions and relevant governments who collaborated in this barbarism, can be judged now on a par with those who co-operated with the operation of concentration camps in Eastern and Central Europe in the 1940s, and since then in other warzones.

I can still remember two boys from my class who spent some time in one or other of those institutions. One of them, Henry, had a haunted look like one sees sometimes in historical photographs from Auschwitz; the other, John Joe, had a look of defiance and mistrust that was likely to lead him into further trouble. I have not seen them or even heard of them for nearly sixty years, and I hope that their lives improved after they left school.

This aspect of schooling remains, for me, one of the terrible aspects of my early education. While I came through the national school system successfully, loved almost every day of it and looked forward to nearly every new day, I recognise that some of my fellow pupils were let down by the school and its high standards, ending up in hell on earth.

I don't blame Mr O'Ceilleachair or any other teacher for what happened to these boys; perhaps the boys themselves did. I can try to understand it from their point of view, but Belgrove National School and my primary education was a happy time for me and helped to lay solid foundations for my subsequent education – both formal and informal – and my professional career.

The teacher that I had in sixth class was the late Mr J. Desmond Millett. In my opinion he was exceptionally good: a very helpful motivator and communicator, learned and intelligent, and very encouraging of me. He was also in charge of the school choir and musical director of the operettas, which were part of the annual school concert. He wasn't particularly small but my recollection is that he had a habit of standing on his toes.

Some years after I left Belgrove, Mr Millett also left; he joined the priesthood and, as far as I know, spent the rest of his life ministering to the spiritual life of parishioners in England, principally near Bristol. An old friend of mine recently gave me his address, where he was still ministering as Canon Millett until his death in September 2021 at the age of 92. I had written a letter to him a few years earlier. I'm not sure that he ever received it or was in a position to reply, but I did receive another letter from him. In my letter, I thanked him for his contribution to my life and told him that I recognised how he operated on the basis that 'Education is not the filling of a pail but the lighting of a fire', a phrase that has been ascribed to W.B. Yeats. At the time I didn't recognise the difference between education and learning, particularly for an examination. It was probably after I finished university – doing a little tutoring and lecturing myself, as well as helping to train young lawyers in my office – that I was conscious of the distinction.

As I said, I enjoyed primary school, and most of my memories are happy ones. The teachers did dispense physical punishment, however, and undoubtedly some boys were punished more than others. Mr Kelleher had a bamboo cane, which he often had with him and used to punish boys when he thought it necessary. He kept the cane in the sleeve of his suit jacket, and it invariably showed as a bulge at his shoulder. When we saw Mr Kelleher coming, we always looked to see if there was a bulge at his shoulder. If there was, trouble was on the way; if not, we could all relax.

I cannot remember any boy who went through five or six years in Belgrove without having received some physical punishment. Nevertheless, from chatting to boys in other schools, both at the time and later, I know that the punishment administered in Belgrove was less severe than in most other similar schools.

A campaign to outlaw physical punishment in schools was started a few years later by Dr Cyril Daly, whose children had been attending another local school and had been physically punished. He had them moved to Belgrove, which he obviously considered more civilised than their previous school. His campaign was initially opposed by the Department of Education, teachers' unions and school managers, who were usually the local parish priests, but it was ultimately successful: physical punishment was outlawed, and schools are now a more civilised and less frightening place than they used to be.

I enjoyed success academically and in extracurricular activities. The latter were principally sports, the drill display and the school concert, but I did sometimes participate in the school choir. I represented the school on a few occasions on Radio Éireann, including on *The School Around the Corner*, a well-known programme of the time presented by Paddy Crosbie, and on an Irish-language discussion program. I also attended Latin and French classes after our usual class hours in the last two years at Belgrove.

Nevertheless, my best achievements were on the football field. I got my place on the junior (under twelves) Gaelic football team when I was in fourth class and still under 10 years old. Many of our games were played in the Phoenix Park, Cabra, Ringsend, Mount Merrion and other locations, which required two bus journeys. Others were closer – in St Anne's Park or Fairview Park – but it was exceptional for any location to have indoor changing facilities, so we togged out on the side of the football pitch; this was a time before tracksuits, and it sometimes occurred that after a rain shower you pulled a wet sweater and trousers over the football kit and then got the bus home.

It was in the Phoenix Park that I first experienced the dividing line between where it rains and where it doesn't. Our team were getting dressed after a match and spread out over a thirty-square-yard area. Some of the guys were getting wet, including me, and others less than three feet away were dry. Obviously, this must occur in any given downfall – unless it were to rain all over the world at the same time – but it was the first time that I noticed it, and it stuck in my memory.

It was towards the end of that school year, 1958/59, that I had the accident referred to earlier – when I was knocked off my bicycle by a car outside the school and broke my right leg in a couple of places. As a result of that, my leg was in plaster of Paris for a long time; even when it was taken off, my use of that leg was very limited for most of the summer of 1959. I tried not to let that totally inhibit my having fun and learned to kick a football with my left foot – so that when I went back to school in September 1959, I was more adept with my left than my right. Mr O'Kennedy and Mr O'Dea, his assistant, were delighted with my recovery and made me into a centre half-back, which was entirely new to me, as I had always been a forward. We did well that year but were defeated on a few occasions and didn't reach the playoffs. With practise, using my right foot again, I gradually became two-footed.

At the start of the following year, we were told that the under twelves team would have a new coach, Mr Seán Kelly, who had joined Belgrove as a teacher one or two years previously. I was appointed as the team captain and reverted to the forwards. Seán adopted a different approach to skill practice, tactics and physical fitness, which was novel for us – and I guess novel in the game generally. He had completedd an extra degree in sports and PE, and was anxious to test his new ideas on us. It was probably the first time that we were coached on the importance of space – creating it by moving around much more when off the ball and then using it productively rather than relying solely on the more basic skills of catch, solo run and kick. We went through the season unbeaten, won a semi final and ended up in the final of the Clann na nGael cup on 25 March 1961 in Croke Park, playing against Cabra National School. This created great excitement in the school, and at least one new song was written for the supporters to sing from the Cusack Stand.

The team that day was Vincent Humphries in goal; Alan Connolly, Tim Moore and Liam Dunne in the full-back line; Gerry Moore, Finbarr Crowley and Garvan Donnelly in the half-back line; Paddy Gogarty and Andy Fottrell in midfield; Brian Mangan, Stephen O'Sullivan and myself in the half-forward line; and Dick Sherlock, John Daly and Mick Gaffney in the full-forward line. The subs were Brendan Malley, Fergus Cronin, Kevin Williams, Brendan Moylan, Mick Joyce, Tim Donovan and Tony Doherty.

This was definitely the highlight of my sports career up to then, and nothing that I have achieved since came close. I'm not sure how the rest of the team feel about that occasion, but Paddy Gogarty did win All-Ireland finals with Dublin in the mid-1970s, so maybe that surpassed the Clann na nGael cup for him. We won the final by 2-7 to 2-2, the first time that Belgrove – or Clontarf, as we were called – had won any schools cup.

After the final whistle, I was presented with the cup. The team then carried me shoulder-high around the pitch in Croke Park and over to where our parents and fellow pupils were standing. My parents and older set of siblings were there, as was my paternal grandfather. It is only now when watching my own grandchildren play games that I realise how proud he was of me; it gives me a lot of pleasure now to think that I was able to give him that moment of pride and joy a couple of years before he died. Unfortunately, five of the team that played that day have since died also.

At the annual school concert a few months later, the main part – other than the usual operetta – was a pageant of acting, marching and singing about the team and our victory. It was strange to see someone on stage acting as me; I cannot remember who had the part, but equally, I don't remember being impressed with his representation. Seán Kelly was doubtless largely responsible for our victory, but he tragically died a short time later, drowning in a swimming pool in a university in the USA, where he was doing a postgraduate degree in PE.

As I stated earlier, I also prospered academically, tending to be top of my class in term examinations. I remember, over Christmas in 1960, getting a school report that showed that I received 101 out of 100 marks in geography. The geography teacher in that sixth class was Mr O'Ceilleachair, who put a premium on neatness in paper work, allowing 3 marks for it – a premium that facilitated the ostensible impossibility in my own results. For the primary certificate examination at the end of that school year – a national examination – I was awarded 100 marks out of 100 for mental arithmetic, 100 out of 100 for arithmetic, 198 out of 200 for English and 196 out of 200 for Irish – an average of 99 per cent. I was later told by Mr O'Ceilleachair that it was the highest aggregate mark in the country. Whether it was or not, Mr O'Ceilleachair was almost as pleased as I was proud.

In advance of the primary certificate examination, most of the boys in the class – myself included – had done a number of entrance exams for various secondary schools, including a few boarding schools, and I was offered scholarships of varying value in a number of them. In the end, my parents, with my approval, decided to send me to the local secondary school, St Paul's College, on Sybil Hill, Raheny, which was situated on the edge of St Anne's Park and was within easy cycling distance. I think the annual fee in 1961 was £40, but my parents were charged £25. When I received my primary certificate results, my father bought me a new red three-gear bicycle with straight handlebars. I was now ready for the next phase of my education.

Not everybody was impressed by my achievements and on a couple of occasions I was attacked by a group of fellow pupils when they got me on my own in a quiet area. These guys punched me and kicked me, saying, 'you think you're great but you're a f—ing goody goody.' I got away from them the first time but was caught again a week later and the same thing occurred. My pride may have been hurt, but I didn't suffer anything more serious. I knew the guys who attacked me; they were known as 'puzzlers', as they came from the Conquer Hill and Brian Boru Avenue area of Clontarf, which was known as 'the puzzle'. I met many of them over the next few years around Clontarf, but I never said anything about the incidents, nor did they. I suppose it was a form of bullying, or attempted bullying, but I guess I had sufficient self-confidence to be unaffected by it

Author's father and mother, Joe and Isabel, on their wedding day in September 1947.

Proud parents, Joe and Isabel, with author at 8 months old, in the
garden at Nottingham Street.

Left: Author on first birthday, 1949.

Below: Author not as happy having to share the limelight with siblings Bernie and Joe, 1952.

Above: Picnic on seafront at Clontarf with father and siblings, 1952.
Below: Holidays at beach in Rush, County Dublin with father and siblings, 1952.

Above: Author's father, Joe, after receiving parchment on admission as solicitor, 1953.

Left: Author after receiving parchment on admission as solicitor, 1972.

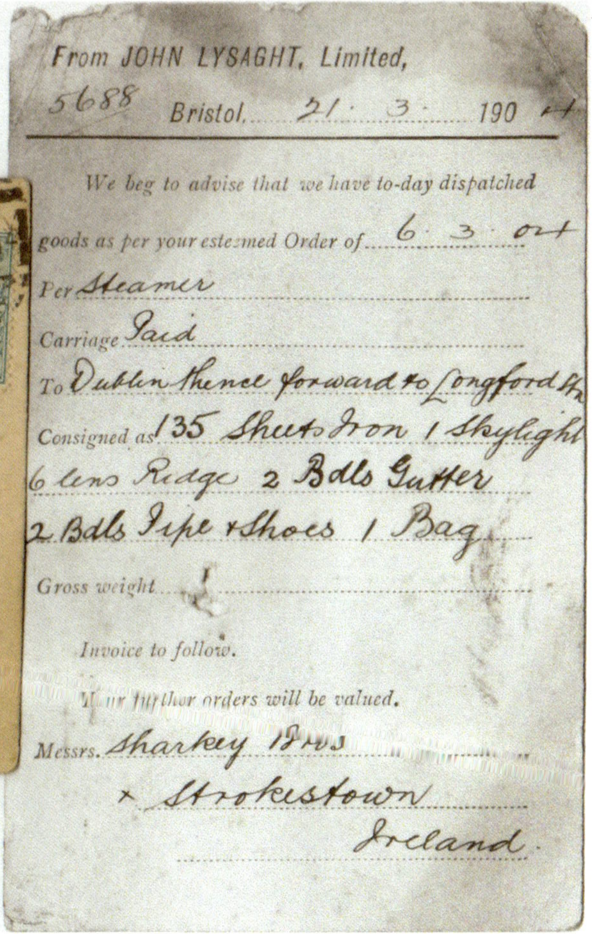

From JOHN LYSAGHT, Limited,

5688 Bristol, 21. 3. 1904

We beg to advise that we have to-day dispatched goods as per your esteemed Order of 6. 3. 04

Per Steamer

Carriage Paid

To Dublin thence forward to Longford &c

Consigned as 135 Sheets Iron 1 Skylight 6 lens Ridge 2 Bdls Gutter 2 Bdls Pipe & Shoes 1 Bag

Gross weight

Invoice to follow.

Your further orders will be valued.

Messrs. Sharkey Bros
× Strokestown
Ireland.

Left: Grandfather Sharkey before his wedding, 1911.

Below: Wedding party including Grandfather and Grandmother Glackin and their extended family, c.1940.

Opposite: Despatch note for goods to grandfather, John Sharkey, Ironmonger, Strokestown, 1904.

Right: Author as captain of Belgrove N.S. Clontarf U 12s 1960 – 61.

Below: Belgrove N.S. Clontarf U.12 gaelic football team winners Clan na Gael Cup, 1961.

Above: St.Paul's College Maths class 1962 with Fr Gardiner.

Below: St.Paul's College Prizewinners, 1966.

PRIZEWINNERS

Back Row: J. Foley, D. Kiberd, A. Williams, H. Duffy, B. O'Kelly, M. Mohan, D. Branagan, C. Connolly.
3rd Row: A. Lacy, J. Cowan, K. O'Brien, E. Brennan, M. Clynes, B. Rae, C. Lennon.
Seated: P. Campbell, G. McElroy, P. Lyons, T. Barragry, J. Glackin, J. Keehan, P. Flanagan, P. Lacy.
Ground: T. Larkin, P. Gilmour, L. Tobin, D. Gilligan, A. Smyth, J. Gordon, G. Howard.

Above: Author and Glackin siblings, 1967.
Below: Author and Glackin siblings, 2019.

SECONDARY EDUCATION AND TEENAGE YEARS

St Paul's College, Raheny was a relatively new boys' secondary school. It was opened in 1950 on land granted by Dublin Corporation to the Vincentian Fathers in order to establish a secondary school in the rapidly expanding north-eastern suburbs of Dublin. It was situated on Sybil Hill, which was strictly in Raheny parish – and Raheny was its address – but it was really in Clontarf and on the edge of St Anne's Park. The school was originally located in a large mansion-style house, Sybil Hill House, but a new modern school was developed very soon afterwards and the old house became 'the priest's house', for those teachers in the school who were priests and for priests who had retired or were on temporary leave from missionary work in Africa.

The school had five or six playing fields at the rear, as well as a church and hall, and tennis and basketball courts. There was a large concrete area, which was used for playing soccer and other games at break time, and a large bicycle-parking area. All of the land had been part of the former Guinness family estate; it adjoined the remainder of that estate, which had been granted to Dublin Corporation for the further development of St Anne's Park as recreation grounds. Considerable controversy and upset arose nearly sixty-five years later, when the Vincentians sold the playing fields – which they had been granted for close to nominal consideration – to a developer for intensive housing.

In secondary school, there were a number of changes from the practices and procedures that we were accustomed to at national school which were immediately obvious. The first was that all the boys wore a kind of school uniform: a school sweater and tie – or a purple school blazer – and grey long trousers, we having had short trousers until then. Instead of one teacher for almost all subjects, as in primary school, there was a different teacher for each subject, with only a few exceptions – when, for instance, the priest who taught religious knowledge might also teach another subject. The curriculum was more extensive than in primary school. In addition to English, Irish, geography, religious knowledge and mathematics – which included not only arithmetic but also algebra and geometry – history and Latin were compulsory, with an option of two choices from science, French, commerce and drawing.

The classes were streamed based on results in the entrance examination, so that when I started in 2.3, there was also a 2.2 and 2.1, but we were all considered second year pupils – first year being for boys who had come through the prep school and had not done their primary cert exams. Many of my friends from Belgrove National School came to St Paul's at the same time as me, but there were also boys from other primary or national schools in the area, such as Killester NS, Raheny NS, Marino NS St Joseph's in Fairview and St Fintan's in Sutton. Others came from further afield, such as Portmarnock, Malahide, Donabate, Rush or Lusk, or from the preparatory school in St Paul's. The latter were always considered posher than the boys from the primary or national schools, as their parents had paid for their early education, whereas the national schools were free.

At that time there were fees payable in St Paul's, and indeed in all secondary schools; it was only after we left school that free secondary education was introduced by the late Minister for Education Donagh O'Malley in 1968. One effect of the streaming process and the introduction of boys from other schools was that my position as first in class, which I had become used to in national school, came under pressure. Although I was never out of the top three of the class overall, and was first in a number of subjects, only once or twice was I first overall. Two of the boys who regularly topped the class ended up as successful academics – one a senior lecturer in English Literature in Glasgow University, the other a senior lecturer in veterinary medicine in UCD. Many others in the class became successful in later life in a variety of careers and businesses, including one internationally renowned artist based in Canada, but the two who topped the class continued the aptitude shown at this early stage as they moved on to academic careers.

Another difference from national school was the longer school day. In Belgrove our classes ended at 2.15 p.m., unless one was doing the optional Latin or French class; in St Paul's, classes ended at 4 p.m., save on

Wednesday when they finished at 12.50 p.m., and on Saturday when they finished at 12.30 p.m. but church prayers then continued until 12.50 p.m. Getting up for school on a Saturday was initially an unwelcome novelty, but as classes were usually followed by rugby or basketball practice, or a match against another school, it didn't seem so bad after a while.

My father had always worked on Saturday mornings – as, indeed, did most other workers. I think that the five-day week wasn't introduced until the early 1960s. For this reason, there was some overlap where my father and I were the only ones at home who had to rise early on Saturdays. Although the school day was longer, it was offset by a longer lunch break. What's more, it was possible for me to cycle (or sometimes walk) home, have my lunch, listen to the radio (usually *The Kennedys of Castlerosse*), finish off some homework for the afternoon classes and be back at school for 2 p.m., when classes resumed.

During the weekdays, I tended to know what lunch I would have by the day it was: on Tuesday, minced meat with onions; on Wednesday, Irish stew; on Thursday, liver; and on Friday, fish – or when I stopped eating fish, fried eggs. Meat was not eaten on Fridays because Christ had reportedly died on a Friday and the Church had ruled that, as penance, no Catholic could eat meat on that day on pain of 'grievous sin'. It was not that fish was seen as more wholesome or healthier than meat; it was because the Roman Catholic Church in Ireland had ruled that abstinence was necessary.

Many religions seemed to have some quirky rule about food, as I subsequently learned that neither Jews nor Muslims eat pork. I accepted this restriction on eating meat on Fridays as a given; at least until my mid-teens, I never thought of questioning its rationality. Indeed, my recollection is that I accepted all the teachings of the Catholic religion without questioning them, regardless of their sense or reason. I was, in all respects, a good Catholic boy, serving Mass (both in St Gabriel's, my local church, and at the priests' house in St Paul's), observing Lent and days of abstinence, regularly attending Mass, confessing my sins to a priest, receiving Communion and feeling guilty for sins committed or wished for, particularly as puberty set in.

This was all recognised and appreciated by the priests in St Paul's, who I think began to see me as a possible recruit for the priesthood. It was hinted a few times over the years, but I didn't realise they were hints until later, when a more explicit comment was made about my possibly 'having a vocation'. When I thought about that for a very short time, I realised that it was not for me as there were three main obstacles: first, I liked girls, and this seemed to be verboten for priests; second, I hated snakes and didn't want to be sent to Africa as a missionary, where I would have to encounter the reptiles every day; third, I knew that I didn't have the patience to be a teacher, which seemed to be the only alternative to being a missionary. So that quickly got put aside when considering career options, which I probably started to do from age 15 onwards. I have no idea now whether any other boys in my class were prompted in this way, as it was not something that we talked or openly worried about.

Nevertheless, my 'sanctity' didn't do me any harm with the priests in St Paul's. I was favoured in many ways, and in my last couple of school years I held positions in some of the religious-based societies. For example, I was secretary of the Altar Society, which set the roster for altar servers for Masses in the priests' house and ceremonies in the school church or hall. I was also chairman of the Patrician Society, which was a religious, morals and ethics discussion group. This gave me my first experience of chairing and moderating the discussion of ideas, which was very useful experience for later life. Although I later realised that all of this religion was irrational nonsense and its practice was a form of brainwashing, I don't believe that my involvement in these societies caused me any long-term harm. It didn't stop me becoming an independent thinker, even though it may have delayed it, and as I said earlier in a slightly different context, *Je ne regrette rien.*

Nevertheless, religion was only a small part of my life at St Paul's. It was during my time at St Paul's that I developed from a young schoolboy through my teens to young adulthood. Though much of one's personality is formed at a younger age, these years between 13 and 18 are hugely important in self-development. I believe school played a positive role in my life, but I recognise that it wasn't so for everyone. Family and home environment also plays a huge part, but I think that the role played by friends and schoolmates is probably underestimated.

I was lucky in having the friends that I did; most of my close friends now are from friendships I made during my late teenage years. I am glad to be able to say that I am still in touch, to a greater or lesser extent, with most of the sixty to seventy boys who were in my year in St Paul's and are still alive. Unfortunately, a number of them have passed away, and the causes of death have ranged from the Vietnam War to a car crash to an accident on a submarine to more typical causes, such as cancer and cardiac arrest.

As I said, my experiences were positive, but some boys were bullied by teachers, or worse, by school colleagues. The latter sometimes involved taunting about shape, size, perceived sexual orientation, accent and any other aspect that involved a difference from the norm. I regret that I was one of those who taunted others, and I only hope that it didn't cause too much distress. I myself had a nickname from the time, aged 10, that I broke my leg and rapidly put on weight from lack of activity and increased eating during my recuperation. Someone called me 'Tubby', and that name stuck throughout my schooldays. I can honestly say that it never bothered me, but I know that in different circumstances it could have.

Our teachers in St Paul's were a mixture of priests and lay teachers. Unlike at Belgrove National School, where I hadn't experienced any teacher less than very good, in St Paul's it was another story – while some teachers were excellent, some were short of that. The president for my first four years there was Fr Thomas O'Flynn, a pleasant gentleman who was statesmanlike in his demeanour and always seemed calm and in control. Most of the teachers and priests had nicknames, but the only name that I can remember for Fr O'Flynn was 'Father Tom'. Other priests were Frs. O'Hanrahan, Kehoe, Gardiner, Johnston, Harbison, Woods, Briscoe, Raftery, Harris, Crowley and Steen. Fr Steen arrived as we entered sixth year – our final year – and took over as president from Fr O'Flynn. For whatever reason, I didn't really get on with him. Fr Crowley, who was known as 'Growler', was not very popular but I never had any problems with him throughout my time there. I was in his class at different times for English, Latin and religious knowledge, and I considered him erudite, encouraging and a good communicator. Though he was from west Cork, he didn't sound like it, at least as we perceived it. He looked like the actor Charles Laughton, with big jowls and a forbidding demeanour, but in reality he was very pleasant.

Most of the priests had a role in coaching sports or organising other extracurricular activities. The main sports were rugby and basketball from September to March, and basketball, athletics, tennis and cricket for the remainder of the school year. Fr Harris, nicknamed 'Jet' after the drummer in the Shadows, a popular band of the early sixties, organised an electronics club, and Fr Gardiner, affectionately known as 'Charlie' after a cartoon character (but mainly because his name was Charles), organised a camera club. Fr Crowley organised the Altar Society and a religious sodality, while Fr O'Flynn organised the debating societies, particularly for the senior boys. After he left, Fr Raftery looked after that society, which was officially known as the Literary and Historical Society.

Although I liked physics and chemistry, I didn't join the electronics club or camera clubs – sports were my priorities and took most of my spare time. I regret somewhat not joining the electronics club; becoming familiar with the basics, I might have had a better understanding of the technology developed since. Many of the boys in my class who did join that club ended up working in the broad computer and electronics industry in later life.

I had started playing rugby shortly after joining the school, and loved it from the beginning. In terms of skills, tactics and rules, it was very different from Gaelic football, which I had been playing since I could run, so it took a little adaptation. One of the boys who started rugby with me on the same day – when our coach was Fr Briscoe – was Kevin Mays, who later went on to be capped for Ireland in 1973 in the second row.

Kevin was always a giant as far as I was concerned: he was always big, and I was always relatively small. But he was a gentle giant, with amazing athletic ability – he was outstanding at rugby, basketball, cricket and the field events in athletics. Many of us actually suffered injuries in training trying to tackle him until we learned the proper technique but even then it was very difficult for young under thirteens to stop someone who was probably six feet, two inches and nearly thirteen stone when he was under twelve years of age. I never became a good or reliable tackler, and maybe it was my first unsuccessful attempts on Kevin that were to blame. I knew what to do but wasn't always brave enough to do it.

Besides rugby, I also started basketball – and when there wasn't rugby training, we had basketball coaching. In fact, as there was a basketball court in the school playground, we often played there during our mid-morning break if the older boys allowed us to do so. Although soccer wasn't an official sport, many of the boys played it in the school playground at break time; even though I often joined them, it was never a game that I really enjoyed playing.

Academically, I seemed to be progressing. At the end of fourth year, which was my third year in secondary school, I sat the intermediate certificate examination – or 'Inter Cert', as we called it. At the time it seemed to be the most important exam in our lives, but once it was over, we realised that much more important tests lay ahead. I performed well, although I didn't match my results from the primary certificate examination.

In St Pauls College, we had an annual sportsday, which was always a big occasion for the students, teachers and parents, and provided an informal occasion for parents to meet the teachers and other parents in a social setting. There was also an annual opera, with a different Gilbert and Sullivan production each year – including *Iolanthe*, *The Mikado*, *The Pirates of Penzance* and *H.M.S. Pinafore* – to which parents and families were invited. So it wasn't all academic activities during my time there.

A significant number of boys ended their secondary education after the Inter Cert. Others stayed back to repeat the year, as they were a year younger than the median and would otherwise have been finishing school at 16 years of age – which many teachers and parents considered too young. Indeed, others stayed back after fifth year for the same reason but didn't have to repeat the Inter Cert. Of those who left after the Inter Cert, some went to boarding schools, some went to vocational schools and started apprenticeships as tradesmen, and some went into family businesses. As they missed the last two years of bonding at school as senior boys, they tended to lose touch and fewer of them have stayed in contact with the rest of the class.

The leaving certificate cycle lasted two years – after the Inter Cert, we went into fifth year. At this stage, the streaming of pupils – that applied for the first three years – continued but with a key variation: streaming was now largely based on whether one wanted to do the honours or pass course. I decided to try the honours course in each subject, of which there were six – or seven if physics and chemistry were taken (as they were two separate subjects but only counted toward one final exam). I would have liked to continue studying history and geography, which I enjoyed, but the timetable didn't allow for it – choices had to be made between groups of subjects and it didn't allow for additional disciplines.

The issue of whether Irish should be compulsory was topical at the time, as it still is. I recognise now that some pupils were seriously stressed over the fact that they had to learn Irish, oral and written, but at the time I didn't have any sympathy for them. I didn't have a difficulty with Irish, and attributed that to the encouragement from home and the excellent basic learning I received at national school. I was a member of the Cumann Díospóireachta, the Irish debating club, and a part of the teams that competed in inter-school Irish-language debating competitions. I still like the language and can understand an Irish-language discussion on radio or television, but I abhor the cultural purist Gaelgeoirí who consider non-Irish speakers as in some way less Irish and insist on having Irish translations on every road sign, train, tram and bus communication, and official notice.

There was physical punishment in St Paul's, as in Belgrove, but individual teachers didn't have the right to administer it. A teacher who wanted to have a boy punished had to write a note and give it to the boy in question; that boy then had to take it to the dean of studies, who was in charge of discipline and was the only person entitled to dole out such punishment. It was a fairer system than in the national school: a boy wouldn't be struck in temper or spite but only after due consideration by the dean of studies.

In sixth year, I was appointed as one of the school prefects, of which there were twelve. We had a role in ensuring compliance with the disciplinary measures imposed by the dean of studies, and we also had an opportunity to influence the dean and the president on school issues generally. We were perceived as a form of liaison between the pupils and the management.

As it happened, 1966 – when I was in sixth year – was the fiftieth anniversary of the Easter Rebellion, and various commemoration events were held in the school – and in schools generally. I was involved in many of the commemorations. I won the school prize for essays, in Irish and in English, on themes based on the fiftieth anniversary. In a national essay contest, I was highly recommended. In the early morning of 8 March 1966, Nelson's Pillar, which had stood at the centre of O'Connell Street since 1809, was blown up by a group of IRA members. I remember getting a bus into the city after school that day to see the ruins. It wasn't totally destroyed at that stage, and it took another few days for the remains to be demolished by the Irish army, making the area safe. The column had been one hundred and twenty feet in height, so to see it almost totally razed to the ground was impressive. At the time, I didn't know that an important painting of the ruins was made by Lady Glenavy, who must have painted it at the scene; I would buy it years later at a charity auction in James Adam & Sons Art

Rooms, together with a large block of the original pillar, which was made of Wicklow granite. I have them both at home still, and every time I look at them it reminds me of that day and, to some extent, of that year.

But my teenage years were not all spent at school. This was the time when girls became interesting – as distinct from a few years earlier, when they were a nuisance who spoiled fun and got in the way of any mischief that we had planned. This was the time when I became interested in pop music, listening to Radio Luxembourg when I could, and when my father allowed me. I know that he couldn't stand most of what I wanted to listen to; it was only when my own son, Shane, became an avid music fan, in the 1980s and 1990s, that I began to sympathise with my father, but unfortunately he had died by then.

Although I liked the Beatles, I preferred the Searchers and the Rolling Stones. Elvis Presley and Cliff Richard were big stars – it took a few weeks and lots of Brylcreem trying to style my hair like Elvis before I realised that it was impossible and went back to being me. I don't think that since then I have ever tried to copy or look like somebody else, famous or otherwise. Clontarf GAA Club organised *céilithe* in the hall of Belgrove National School on Sunday nights for a few months over a couple of years, and that was my first opportunity to mix with girls who weren't immediate neighbours. It was good fun, but entirely innocent.

We all graduated from there to the hops, or discos, in Clontarf tennis club on Oulton Road. I was never a member of the tennis club, but for two summers, between 1965 and 1966, my pals and I were there a few times a week. In the summer of 1966 and for a few years afterwards we were regulars at the dance in the cricket club on Castle Avenue, which was also the rugby club. I went out with girls on a few occasions, but it wasn't until I left school that I had a girlfriend that lasted for more than two or three dates. At the time I felt there were lots of fish in the sea, and I enjoyed meeting different girls rather than being tied to one.

In the summer of 1963, when I was 14, I went to an Irish college in Ballingeary, County Cork with a group of friends for a month. My younger brother Joe and my sister Bernie were there too, but we lived fairly separate lives while there – not necessarily deliberately, but we had different residences, classes and friends. Although I had been to an Irish college in Kilmacurragh in County Wicklow for two or three weeks in the summer between primary school and secondary school – which was boys only, and more like a boarding school – the month in Ballingeary was the first time that I experienced teenage freedom.

Like many of the others there, I hated it initially; for the first week, some of us were planning on escaping back to Dublin if our requests to our parents for rescue were ignored, but that changed radically after the first weekend away. Many of the other students there were from Cork, Tipperary and other parts of the country as well as from Dublin. It was a time when I know that I matured in a lot of ways, as I met many people who were strangers at first but good friends by the time we left to go home at the end of the month. Indeed, by that time we were very sad to be going home, and tears were shed by many of the girls.

As with many Irish teenagers, a month in Irish college was a rite of passage, somewhat similar to the American concept of holiday camp; my own children also spent a month in such a college many years later, albeit not in Ballingeary. Even though we swore at the time of leaving that we would return the following summer, neither I nor any of my friends did so. Other plans got in the way in the years that followed, but it was an experience that I never regretted and an important stage in my personal development and that of other teenagers who didn't experience boarding school.

Holidays during my early years were usually with my family. We initially went every year to Strokestown to my Sharkey grandparents and stayed in their house, helping in the shop, making hay in the fields, saving turf on the bog for winter, driving cows from their fields outside the town and up Church Street to their house's yard for milking, collecting eggs from the henhouses, and playing football and hurling on the wide street. My grandparents had a cobbled yard at the back of their house and a long garden behind the outbuildings. There was an old broken tractor in the yard and this served as an early form of climbing frame for us. My grandmother tended the garden diligently with a combination of flowers and vegetables. Her favourite flower was the dahlia and she prided herself on her varied display of them. Anytime I see a dahlia now it evokes pleasant memories of my grandmother and of our holidays in Strokestown.

I visited the house recently and was graciously shown around by the daughter of the present owner. Again, it brought back pleasant albeit sad memories when I realised that so many of those who I associated with those holidays were long gone and I was now older than my grandmother had been when I last saw her there. One thing that I noticed was that the outbuildings and lofts were bigger than I had envisaged – I could better understand why the Black and Tans had tired of their search for guns back in 1921.

Other holidays were in my Aunt Bridget's house in Kilsallaghan, but that was on my own or with my brother Joe. Although only about 15 miles from the city centre, it was deep in the countryside. The farm, Colmcille Fruit Farm, was the site of the first rural electrification connection in Ireland, in 1947, which was just before when I would have first visited. What I do remember was a windmill that generated electricity for the very extensive greenhouses they had, for growing tomatoes, cucumbers and gladioli. There were also very large orchards with apple trees that my Uncle Patrick had sourced from his home in County Armagh, along with fields of strawberries, raspberries and gooseberries. There was always something interesting to do there on holidays. This included picking tomatoes and other fruits and then accompanying my uncle – and later my cousins Aidan and Kierie – in a lorry, bringing their produce into the Dublin Fruit Market to Hugh McNulty and his son, the wholesale merchants that they invariably used.

At some stage we started going also to Enniscrone in County Sligo. My mother's sister Margaret was married to Joe McManus, who became the garda sergeant in Enniscrone, and we visited the McManus cousins for a few years. Enniscrone was then a small, sleepy but very pleasant seaside resort; there was a magnificent beach and high sand dunes (including the Valley of Diamonds), as well as other seaside amenities that kept us occupied while there. The resort has grown significantly since the early 1960s, and now also has a superb eighteen-hole championship golf course.

Foreign holidays were not even discussed with us; in fact, it was 1965 before my parents themselves went on a holiday to Europe, visiting Sorrento, Capri and Rome. As I wrote earlier, I was in Holyhead in Wales for a few days when I was 4 or 5 years old, but I wasn't out of Ireland again until I was 18 or 19. Nonetheless, as my friends were not regular travellers either, I did not notice that I was missing out on anything special. Times change, as do our interests and aspirations, and from my mid-twenties, foreign travel became the norm.

SUMMER JOBS, TRAINEE ACTUARY AND CAREER CHANGE

As mentioned earlier, I was beginning to think of my future career after school from about the age of 15 or 16. I considered a wide range of professions with the help of a book on careers that my father had bought for me. I was wise enough to consider potential job satisfaction as an important criterion; however, earning capacity was a major factor for me, and that ruled out some career paths immediately.

I had gained plenty of work experience during summer and Christmas holidays since my early teens. Indeed, before I started secondary school, I had worked at fruit picking on a few occasions while staying at my uncle's fruit farm in Kilsallaghan, County Dublin. In the couple of summers that followed, I had worked a few days a week for a couple of weeks in Lamb's fruit farm in Donabate, which was easier to access than Kilsallaghan; a few friends and I were able to get the train from Killester to Donabate and walk to the farm from there. I was put off continuing with the venture after one of my friends was robbed by a gang who attacked us as we walked back to the train one evening. They knew that we had just been paid for the work, as they were also fruit pickers, but they were bigger and tougher than us. We decided not to return. Having seen what some guys did to add weight to the containers of fruit they collected, I wouldn't eat unwashed fruit no matter how attractive it looked on a shelf in a shop or in a stall.

My mother used to work in Macy's department store on South Great George's Street before she got married, and one of her former colleagues had become the general manager. She called him and got a job for me; I worked for two weeks as a general dogsbody, doing odd jobs and helping out whenever anyone needed a little assistance. I enjoyed the work, meeting new people and feeling useful – as well, of course, as earning a little. On the Friday of my second week, I was working in the basement, keeping an eye on a fire in a large incinerator where paper and packaging and other waste material from the store was burned. I had to open the door or gate regularly, stoke the fire and feed it new material. In the course of doing so, I was called up to one of the store departments to collect more material. I was only gone a few minutes when alarm bells started ringing and smoke appeared, bellowing from the stairwell to the basement. Within a few minutes, the store had to be evacuated and the fire brigade arrived.

If that had happened on a Monday morning, when there were few in the store, it might have been overlooked; however, on a busy Friday afternoon the amount of business lost – never mind the damage caused by the fire and its extinction – was too much for even my mother's friendship with the general manager, and I wasn't asked to extend my work for another week. Apparently, when I left the fire and went upstairs, I hadn't closed the fire door properly; some burning material had fallen out and spread to other waste material that was yet to be thrown in the fire. I didn't have to take all the blame, and in fact the damage was not too bad – and it was probably covered by insurance, although I didn't know that at the time.

The manner in which my subsequent career developed meant that I never had to fill out a curriculum vitae indicating that I had worked in Macy's – risking my prospective employer seeking a reference – nor had I ever to answer a question in an interview that would have revealed the incident. So it did not adversely affect me, even when working at other department stores as I continued my holiday working career. The next position that I got was the following summer in Switzer's department store on Grafton Street, which I got again through the good offices of my mother; she called a cousin of hers, who was one of the department managers.

Unlike in Macy's, I was put on the floor in the household department, selling bed linen, sheets, blankets, towels and similar goods after approximately one hour's training. I was out of my depth and knew almost nothing about what I was selling – the brands, the quality, the price or anything of relevance. Nevertheless, I managed to make a few sales, which earned me commission as well as my basic pay, so I was delighted with myself. The part that I found most difficult was wrapping the sold items neatly. I couldn't manage it, and even today, nearly sixty years later, when using sellotape rather than string, I find it very difficult to wrap anything neatly and without bulges. When I turned up the following week, I found that I had been moved to the books department, where I spent two weeks selling books.

In addition to getting paid well, I had lots of time to read and watch people strolling up and down Grafton Street, as the book department was at the front of the store. Switzer's was where Brown Thomas is now, the latter having bought Switzer's some years later, moving across Grafton Street from its previous location. Macy's department store is long gone; it survived my attempt to burn it down but was not around for much longer either way as it was closed down a few years later. Another even larger department store, Pims – also situated on South Great George's Street – found that, from the mid-1960s, Grafton Street and its immediate side streets had become the centre of retail shopping in the south city at the expense of South Great George's Street and its side streets, and it too closed down. I worked in Switzer's again for a week around Xmas later that year and for two weeks in the following summer of 1965.

After my first stint in Switzer's, I got a job working in the photographic department of Roche's Chemist on Grafton Street. I worked there for two weeks in the summer of 1964 and for a week over the following Xmas holidays. John Gunn, who managed the photography department (and may have been a shareholder in the business), was a most pleasant gentleman, and he tried valiantly to teach me the details of cameras and their operations – shutter speeds, light meters and so on – but I was a poor learner. I do remember the enthusiasm with which he discussed these details with customers who knew and understood what he was saying. John had what was probably the best selection of cameras at the time, and I can remember the brand names, many of which are still in existence even though they may be made by different manufacturers now: Canon, Minolta, Pentax, Leica, Olympus, Nikon, Kodak and Zeiss Ikon. This was before Polaroid instant cameras became popular in Ireland, and long before digital cameras were seen or heard of.

I was very much a relief worker while John's assistant was away on holidays. I looked after the shop while John was on his morning break and during lunch. I didn't pretend to know more than I did; if customers had queries of even a vaguely technical nature, I suggested that they come back when John would be there. But I did sell a few cameras to persons who knew exactly what they wanted. I also sold film, took film in for developing, and handed out photographs when they were ready.

When I went back to Roches for the Xmas holidays, the assistant had returned, so there were three of us; it was a busy time, but I didn't have to be left on my own. John knew what my limitations were. John remained a good friend, and when I could afford a good camera and cine-camera in later years, I invariably went to John for advice and to make a purchase. He had opened his own new photography shop in Wexford Street by that time, but he himself did not change. In each of my other holiday jobs, people were addressed formally, so it was 'Mr O'Reilly' or 'Miss Keegan', although as the boy, I was addressed as John; but with John Gunn it was informal and everyone was addressed by their Christian name.

I didn't envisage any of these holiday jobs as steps into a career in the retail business – they simply paid for my pocket money. From an early stage, I wanted to be independent and have my own resources, particularly as I was the eldest of seven children and didn't believe that I should be dependent on my parents for indulging my leisure and pastimes.

Career guidance was arranged during the first term of sixth year in school. It involved talks by past pupils on different careers, aptitude tests, filling out forms and an interview with the career guidance counsellor. In the form we had to set out our career ambitions and list three careers that we were interested in pursuing. I can still remember the three I listed: playwright, farmer and solicitor. The counsellor was quite forthright in telling me that the only career that might meet my ambitions was that of a solicitor; he said I had the aptitude and attributes appropriate for it, and the advantage of having my father as a solicitor before me.

The life of a playwright appealed to me because I fancied myself as a writer, and I also fancied the bohemian lifestyle that seemed to be involved – even though I was never remotely bohemian. Being a farmer appealed to me because I saw it as a relatively easy life, with a pleasant lifestyle; but I wasn't envisaging myself as a small farmer and didn't take into account how I could become a big farmer. So the clear recommendation for me was to become a solicitor. In fact, that was a relief because I had come to that conclusion myself. If anybody over the previous twelve months had asked me what I wanted to do, I would have answered that I hoped to study law and practise as a solicitor.

When we started the leaving certificate cycle at the beginning of fifth year, a new mathematics curriculum was introduced. In addition to the former elements of arithmetic, algebra, geometry, trigonometry and calculus, we now had set theory, statistics and probability. I really enjoyed mathematics and was achieving good grades in fifth year. That continued into sixth year, when we had the new principal, Fr Steen, teaching us. It was only toward the very end of the school year and after I had completed the leaving certificate examinations that I considered a career involving mathematics and looked at the possibility of training as an actuary.

I knew vaguely that Irish Life, where my father was a solicitor, had a training scheme for actuaries. It involved working in their actuarial, pensions and investment departments while studying for the Institute of Actuaries examinations. My father had arranged a solicitor's apprenticeship for me with a colleague and acquaintance of his, Frank Plunkett Dillon, who was a senior partner in the firm Ryan, Scallan & O'Brien, and of whom my father had a very high regard, but when I indicated that I wished to apply to train as an actuary, he did not stand in my way. I got accepted for the actuarial training and he had to explain to Frank that I had changed my mind. One factor that influenced me to some extent – although it is difficult to quantify – was that I would be earning and could contribute to the family coffers rather than be a drain, as would otherwise be the case. A more important factor, however, was the independence that I would gain.

I had bought my matriculation for entry to university, as was the norm for anyone who had passed the leaving certificate in specific subjects such as English and Latin, but in mid-September I started in Irish Life, in the OB (Ordinary Branch) Actuarial Department. I was to receive a salary of £520 per annum, or £10 per week – a significant sum at the time – although as a 'salaried employee' I was paid monthly. I was delighted with myself, and even when all my pals started in UCD or Trinity in the following two weeks, I didn't have any regrets.

I enjoyed the work, which included dealing on the phone with queries raised by clients or life assurance salesmen, replying to letters and working on calculations using actuarial tables and investment growth factors. I had been told shortly after I started that I would have to sit a preliminary examination in various mathematical subjects in order to become a student member of the Institute of Actuaries. The first opportunity was in

November, just two months away. I anticipated having to undertake many examinations to qualify as an actuary, but I didn't expect to have one so soon.

The institute was London-based. There was no Irish institute – or even branch – as there were less than ten actuaries in the country at the time. On checking, I learned that trainees in England who had achieved a C grade or higher in A Level mathematics were exempt from the preliminary examination. I wrote a strong letter to the institute, pointing out that the recently introduced curriculum in Ireland was at least as comprehensive and difficult as the syllabus in place in the United Kingdom. I opined that it was now discriminatory not to allow the same exemptions for an A grade in the Irish leaving certificate, and thus I was applying for an exemption.

I received a reply a few weeks later, which was about two weeks before the exam. It stated that my letter would be brought before the board of the institute for consideration, but that the board would not be meeting again until December; it suggested that I sit the exam in November to be safe. I did, getting down to serious cramming for a couple of weeks. It was difficult, and the format and structure of the questions was quite different from the leaving certificate, albeit it was the same subject matter.

I was confident enough afterwards to believe that I would pass the examination; therefore I was surprised, when the results were issued in early January, to learn that I had not passed. This was the first time in my life that I had failed an examination. The sense of failure was exacerbated by a letter received a couple of days later which stated that the board were impressed by my appeal for exemption and that from then onwards the Irish leaving certificate would have the same status as the A Levels. It added, however, that as I had sat their preliminary examination – along with two colleagues who were in the same position as me – and had failed, they could not apply the exemption to me; I would have to resit the examination, the next one of which was in May 1967.

I failed that, and failed again in November 1967, when trainees who joined the year after me had got exemptions based on my pleadings. Within Irish Life – and in particular the personnel department, which was responsible for our training – there was considerable sympathy for my predicament, and I was encouraged to try again the following May. I did and failed for the fourth time, which was the limit on the number of attempts that a trainee could make. Before the results had been issued, I applied to sit the A Level mathematics papers, as I had discovered that it was possible to do so even though I lived in Ireland and had not attended a UK school. Those examinations were in June; when the results were issued in August, I found I had passed with a grade that would have exempted me from the preliminary examination. But by then I had decided that I didn't want to pursue a career as an actuary, and I didn't even send my results to the institute.

I had handed in my notice to Irish Life and was paid my final month's salary, which had been increased since September 1967 to £572 per annum, or £11 per week. I was also repaid my pension contributions, which amounted to approximately £50. I was cash rich but qualification poor. With the help of my parents, who were now worried that their promising son had become a failure, I considered the alternatives. My mother suggested that I consider studying medicine; I thought about it for a short while, but I quickly decided that I should go back to my original choice and start to study law. On reflection, I'm sure that I wouldn't have made a very good doctor, but thankfully my two daughters have become consultant paediatricians, the obvious influence of their mother.

I think that my father was silently relieved about the change in my career path, as he preferred those of his colleagues who were solicitors over those who were actuaries. I had multiple emotions: disappointment that I had failed at what I had tried, relief that I was getting out of it and excitement at starting something that I was sure I would enjoy. Looking back, I knew that I had jumped into actuarial training without much research or thought, whereas I had thought about becoming a solicitor for a long time and knew what I was getting into, or at least I thought that I did.

My father contacted Frank Plunkett Dillon again, who just shortly beforehand had merged the firm Ryan, Scallan & O'Brien with Thomas Gerrard & Co. to form Gerrard, Scallan & O'Brien and had moved to new offices at Hainault House, 69–71 St Stephen's Green, just around the corner from UCD, which was then on Earlsfort Terrace. The one problem that I then encountered was that my 'bought' matriculation and leaving certificate of 1966 were out of date for the Incorporated Law Society because of a change in regulations; I would have to do the leaving certificate again or sit for the society's preliminary examination, which was effectively the same thing for me and would be very difficult in subjects such as English, Irish,

Latin and French – subjects that had different novels and dramas each year on which the examinations were based. It would be impossible to cram for all these within a couple of weeks.

Again my father came to my rescue. He knew the president of the Law Society and persuaded him to have the education committee grant me a discretionary exemption based on the results that I had achieved in my leaving certificate two years earlier, and on the fact that I had continued studying for the next two years, albeit not in university. Being granted that exemption was a massive relief; it meant that, in theory – on the assumption that I worked diligently, attempted all my law degree and professional examinations at the first possible opportunity and passed them for the next four years – I could be admitted as a solicitor in four years, which was the minimum period.

One interesting sequel to this series of events, which was not entirely dissimilar from my father's situation nearly twenty-five years earlier, was that the only recurring nightmare I have had over the fifty years that followed involved me cramming for school subject exams in order to start studying law. I would be among a mixture of guys who had been in school with me and guys who were in my law class in university; I would be aware I wasn't ready for the exams, wondering in a panic what I was going to do next. Either that or I would be cramming for the law exams and suddenly realise that it was school subject exams that I had in the morning, again panicking.

I would awake from my nightmare and realise to my relief that I was long qualified as a solicitor and didn't have to worry about exams again – or, in the later years, that I was finished my career and was actually retired. Obviously, this period and the subsequent law examinations caused me more stress than I recognised at the time, but the stress got stored in my subconscious.

The fact that I seemed to be better at pleading a case to the Institute of Actuaries on quasi-legal grounds than I was at doing their mathematics examinations encouraged me to accept that I was right to change career. Career changes were not as common then as they are now, but I knew that many of my peers had tried a course and when they didn't get through first year examinations, they switched; this applied particularly to those who started studying medicine and didn't pass their pre-med exams.

Nevertheless, one of my closest friends, Cormac Hughes, who had been in class with me since age 6, had the quickest change that I have ever heard of. Cormac, like me, was to study law in UCD in October 1966, and like me, his father had arranged an apprenticeship with a solicitor friend. Cormac went into Earlsfort Terrace on the appointed day to register for the Bachelor of Civil Law course – or BCL, as it was known. He realised that the queue was much longer than that of the commerce degree course, where more of our friends had queued, registered and were on the way out to O'Dwyer's pub across the road. Cormac has more or less the same amount of patience as me, so he left the queue for law, joined the commerce queue, registered and met up with our friends in the pub. He duly completed a three-year degree course, was conferred with his BComm degree and later completed accountancy examinations, becoming a successful businessman. It was some time before he told his father what he had done, by which point it was too late to reverse.

That two-year period in Irish Life was very enjoyable in many ways. Our offices were on Mespil Road, and at lunchtime my new work friends and I would often have a pleasant walk along the canal or down to Leeson Street Bridge, along Upper Leeson Street to Burlington Road and back to Mespil Road, or alternatively to Baggot Street Bridge, along Baggot Street to Waterloo Road and then back to Mespil Road via Burlington Road. Before this I didn't know the city, and particularly this area around the canal, very well.

I didn't drink alcohol at the time, even though I was a frequenter of pubs in Clontarf and in the city. My colleagues in Irish Life chose the Crooked Bawbee as their regular. It was at Baggot Street Bridge on the corner of Upper Baggot Street and Mespil Road, and we often went there on a Friday evening or up to O'Briens at Leeson Street Bridge. Many of my colleagues were regular customers of Joe Byrne's bookmakers shop across the road, but I never got that gambling bug – though I was investing in stocks and shares from that time, which on reflection wasn't much different.

On Saturday nights, I would go with my Clontarf pals, who were now in UCD, to the Literary and Historical Society (L&H) debates in the old Physics Theatre on Earlsfort Terrace, skipping back and forth between there and any of the pubs at the bottom of Leeson Street – O'Dwyer's, Hartigan's or Kirwan House. The entertainment at the L&H was superb; although intellectually stimulating, it was never taken too seriously – and most importantly, it was free. We often went from there to the Olympic Ballroom on Pleasant Street, off Camden Street, where the Students' Representative Council held a dance during term time. Outside term time, if we weren't going to the cricket club in Clontarf, we would meet in the Crooked Bawbee and then go to a dance in Bective, which was the clubhouse of Bective Rangers in Donnybrook. If there was money left between us, and the person who had most money wasn't leaving a girl home, we would share a taxi at the end of the night. Alternatively, we would walk home from Donnybrook to Clontarf. This group consisted of Cormac, Paul, Jimmy, Kieran, Alan and Cormac – the core group - but we were usually joined by four or five others but they would not all be with us every week.

On some Saturday nights, one of us would have use of our father's car, but that happened very seldom in the first couple of years. In Irish Life there was an annual Christmas party for the staff; it was at my second year's party that I had my first pint of Guinness, and my second, third and fourth. I didn't realise that it would be immediately obvious at home, but on the following morning, when I surfaced for breakfast, my mother could obviously smell the sweat and boozy breath before I got a chance to wash it off and she asked me if I had started drinking. I told her that I had; she didn't seem upset and merely advised me to be careful. I was 20 years old at the time, and most of my close friends had begun drinking two years beforehand, starting before they left school. The fact that I was now drinking pints and liking them didn't have any major impact on my life, as I was already a regular in pubs – the only real difference was that I stopped drinking Cidona, and I'm not sure if I ever drank it again in a pub.

During the summer between leaving Irish Life and starting in UCD, I went to London with a friend of mine, Leslie. It was my first visit to London and my first flight. I had been to Liverpool and North Wales on a couple of occasions, but I had travelled by ferry. The flight to London was a USIT chartered flight scheduled to land at Gatwick, but it actually landed at a small airport on the south coast of England, which was probably a former RAF airfield. We were bussed to the centre of London, but it was quite late when we arrived. Leslie and I were due to go to Ilford to stay overnight with his aunt, yet by the time we got to the train station, the last train to Ilford had departed. Ilford was about an hour's train journey from central London. We went on the Underground, or tube as it was known, for part of the way, hoping to get a bus from there to Ilford; however, when we got to the bus stop, we discovered that the last bus had also departed.

We were now in a suburb that I had never heard of. I only knew that it was in north London because I vaguely knew that Ilford was north-east of central London, and even though Leslie had been in London before, he had never been in this part either. We tried a few guesthouses, but they were either closed or full, certainly to a couple of 'paddy' students. We weren't desperate, as the evening was warm and it didn't look as if it would rain, so we went into a park with the intention of sleeping on benches. We had just settled down and made ourselves comfortable when a park ranger came up to us and ordered us to leave; he told us the park had closed at midnight and rough sleepers were not allowed.

We left as ordered, while probably trying to explain – to no avail – that we were good middle-class students and not hobos. The ranger could not help us with advice on what to do other than to go to the police station and ask them to let us stay. We didn't want that, and one of us came up with the bright idea of sleeping on the steps leading down to the tube station that we had left an hour earlier; we went back, used our rucksacks as pillows and tried to get some sleep, keeping one eye open for thieves.

The station was closed, but a draught was blowing from the tunnel up one set of steps and a breeze was blowing leaves and litter down the other, so sleep was close to impossible. We arose when the first commuters of the day came to the steps, saw us and stepped around us or walked down the other side. We got the first train back into central London, to either Paddington or Liverpool Street. As we were both feeling grotty after the night, we headed straight to the washrooms and proceeded to shave and have a quick wash and splash at a handbasin.

At the wash hand basin beside me, I noticed a guy mainlining and creating a bit of a bloody mess. That was the first and only time that I saw someone doing that; when he saw me looking at him, he threatened to stab me with his needle. I hardly knew what he was doing – and would probably have been able to defend myself, as he was 'out of it' – but I was very uncomfortable and so grabbed my clothes and got out of there quickly;

Leslie, who hadn't seen the incident, followed me. We had breakfast, found a guesthouse – where we booked in for a few nights – and went sightseeing.

That evening we went out to Harlesden, where our friend Cormac Hughes was staying while working on a construction site for the summer. I knew Cormac's address, but he didn't know that we were coming, so we 'bumped' into him as he got home, much to his surprise. We went to his local pub in Kilburn, and I had my first pint of bitter, which lived up to its name. Cormac then took us to his favourite Turkish restaurant, which had nice but unusual food and no floorboards, so getting in and out was a little dangerous. After a few more days in London, I left for Liverpool, spent a few days there with family and then headed home to get ready for the next phase of my life as a law student.

UNIVERSITY AND STUDYING LAW

As I was starting to study law two years after my original intended start date, I was determined to qualify as a solicitor in the minimum time possible, which was four years. It was possible to qualify as a solicitor without completing a law degree, and some who qualified with me had not done so, but I wanted to achieve both.

The schedule to achieve admission as a solicitor within the minimum four years was tight. My lectures for the BCL degree started in early October 1968; the first year degree exam was in June 1969; second year lectures started in early October 1969, as did lectures for the first solicitors' exam of the Incorporated Law Society; the second year degree exam was in June 1970; the first solicitors' exam was in September 1970; third year lectures for the degree and the lectures for the second solicitors' exam started in October 1970. The latter were held in Andrew Street, in an old deconsecrated church, and they were more practically oriented.

In September 1971 we sat the degree exam in UCD, and in October we commenced lectures for the third and final solicitors' exam and for the bookkeeping exam conducted by the Law Society. Although I hadn't originally scheduled for it in my plan, I also commenced lectures for a new Masters Degree course in UCD (LLM). In February 1972 I sat the second solicitors' exam; in June 1972, I sat the second Irish exam for the Law Society and the bookkeeping exam and also the exam part of the Masters Degree course; and in September 1972, I sat the third and final solicitors' exam for the Law Society.

This schedule applied if one passed all exams at the first sitting, which thankfully I did; however, some of my class attempting the same schedule had to repeat one or more of these exams as well. That adds up to nine exams in four years and doesn't include the first Irish exam, which had to be passed before one could commence the apprenticeship and the courses for the Law Society exams. All of these exams, except the bookkeeping and Irish exams, had multiple subjects, so the number of days spent doing exams in the four years was exhausting – as, of course, was the waiting for results.

Some of the subjects for the two sets of examinations overlapped, such as the law of contract, real property law, criminal law, law of evidence and law of torts. The degree course also included some more academic subjects, such as jurisprudence, Roman law, constitutional law and European law, while the solicitors' course included practical or applied law, such as conveyancing law, court practice and procedure, company law and commercial law. Where subjects overlapped between the two, the approach to exam questions, and presumably the marking, was different – so it was not taken for granted that because one passed or even got honours in one subject, one would necessarily repeat that result in the Law Society exam in the same subject.

For that reason, in Summer 1970, having completed the degree exams in June, a few of us engaged a young barrister, Peter Sutherland, to give extra tutorials and help us to cram for the solicitors' exams due in September, which were in law of contract and law of torts. Peter, or 'Suds', had an amazing method of cramming to assist detail memory retention of case law. I had never experienced that type of cramming previously, but it worked and all of us got through with ease. Around that time, Suds became involved in the Arms Trial – a controversy involving government ministers and an army officer regarding an attempt to import arms into Ireland for use in Northern Ireland – as junior counsel for one of the defendants; his barrister's practice took off rapidly, so we were the last group who benefitted from his unique methods. That was the first of numerous dealings that I had with Suds, both professionally and personally, over the next forty-five years.

Having described the optimum time to qualify and be admitted as a solicitor, I am not complaining – that was my choice. It was also my choice to undertake an active apprenticeship from the beginning. Many of my fellow students staggered their professional exams and took an extra year or two to finish; some didn't start their apprenticeship and Law Society courses until they finished their degree. Many others did not have an active apprenticeship.

I, however, having spent two years as a trainee actuary, was determined to learn as quickly as possible and once more become financially independent of my parents, who at that stage also had my siblings coming on to be educated. By agreeing to attend the office as often as I could – and there was no minimum time laid down – I was paid £3 per week. Although it was a big step down from the £11 per week that I was earning in Irish Life, it was probably more than what any of my fellow students were receiving; some of them were not only unpaid but also had to pay a significant premium to their master, either in a lump sum or in staged payments.

The fact that my master's office was at 69–71 St Stephen's Green, in Hainault House, and within three hundred yards of the university on Earlsfort Terrace, was a great advantage – albeit it also had some disadvantages. A great advantage was that I could go into the office and work between lectures and on days when I didn't have any lectures; with this level of accessibility, I was able to gain experience of the actual application of law from an early stage. The disadvantages included the fact that I had little excuse if there was a clash between doing something for the office and doing something that was extracurricular.

One example was my joining a student protest march that went from the university on Earlsfort Terrace to the Department of Justice at 65 St Stephen's Green, stopping almost under the windows of my office. On the following morning, one of the secretaries, Miss McSharry – who was a gentle, polite lady, probably in her sixties at that time – commented to me that she had seen somebody who looked very like me taking part in the demonstration, adding that she couldn't believe that it might be me. I managed to get out of the conversation without admitting or denying that it was me, but it reminded me to be careful about keeping my growing political radicalism separate from my nascent professional career; Gerrard, Scallan & O'Brien was a large commercial law firm with many clients who would not welcome having a radical student looking through their files.

Not all of the work that we carried out in the office involved training to become a solicitor. On one occasion, myself and Bryan Strahan, who had started at more or less the same time as me, were asked to arrange the move of a large boardroom table from the previous offices of Ryan, Scallan & O'Brien on 86 Lower Leeson Street to our new offices about three hundred yards away. The merger of the two constituent firms had only been effected a few months earlier, and some archived files, library books and furniture had not yet been moved when Bryan and I first started there.

We managed to manoeuvre the table out of 86, as it was known. Because it was on wheels, we pushed it down Leeson Street, across the junction at Earlsfort Terrace and over to Hainault House – much to the amusement of some of the traffic on Lower Leeson Street, which was a two-way street at that time, and to the annoyance of others who were being delayed. We felt more like furniture removers than apprentice solicitors, but we were commended by the partner who had asked us to arrange the removal for our speed and enterprise in achieving it without any cost to the firm. I guessed that there was another objective: to teach us that practising law was not all glamour and prestige.

One of the senior partners, Denzil O'Donnell, sometimes asked one or other of us to do some personal errands for him. I can particularly remember that Denzil had a Remington Rand electric shaver that gave him a lot of trouble; I had to bring it back to the Remington Rand service centre on Camden Street on a number of occasions. Other non-legal duties for the firm included bringing lodgements to the bank, which was the National Bank on College Green and Suffolk Street. In 1969, the bank merged with Hibernian Bank to form the Bank of Ireland Group, the National Bank having been taken over by Bank of Ireland in 1965; nevertheless, our branch was always referred to as the National Bank.

When I started in 1968, the office notepaper included the telegram address; it was at least a year before we obtained a telex machine, which was like a ticker tape, and the telex address was added. Within a few more years, the telegram address was removed and telex became pervasive. Then the advent of the fax or facsimile machine followed years later, which took over from the telex until it too became redundant after the advent of emails. Nevertheless, quite a lot of post was delivered by hand – particularly legal documents being delivered to other solicitor's offices – and it was part of the duties of the apprentices to assist in the post room with the by-hand deliveries, especially if there were staff shortages because of illness or vacation, or there was some urgency. It was not intellectually stimulating, but I got to know the centre of Dublin very well, so I didn't complain. This role was later made redundant by the introduction of the Dublin Document Exchange.

Bryan and I had our seats in the office library, and for some time we were joined by a young solicitor assistant. The firm soon took additional space in the building by leasing the rear of the second floor (it already had possession of the front). It was not all needed immediately, and three rooms at the rear were sublet to a company, Universal Exports, owned by a successful and flamboyant business man, Oliver Caffrey. Other tenants in the building at the initial stages were Citibank, Kennedy Crowley, Chartered Accountants and Duggan Insurances, but there were fairly regular changes – the principal one being Kennedy Crowley moving to Harcourt House in Harcourt Street, freeing up nearly three floors. Gerrard, Scallan & O'Brien was expanding also, and was lucky to be able to expand within Hainault House by taking over leases as others left, subletting initially and then taking back the sublet space – but that was all in the future.

Back in the late 1960s, being in the library had advantages. It was where the incoming post was sorted in the morning, there was plenty of movement in and out, and it was easy to get to know everybody in the firm. We weren't giving legal advice or interfacing with clients, but we were sometimes used as a research resource, made to do filing, or given finished files to tidy up and be archived.

One of the jobs that I enjoyed doing, at least for the first few years, was assisting the court clerk Joe Sharkey. Joe wasn't a solicitor, but the office could not have functioned successfully without him. As well as attending at the court offices, getting court documents stamped and then filed, he also went to the Companies Office, the Land Registry and the Registry of Deeds every day and to the Land Commission once a week. Joe was an expert at what he did, having started as a junior office boy for the father of Ted O'Brien – now one of our senior partners – many years previously. He was very affable and popular with everyone he dealt with, so he smoothed the path for those like me who helped him from time to time. Knowing people in all these government offices made life easier when I later qualified as a solicitor; at times I relied on favours or advice from them on how to resolve some particular procedural problem.

In 1968, when I commenced as an apprentice, there were seven solicitors in the firm, all of whom were partners. By the time my apprenticeship was completed four years later, there were an additional three assistant solicitors; when I joined as a solicitor in January 1973, there were four – and one of those became a junior partner a month later. Unlike other places where I had worked, where people were called by their formal 'Mr' or 'Miss', as in

Switzer's, or first names, as in Gunns and Irish Life (save when addressing a much more senior person, when the address was again 'Mr' or 'Miss'), in Gerrard, Scallan & O'Brien, it varied quite a lot. The partners were known by their initials, so there was D.O.D., E.J.O.B., F.P.D., T.H.C. and so forth, but they were addressed by their first names; most of the women were addressed by their first names, but the older ladies were addressed as 'Miss', so there was Miss McSharry, Miss Rowe and Miss Donnelly. Nonetheless, generally it was quite informal, and a very pleasant atmosphere prevailed. Interestingly, the name of the firm was often shortened to the initials GSOB; many people knew it by this name over the next thirty-five years.

In my first year at university, even though it was a three-year primary law degree, there were only two law-related subjects: Introduction to the Legal System, taught by Professor John Kelly, who was the Dean of the Law Faculty; and Legal and Constitutional History, taught by Geoffrey Hand, who became Dean of the Law Faculty in 1970, when Professor Kelly became a senator. Both of these subjects were fascinating and both lecturers were excellent. Geoff Hand had a very pleasant lisp and couldn't pronounce his Rs; we used to laugh at his attempts to pronounce 'rotten boroughs' in the context of English constitutional history and its equivalent in early nineteenth-century Ireland.

We also had three other subjects from the arts faculty – classes that we shared with students from that faculty and the social science faculty. There were various sets of options to facilitate the scheduling of lectures, and I chose history, economics and philosophy. Many of my fellow students chose English, Irish or one of the continental languages, but I reckoned that the subjects I chose were the most suitable for me and my chance of getting through the first-year exams and on to real law.

My assessment was correct; I thoroughly enjoyed the history and philosophy courses, although the economics was a little dry. Among the lecturers we had were Des Norton and Cormac Ó Gráda in economics; Philip Pettit, Denis Turner, Paddy Masterson, Fr Bertie Crowe and Dr Desmond Connell (later Cardinal and Archbishop of Dublin), who lectured on various aspects of philosophy; and Ronan Fanning in history.

I had studied history in secondary school up to intermediate certificate level, but there was no real comparison between that and the university course. Significantly, we now studied English history of the nineteenth and early twentieth century, which we hadn't done at school, and the concentration in Irish and European history was less on battles and their dates and more on the politics as it evolved. The course on English history was complementary to the course on legal and constitutional history taught by Geoffrey Hand; they both helped us realise that although imperial Britain had oppressed Ireland for centuries, the ordinary Englishman was often just as oppressed and not really much different from the ordinary Irish person.

Philosophy was intellectually stimulating and very different from any subject that I had studied previously. It was one subject which had a noticeable number of trainee nuns and priests in the class, and there is no doubt that there was an underlying Catholic ethos – particularly with metaphysics and epistemology, taught by Dr Connell and Paddy Masterson; however, the lectures by Philip Pettit and Denis Turner were more secular and political. To some extent, the philosophy course was self-indulgence for me, as I would tend to be reflective; I found the exams relatively easy and did well at the end-of-year test. Interestingly, my son, Shane, later studied philosophy in Trinity College and eventually graduated with a doctorate in philosophy from Leeds University; he is now an academic philosopher in Exeter University.

Most of UCD was based in Earlsfort Terrace in the city centre during my undergraduate years 1968-1971 with only the Engineering faculty in a separate building off Merrion Street and the Science faculty which had moved to the new campus at Belfieldin 1964. The building at Earlsfort Terrace, which now houses the National Concert Hall, was grossly overcrowded by 1968 but nevertheless had a charm that was reminiscent of the older English universities and indeed of Trinity College Dublin, also in the city centre. The Front Hall was a great meeting place for students, both new and experienced alike and was sometimes compared to a train station. Paddy Keogh, who was the head porter in Earlsfort Terrace and who had an office just inside the main entrance door, was known to nearly all the students there, and he got to know many of them himself.

However, as Earlsfort Terrace was bursting at the seams, the college authorities wished to move as many as possible and as quickly as possible to the new campus which was being developed at Belfield which was a few miles away. In the few months before I started life as a student, protests were beginning to simmer due to various concerns that students had including that the proposed move to Belfield was not properly planned. This came to a head in November 1968 when it was realised that the Arts faculty was to move to Belfield from the commencement of the 1969 academic year but that there were no student facilities such as library, restaurant, bar, or students union building. Thus commenced what became known as the Gentle Revolution and the first of the sit ins in Earlsfort Terrace. In fact, the Arts faculty did not move until September 1970. I spent my three undergraduate years in Earlsfort Terrace, as the Law faculty did not move until the following year.

As we came to the end of first year and late spring 1969, and as exams began to loom ahead, many of us took to studying out in the Iveagh Gardens, which were behind the university and stretched from the rear of Earlsfort Terrace to the rear of Harcourt Street, and from the rear of the southern end of St Stephens Green to the rear of Hatch Street. There was a great, relaxed atmosphere there; besides studying while sitting under the trees, there were good football matches to let off steam and great informal concerts when some of the guys brought their guitars and entertained themselves and the rest of us.

One of the guys in my law class was Bill Whelan, who was a brilliant guitarist and singer, and who later – after he found the law business too boring – made a very successful career in the entertainment business. He is most famous for his composing and musical directorship of Riverdance, but has been involved in a myriad of other musical ventures also. Another good guitarist and entertainer at the time was Neil Jordan, who was studying arts but whose girlfriend was studying law in our class. Neil later achieved fame as a writer and a film director; among his novels was one in which he dealt very well with his time in Belgrove National School, where he was a pupil two years behind me.

As another songwriter once wrote, 'Those were the days my friend, we thought they'd never end' I continued using the Iveagh Gardens for study and relaxation in the summers that followed, but it never seemed to be as good and carefree as that first one. On one occasion Dramsoc, the college drama society, put on a play at lunchtime on a beautiful, idyllic day; it was staged in the part of the gardens that had the form of a natural open-air amphitheatre. The star of the play was a young Jeananne Crowley, who later had a very successful international acting career – in film, television and on stage – and if I'm not mistaken, another of the stars of that production was Barry McGovern, who also had a very successful career as an actor.

It wasn't until we commenced the second year of the degree course that we experienced actual legal studies. Professor Kelly's course in first year, Introduction to the Legal System, introduced us to the difference between the common and civil law systems, and the modern court system. The sources of law in the common law system comprised written and unwritten law. Written law was the constitution – or Bunreacht na hÉireann – and legislation, primary and secondary; unwritten law was judge-made law, based on precedent, relying on the principle of stare decisis.

Common law applied in the United Kingdom, Ireland, the United States and the Commonwealth, where unwritten law predominated. The civil law system, which applied in most of Europe, relied on codified law, following the approach of the Code Napoléon – in that system, legislation predominated.

There were also other systems, such as socialist law on the one hand and religious and traditional law on the other; religious law applied in Muslim countries and traditional laws in many African countries. But these were not taught in any detail at undergraduate level. We had been taught the difference between public law, comprising constitutional law, criminal law and social welfare law, and private law, comprising the law of contract, the law of torts, the law of property – both real and personal – and the law of trusts and the law of succession, and also the difference between civil and criminal proceedings – but it was very much an overview.

The law of real property, which we started in second year, was reputedly very difficult conceptually, and so it proved. In itself it is an academic subject based on concepts going back to the Norman Conquest and feudalism; the main object of learning this subject is to lay a foundation for the study of conveyancing, which is the practical application of real property law and used for the transfer of ownership of land and buildings – the bread and butter of many solicitors' practices. At the time, there was no Irish textbook on the subject; the textbook that we used was Megarry's *Manual of the Law of Real Property*. It was an English textbook, and while fine for all the conceptual matters, when it came to twentieth-century current law the English legislation of 1925 that was dealt with in the book was not mirrored closely in Ireland, so there was greater reliance on the lecturer and tutorials. My father, who was a specialist conveyancer in his work, was of considerable assistance to me in this subject and was able to answer any questions I had.

Professor Kelly taught us constitutional law and Roman law. He was the author of the seminal work on the Irish Constitution, *Fundamental Rights in the Irish Law and Constitution*, which was the only textbook on Irish law that we had on a reading list in our three years of study for the degree. Professor Kelly was the best lecturer or teacher that I had experienced since the start of my education, surpassing even Desmond Millett, my great primary school teacher; I considered myself extremely lucky to have had him for four subjects over the three years, as he also taught jurisprudence in third year after he had stood down as Dean of the Law Faculty and joined the Senate.

As Professor Kelly stated in the foreword to the second edition of his book in May 1967:

> In the six years which have elapsed since the first edition of this book appeared the Irish courts have pronounced decisions in constitutional cases which rival, in number and weight, those of the whole preceding period since the Constitution was enacted in 1937; and as these pages went to press, some further important cases were pending. Both Bench and Bar are increasingly tending to fertilise Irish jurisprudence by implanting in it concrete propositions evolved from fundamental principles, and the rate of development over the next few years is likely to be rapid, particularly, perhaps, in the areas of access to the courts'.

As well as being extremely modest in not noting that he was the single most influential figure in that increase, and the effective creator of Irish constitutional law as a source of litigation, he was remarkably prescient in his forecast of the future development of the law. The subject was very interesting in itself, particularly when comparing its dynamic development to the slow development of the law of real property and its interfacing of public and personal rights, which often clashed; what's more, the erudition, fluency and enthusiasm of Professor Kelly in his lectures made it the most engrossing law subject that I studied in my four years as a student. The issues covered included the individual rights as set out in the constitution – personal rights, property rights, family rights, education rights and religious rights – but as Professor Kelly argued, and as the courts accepted in due course, there were other rights inherent in the Irish Constitution, such as the right of personal liberty; the right of bodily integrity; the rights of freedom of expression, of assembly, of association; and political rights.

These rights were elaborated on and extended in subsequent case law – and they continue to be elaborated today. Such extended fundamental rights have been claimed in many kinds of situations, most of which Professor Kelly could not have imagined, including in cases where I was one of the codefendants with the Attorney General and the Irish State in 1991 and 1992. Besides this aspect of constitutional law, which was the most interesting, we became familiar with the written Irish Constitution, Bunreacht na hÉireann, and its many other provisions, political, administrative and legal.

As mentioned, Professor Kelly also taught Roman law. At the outset, this did not strike me as an important or interesting subject, but he again used his erudition, articulation and enthusiasm to transform the subject for me; he made me realise the huge influence that Roman law had not only on the civil law systems but also on common law in the UK and consequently in Ireland. One only has to look at the Latin terms that are used every day in our law and courts to accept that. A list of the more common terms are: *de facto*, *res judicata*, *ratio decidenda*, *obiter dicta*, *stare decisis*, *nemo dat quod non habet*, *mens rea*, *actus rea*, *certiorari*, *mandamus*, *bona fide*, *uberrimae fidei*, *onus*, *animus ferae naturae* and *animus mansuetae naturae*, *chattel*, *habeas corpus*, *res ipsa loquitur*, *quasi*, *quia timet*, *volenti non fit injuria*.

The Gentle Revolution of 1968 in UCD was over quickly, without much tangible change except for the introduction of staff student committees in each department. Towards the end of our first university year, at a meeting of our law class, Finbarr Crowley and I were elected to represent our class on the law faculty committee. I don't recollect there being an election and think that we were the only persons nominated.

Coincidentally, Finbarr and I knew each other well, although we were not close friends. We had both been in Belgrove National School and in St Paul's College, albeit Finbarr was a year behind me. But we caught up with each other in university. Finbarr was on the school football team with me when we won the final in Croke Park, and we were to have many further dealings in the future – personal, business and sporting. In any event, the staff student committee began to meet once a month, with two or three staff and two representatives from each year. It is hard to claim that we achieved anything tangible other than assisting in coordinating the move of the Law faculty to Belfield and reducing the disruption caused, but we probably had some influence on the timing of tutorials, the numbers in each tutorial class, the scheduling of examinations and the gaps between subjects, making them more amenable than previously.

I stayed on the committee for three years, including the postgraduate year. For me personally, the highlight was regular meetings with Professor Kelly, who was on the committee while we were in second year but stood down for the following year. He was very entertaining and humorous, as well as erudite; he was also very practical, and I developed a good relationship with him. I didn't know at the time that he was the brother-in-law of one of the partners in GSOB – so that in later years I met him socially on a few occasions – nor did I know that he would become one of the most important politicians of the late twentieth century.

He was a senator from 1969, before becoming a TD in 1973; and he became parliamentary secretary to the Taoiseach, Liam Cosgrave, on his first day in the Dáil. At different times he served as Attorney General, Minister for Trade, Commerce and Tourism and Minister for Foreign Affairs. Unfortunately, he died suddenly at the age of 59 in 1991. He made some of the best, yet witty, speeches in the Dáil that I had heard and was in every respect a hugely important contributor to Irish academic and political life in the second half of the century. I have always felt exceedingly lucky to have had him as a lecturer for each of three years, and to have known him outside that as well.

Other lecturers that we had at undergraduate level included Jim Brady, Peter Shanley, Nial Osborough – a very good and witty but unorthodox Belfast man – and Professor Rory O'Hanlon, who lectured in Criminal Law and Evidence and later became a highly regarded High Court judge, as indeed did Peter Shanley. I came across Professor O'Hanlon many years later, when he was the judge in one of the series of cases arising in the Telecom inquiry, when I was a co-defendant with the Attorney General.

The main debating society in university was the L&H, which welcomed students from all faculties. In addition, however, each faculty had its own society, the Law Society being associated with our own faculty. I was on the committee of the Law Society for one or two years; my main function was to convene debates and arrange guest speakers for them. The guest speaker was usually one of the university lecturers or a government minister. Among some others were Cardinal Conway, Father James McDyer (from Glencolmcille in Donegal) and Austin Currie, who was one of the founders of the SDLP in Northern Ireland and a member of the Stormont parliament for East Tyrone. Austin's father, Johnny, was, as I mentioned earlier, a childhood pal of my father in Edendork; after his contribution to our debate, my parents hosted a party at our home for Austin and the other speakers, as well as the committee of the Law Society, and I know my father enjoyed meeting Austin and chatting to him about his family and about Edendork.

On another occasion, I had invited Seán Flanagan as guest speaker; he was a solicitor and the then Minister for Lands. After the debate I was chatting to Mr Flanagan and learned that he lived in Clontarf. We exchanged some chat about Clontarf, and when he learned that I lived there too, he offered me a lift home in the ministerial car. I accepted the invitation, but as we left Earlsfort Terrace, he told his driver to go home via Groomes Hotel. He explained to me that a few of his colleagues were there and he wanted to meet them about some matter. I had heard about Groomes Hotel and it being the effective headquarters of Fianna Fáil, so I didn't object. As well as having free pints for a couple of hours, which is like winning the lotto for a student, I met half of the government ministers, who were in casual mode and all very friendly and welcoming. Mr Flanagan eventually decided to leave the informal gathering, and he and his chauffeur got me home safely. I never got back to Groomes Hotel, but I knew now that the stories about it were true.

I found my four years in university intellectually liberating. It was the most interesting time of my life, and I thoroughly enjoyed it. Everything could be challenged, nothing could be taken for granted – whether religious beliefs, political affiliations, socio-economic background or personal ethics. Much of it was fun, but to achieve success in all the exams on first attempt also required a lot of study and work. That suited me, and I thrived in the environment. Rather than leave intensive study to the last term each year, as some of my peers did, I tried to spread it out over the entire year and regularly used the library for studying and enjoyed it. Sometimes the library became busy particularly in the last few months before the end of year examinations and it was not possible to get a seat and desk. I had been tipped off that the library of the medicine faculty tended to be quieter, not because the medical students did not use it regularly, but there tended to be space there as some medical students were out training at hospitals.

As I travelled to and from Earlsfort Terrace by bus, I read textbooks or reviewed lecture notes if I was on my own; I was a diligent student when studying but a diligent participant in extra curricular activities when I wasn't taken up with work.

At the end of the final term in third year, one of my friends suggested going on a trip to Lough Derg in Donegal; the excursion was in essence a religious pilgrimage with penitential aspects. I was already aware of it, as my mother had gone on a trip there at least once in the previous years, and my aunts Bridget and Alice did so annually. I'm not sure what attracted me to the trip – I don't think it was the religious aspects (though I suppose if I thought it would give me any assistance in my forthcoming exams, I would have been interested). More likely, it was the novelty of the trip and the anticipation of having some fun with some friends that persuaded me to go. It certainly was fun, as we raced each other around the penitential exercises that we had to undergo, stayed silent when obliged to do so, fasted for three days with limited and basic tasteless food, and then sang and chatted when we could. I remember very little of the trip or those who were on it with me, but I do remember Andy O'Rorke, Hugh O'Donnell and Marie Browne, now Marie Dillon, and think we all had fun. It was supposed to be very religious focussed. I wonder if anyone else on the trip – most of whom I haven't seen for many years – has turned out with the same views on religion as me.

The late 1960s was generally a time of significant change, and young people were at the forefront of that movement. The Vietnam War, the Cultural Revolution of Mao Tse-tung in China, the coming to adulthood of the post-war generation in Europe and the increasing use of recreational drugs all combined to nurture a period of rebellion, and although there was very little violence among students in Ireland, we could see on television the violence in the USA, Vietnam, Germany and France – and as the decade came to an end, in Northern Ireland.

Some of the student leaders in Dublin from this period have since gone on to success in business, politics, journalism and other professions. I remember how Ruairi Quinn, who became a very successful architect and politician, had the nickname Ho Chi Quinn, while Eddie O'Connor, who has had a very successful career in business – and is now undoubtedly a capitalist, albeit one with a social conscience – was known by other students as Red Eddie when he became president of the Students' Representative Council in UCD in the late 1960s, copying the nickname of his French counterpart, Daniel Cohn Bendit, who was known as Dany le Rouge.

Achieving a good balance between all the elements of college life was my target – and it was a balance I continued to pursue with various interests in my later life.

As I said, I really enjoyed myself. Although often offered drugs, I never even smoked a joint, and haven't indulged in any since. I have been with student friends as they came out of psychedelic trips and have had them describe the sensations to me; I found it sufficiently scary and off-putting that I determined not to take any risks, and so I never touched anything that might possibly lead to a dependency or addiction. Alcohol was enough for me, and I was a regular in one or other of the pubs at the bottom of Leeson Street when I could afford the time and money.

In early October 1970, while walking up Grafton Street, I met an old friend, a recently qualified barrister, coming in the opposite direction. Having shaken hands, we started catching up on each other's recent activities, including his commencement to practice in the Four Courts. We were approached by two gentlemen; they politely interrupted us, asking if we would approach each other again and repeat our handshake, as they wanted to film it. They explained that they were making a video advertisement and thought that the image of two friends meeting, smiling and shaking hands like we had just done would be perfect for a scene. We repeated our greeting a couple of times, which they recorded, and they asked us to sign a piece of paper, giving our names and home addresses. We both did so without reading it, which was a little naive for a barrister and a law student. A month or so later, when I had totally forgotten the event, I received a letter from Kenny Advertising telling me that the recording was to be used in an advertising campaign for Irish butter, shown on television and in cinemas.

I telephoned the agency the following morning and asked if we were to be paid a fee for our participation. The answer was no – that we had signed a consent form at the time. I threatened to block them from using the recording unless we were paid. My friend, however, didn't want to do so; he was concerned that by taking a fee for it, it could be in breach of Bar Council regulations. So I dropped my claim. I was merely looking for a few pounds to augment my pocket money for a couple of weeks.

A few weeks later, I was watching television at home with my parents and siblings when the butter ad appeared. Our meeting and greeting on Grafton Street was featured; it was overlayed with a commentary of a real friendly Irish greeting and followed by a commentary on how Irish butter has a real Irish taste. My parents and siblings were impressed and surprised, as I had forgotten to tell them about the lead into the advertisement. Later that evening, I took a girl who I had recently met on a first date; we went to see a film in the city centre. To my surprise, the ad came on the big screen. The girl saw it, looked over at me, back at the screen and broke out laughing. I think it made a good impression, because later that night she invited me to her graduation ball, which was held a few weeks later. So I mightn't have got paid by Kenny Advertising or Bord Bainne, but I got some fun from the incident.

By the end of 1972, I had completed enough exams for a lifetime and was ready to enter the working life of a solicitor; however, towards the end of my undergraduate days, I did experience some different extracurricular activities.

FLAC, POSTGRADUATE STUDY AND LECTURING IN THE INSTITUTE OF PUBLIC ADMINISTRATION

In 1969, a group of law students, realising that there was a serious social problem because of the lack of access to legal advice, formed the Free Legal Advice Centre (FLAC), operating from Ozanam House, the headquarters of St Vincent de Paul in Mountjoy Square in Dublin. This group included Vivian Lavan, subsequently a High Court judge; Denis McCullough, subsequently a successful senior counsel; and David Byrne, subsequently the Attorney General and a European commissioner. This was the start of a remarkable organisation that recently celebrated its fiftieth anniversary.

As I entered third year law in October 1970, I was approached by some of the students from previous years who were involved in the organisation, and they asked if I was interested in helping. I did and quickly got involved, attending the advice centre once a week. Initially, I was sitting in with a more experienced student, but I was soon interviewing and operating cases myself – referring them, where necessary, to one of a panel of solicitors and young barristers who had volunteered their services. This panel included the founding members, who were now qualified barristers. It was an eye-opener for me, and indeed for those of my fellow students who had also joined, as we had not experienced the type of problems now presented to us.

These included criminal cases that the State Free Legal Aid scheme didn't cover, eviction cases where families were being thrown out of their flats or houses without having a place to go, social welfare claims cases that had been rejected, domestic violence cases and marital separation cases. In my first few months, I paid my first and only visit to Mountjoy Prison in order to interview two young itinerants who had been refused bail and legal aid and needed assistance with an appeal. In another case, when a young wife was applying for a separation – on which I advised with the assistance of a solicitor volunteer – I was threatened outside the courts by her husband. The lady had come to the advice centre one night, bruised and frightened. She had been beaten by her young husband on numerous occasions and had decided that she wouldn't take any more.

This was a shock to me. Maybe I was innocent, but such incidents were not much publicised at the time, and neither I nor the other students would have had experience of this type of violence previously. We were not trained as interviewers – nor as social workers, psychologists or marriage counsellors – but nobody else was addressing what was manifesting itself as a major social problem, and we coped as well as we could in this case and hundreds of others over the next few years. In this particular case, the husband was haranguing the wife outside the court as I arrived. He was calling her a common prostitute of the docks area, where she lived in a tenement house on Commons Street (now in the middle of the International Financial Services Centre, but then in a very poor area of the city). I didn't hear what she said to him, but he attacked her with his feet and fists. I intervened, and probably because I was more or less the same size as him, he stopped. Nevertheless, he threatened that he would get me on my own some time and 'f—ing do' me. I can't say that he frightened me, but I did realise that he was a docker, and all dockers had the reputation of being tough.

In the middle of the year, FLAC extended by opening two new centres. One was in Molesworth Street in the city centre, in the offices of the Irish Society for Prevention of Cruelty to Children (ISPCC), with whom we had started to work closely; they, in their work, had come across many cases of domestic violence where legal advice was needed for their clients, who couldn't otherwise afford it. The second centre was in Rialto, in a community centre. I was appointed as director there, and in addition to taking cases myself, I had the role of arranging the roster of students to attend the centre and to liaise with the panel of barristers and solicitors.

In mid-October 1971, as FLAC's annual general meeting was approaching, I was asked by the outgoing chairman, Brian Gallagher, if I would take over as chairman of the organisation for the following year. I met and spoke to him about the role, was flattered to be entrusted by peers that I admired, and probably foolishly agreed to undertake it. I started almost immediately. He didn't tell me about the public relations aspect of the role. Within a week I had two journalists looking for interviews about FLAC. They wanted to know about the problems we were dealing with and our views on the lack of appreciation at government level; they also had questions about the extent of domestic violence and unhappy marriages in the country.

In one of the interviews, I was quoted as saying, 'Apart from physical abuse, some husbands wage a sort of psychological warfare against their wives.' I was not used to the level of personal interest that the media had in me; I spent quite a lot of time over the next year dealing with the journalists who wanted more interviews or wanted my comments on statements made by others, including government ministers. The journalists that I dealt with included Frank Byrne, Don Buckley, Elgy Gillespie, Ciaran Carty and Mary Punch. It was a strange experience, but it served me well twenty years later, when I found myself in the middle of another media storm during the Telecom inquiry. Not all the publicity was favourable, and there was kickback when vested interests, including parts of the Catholic Church, did not like the lid being lifted on a major social problem that they considered their field and wanted to have kept quiet.

We opened new centres in Ballymun, Ballyfermot and Dún Laoghaire. Getting them established and then having them manned by the appropriate students required much organisation and time. Other areas were approaching us to open centres there, but we were stretched too thinly. As the number of cases that we were dealing with, and which necessitated hearing in court, was growing exponentially, it became obvious to me that an office in the Four Courts building was advisable – if not essential – so that barristers could meet the litigants before their case went into court.

These litigants were very vulnerable. Some women were seeking a judicial separation or a court order for a monetary allowance. They had to attend court, often on their own, and had to run the gauntlet of their husband and his friends around the courts as they tried to consult privately with their assigned barristers. It was difficult also for the barristers to take instructions from the client in public areas, unlike with clients who could afford to hire a private meeting room. Peter Kelly, who worked in the Four Courts offices at the time, and who subsequently became a successful senior counsel and president of the High Court, was very helpful and sympathetic to our position; he identified some rooms in the building that were not being used.

Someone else tried to put me in touch with the Minister for Justice, the late Des O'Malley, who had ultimate authority over the Four Courts building, and I eventually had a meeting with him in the Department of Justice. I did not make any progress with him. I know he was extremely busy with the Troubles in the North and subversives in the South (it was around the time of the Arms Trial), as well as many other important matters in his department; although he was polite and courteous, he seemed distracted and was not inclined to intervene with the civil servant in charge of the Four Courts building, and so I didn't succeed with that initiative.

Much of my time was spent on administrative matters and trying to establish an administrative system for what was becoming too large for the part-time and untrained backup that we had. In addition to visiting one or more centres each week, we had FLAC committee meetings every couple of weeks to deal with the issues that were arising, such as dealing with the requests for new centres, extending the panel of volunteer solicitors and barristers, and assigning barristers to the cases being dealt with by the younger students. We were also trying to draft a constitution and rules for the organisation, which had far outgrown the original framework.

During this time, I was studying for the second solicitors' exams, attending lectures for the third solicitors' exams and the bookkeeping exam, attending lectures and studying for an LLM degree, tutoring first year students in Introduction to the Legal System and trying to get some work done in GSOB. I was also helping law students in Galway to establish FLAC in that city, and that involved a couple of trips there. In addition, I was asked to give speeches; for example, at their annual seminar, I addressed the ISPCC on the role of FLAC, the legal position on custody of children, guardianship of infants and maintenance for deserted wives.

I realised during this period that I was putting myself under a lot of stress; I knew that I was not sufficiently unemotional about the myriad of difficult cases that I was involved in directly or indirectly to the extent that I was ultimately responsible for ensuring that the clients got some level of advice and representation. I was getting great support from students around me, including Susan Denham, later Chief Justice; John Rogers, later Attorney General; Brian McGovern, later a judge of the Court of Appeal; David Molony, who I later nominated to succeed me as chairman and who later became a TD for Tipperary North, but who died very young; and Barry O'Neill, George Gill and Guy French, who all subsequently became very successful solicitors.

One of the young social workers from St Ultan's Children's Hospital that I dealt with regularly at that time – in relation to guardianship of infant issues – was Frances Ryan, who I had known in university. Later, as Frances Fitzgerald, she became Minister for Justice, succeeding Alan Shatter, who coincidentally had succeeded David Molony as chairman of FLAC. More than forty years later, I met Frances when she, as a local TD in Dublin West, and I, as president of Leinster Rugby, cut a ribbon together at the opening of a new development at Clondalkin Rugby Club, which was in her constituency.

Despite the assistance that I was receiving from colleagues, I was finding it overwhelming, as I was also trying to carry on the usual social life of a 23-year-old. I didn't have time to engage in sports, which was very important to me, and in April I told David Molony that I was resigning as chairman as soon as I could and that I wanted him to succeed me. He rallied some of the other leaders, who tried to persuade me to stay on for another six months, but I wanted to have the annual changeover to occur before the summer rather than after it, as was the case for me. I also explained that I would have to reduce my case involvement; I had realised that my personality was not suited to family law matters, as I tended to get too emotionally involved.

I had been interested in the subject of family law and had taken it as an optional subject in my masters program, so my involvement was rewarding for me – I learned early in my career that I should not continue with that area of law, as it did not suit my temperament. I did continue my involvement in FLAC, however, and attended a newly opened centre in Finglas on a monthly basis for the next three years as a supervisor and mentor to the students then assisting there. I also continued to attend FLAC's general meetings for the next few years, but my involvement lessened as I became busier with my professional and personal life.

In the meantime, I had submitted a handwritten four-page memorandum to the partners of GSOB just before I left for exam study leave at the end of December 1971; the document included my suggestions for improving administration and profitability in the firm. Part of my motivation was that I was not spending as much time in the office as I had hoped – and the partners had probably expected – after I finished the primary degree, and I wanted to contribute something tangible. I knew, in submitting the document, that there was a risk that I would be considered cheeky – that I had gone beyond my pay grade on issues that should not concern an apprentice – but I could see that the three constituent firms of GSOB had not integrated. I discerned three different systems operating in some areas, particularly on simple issues such as the procedures for opening new files, indexing them and then closing and archiving them, but also on more commercial issues such as the method of measuring the value of the work completed, or in progress. I also suggested that the partners consider the advisability of upgrading our accounts system by more computerisation.

Despite my reservations, my efforts prompted the opposite reaction. In late February, when I returned to the office after the exams, I was approached by one of the senior partners, who seemed to look after administration of the firm. He asked me if I had considered what I wanted to do after I qualified later in the year. I told him that, to the extent I had seriously considered it, I wanted to go down to a country town and practice there, as I reckoned that I would get good all-round experience in such a firm and could then decide on what areas of practice I wanted to concentrate; I also told him that I wanted to take it a bit easier than I had been doing up to then. He told me that the partners were very impressed with me; he offered me a job when I qualified, 'leading to partnership', and told me that he was increasing my salary to £10 per week, with immediate effect. He told me that I would get the opportunity to try different areas of practice in GSOB and would get as varied an experience there as anywhere. I asked for time to consider this, as I was flattered and did not expect it; I reverted to him a few days later and told him that I would accept his offer.

With my future now looking more settled, I went back to lectures, studying, tutoring and FLAC with a new horizon; subject only to my difficulty with the FLAC chairman's role, I was able to move on to the remaining exams and finished them in September 1972. After the final exams were finished, I went to the west and south-west of the country on a good holiday to wind down. When the results were published, I had passed and my apprenticeship was completed. I had to get various forms completed and signed by my master, Frank Plunkett Dillon, to the effect that I had attended the office regularly during my apprenticeship, that I was an appropriate person to be admitted as a solicitor and that I could be safely let loose on clients and judges. The admission ceremony took place later in November, and I received my parchment. It was a long and circuitous journey, but I was very proud of my achievement and qualification – as were my mother and father, who attended the ceremony with me.

Between the end of the second law exam in February and the time that I took study leave for the final exam, the work that I was asked to do in GSOB was more demanding and interesting, and I was being given more responsibility – responsibility consistent with my being employed as a solicitor when I qualified. One of the principal tasks that I dealt with was assisting a senior partner in representing Hammond Lane Industries Limited at a Fair Trade Commission inquiry into the steel industry in Ireland and, in particular, the practices of Irish Steel Limited, which was a semi-state company. We had a senior and junior counsel working on the case also, and I enjoyed the work and experience very much. Later that year, when I was discussing with the Law Faculty in UCD a topic for my thesis – which was the second part of the masters degree course – I suggested doing it on the Fair Trade Commission, and fair trade generally, but this was not acceptable to the professor, who did not consider it sufficiently academic. It would have made me an early authority on competition law, which was introduced into Irish law shortly afterwards – upon Ireland's accession to the European Economic Community (EEC) – but I know now, looking back, that it would have narrowed my focus unduly, and my subsequent career would have been very different. Twelve months later I suggested doing my thesis on insolvency law, but in the end I never got started on it, as I had become engrossed in practice; I let the thesis, and consequently the possibility of obtaining a masters degree, lapse.

In September 1972, I received a call from one of the executives in the Institute of Public Administration asking if I would consider taking a position as a part-time lecturer in law to those undertaking the diploma in Public Administration. The person who had been lecturing for the previous year, Mary Finlay, later a Supreme Court judge, had to stand down due to work pressures. I had to scope the position, try to ascertain how much time would be involved in preparing for and giving the lectures, but after talking to Mary and getting more information from the institute itself – on the number of participants, local and external, the purpose of having law in the course and the structure of the academic year – I agreed to undertake lecturing a course titled Introduction to Irish Law.

The diploma was designed for civil servants and persons in the public service, such as health authorities, local authorities and some state-sponsored bodies. There were approximately fifty participants; half of them were to attend lectures, and the other half were to get the lectures and other course material by post. These latter external participants lived in different parts of the country and could not come to Dublin for weekly lectures, hence the remote access basis; if they had queries or comments, they posted them back to the institute and they were passed on to me to prepare a response.

The course covered part of what was in the university degree first year course on Introduction to the Legal System: the basics of constitutional law and Bunreacht na hÉireann, contract law, torts, criminal law and property law. I had never seen myself as an academic, and I tried to make the course as practical as possible for the participants rather than trying to be an academic. That was also the advice from my predecessor, Mary, and it suited me. Nor had I envisaged myself as a teacher of any sort, and yet I was now following on from my year as a tutor in UCD.

Whereas giving the lectures each week and preparing for them wasn't a problem for me, I hated reading through and correcting essays and exam papers after the first two in each batch; I can understand the frustrations of my son, Shane, who has to deal with batches far in excess of what I did in his capacity as a university lecturer. Nevertheless, he does it because he is an academic lecturer by profession; I was doing it to earn some money.

That was less of an issue after January 1973, when I had qualified and started working as a solicitor, but it was very welcome for the first term up to Christmas 1972. When the course ended in May 1973 and the exam papers were corrected, I notified the institute that I didn't want to continue teaching the course in the following year. I assumed that would be the end of my teaching, but in fact I was asked by the Incorporated Law Society to teach a practical module in the company law course a few years later, after it had altered the solicitors' training schedule and courses. I was also asked to give grinds to friends in GSOB and UCD who were a year behind me, and over the next twenty years I had many requests to lecture or address various conferences both national and international, most of which I accepted.

GETTING ESTABLISHED QUICKLY: LIFE AND SOLICITOR'S PRACTICE, 1970s

I commenced working as a solicitor on 2 January 1973. On the first morning, I met with Tim Crowley, the senior partner who had first offered me the position the previous February. Tim was a charming person, but he had a fierce temper. He didn't stay still for long enough to finish what he started, and at times seemed hyperactive, but he was a very successful rainmaker, or – more correctly – generator of new business. I got on very well with him but knew that others in the office, for whatever reason, didn't. That morning, Tim told me that I would have a starting salary of £2,000 per annum. There was no negotiation; in fact, there was no need for negotiation, as I was thrilled. It was nearly four times my finishing salary in Irish Life just four years earlier; even allowing for inflation, I felt that I had caught up quickly in salary terms with where I would have been if I had persisted there.

My official title was assistant solicitor, and over the next few days I was handed a ragbag of files, only a few of which had commenced recently – most were files that had got stuck on some partner's desk for various reasons and needed fresh enthusiasm and momentum to be progressed. Many of these latter cases were probate cases that had come to a temporary halt because there were unexpected difficulties that required action or responses from a third party – whether an executor, a government department or a beneficiary under the will – and by the time the action was made or response had come, the solicitor dealing with it had moved to some other case and was now too busy to pick up the older probate file again.

As I soon came to know, probate practice is best undertaken as a specialty area, and although many smaller solicitors firms required a solicitor to be conducting a wide range of practice areas, probate did not suit solicitors whose main practice was commercial or business law. I had touched on this in the memorandum that I submitted to the partners more than a year previously, but I now found that I was a dumping ground for many of these older probate files.

I rebelled a little, and within a year or so – as I had suggested – the firm employed a full-time probate clerk, Paddy Nolan, who was an expert in that area and very efficient and diligent, albeit not a qualified solicitor. For my part, I was able to escape from probate. In reality, there was little resistance from the partners and it just needed a gentle push from below. The senior solicitors continued to interface with the clients when taking instructions for a will and during the initial meetings with the executors, but they then passed the file immediately to the probate clerk to progress and finalise the case, and the system became more efficient and less stressful.

Among the files that were given to me in the first few days as a solicitor were those related to the liquidation of Shannon Travel Limited and three related travel and car hire companies, which were one half of a bigger group, Hibernian Transport Group, the other half being Palgrave Murphy Limited and related shipping and stevedoring companies. Niall Crowley, the senior partner in Kennedy Crowley Chartered Accountants and an older brother of Tim, was the official liquidator of the Shannon Travel half; Russell Murphy, another chartered accountant, was the official liquidator of Palgrave Murphy Limited and of the holding company.

Frank Plunkett Dillon had been retained as solicitor for Niall Crowley, and Russell Murphy had retained William Fry solicitors. The Shannon Travel and Palgrave Murphy businesses had become hopelessly intertwined, with money paid by clients of the travel companies being used by the other companies for various purposes, such as payment of wages and payment of other creditors and banks; the shipping and stevedoring companies had run into cash flow difficulties and then insolvency. The back office administration and bookkeeping did not accurately, or at all, reflect what had been occurring.

The position was very complicated and gave rise to many new issues of law for which there was no ready precedent, but due to significant work pressure on Frank – including the merger of Roadstone Limited and Irish

Cement Limited to form Cement Roadstone Holdings, the much increased work arising from the merged company and then the acquisition by Bula from under the noses of Tara Mines Limited of the ore-rich lands of Patrick Wright near Navan – the Shannon Travel work had lost momentum and there was a large backlog of issues for which the liquidator and his staff were awaiting responses.

These files had a significant effect on my future career – as they did for the young solicitor working on the Palgrave Murphy files, Frank Sowman. We didn't know it at the time, but our paths were to cross and run parallel many times over the next forty-plus years, with the most recent occasions being related not to law but to rugby. The liquidation of the Hibernian Transport Group companies went on for over ten years, and many trainee accountants in Kennedy Crowley, and subsequently Stokes Kennedy Crowley, who later became partners there or in other firms, or became successful businessmen in later life, cut their teeth on the Shannon Travel files.

When I was studying law, one of the most boring subjects that we had was the Law of Equity and Trusts. We hardly touched on the topics of constructive and implied trusts, but what fascinated me when I started to practise was the elasticity of the concepts and the way that we were able to argue and establish the existence of trusts and consequent tracing in ordinary commercial life – what we termed as order and benefit in the Hibernian Transport Group intertwining of businesses. This had significant consequence not only in these cases but also in other insolvency cases for many years subsequently, and probably still has.

I got stuck into these Shannon Travel files, started dealing with the outstanding queries, many of which required advice of junior and senior counsel, and which ended up in major litigation between the representatives of the different interests; within a short time, I had been given direct responsibility for this matter within GSOB, albeit with plenty of advice and assistance from Frank. This case not only accelerated my promotion to junior partnership in GSOB, which was offered to me in August 1973 – only eight months after I had started – but also established me as a specialist insolvency lawyer, and over the next fifteen years I was involved in one capacity or another in most of the major corporate insolvencies in that period, as indeed was Frank Sowman. Again, it was a series of lucky and unplanned events that played a huge part in my subsequent career.

Nevertheless, insolvency and probate weren't the only areas that I was involved in from an early stage. Some personal friends appointed me as their solicitor to deal with the conveyancing aspects of their first house purchases and the contractual issues they were having on a variety of matters. I was also handed cases of company law, employment law, personal injuries, commercial leases, pension trust deeds, property purchases, contract disputes and licensing issues; and I was also involved in the District, Circuit and High Courts. I was certainly being given the variety of experience that had been promised to me when I was first offered the job back in February 1972.

From September 1973, as a partner – albeit a salaried rather than a profit-sharing partner – I was now listed on the notepaper and was entitled to attend and contribute to partners' meetings, which were held monthly. My salary was significantly increased, as was my cash flow – as being now classified as self employed, I was no longer on PAYE but had to pay income tax once a year on a deferred basis. Salary was now treated as monthly drawings, with a reserve being built up to pay the tax when it became due at least twelve months later and to build up capital in the firm. I was now able to resume paying a financial contribution at home; I had done so from the time I first started earning as a secondary school student, but I had taken a break while I was at university and then paying off a small student loan.

I had bought my first car, a secondhand Fiat 128, registration number 927 YI, in August. On the first Saturday after I got the car, I went for a drive with my brother Joe and friend Kieran Forde. I wasn't going anywhere in particular, but I wanted to give the car a good run and thought that the Naas dual carriageway would be best to check it out. I intended to go as far as Naas and then return, but on the way we noticed that smoke was billowing from the exhaust. I decided that it needed a longer spin, so I continued past Naas. The smoke continued, and one of us remembered that there was a main Fiat garage, Finlays, near Monasterevin. Even though it was a Saturday afternoon, the garage was open. A mechanic checked the car and advised that it needed a new oil filter. Once acquired, I wanted to test whether it was fixed. I rationalised that if I drove further along the road and the problem persisted, I could call back to this garage.

I drove further, and thankfully the smoke had stopped. But I didn't. Shortly after leaving Monasterevin, I thought of going to the Fleadh Cheoil, which I knew was on in Listowel, about 140 miles away. I consulted with Joe and Kieran, and they agreed that I should proceed. Later that evening, tired, hungry and thirsty, we arrived in Listowel. We parked the car along a sidestreet, got something to eat and went into a pub for a drink. The reason that I remember this evening is that I got a craving for a cigarette. I had not been a regular smoker and had never felt such a craving. I got a cigarette from Joe or Kieran, smoked it, and have never smoked another cigarette since, nor have I had any craving or inclination to do so. We slept in the car, bought toothbrushes and toothpaste, and headed home on Sunday morning to be ready for work on Monday. The car never gave me further trouble, but a couple of years later I upgraded it for a newer, bigger model.

One of the major transactions with succeeding court actions in 1973 and 1974 was the Bula case with Tara Mines, relating to the ore discovery referred to above. Frank Plunkett Dillon was the legal adviser to Bula, and it enjoyed initial success, winning a significant High Court action in March 1974. Because Frank was involved, I had a peripheral involvement in the case, which was very divisive publicly and politically, as it involved an allegation of 'claim jumping' on the one hand and oppression by undue influence on the other. As it ultimately transpired, Bula ended up in twenty years of litigation – but GSOB was long out of it by then, as our direct client, Tom Roche, had left the company.

The full Bula saga is sad. It resulted in a family split, a divorce and a manic obsession, but people sometimes wondered how Bula got its name, which was not very imposing in the way that Tara Mines was. The truth is that GSOB, as part of its practice, operated a company formation and shelf company business. It formed hundreds of companies with the minimum two shares issued to partners; when a client wanted a company for their own business purposes, it was immediately available. The two shares were transferred to the client, and the existing directors – who were two solicitors in the firm – co-opted two new directors nominated by the new owner and usually resigned immediately.

The only difficulty experienced by the solicitor who operated this business was not a legal one – it was in coming up with names for the companies. Each company, when formed, had to have a name not already used, and it was not known at the time of formation what it would be used for, so a name was invented for it. When bought by the client, it usually had its name changed to match that of the client or his business, and the change of name was filed in the Companies Registration Office (CRO).

Bula was the name of a racehorse that won the Champion Hurdle at Cheltenham in 1971 and 1972 and was used as the name of a shelf company. If the person in the CRO who registered the company had any interest in horseracing, it might not have allowed it, but obviously he didn't. In this case, when the company was called for by the client, it had to be used in a contract immediately – there was no opportunity to have its name changed before its first use, and hence the name stuck. There were other examples of the original name being retained for similar reasons, but probably none as well known as Bula Limited.

Since September 1973, as a partner, I was now taking direct responsibility for many of the cases that I was dealing with. The business of the firm was growing rapidly, and while we were all generating new business, the existing clients of the firm were themselves expanding their businesses, buying new businesses and investing in new employees, premises, plant and machinery.

The senior partners of the firm – Denzil O'Donnell, Ted O'Brien, Frank Plunkett Dillon and Tim Crowley – had built successful firms before the merger in 1968, and their clients provided a very solid base on which the firm could, and did, grow. Denzil and Ted each acted for many of the professional class that had developed in Dublin after the state's independence in 1921; Denzil – through his former firm, Thomas Gerrard & Company – also acted for some of what I considered the landed gentry, but had also built up a good commercial law practice and acted as legal adviser in the establishment of Banque Nationale de Paris (Ireland) Limited and Algemene Bank Nederland (Ireland) Limited in the early 1970s, and the firm acted for these banks, among others, for many years afterwards.

Frank, whose grandfather had started the firm John L. Scallan & Co. in offices in Suffolk Street before the end of the nineteenth century, was the partner that I knew best; he was the master to whom I was apprenticed and the one who mentored me most during the early years, before I became a partner myself. Frank's father, John Plunkett Dillon, had married John L. Scallan's daughter around 1920; he took over the management of the firm, building a very successful commercial practice.

John had recognised that as the country emerged from the depression of the 1930s and 1940s, indigenous Irish businesses needed access to new capital to grow. He and Frank, when the latter joined him in the mid-1950s, identified a number of successful but undercapitalised businesses that could become public companies and get a listing on the stock exchange. These included A.H. Masser, Castle Sand Company, Irish Wire Products and Gypsum Industries, all of which had grown significantly – and had strong and dynamic leadership – by the time that I qualified.

Tim Crowley was, as I wrote earlier, a 'rainmaker'. Through his family, who were the Crowleys of Kennedy Crowley, and through the family of his wife, he had great business connections and introduced lots of interesting opportunities to GSOB.

One of the junior partners – who took over the banking business from Denzil – developed our expertise and reputation as banking and financial services lawyers, which reputation continued up to and beyond the establishment of the International Financial Services Centre (IFSC) in the late 1980s and 1990s.

In the last quarter of 1973, I was brought into a property acquisition programme for a proposed major redevelopment on South William Street and Clarendon Street. It was started off by the acquisition of control by Kilbride Holdings Limited of the share capital of Ferrier Pollock Limited, a public company quoted on the stock exchange. Ferrier Pollock occupied Powerscourt House on South William Street. It was a wholesale drapery company, selling ladies underwear and garments. It is impossible to believe now when one visits the Powerscourt Centre that in the early 1970s it was stacked high with brassieres, corsets, knickers, house coats, aprons and various other garments for ladies; the scene was quite chaotic, and even though the business had been carried on there for over a hundred years, nothing seemed to have been done to the interior of what was originally the townhouse of Viscount Powerscourt and the Wingfield family.

Perhaps in retrospect, it is better that it wasn't changed much previously, as it was eventually transformed into the Powerscourt Centre in what was one of the best restorations of any building in the city. Most people have forgotten the existence of Ferrier Pollock, and have only heard of it in the context of the famous story about Brendan Behan. Brendan was touring England universities after his recognition as an Irish literary figure. He was asked by a student if he could explain the difference between prose and poetry. He thought for a second and replied:

There was a young man named Rollocks
Who worked for Ferrier Pollocks.
As he walked on the Strand
With his girl by the hand.
The tide came up to his knees.

'Now that's prose,' he added. 'If the tide had been in, it would have been poetry.'

The acquisition programme involved the purchase of 60–62 South William Street and some buildings on Clarendon Street through Blackglen Limited, a subsidiary of Kilbride Holdings. Each of these properties was occupied by a myriad of mainly small agency businesses which had one or two offices in a warren of corridors and floors. This was the centre of what was known as 'the rag trade', and most of these businesses were on relatively short leases or licences. All had to be bought out – by compensation for surrendering their lease, or for actually selling their interest if surrender was not feasible – and others stayed on but their leases expired and they either left voluntarily or were ejected if agreement could not be reached.

There were only a very few situations where ejectment proceedings had to be commenced, but over the course of a few years, vacant possession was obtained, and in some cases the occupiers were allowed back into possession on short-term licences. Kilbride's long-term plan was to develop a major centre, or mall, running from the rear of the Wicklow Street buildings up to Coppinger Row and between South William Street and Clarendon Street; it was also to include a large property owned by Switzer's on Clarendon Street. An option agreement was entered into with Switzer's, but in the interim, planning permission was refused and the only major change that came out of all the work and time that went into the multi-year project was the redevelopment of Powerscourt House, which in fact was not carried out by Kilbride Holdings but by Power Securities. The business of Ferrier Pollock was moved to a new building in an industrial estate – and that building, with its new tenant, was then sold to an Irish Life property fund.

I was getting a lot of referrals in the corporate insolvency area – receiverships and voluntary and official liquidations. These included EC Handcock Limited, a distributor of electrical equipment, and W.E. Berney Limited, which traded as Berney Mastervision and had multiple premises throughout the eastern half of Ireland from which it leased televisions; it was probably the first or second biggest company in that business at the time, and the most common way of acquiring a television in the early 1970s. There were a huge number of leasing contracts, which were in fact the main asset, as most of the multiple premises occupied by it were held on leases either on the main street in towns or in shopping centres at a full market rent and had little or no capital value.

Another receivership that I considered significant, because the business was saved, was Galway Crystal Limited, which was located just outside Galway city on the Dublin road. Galway Crystal made beautiful products of cut glass and was a competitor of the better-known Waterford Glass, which was considered in the market as a premium product. Since then, there has been a large increase in the number of cut-glass factories – indeed, ten years later I was involved in the receivership of Cavan Crystal, another competitor, albeit also less well known. Galway Crystal was successful in making lovely products, but it was not profitable; it ran out of money, and the bank appointed Laurence Crowley, a younger brother of Niall, as receiver and manager.

Laurence decided to continue to operate the business with a view to selling it as a going concern, which was likely to get a better return for the bank and hopefully the other creditors. He quickly noted how stemware that was cut in one building or shed before being brought to another building – across a yard for polishing and packaging – had a high breakage level, occurring apparently between one building and the other.

On inspection, it was obvious that the path across the yard was rough and uneven. By having a layer of tarmac applied to that pathway, Laurence was able to return the business to profitability and to sell it on successfully. Unfortunately, it did go into liquidation again around ten years later, but for different reasons. After Laurence figured out how to get the business back to profitability, he gave me the opportunity to buy six whiskey and six brandy tumblers at cost price. I was delighted to do so, and I still use them regularly – and much to Mary's chagrin, prefer them to the Waterford Glass tumblers that we got as wedding presents or won as golf prizes in the intervening years.

By October 1974, Joe Sharkey, our court clerk, had become ill with emphysema and had to retire. Sadly, he died a few months later, in February 1975. Although I wasn't the main litigation partner or the main conveyancing partner, I was given the task of interviewing applicants to succeed him – probably because I was the partner most familiar with his role, being the most recently qualified partner. It may not have struck me as unusual at the time, but all the applicants were female. We found a very good candidate; although she was never going to replace Joe and his contacts in the various government offices, she did a very good job for us for a few years, until she got married and decided to change career.

My workload continued to be varied, but as I became more and more busy, I became more and more frustrated with the court system, and then with litigation in general. I disliked many of the formalities involved – the wigs and gowns, and what I perceived as the undue deference given to judges, many of whom seemed to be working for only four hours a day. I knew that most of the High and Supreme Court judges had to research and then write their judgements when the court wasn't sitting, but there were too many cases when the simplest judgement was taking an inordinate time.

When added to the other inefficiencies in case management – when cases were fixed and then postponed, or hearings were commenced and then adjourned because a barrister or judge had another case in another court – and the general waste of time involved with most court applications, I found that it didn't suit my lack of patience. Although I didn't avoid courts completely – as that was almost impossible, particularly because of the wide spectrum of legal issues that arose in most insolvency cases – I did decide early on that I did not want to specialise in litigation, whether commercial or personal injuries. Although it was very lucrative, it was not intellectually stimulating.

In 1975, I acted for Kildare Street Club in the sale of its club premises at the bottom of the street. It was sold to a property developer, Norwest Holst, which I presume had the intention of demolishing and redeveloping it. Nonetheless, that has not happened since, and the building now houses Alliance Francaise, a French language school and cultural centre, which got the opportunity to expand its business when planning permission was not forthcoming for the demolition. Kildare Street Club had earlier merged with University Club, situated on St Stephen's Green; it used the proceeds of the sale of its property as a dowry, funding refurbishment works in the new clubhouse. I joined the newly merged Kildare Street Club and University Club a few months later, and used it regularly for many years at lunchtime; however, as I had stopped using it almost altogether by the late 1980s – because of work pressure and shorter lunchtimes – I resigned my membership in the early 1990s.

In 1975, I was also involved in two large insolvencies (as well as many smaller ones). One was Cahill Printers Limited, a long-established print works on East Wall Road that, *inter alia*, had the contract for almost all of the Government Publications Office documents; the other, Cork Shoe Company Limited, a shoe manufacturing company that was not long established but had quickly become a successful business – perhaps too quickly, as it ran into financial difficulties. Its owner, Paul Duggan, fought valiantly to save it, and then fought with the receiver; unfortunately for him, he was unable to raise the finance to save the business or its related company, Cork Rubber and Manufacturing Company Limited. Another company, Macroom Shoe Company Limited, collapsed at the same time, but its owner, Noel Duggan, survived by developing the premises – which he himself had owned and leased to his company – into an international equestrian and entertainment centre that many years later hosted the Eurovision Song Contest.

As it transpired, 1975 was a significant year in my life for many reasons. I bought my first house for £12,700 and got my first mortgage, borrowing £9,000 from Irish Permanent Building Society and £3,000 on a term loan from Bank of Ireland. It was also the year that I met Mary, my wife, and started 'going out with her'. It was also the year that my uncle John (Glackin) died, my uncle Patrick (Donnelly) having died the previous year; it was probably the first time that I realised the generation just ahead of me was mortal. My sister Bernadette was getting married at the beginning of July and moving to Limerick, and a little earlier, my brother Joe, who had qualified as a dentist, moved to Kent in England to work.

The confluence of some of these events, with me indicating that I intended to move to my new house, upset my father greatly. I believe that he also realised that he was only a couple of years from retirement, and he seemed to suffer a depression. Luckily it didn't last long, and he soon reverted to his cheerful usual self. It was also the year when one of my partners, Bryan O'Flaherty had a serious car accident. Bryan's principal work was acting for Roadstone Limited, a subsidiary of Cement Roadstone Holdings (or as it was subsequently called, CRH) in its property acquisition programme around the country; he also dealt with all their litigation.

I was asked to take over Bryan's workload in addition to what I had been doing. Although I had done some minor work for Roadstone previously, such as applying for licences for the Roadstone Sports and Social Club and representing some of their employee drivers for road traffic charges, this was the first substantive work that I did for the company. It became a substantial and interesting part of my workload for the next few years; indeed, CRH plc became the major element of my work from 1993 onwards.

The following year, 1976, continued to be a busy period; the government introduced new capital and corporation taxation, including wealth tax and capital gains tax, and I continued legal education, with seminars and conferences becoming regular events. One of the organisations that arranged seminars and conferences on various topics was the Society of Young Solicitors (SYS); having been an attendee at a few of their weekend conferences, I was invited to join the committee in early 1976 and in October 1977, I was chairman of the subcommittee that organised and ran the SYS weekend conference in Sligo. The society had been operating for seven or eight years, and this conference was the first time that it had gone to the north-west. It wasn't that I had any particular affinity to Sligo or Donegal, but I thought that the conference venue should be a little different from the usual Galway, Killarney, Kilkenny, Waterford and Kinsale venues; as I had the call as chairman, I exercised it and we had a great conference assisted by the North West Tourism Board, which I had brought on board. I then served as chairman of SYS, and in the early 1980s I got involved in the organisation of the annual conference of Association Internationale des Jeunes Avocats (AIJA), the related international body, which was held in Dublin.

In 1976, I was involved in a number of new insolvency cases. One was the liquidation of Kyteler's Inn, a very old pub and restaurant in Kilkenny where the liquidator was Declan O'Connor of Reynolds McCarron; another was Ashbourne Properties Limited, which owned the Roxboro Shopping Centre in Limerick, where the receiver and manager was Maurice Tempany of Griffin Lynch, which later became Ernst & Young Ireland. I was also involved in the liquidation of Knockmeal Co-operative Society, based in County Waterford, which owned property and land throughout the rural parts of the county; the liquidator in this case was Laurence Crowley. Another interesting transaction was acting for the Dominican Convent Cabra in the sale of a site to the Holy See for the construction of a nunciature for the Papal Nuncio. This involved dealing with the Archbishop of Dublin, as well as the Holy See represented by the Nuncio, as the formal consent of the archbishop had to be obtained and this also required correspondence with the Vatican.

An interesting character that I was introduced to – and who wanted to buy a property in Ireland for greyhound training and breeding – was Denny Cordell Lavarack. Although born in Argentina, Denny grew up in England and became a very successful record producer. He produced hit singles for the Moody Blues, Procul Harum and Joe Cocker; he also later worked with Bob Marley and Tom Petty and their bands. Denny left the music business after he came to Ireland. He got involved in horse breeding and training after he gave up the greyhound breeding, but he continued to associate with many of those involved in the music business, and trained a horse for Ron Wood of the Rolling Stones.

Denny went back into the music business in his late forties, working in A&R for Island Records. He was credited with promoting the Cranberries – who had been discovered by his son – in the USA. He also produced an album for Marianne Faithful during this period. He had originally rented a property in Colvinstown near Kiltegan, County Wicklow, along with his friend Maldwyn Thomas, for his dog breeding. Sometime later, however, he bought a lovely property, Corries House in County Carlow, for his horse breeding. I lost touch with him after he settled in Corries House; I couldn't continue to act for him due to a conflict of interest. He was a larger-than-life personality and became well known in the equine business in Ireland before his premature death in 1993 at the age of 51.

In the summer of 1976, I went with Mary to the south of France on a fly-drive holiday, collecting a car at Marseilles airport, driving across the Riviera, and stopping at many of the towns and resorts along the coast. From there, we went into Italy, where we visited Pisa, Bologna, Florence and Venice, driving back around Mont Blanc to Lyons airport, where we returned the car and flew home. We had nothing planned other than the hired car and the flights in and out of France, so we were free and easy. We could stay an extra day or night in a location if we so wished, or sleep in the car if we had to – which we did. It was my first trip to the south of France, and I fell in love with it – its sea, sun and mountains, its special shade of blue light, its beaches, its food and wine. We stayed in a variety of locations, including camping sites, city hotels and (just the once) a beach, seeing sights that I had read of but had not experienced previously.

Our car was a small Fiat 600. It took us up and down some very twisting hilly routes as I got used to driving on the right-hand side of the road for the first time. At Palm Beach nightclub and casino in Cannes, I proudly parked our little Fiat among the other patrons' Porsches, Ferraris, Alfa Romeos, Lamborghinis, Daimlers and Maseratis. On the Saturday night that Eamonn Coghlan ran in the Olympic 1,500 metres final, we couldn't find a television in Monte Carlo that was showing the event. We had to race back to our guesthouse in Menton, simulating the Monte Carlo rally; we barely got there in time and were hugely disappointed, as he finished fourth and outside the medals. When we returned home after nearly three special weeks together, we both realised that we could probably live with each other for the rest of our lives. In November that year, we got engaged.

For me, 1977 was another significant year. I got married on the last Saturday in June, in Kilworth, County Cork, where Mary had grown up. We had our wedding reception in Aherlow House Hotel, which was about 30 miles away. I drove the wedding car, which was actually my own car, from the church to the hotel, but when I went to park in the space reserved for the bride and groom, I was directed elsewhere; the attendant didn't think that we were the married couple, never previously having seen the groom taking the role of chauffeur. Only when Mary got out of the car and he saw her wedding dress did he allow me to park there. Everything else went smoothly, and we had a very enjoyable day with friends and family.

After the wedding, we flew to Scotland for a short honeymoon, as Mary could only take a week's holiday, it being near the end of the school year. I had booked another fly-drive holiday and thought I had it well planned. Neither of us had been to Scotland previously, but we loved it there. The only problem was the strict Sunday observance rules that applied there at that time; the only restaurant that was open in Helensburgh, where we spent our first night in Scotland, was a small and not very inviting Chinese.

I had overlooked that in my planning, but everything else surpassed our expectations. We drove through the Highlands and spent a few days on the Isle of Skye before driving over to Edinburgh, flying home from there on the following Sunday morning.

Later that year, I sold my first house in Malahide and, with Mary, bought a house in Sutton.

During the year, I started advising two new clients, Benny Hyde and J.C. Savage, who became good friends and clients over the following years. Benny owned a successful company in the construction sector, and J.C., who lived in Swords, was in the course of developing Swords Shopping Centre and asked me to take over the legal work involved. He was a friend of my cousin Kierie Donnelly, and I had met him at Kierie's wedding a couple of years earlier; I then met him again when Mary and I were on our proper honeymoon in Marbella.

Mary and I were roughing it, touring around the south of Spain in a rented car without having booked accommodation in advance – which resulted in having to spend some nights in quite a small car. We bumped into J.C. one night and chatted for a while; he found us a hotel for the night and the rest of our holiday, and he brought us to his favourite local bar, The Blue Cat, where we met lots of his friends and where he was the life and soul of the bar – which was the case no matter where he went. We ended up becoming good friends until his premature death in 2011, more than thirty years later.

Another new client who was introduced to me during that year was Pat Darcy, who owned a company, Metallurgical and Materials Testing Limited, trading as Metlabs. It was probably the first time that I had no understanding of the business that a client was conducting, but I knew it was successful. Pat Darcy stands out in my memory, because a few years later I received a phone call from him as he was being driven to a meeting in Saudi Arabia. It was the first mobile call I had received; in fact, it was the first time that I had heard of a call being made from a car.

Hammond Holdings Limited, a long-established client – a public company listed on the stock exchange – was becoming very active in 1976 and 1977, expanding from its original base as a scrap metal company and property investor to a manufacturing and distribution company. It entered into agreements with companies such as Pitco Frialator, Southbend

International and Medicare, and – led by J. Dominic Murphy – was actively looking for new opportunities.

In August 1977, I was told about a new transaction with Hospital & Kitchen International (HKI), a Canadian company. HKI had started as a manufacturer of stainless kitchens for hospitals, but it achieved its rapid growth and success when it got the contract to build the kitchens for McDonald's, initially in Canada and then for North America. As McDonald's expanded into Europe, it wanted HKI to follow it and manufacture all its requirements for the continent. It had decided to look for a joint venture partner, and the Industrial Development Authority (IDA) had introduced it to Hammond Holdings. Hence, I was asked to draft a joint venture agreement; this was new for me, but it was required urgently, as Dominic knew the old adage, 'If you control the paper, you control the negotiations.'

Negotiations developed over the next few months, and became more intense in late October when the Canadians and their lawyers arrived. We had three straight full days – Wednesday to Friday evening – of negotiating and drafting, which involved postponing some work and having to delegate further work to other partners. Negotiations resumed on the following Monday – but less intensely, as the Canadians had gone to London for a few days. They returned on the following Thursday with an ultimatum: that the joint venture agreement – or JVA, as we were calling it – had to be signed before they returned to Toronto the following Sunday.

We started again at 8.30 a.m. on Friday, worked through Friday night and eventually signed at 12 noon on the following day. Much of the negotiation was on the issue of what occurs if the parties have a dispute and want to separate, as the Canadians had the specific technical expertise and market knowledge, and might have had a tactical advantage if there was such a dispute. David Massie, the Canadian lawyer for HKI, maintained that the most important provisions in a partnership agreement for a joint venture company such as this were the arrangements for divorce if the parties fell out. I thought it was a great position to take, and used it on many occasions over the next thirty years.

A celebratory dinner had been arranged for 8 p.m. that evening. I went home for the afternoon, went to sleep and, according to Mary, was ranting in my sleep about the 'JVC'. Mary, of course, had no idea prior to this what a JVC was, and she was worried. I woke up and explained when asked what

I was talking about in my sleep; we then went to the dinner. It was only then that Mary realised the stress that I was putting myself under.

The new joint venture company that we negotiated is still in existence, and still very successful, but its ownership has changed significantly in the meantime. It was decided a few weeks after the agreement was signed that I could not continue to act as solicitor for the joint venture company as well as Hammond Holdings, so for the joint venture company I recommended Laurence Shields, who I knew from university and who had recently set up his own firm with two colleagues. As Laurence said many years later, he owed me a referral from back then; in 1991, the payback came when Laurence recommended me to Des O'Malley, the Minister for Industry and Commerce, to be appointed as inspector, under the Companies Act 1990, to Chestvale Properties and Hoddle Investments in relation to the sale of the Johnston, Mooney & O'Brien site and the involvement of Telecom Éireann.

Another significant case for me that year, 1977, was my appointment as solicitor to Declan O'Connor and Bernard Somers two partners of Reynolds McCarron, an accountancy firm who were reviewing the business of Lakeglen Construction Limited. The latter was a very large house-building company that was working as a contractor, through the National Building Agency, for local authorities' housing programmes; however, it had run out of money. We advised the main creditors that we could operate an informal Chapter 11 administration. Chapter 11 was a USA insolvency procedure, not available at the time under Irish law. The proposal required agreement from the main creditors, who formed a creditors committee and became the 'moratorium creditors', and the company directors and management.

In the course of this work, I met a businessman from Donegal who told me that coincidentally, his nickname as a teenager was Glackin. He represented W. & L. Crowe Limited, part of the Gallagher Group. He later introduced me to two builders, which quickly led me to invest in, and become involved in, Lark Developments; I would stay involved as a shareholder and director with that company for eighteen years.

During the year, Laurence Crowley was appointed receiver and manager of Continental Irish Meats Limited, a company based in Waterford that operated a burger-manufacturing business. It brought in large numbers of cattle, butchered them and then made the burgers in huge quantities. When the receiver was appointed, two cattle dealers who had recently delivered livestock applied to the High Court for injunctions, restraining the receiver from dealing with the cattle supplied by them.

These applications, and others that followed, led to lengthy and intense litigation over the next couple of years; it also resulted in some new law being enunciated by the courts on the concept of reservation of title. This concept was a blend of equity and contract that hadn't been dealt with by the Irish courts previously, and had only recently been dealt with in the English courts, the other common law system which most influenced the Irish courts. The cattle dealers' claim was that they retained ownership of the cattle until they were fully paid for. This was a relatively simple concept and although not then common to have it provided for in contracts, there was no legal reason not to do so.

The claims in these cases went further, and they asserted that they became the owners of the burgers until they were paid for the cattle. That was a more complex issue, as we maintained that the meat from the particular cattle had been mixed with the meat from other cattle, was unidentifiable, and had also been mixed with spices and whatever else went into the manufacture of the burgers. We ultimately won the case, but in the course of the preparation for it I learned too much about what went into the manufacture of the burgers and it put me off them. In the forty years since then, I reckon I have eaten less than twenty burgers that weren't homemade.

One case from the Continental Irish Meats receivership that went to the Supreme Court related to monetary compensation amounts (MCAs) payable through the Department of Agriculture that arose from the EEC common agricultural policy and whether the bank's charge extended to the MCAs. Again, this was new ground for me – but also for the courts and for the barristers that I used for the court cases, Peter Sutherland BL, who was the junior counsel, and Henry Barron SC, who was the senior counsel. Peter later became the Attorney General and an EU commissioner, and Henry later became a Supreme Court judge.

My father retired from Irish Life in March 1978; as we had need in GSOB for more experience in our property department, we offered him a consultancy. He was delighted to accept and continued working part-time for us until his illness in early 1982. He took on some of the difficult conveyancing cases that arose, including advising the purchaser of An Grianán Estate in County Donegal, reputedly the largest farm in the country.

It was in 1978 that I bought a new car for the first time; in fact, I only did it twice more over the next forty-three years. It was a lime green Toyota Celica Coupe, but after 1985, when I bought my second new BMW, I allowed someone else to take the first year's depreciation and I only bought used cars, albeit some very nice ones.

The Lakeglen project was taking up a lot of time, and as not all creditors – particularly the Revenue Commissioners – supported the informal administration, it also involved a series of court applications and ultimately ended up in liquidation. Nevertheless, it was successful: a large number of houses got finished, building workers could continue their employment for longer and the moratorium creditors significantly reduced their indebtedness.

John Donnelly of Deloitte, Haskins & Sells was appointed by Algemene Bank Nederland to investigate Eurobrand Limited, which was a distributor of grocery products in Europe that operated from Dublin. He asked me to advise him and on the basis of the bank's suspicions, we guessed that there was a teeming and lading fraud being carried on. I engaged a private detective to report on movements over the first weekend at the main warehouse; we deduced from that report and the bank statements that, indeed, there was fraud.

A court application quickly followed to have John appointed as provisional liquidator, and subsequently as official liquidator, and litigation then ensued in Dublin and Manchester over the next few years. The timing of the appointment of a provisional liquidator was opportune, as the fraud was about to escalate. Nevertheless, considerable obstruction and obfuscation followed, and it took quite a bit of persistence by the liquidator and his colleagues to unravel the situation and restore proper accounting records for the company.

In early 1979 the Shah of Iran fled the country, Ayatollah Khomeini took over as leader and the second petroleum crisis in six years commenced. It is hard to imagine now, but petrol was in seriously short supply – there was a rationing system in operation for customers, as there was for the suppliers and retailers. Panic ensued, and the price of petrol doubled in less than twelve months. Long queues outside petrol stations were the norm, and a spate of siphoning petrol from other people's cars occurred. I took to keeping an emergency supply in a can in the car itself, which was probably very dangerous; but as Mary was expecting our first child in late April, I didn't want to find myself short at the crucial moment when she wanted an urgent lift to the Rotunda Hospital.

As it transpired, I did have enough petrol when the time came, early in the morning of 24 April. Shane was born at 6.45 p.m. that evening, and I can fairly state that it was the most emotional, magical moment of my life, far exceeding what I had been led to believe. We had been at antenatal classes together, and I thought that I had some idea of what to expect; however, I grossly underestimated what was to come. The labour ward was a busy and noisy place, and at one stage my lack of patience kicked in when Mary was in serious pain and the epidural that had been promised to her was not forthcoming.

I threatened to look for the obstetrician myself and bring him back with me to the room where Mary was. This simple threat was sufficient to stir the head nurse to call him and ask if the epidural could be administered then. He said it should already have been given, and it duly was. I was not very popular with that nurse for the rest of the day, but that didn't bother me in the slightest. Shane was safely born, and we took him home a few days later. I knew that I was never as proud and happy as that day, but I didn't know that it was to be repeated twice more within a few years with the birth of my two daughters, Louisa and Sinéad.

At the Chartered Accountants Dress Dance at the beginning of February 1979 – to which Mary and I had been invited by Dominic Murphy, who was on the organising committee – there was an auction, the proceeds of which were to go to charity. The first item on the list was a portable TV, which at that stage was relatively unusual, but I thought it would be a nice present for Mary when she was nursing our baby to be.

I didn't hear the auctioneer commencing the auction and proceeded to bid vigorously for the TV. It was knocked down to me eventually, or so I thought, at a price that was more than I anticipated, but I consoled myself with the thought that the proceeds were for charity. It was only at the last item of the auction, when I heard the auctioneer announce the bidding for the TV, that I realised that he had auctioned the items in reverse order and that what I had been bidding for was a case of champagne. I didn't tell anyone at the time of my mistake, but I had to inform Mary when she told me on the way home that she thought I was stupid to have bought the champagne. My explanation didn't change her mind. We did get to enjoy some of the champagne when Shane came home a few months later, but as neither of us were regular champagne imbibers, it lasted until the following Xmas.

My friend J.C. Savage sponsored a golf outing for Swords Community Council in September 1979; he invited me to play, and to the dinner afterwards. One of his guests was the local TD and junior government minister Ray Burke. There were about ten persons at the guest table and afterwards I took an order from the guests at our table for the bar, went up, joined the queue bought it and brought it back in two or three lots. The minister beckoned me over in the middle of my delivering the drinks; he told me that this was his round and he would pay for it. I declined. When he insisted, I told him as politely as I could, but perhaps using an expletive, that if he wanted to buy a round, 'You go to the bar and queue like everybody else here.' He was not accustomed to not getting his own way in his own constituency, but he didn't say anything to me. He did tell J.C., who wasn't at the table at the time; J.C., who was an old school friend and supporter of the minister but who was very independent of him, thought that my response was brilliant and still recounted the incident with pleasure thirty years later. Shortly after that, J.C. bought O'Toole's pub in Swords, renovated it substantially and reopened it as the Lord Mayors – named after his father, who had earlier that year been elected as Lord Mayor of Swords.

During this year, 1979, I also advised Pat Donohoe who established a new business, Donohoe Lift Engineering Systems Limited, and obtained a licence from Schindler – one of the main lift manufacturers in Europe but which hadn't been present in Ireland previously. He then challenged Otis Lifts, which at the time was the largest in Ireland, and proceeded to build a very successful business. Unfortunately, it ended in tragedy many years later; his son Patrick was accidentally killed while doing holiday work for the company at a time when Pat had sold the business and was operating a post-completion earn out. He was an entrepreneur engineer, and over the years he started a number of new businesses; he was always full of new ideas and always a very pleasant client to work with. He never recovered from Patrick's tragic death, however, and died suddenly at much too young an age.

In 1979 I continued on the Law Society's company law committee and on the education subcommittee, as well as the SYS committee; so much of my extracurricular activity was law-related. In preparation for the course on compulsory liquidations, which I gave to the trainee solicitors with Anthony Collins, another insolvency lawyer, I had to write our role-playing scripts. Anthony and I used these to demonstrate how to deal with a client who either wanted to put a customer in liquidation or wanted to put his own company into liquidation; we then watched CCTV video recordings of ourselves to try to improve our performance. It was a strange experience but proved very useful when it came to the actual course. It was the nearest that I came to becoming the playwright that I had listed as a career option before I left school thirteen years previously, but it didn't persuade me to change career again.

By 1979, my partnership profit share had increased and I was now entitled to 80 per cent of the senior partners' profit level, which was a significant amount. Nonetheless, one of my colleagues was not pulling his weight; he had a drink problem, and I had to regularly cover some of his work as well as my own. In addition, some important work that had been delegated to him was not being progressed satisfactorily, and it was damaging the reputation of the firm, adversely affecting all of us. I suggested to the senior partners that this situation should be reflected in our relative profit shares.

When it wasn't acted on, I started to think about leaving the firm and setting up my own practice; I didn't say anything, however, as I hadn't done anything concrete about it. I was told that the senior partners had had a serious talk with that partner and had given him an ultimatum, as I wasn't the only one that had noted the subpar performance. That satisfied me, I stayed and that particular partner did alter his behaviour. He became a very important and successful partner for the next fifteen or sixteen years, but unfortunately his old woes returned again; though we made allowances, we could not let it continue when he became erratic and had to be confronted. This saga ended in the mid to late 1990s, with his sudden resignation from the firm. It was a pity but the best outcome for us, and indeed for him.

FAMILY GROWS: LIFE AND SOLICITOR'S PRACTICE, 1980S

The start of the next decade brought new insolvency cases, such as Munster Chipboard Limited, based in Scariff, County Clare, where I advised the receiver, Ray Jackson of Stokes Kennedy Crowley. The company's business was sold later in the year to another company which operated a successful business there for many years.

I also advised the liquidator of Birr Fabrics Limited. The business of Birr Fabrics Limited was eventually sold to a French company, which established a new company, Max Birr Limited. Before the sale, however, I made a quick dash to Condrieu in the middle of France to meet the eponymous Max and his father; they had a business there but were interested in investing in Ireland. The liquidator, Declan O'Connor, and I left Dublin Airport at 5.10 p.m. for Paris; we then flew to Lyon, where we arrived at 10 p.m., and too late to enjoy its gastronomic delights. The next morning, we drove to Condrieu, which was about 40 kilometres south; we met Max and his father, and negotiated through the day, agreeing a deal. We got a flight back from Lyon at 18.25 p.m., flying to London and then Dublin, where we arrived around 10.00 p.m. The flight was due to arrive a little earlier, but some problem arose with the landing gear on the plane, and we had to make a very bumpy emergency landing. We both thanked the pilot when we did eventually disembark, as clearly it could have been more difficult. That was the first of at least three occasions over the next thirty-five years when I had a scary landing; although on that first occasion I was still a believer of sorts, I don't think I resorted to praying. Max Birr Limited then operated successfully for many years afterwards.

Other cases in that year where I advised the liquidator or receiver included the liquidation of the South County Hotel in Stillorgan, County Dublin, which subsequently became the Stillorgan Park Hotel, and James O'Keeffe Limited, which was a timber merchant business in East Wall, Dublin. Work continued on many of the older cases, including Shannon Travel, which had been suspended pending a Supreme Court decision involving the parent company, Hibernian Transport Group.

I also acted for the first time for Fiat Trattori, a division of the Fiat Group; it sold agricultural tractors throughout Ireland. Its main distributor, Bamford (Ireland), a subsidiary of the JCB manufacturer, got into financial difficulties and ultimately went into liquidation. I met with two of their international marketing executives, Guido Alvera and Armando Moresa, and began a relationship that lasted for most of the following ten years, as Fiat Trattori developed a new distribution network in Ireland. We got on very well socially, and I was invited on a number of occasions to visit their home city of Modena to see the Ferrari works and testing; however, I didn't take them up on it.

I first went to the United States and Canada in 1980. We went as a family – Mary, Shane and I – and visited Seattle and Port Townsend in Washington State (where Mary's brother, Jim, lived with his wife, Noreen), along with San Francisco, Vancouver and Toronto. We came home after three and a half weeks, the longest holiday I had ever had up to then.

John Donnelly, who I had worked with during the previous year on the Eurobrand Limited case, was also the Finnish consul in Ireland; he introduced me to the Portuguese Ambassador, who was looking for a new legal adviser. The ambassador at that time was Dr Mario de Melo Freitas, a very pleasant gentleman, and one of the many ambassadors that I met and worked with over the next twenty-eight years.

Finally, it was the year that I first advised Irish Cement Limited, which was the other half of CRH plc. Until then, it had retained its own separate legal advisers while GSOB had acted for the Roadstone Limited half and for the parent company, CRH.

Early in 1981, I badly sprained ligaments in my right ankle while playing squash. I had used squash, particularly at lunchtime, as a safety valve; it was my principal mode of exercise other than a little golf. Although it wasn't the end of my squash playing days, I didn't play for a few months and got out of the habit of regular playing. Mary was expecting again, and our daughter Louisa was born on 3 June at 10.40 p.m. In late February, Mary and I went to Puerto Rico in Gran Canaria for a week in the sun. It was a pleasant break, and while there we met another young couple, Pat and Dairine Trundle, who have remained good friends of ours up to the present time.

In early April, Laurence Crowley was appointed liquidator of Galway Concrete Limited, which was based in Oranmore outside Galway and was owned by the Coyle family. Unlike some insolvency cases, which involved an element of bitterness and resentment, this liquidation was relatively amicable, and I got to meet Donnie Coyle and his son, John. They also owned Renvyle House Hotel in Connemara, where Mary and I had spent some holidays in the preceding years. Renvyle was renowned for its great entertainment and singsongs, led by the manager Hugh Coyle; it attracted a wide and varied clientele from all parts of Ireland and abroad.

On our holiday there in early September 1981, John Coyle – with whom I had been chatting – called on me to sing. I was anticipating being called on by Hugh, who had heard me singing before, so I had my party piece ready. Later in the evening, I noticed a group of three or four younger guys in the bar who were singing along; I recognised one of them, Joe Duffy, and suggested to Hugh that he call on him to sing. I only knew Joe through his earlier presidency of the Union of Students in Ireland, and I think he was then a trade union official.

In mentioning his name to Hugh, I was verbally accosted by Des O'Malley, a former government minister, who was with Hugh and was a regular visitor to Renvyle with his family and friends. Des said to me and Hugh – and Bobby Molloy, who was also there – that Joe was a radical socialist and that Hugh shouldn't be encouraging him by asking him to sing. I told them that that was ridiculous, and Hugh did ask Joe to sing, which he did and very well; as far as I can remember, he sang 'The Town I Loved So Well'. That was the second of my meetings with Des O'Malley, and although we bumped into each other on a few occasions in Renvyle and in Connemara Golf Club over the next few years, that night was never mentioned.

It was on Tuesday, 29 September 1981 that I had the accident in The Royal Dublin Golf Club. Two friends, including Cormac Hughes, who used his new car, took me to Jervis Street Hospital; although an ambulance had been called by the golf club, they wanted to get me to hospital as quickly as possible. Cormac subsequently regretted that, as his new car was badly bloodstained. When I was taken into the A&E department, I was ignored by the triage team; I hadn't come by ambulance and therefore, according to their system, could not be badly injured.

The two guys insisted on my being seen, and eventually one of the nurses examined me. Everything was calm until she pulled off the gauze protective covering that Dr Frank O'Driscoll had applied. The blood spurted, hitting her in the face; she roared for assistance and a stretcher. A few nurses and doctors came running, and I knew then that it was more serious than I had earlier thought. I was operated on that night, and was then detained for five days. After the first day, I was able to work from my hospital bed, the necessary files having been brought in to me, and even though there were no mobile phones at the time, I had a landline phone beside the bed and only missed one day's work from the incident.

I also had time to reflect on what had occurred and quickly realised that the table design was dangerous; the glass, when impacted, broke into long shards like daggers rather than shattering into much smaller pieces, as would happen with a car windscreen. I contacted Royal Dublin, who told me that they had bought the tables in Switzer's Grafton Street a few weeks previously, when redecorating and designating the Christy O'Connor room.

Sometime after I went back to work, during one lunch time, I went to Switzer's furniture department and saw a number of the same tables. I spoke to the department manager and explained to him what had happened – and that I thought they were dangerous and should be withdrawn. He shrugged and more or less told me that I was raving. I then contacted the Institute for Industrial Research and Standards, explained to them what had happened, and they agreed that the table design was dangerous. I then wrote a legal-style letter to Switzer's, albeit on my own notepaper, not indicating that I was a solicitor. I insisted that the tables were dangerous – that they should be tested, and if I was correct, that they should be withdrawn. I added that if they did not do so, I would sue them for the damage to me; I further added that the adverse publicity that the case would get would be damaging for the company.

I wasn't demanding compensation for damage, but I was requesting that the tables be withdrawn from sale. I succeeded, as Switzer's wrote back to me within a week, informing me that they had tested the tables; although they did not fully agree with me (obviously, on legal advice, they did not want to leave themselves open to compensation claims from me or anyone else who might have had a similar experience), they were withdrawing them as a precaution. Although I didn't follow it up, other than to check that they had changed the tables in their showrooms, I presume that they reverted to the manufacturers and had the specification changed. There was never a glass table in our house since then.

Later in that year, Hugh Cooney, who I had met a few years earlier – and again at the time of Louisa's birth, as his wife, Nuala, was about to give birth to their son, also Hugh – was appointed as liquidator of Irish Pharmaceuticals Limited, a company listed on the stock exchange; it was a wholesale distributor of pharmaceuticals and owned mainly by pharmacists. Hugh asked me to advise him. This was the first of many involvements with Hugh, personal and professional, and we became good friends.

I was also introduced to David McMurtry and his brother, Peter. David was from Clontarf originally and had established Renishaw Electronics Limited, a successful business in England; I later advised Peter on the setting up of an Irish subsidiary aided by the IDA. Renishaw has since grown into a multi-billion stock exchange-listed company, but even in 1981 – when the company was just seven years old – it was obvious to me from the demeanour of the persons involved that it was likely to be very successful.

In late November 1981, I was approached by Cormac Crawford – who at that time was one of the senior executives in Banque Nationale de Paris (Ireland) – about concerns he was having about one of the bank's clients, Euroterminals Limited, and a related company, Precision Materials Limited. A series of meetings ensued, and Breffni Byrne – a partner in Arthur Andersen – was also engaged by the bank. There were indications of fraud, and the trail led to Boston and Toronto. This soon led to a hurried trip by me, Cormac and Breffni to New York and on to Boston. We had one unsuccessful meeting in Boston on the morning that we arrived; we decided that we needed to get to Toronto, but we couldn't get a flight until early on the following day, Saturday, 12 December.

That gave us time to have a quick tour of Boston and a trip to Harvard University campus in Cambridge just outside Boston. Walking around the campus of Harvard was the first and only time since I left UCD nine years earlier that I felt I would like to go back to study. It was idyllic; covered in snow, it seemed so conducive to study and research. Rather than get lost in this reverie, I continued with the others on what transpired to be our wild goose chase to Toronto. The meeting there, however, also proved unsuccessful. The only consolation was getting to see an ice hockey game between two great rivals: the Montreal Canadiens and the Toronto Maple Leafs. I had seen ice hockey once or twice on television but had no idea that it was so fast, skilful and rough. Two players stood out for us: Guy Lafleur of the Montreal team, who was long-established and coming to the end of his career, and Wayne Gretzsky of the Toronto team, who was young and at the start of his legendary career – and already a fantastic player.

We also got to see Niagara Falls before flying back to New York, toured New York and flew home. It was largely a waste of time, except that I saw New York and Boston for the first time and struck up a great friendship with Breffni Byrne, which lasts to the present time. We were told one interesting thing on the trip by a Canadian lawyer who was advising the Canadian parent company involved. He said that when they applied to the IDA for a grant to establish in Galway, it seemed that they were initially refused; it transpired that they were, but one of the inhouse professional advisers in the IDA offered to ensure that the decision was overturned – that the application would be granted – if a fee was paid to him in cash. The Canadians were shocked at this, as were we, and we were given the name. The person left the IDA soon afterwards and went into practice with one of the professional firms in Dublin. I never learned if his leaving the IDA arose because of this issue, and I never asked.

The following year, 1982, was important for me: I became involved in a series of high-profile insolvency cases, as well as other interesting projects. The building company that I had joined commenced building its first houses, and I found the dream site for a new home for my family. But all of this apparent success and progress was totally overshadowed by my father's illness, which manifested itself in early February, and by his death in mid-July.

He had been working on Friday, 4 February, and I still have the notes that he had made of some research he was doing in the Land Registry; he went into hospital on the following day and never got back to his office, although he did get home twice before being hospitalised for the final time.

He underwent three operations between February and June, and although I had some doubts about the efficacy of his early treatment, he died of cancer at the age of 69, which was much too young.

My last clear memory of him before his illness manifested itself was in mid-January. There had been very heavy snow falls for a few days, the snow hadn't melted, and Dublin almost ceased operating. In particular, Sutton and Howth were badly hit; even getting to the shops posed problems. My father arrived one morning, having battled through snow drifts and dangerous roads with grocery provisions. It reminded me of the time, in 1954, when my grandfather waded through the North Strand floods to reach us and get us out to Marino.

On 8 March I was asked to act for Butlins Limited, which had decided to sell their entertainment and holiday complex at Mosney; it was their only business in Ireland and therefore almost iconic to many persons.

On the following day, I was asked to act for Frank Barrett, the senior partner of Arthur Andersen, who was about to be appointed as receiver and manager of Fieldcrest Ireland Limited, a manufacturer of luxury towels and towelling materials. Fieldcrest Inc., a US company quoted on Wall Street, owned 50 per cent of Fieldcrest Ireland; the balance was owned by Bank of Ireland and Carroll Industries, the cigarette manufacturer.

Fieldcrest had established itself in Ireland a few years earlier, and had sought partners with the assistance of the IDA. Don Carroll – who was chairman of Carroll Industries, which had been seeking diversification opportunities – was also governor of the Bank of Ireland's Court of Directors and may have persuaded the bank to invest in Fieldcrest's share capital, as well as provide loans and banking facilities to it. It seemed to be one of the IDA's major successes in the early 1980s and involved investment of $55 million; a huge factory of 50,000 square meters was built in Kilkenny, employing 630 people.

Nevertheless, the project was too big and the production capacity was far in excess of demand for the luxury goods. Significant losses were made from the beginning, and the bank lending department lost patience and eventually called in the receiver. It was a very delicate situation because of the project's and the shareholders' high profile. Intense and lengthy negotiations with the receiver took place on a myriad of issues, legal and commercial, with a view to saving the business. But the co-operation of

Fieldcrest Inc., which owned the intellectual property, was essential. Frank Barrett and I were summoned to New York on 23 March for urgent meetings with the senior management and Fieldcrest Inc.'s lawyers in their offices on Wall Street on the following day.

Frank decided that the only way to get there in time – as the Aer Lingus flight to New York had already departed – was to fly to London and get the 6 p.m. Concorde flight to New York. This we did, and when we got to JFK airport, we got a helicopter to the heliport on East 34th Street on Manhattan as part of the Concorde deal. This was my only flight on Concorde, my first in a helicopter and only my second time in New York.

I initially felt slightly apprehensive when we met early on the following morning; although I had dealt with many foreign lawyers, including many from the USA, Wall Street still had an aura of dominance and superiority. I needn't have been concerned: the lawyers were no better or worse than many I had already dealt with, and I was not bullied or intimidated. Neither, however, were we successful in persuading Fieldcrest to invest further funds or provide guarantees for the Irish company's further borrowings. Nor did we convince them to allow the receiver to assign the license agreement for the intellectual property if he found a buyer for the business. Although negotiations continued over the next few months, all efforts to save the business were unsuccessful and the company closed down in mid-June 1982. The factory and surrounding lands were eventually developed into a successful industrial estate.

On 1 April, I was asked to advise a moratorium creditors committee of MFN Construction Limited, a company engaged in house-building for the National Building Agency. It was very similar to the Lakeglen Construction situation of a few years previous, and this work continued for a few months.

On 30 April, Laurence Crowley was appointed as receiver and manager of the Gallagher Group, which was the largest house-building and property development group in Ireland; it consisted of fifty different companies, including two banks and some manufacturing companies. The chief executive of the group, Patrick Gallagher – a son of the founder Matt Gallagher – was a flamboyant high-living character, regularly in the newspaper social columns, but when I saw him in the bank's boardroom, when he was told that his group was going to be put into receivership, I felt sorry for him as he broke down and sobbed inconsolably.

Laurence retained me as his solicitor for approximately half the companies and retained two other firms for the other companies. The work in some of these receiverships went on for five or six years, but it was very intense for the first year. Some of the companies went into liquidation, including the banks; in fact, Patrick Gallagher was convicted in Northern Ireland and spent time in jail for banking offences.

On 26 May I was to meet two of John Donnelly's clients in Cork. They were two brothers who owned a very successful retail and wholesale business in Cork city; they had fallen out, and the company business needed restructuring to facilitate the brothers' differing aspirations. I had meetings in Dublin that morning and planned to get a flight to Cork airport at two o'clock for the meeting at half past three. It seemed an interesting and lucrative assignment, but I knew that I had to be on time for the meeting, as John Donnelly wouldn't accept a non-appearance – he had stuck his neck out by suggesting a Dublin solicitor.

I got delayed in traffic on the way to the airport – having left my office too late anyway – and missed the Aer Lingus flight. Rather than panic or try to make excuses, I went over to the Iona Airways desk and hired a private flight to Cork, getting to the meeting on time and having the flight await my return.

The cost of hiring the private plane was significant but it was well covered by the fee that was generated by the work involved – and more importantly, I didn't upset John Donnelly. In fact, just two months later, he was appointed receiver and manager of James J Murphy & Company Limited, the well-known Cork brewery founded in 1856, and he asked me to advise him. This was one of the largest receiverships that I was ever involved in, and the third major one of this year. I knew that if I hadn't been lucky enough, or perhaps resourceful enough, to get that Iona flight to Cork, I wouldn't have been asked to advise in this case.

The Murphy case was very interesting, as in addition to the brewery business that had to be continued, the assets included mortgages over many of the pubs in Cork city, in the county and in the rest of Munster and a significant number of them were in arrears, the payments for product and for the morgage being sometimes unclear. Negotiations were entered into with some potential purchasers of the business, but eventually some progress was made with the most likely purchaser: Heineken N.V. After some detailed negotiations in Dublin, Cork and Amsterdam, the business was sold to Heineken and its name was changed to Murphy Brewery Ireland Limited. It was subsequently changed to Heineken Ireland Limited, and it continues to brew Murphy's stout, Heineken lager and other Heineken products up to the present time.

Before the end of 1982, another major insolvency case occurred with the appointment of a receiver and manager, Bill Horgan, of Arthur Andersen, to Polaroid Ireland Limited, which had a very large modern factory in Newbridge, County Kildare. It was the largest factory building that I had seen, but it never achieved full production capacity and unfortunately collapsed. I had the opportunity to view the manufacturing processes for the cameras and the film involved, which were impressive and very different from the brewing of Murphy's stout, a process I had observed shortly before. Polaroid Corporation, the owner of the company, was not in a position to further support its Irish subsidiary, and it closed in 1983. Indeed, Polaroid Corporation itself collapsed in 2001, as its technology had become outdated.

As I entered 1983, one of the matters that was high on my priority list was the new site in Baily that I had agreed to buy on the condition that I received planning permission for the house that I wanted on the site. There was outline planning permission and full planning permission for a house to cater for the then owner and her mother, but we wanted a larger house.

Mary and I engaged an old school friend of mine, Jackie Reynolds, as our architect, and we commenced an exceedingly interesting and stimulating process as we worked closely with Jackie in the design of the house. Due to its location, there were various restrictions imposed in trying to avoid blocking sea views of the houses behind us; at the same time, we had to keep the house sufficiently distant from a new septic tank that had to be installed. The site was on a steep slope, both north to south and east to west, and presented many challenges from a design and an engineering point of view.

This was a totally new experience for me, as I have a relatively low visualisation intelligence and found it difficult to envisage some of the ideas and concepts that Jackie was proposing. Nevertheless, we kept at it, eventually getting planning permission for what we wanted in August of that year. The process included discussions with the planning officials; with An Taisce, an organisation that assumed responsibility to conserve Ireland's natural environment and built heritage, and which was very influential in the locality of Howth Hill; and with future neighbours and their architects. We managed to satisfy the requirements of everybody except for one difficult neighbour; he lodged an appeal to An Bord Pleanála, which held up our plans for some time.

In fact, that worked to our advantage, as it gave us more time to consider and review the interior of the house; we were able to make significant adjustments without affecting the planning permission that we had obtained. Jackie arranged for me and Mary to see the 'conversation pit' in the home of Sam Stephenson, another well known architect. This was a new concept to me, and very unusual, but I was impressed with it and included it in our plans. Jackie also had a professional model made of the proposed house and its interior; the latter was particularly helpful to me, as without it I could not imagine the internal details.

With the benefit of the model, I could see a number of aspects that could be improved, including the addition of skylights and the alignment of floor-to-ceiling windows, and we were able to incorporate those refined features. In the end we had the design for a unique house that fitted superbly into a difficult but beautiful site, and Keane Murphy Duff, the architect firm involved, included the house in its brochure in the second half of the 1980s. As it transpired, we were lucky that the permission was appealed – in my opinion, it was another example of my good luck.

In June of 1983, I was going to a conference of the International Bar Association in New York and decided to build a holiday around that trip. Mary, Shane and I flew to Washington, DC via New York, spent a few days there, went to Disney World in Orlando for a few days and back to New York for the conference, staying in the Plaza Hotel; we then went up to Hyannis for a week, back then to New York for another few days and then home. Mary and I enjoyed the variety of locations, but Shane – who was just 4 – would have been happy to stay in the Smithsonian dinosaur hall in Washington, DC and in the Magic Kingdom in Disney World for the three weeks; although he was in New York on subsequent occasions, he never fell in love with the city, probably put off by his early experiences there.

In the office, the legal work arising from most of the insolvency cases that had commenced in the previous few years continued. We now had an insolvency department with three specialists, and relevant work was also allocated to the property and litigation departments. A number of new insolvency cases commenced, the more important of which were the liquidation of Hunting Lodges Limited, which owned Durty Nelly's famous pub at Bunratty, near Shannon airport; Cavan Crystal Limited, another manufacturer of cut crystal glass; and Eurovision Publications Limited, a publisher of business magazines, operated in London but incorporated in Ireland.

The Hunting Lodges case garnered much media interest, as Durty Nelly's was very well known and a favourite haunt of many celebrities. Nonetheless, it did get into financial difficulties, and the proprietary director sought to protect himself at the expense of creditors – mainly the Revenue Commissioners and some leasing companies. The case went to the High Court, and the judge there agreed with our contention that this was a prime example of 'the phoenix syndrome' – that the directors had traded fraudulently while insolvent and that the attempt to put the assets beyond the reach of the defrauded creditors should not be allowed.

This was one of the first cases in Ireland of 'lifting the corporate veil' and the court making the directors personally liable for the debts of the company. The barrister, Peter Kelly BL, who later became president of the High Court, had argued the case for us and was particularly impressive in persuading the judge to effectively create new case law in her decision.

During the year I also became involved in the legal aspects of financing in the production of films and television programming; the principal client was Little Bird Films, which made the *Irish R.M.* and *Wurzel Gummidge*, but others included Lake Films and Heather Films, which made programmes for RTÉ.

I also advised the Portuguese embassy on the purchase of Knocksinna House in Foxrock, their new embassy, and J.C. Savage on the purchase of another pub in Swords, the Harp Inn. J.C. purchased the building from Dunnes Stores, which had bought it with a view to demolishing it and building a new shopping centre there; however, it had failed to get planning permission to do so.

When advising on the purchase of the new embassy, the ambassador's architect and I looked at road plans for the future, as the grounds fronted the Stillorgan Road. This was important, as many years later, Dún Laoghaire

Corporation did include part of the front garden in its plans for the continuation of the Stillorgan bypass and the creation of a dual carriageway as far as the M50. There was a threat of a compulsory purchase order, but I was able to counteract it. Firstly, I pointed out that such an order could not be exercised against the embassy, as its diplomatic immunity protected it; secondly, and more importantly, I argued how it was unfair to drag the embassy into public dispute, allowing it to be blamed for delay in the road construction, as its advisers had done the appropriate due diligence before the property was bought and there was no indication of any plans to widen the roads at the time. Eventually, after some tough negotiation, the embassy was happy to cede some of the garden – but on terms that protected its privacy and compensated it for the inconvenience involved.

I also became involved in the Portugal Ireland Chamber of Commerce. Through this and Portuguese businesses that were referred to me by the embassy, I advised, over many years, on business transactions for Portuguese who were conducting business in Ireland.

The economic recession of the early 1980s continued in 1984, despite the currency depreciation that had taken place in March 1983. I was involved in a plethora of new corporate insolvency matters that ensued. These included Hanlon's Frozen Foods Limited, Walkinstown Trading Company, Reynard Colour Limited, Freezermarket Limited, L.S. Dixon Limited, Altergo Ireland Limited, A. Murdock & Sons Limited, Tara Cooperative Company, Westfalian Carpet Yarns Limited, Bonfield Limited, Kenny Electronics Limited, Welding Plant Limited, Olympic Tank Limited, Realta Quilt Teoranta, Corcoran & Co. Limited and Gourmet Restaurants Limited. The last of these owned the Mirabeau Restaurant, operated by Seán Kinsella and thought to be the top and most expensive restaurant in Dublin at the time. It was jokingly said that when Gallagher Group (one of its best customers) collapsed in 1982, it was inevitable that the Mirabeau wouldn't survive, but in fact it lasted for two years after the former's demise. It was an obvious casualty of the recession, but most of the companies mentioned above were also casualties.

Three other companies that collapsed in the second half of the year were public companies quoted on the Irish Stock Exchange, and I was retained to advise in relation to them. These were Castle Brand Limited in Nenagh, County Tipperary, where the liquidator was Hugh Cooney; Solus Teoranta in Bray, County Wicklow, where the receiver and manager was Laurence Crowley; and Bolands Mills Limited in Dublin city, where the receiver and manager was Ray Jackson. These alone were enough to keep me immensely busy, but I also became involved in other projects, including a joint venture between Bryan S. Ryan and Aircall Limited in a new company, Skytel Limited, which had developed the technology for facilitating phone calls being made by passengers in aeroplanes. Beyond this, there was the further development of Hammond Holdings plc; the first major house-building project of Ballymore Homes, led by Sean Mulryan, to whom I was introduced earlier in the year; and the continued progress of Lark Developments, which by then had bought a tract of land in Maynooth, had commenced house-building there and was negotiating to buy further land in Lucan.

Nevertheless, the major issue for me in 1984 was the birth of my youngest daughter, Sinéad, on 26 August. I brought Mary into the Rotunda Hospital at 3.10 a.m., having collected a babysitter who was on call for us; I then went home to ensure that the babysitter was settled in, checked that Shane and Louisa were okay, and went back to the Rotunda at 5.45 a.m. Sinéad was born at 6.45 a.m., and has probably never been late for any event in her life. The early morning driving to and from the Rotunda put an end to my aspirations of winning the ongoing Captains Prize in Howth Golf Club. I had been in the top six after the first round on the previous Sunday, but I finished well down the field after that Sunday's second round. Nevertheless, that was probably the best Sunday I have ever had, and I didn't blame Sinéad for my subsequent poor score later that day, knowing well that inconsistency was the most consistent aspect of my golf at the time.

In June, Mary and I hosted a drinks party at home and invited an eclectic group of neighbours, clients and friends. Included were Peter Sutherland and his wife, Meruja, and the then Portuguese ambassador and his wife; I introduced the couples to each other, as the ambassador didn't know anybody else at the party at the time. Peter was the Attorney General at that stage, but within twelve months he became an EU commissioner.

That party had an indirectly positive influence on Portugal's future, even though I had never been to Portugal and didn't go until many years later. I didn't realise it until a few years later, when I received a very nice letter from that ambassador. He informed me that when he left his posting to Ireland, he was posted to Brussels and took the lead diplomatic role in Portugal's negotiations to formally join the EU. He thanked me for the introduction to Peter Sutherland that night as he said that when he went to Brussels he contacted Peter, they became friendly so that he was able to deal with him on a personal basis and informed me that Peter was very co-operative and of great assistance at some difficult negotiating sessions. I was surprised to get the letter but very pleased that a casual encounter at a drinks party could have such an outcome.

In February 1985, I got the greatest scare that I have ever had. One Sunday afternoon, Mary and I took the three children out for a walk around Offington Estate, where we lived. Shane was on a bicycle on the footpath about five or six yards ahead of me, Louisa was walking with me and Sinéad was being wheeled by Mary in a pram just behind Shane. We had no need to cross a road, as we could walk around our entire route on the footpath. As we came to a junction, a car stopped beside us and then screeched as it jumped the footpath; it hit Shane full on, knocking him flying into the air, and he landed fifteen yards away in somebodys garden.

As we later learned, the passenger in the car was teaching the driver, his girlfriend, how to drive, but he was totally unqualified to do so and barely knew how to drive himself. When his girlfriend stopped at the junction, she took her foot off the clutch, the car jumped forward, and as she had the steering wheel turned to make a left turn, it had jumped to the left as it mounted the footpath and collided with Shane. I didn't realise at the time what had caused this nightmare attack; I assumed that it was deliberate and only saw Shane being struck and flying through the air. I immediately inferred that he had been killed and that Mary and Sinéad were also dead, but I only saw Shane and ran to him.

I then heard Mary's screams of terror, but saw that she and Sinéad had not been touched. This all unfolded within a few seconds. Shane was lying crumpled up, and my instant thought was that he was dead; thankfully, however, he wasn't. My next reaction, as Mary cradled him, was to attack the attackers and kill them. I'm not sure what stopped me, but I suppose it was the sense that the attack had ended and that tending to Shane was more important.

Our local doctor, David Chapman, was called; to our endless gratitude, he made his way over to us despite the fact that it was a Sunday afternoon and he was not on call. He called an ambulance, and Mary went to Temple Street with Shane in the ambulance while I followed in my car in its wake. He was alive, but the issue was whether he had suffered serious head injuries, as the doctor had feared. Thankfully he was allowed out of hospital on the following day after a battery of tests and observation, and he suffered nothing more than bruising and a few abrasions. He was extremely unlucky to be where he was when the driver lost control, but at the same time he was lucky to have landed on a grassy garden and avoided suffering serious injuries.

A month later, we bought a yellow Labrador pup, named it Cara, and the accident was well forgotten. Cara was a delightful pet for the children, and indeed for Mary and me, and she lived with us for fourteen years before she became ill and had to be put down. We later got a kitten, who the children named Topsy; she outlived Cara by a few years before she too succumbed to old age.

In July of that year, O'Hare Barry, a small but ambitious accountancy firm, invited me to a golf outing in Stackstown. Aidan Barry was a financial adviser to Stackstown Golf Club, which was one of the earliest of the many new golf clubs that commenced in the 1980s and 1990s, but although it had a captive membership of Gardaí Síochána, it had run into financial difficulties. Aidan organised a superb golf outing there and had invited Peter Thomson, the Australian golfer who had won the British Open five times.

Peter was a friend of Aidan's father, and Aidan had also invited Christy O'Connor and J.B. Carr to play with Thomson. After our round, somebody pointed out a young teenager practising on the range who, it was explained, had earlier caddied for one of the guests; it was further explained that he was a son of Paddy Harrington, who had been a great Cork Gaelic footballer and was one of the founders of Stackstown Golf Club. Nobody at the time realised that the young teenager would himself go on to win three major championships, including two British Opens – it was Padraig Harrington already showing the diligence in practice for which he later became famous.

Most of the insolvency cases that had been ongoing over the previous few years continued, and many others commenced; however, there were no well-known cases with which I was involved. I did advise my old club, Clontarf GAA Club, on the acquisition of their clubhouse. The building they purchased was once the old Belgrove girls' school where, thirty years previously, I had spent one and a half school years.

The building work commenced on our site on Baily in early November. It initially involved lots of machinery digging out a level site from the side of the hill, and this levelling of the site and shaping of the field took a long time. In April 1986, while the building work was going on, there was drama as my future neighbour, Jennifer Guinness, was kidnapped from her home a couple of hundred yards away, at the end of the road, by an armed gang of dangerous criminals. The Gardaí, looking for clues as to who was involved and where Jennifer might be, wanted to question all the workmen on my site on what they might have seen or noticed.

None of them had noticed anything suspicious, so they were unable to be of any assistance, but thankfully Jennifer – or Jennie, as I later came to know her – was found after eight days and rescued by armed Gardaí after a six-hour standoff at an apartment in Ballsbridge, Dublin. Jennie's husband, John, who was a very pleasant gentleman, died tragically two years later when he fell to his death while walking in Snowdonia with Jennie and two friends.

I was involved in many more insolvency cases that commenced in 1986; these included the Belton Pub Group and Zhivago Restaurants, which owned the predecessor of Tamango's in Portmarnock. I was also involved in many new business start-ups, such as Oglesby & Butler, Walsh Mushrooms, Doherty Timber, Ospreycare Systems, Kes Security Systems and Eir Nor. The latter was a joint venture between Norwegian investors who had expertise in salmon fish farms – who I advised – with one of the main Irish fish merchants; they developed a number of successful fish farms along the west coast of Ireland over the next few years.

In November 1986, at a special partners' meeting, I was elected as the firm's first managing partner. Another partner had acted as such on a de facto basis when I first joined the firm, but this had ceased some years previously and it was realised by 1986 that it was time to formalise the role. I was honoured to be elected but knew that it was going to add significantly to the responsibilities I already had to my clients.

I had developed a team to assist me in the insolvency cases and the other commercial cases in which I was involved; I had also learned to delegate work referred to me in other areas to other partners. Given all this, I believed that I was ready and able to undertake the role. I smiled inwardly when recollecting the handwritten memorandum that I had submitted to the partners fifteen years previously. Everything that I had written about then had since been implemented, and indeed improved on, but because of the increase in the size of the firm, both in number of fee earners and back office staff – not to mention the development of new areas of law and the increasing computerisation in accounts and in word processing – everything had to be looked at again and indeed kept under constant review.

To begin with, 1987 was a simple continuation of the previous years, with more new insolvency cases to add to those that continued from previous years, such as Irish Jurong Limited, John Jackman Engineering Limited and John C. Parkes Limited. Nonetheless, later in the year a major grocery multiple, H. Williams Limited, collapsed; I was asked by the liquidator to advise him. Before the liquidator's actual appointment, we had a meeting with the recently appointed Minister for Industry and Commerce, Albert Reynolds, who was anxious to ascertain if he could intervene in an effort to avoid the liquidation.

We had to tell him that this was not a matter for us – that it was a matter for the directors of the company and their advisers, and that he should talk to them if he had any proposals that might avoid the collapse. We assured him that if appointed, the liquidator would try to ensure the continuation of the business in the various shops around the country rather than close them down immediately. The hope was that employment could be continued until there was a sale of the business as a going concern.

I also became involved in some new transactions. These included a CRH subsidiary, Premier Periclase, based in the former Irish Cement plant in Drogheda; Masterair Products Limited, which was bought out of receivership by Carlton Productions Limited, a new client ; Kilkenny People Holdings, led by John Kerry Keane, which was looking to invest in new ventures; and Aquascutum plc, which was opening a business in Ireland. But the most significant event for me was the resignation as a partner of the person I had beaten in the election in the previous year; he had been recruited by a client in the financial services sector with a lucrative offer of equity, and so he left us.

This was disappointing for me, as he was the partner who led our banking department, and the financial services sector was beginning to take off. There was no other partner who was in a position to take over his role; I decided that I would have to try to cover the position myself until we recruited a new partner with experience in that sector. Within a very short time, I had to take over responsibility for the banking department. I commenced working on the financing and leasing of aircraft, ships, containers and other large high-value assets with banks already well established in Ireland such as Hill Samuel, Anglo Irish Bank, Banque Nationale de Paris, Hongkong and Shanghai Bank and Irish Intercontinental Bank, as well as newly established subsidiaries of Banque Brussels Lambert and ASLK-CGER Bank, both from Belgium. On 17 November the Financial Services Ireland Association hosted a Docks Financial conference which was the first open conference on what ultimately became the IFSC. I attended, with a number of the banking clients as guests.

The following year, 1988, continued along the same path. The Financial Services Ireland Association hosted a conference in London on 18 March, which was intended to target some of the international financial service businesses based in that city. I invited some of our contacts from banks and solicitors firms in London with a view of helping to promote the new centre in Dublin. The general attitude was that it was not taken seriously, but there was interest in the tax aspects that were outlined. The IFSC was opened later in the year, and an architectural competition started for the development of the docks area. Some of those that I invited to that conference in London later established businesses in the IFSC. It was satisfying to have even a small part in the beginning of what has transpired to be transformational for the financial services sector in Ireland, with benefits for all allied professional services – but even more so for the physical development of the Dublin docks area.

The most difficult issue that I had as managing partner was dealing with partners in whom I and the other partners had lost trust. Reasons for such loss in confidence were various – including a partner's refusal to adapt and extend their range of specialisation, or their failure to do or complete cases. This occurred for the first time in 1988, with one of the senior partners, but unfortunately it wasn't the only occasion over the following twelve years when I had to inform a partner that we would have to terminate the relationship and come to a mutually suitable settlement. These instances would cause difficulties not only with the person themselves but also with their client connections and their families. I believe that I managed to deal with the first two elements reasonably well and was able to retain or at least resume the relationships, but some of the families did not accept the position.

As I had passed over my insolvency practice to colleagues when I took over the banking work, I didn't have any new cases. Nevertheless, this was replaced by other commercial law matters, and I commenced to advise some new clients – including the stock exchange listed Unidare plc, Litho Studios Limited and Perigord Communications Limited, Carbury Mushrooms Limited, National Chemical Limited, and Master Meat Anstalt – on their respective corporate acquisition programmes. I also advised some investor groups and investee companies under the Business Expansion Scheme (BES). I didn't particularly enjoy the banking sector work, but I found the work for these clients more interesting and enjoyable. By the end of the year, and despite interviewing a number of possible candidates, I didn't succeed in recruiting a partner to assume the role of banking partner, so I had little option but to continue in that role.

Earlier in the year, there was a very damaging storm, Storm Kay, which tore off a heavy entrance gate to our home. On the following day I learned that the storm had caused a tree to fall on the Stillorgan Road, tragically killing one of our former apprentice solicitors, John Fay, a very pleasant young man. It was later that month that my neighbour John Guinness fell to his death while walking in Snowdonia in Wales.

In June 1988, I went for the first time, with the family, on the ferry to France and stayed in a mobile home near Les Sables d'Olonne. That was the summer that the Irish soccer team played in the European Championship finals for the first time, and indeed in any finals. The joy of defeating England in Stuttgart in our first match was limited a little by the lack of a working television, so some other fathers and I, both Irish and English, managed to listen to it on somebody's transistor radio. The poor English men couldn't believe what had happened when Ray Houghton scored the only goal of the game, and we Irish felt very proud. A television was found for the next games, and the Irish parents and all the children in the holiday site gathered to watch it and sing the new Irish national anthem, 'Olé Olé Olé'. On the ferry home later in the month, we were joined by crowds of excited but very tired Irish supporters who had spent the previous three or four weeks touring around Germany.

If nothing else, the championship gave a huge confidence boost to all in Ireland just as we were stuck in a long recession and beginning to suffer from major state cutbacks necessary to avoid the country becoming bankrupt. As Dublin was deemed to have been founded in 988, 1988 was celebrated as the millenium of the city, with lots of different celebrations and special events. In September there was a millenium cruise up the Liffey for yachts of all shapes and sizes. We took part in this, with my family, that of my friend Tom Duffy and some other friends on *Bilbo* the yacht that Tom and I had bought in the summer of 1987. In many ways, it was the best family trip we had on the boat during the time that I owned a share in it.

Another busy year followed in 1989. In addition to the financial services work, which continued and expanded – although not as well as if I or another partner had concentrated and specialised in it – I was involved in many new corporate transactions involving acquisitions, restructurings, new inward investments from Europe and the USA, the development of new Irish start-up companies and the establishment of profit-sharing schemes for employees in some of the CRH subsidiaries.

One of these transactions involved a dispute between Munekata and Plastronix Limited, an Irish company owned by Killeen Investments, itself an Irish investment holding company owned by Tim Mahony who also owned Toyota Ireland. Plastronix operated a plastic moulding manufacturing business, which it had set up as part of the deal to compensate for the termination of assembly of Toyota cars in Ireland. It operated under a licence from Munekata, a large Japanese company based in Fukushima. Munekata had become unhappy with Plastronix's operation of the licence, hence the dispute.

After some negotiations, it was decided that Munekata would buy out Killeen Investments' shareholding, and Killeen agreed – they recognised that the licence might be terminated, which would almost certainly lead to large losses for Plastronix and hence for themselves. I was introduced to Munekata by one of the partners of Stokes Kennedy Crowley in late March 1989. There followed intense negotiations on the terms and conditions of the share purchase agreement, which led to the siging of an agreement on 17 April subject to due diligence and any possible regulatory approvals.

The two Japanese executives with whom I was working were very diligent and seemed to be working fifteen or more hours a day. And yet, they were ready every night to be entertained in pubs and restaurants, followed by visits to nightclubs in Leeson Street. I had thought that it was only when they were abroad that senior executives would work and play that hard, but I was informed by my colleague in Stokes Kennedy Crowley that they were much the same at home. The due diligence was completed, the share purchase transaction was finalised on 18 May, and the name of the company was changed to Munekata Ireland Limited.

Although the Japanese were very informal at one level – when they had finished work – they had very rigid formalities, such as bowing instead of shaking hands, even when abroad. To them I was 'Glackin San' rather than John, even after a couple of bottles of wine. I never really understood the formality of bowing and how low one was expected to bow; it was only fifteen years later, when Mary and I visited Japan on holidays, that I began to gain some understanding of their culture.

The Stokes Kennedy Crowley partner who first introduced me to Munekata was a regular visitor to Japan as part of his role to attract Japanese investment into Ireland. He had a good understanding of the Japanese customs and manners, so he helped me to avoid insulting them by guiding me on what to do or say – and what not to do or say. He stayed in touch with the Munekata executives in Japan after they returned, but after that, I only dealt with their Irish management.

I learned from him that the executive who led the negotiations in Dublin – and who was around the same age as me – died of a heart attack within a few months of completing the deal and returning to Fukushima. I was sorry but cannot say that I was surprised, and only learned then that there was a high mortality rate among Japanese business executives in their early to mid-forties who worked long hours and then partied hard.

Other transactions in 1989 included the acquisition of Handipak Distributors Limited by Nokia Ireland Limited, of IFG by Bloxham Maguire Quigley, of National Agricultural Distributors by National Chemical Limited, and of McCormick McNaughton by Iveco. Beyond acquisitions, there were investments into Lir Chocolates Limited and MDS Limited, and various other corporate transactions where I was advising BES fund managers. In addition, I was still involved in advising on the large ticket banking transactions in different parts of Europe.

In 1989, my aunt Alice, whose son John had Down's syndrome, was told by her doctors that because of her own cardiac condition, she could no longer look after John and that he would have to be taken into residential care. John had been a client of St Michael's House for many years but was then in his late twenties and finding a residential place for him was proving a problem. My aunt wished that he go into St Michael's House, and I agreed to approach Pat Molony, the then chief executive there, to plead his case. I told Pat that if he could accommodate John, he could feel free to call on me any time for fundraising, particularly by organising a golf outing.

He did find a place for John, and indeed John is still in the care of St Michael's House more than thirty years later. I was delighted to get a call from Pat six months later inviting me to join a committee that was organising a golf outing in aid of St Michael's House. I joined the committee, which was led by Conor Donnelly, Brendan Coakley and Marcus Magnier – three guys that I knew of through business but hadn't met before. I have since developed huge respect for each of them, as the golf outing has continued annually – and successfully – since then, completing thirty years in 2019. I stayed on the committee for twenty-five years and still maintain an interest in their success and the fundraising that they undertake.

As the firm expanded, the number of apprentices that we wanted to recruit also grew, as we saw that recruiting future solicitors and training them ourselves was the most efficient approach. Many of the other larger firms thought the same way; we all realised that lateral hires tended to be less successful in the longer term, although there were many notable exceptions. The recruitment of apprentices had become a very time-consuming exercise for a few years, and these larger firms – ourselves included – agreed to do the recruitment at more or less the same time of the year, so for a couple of months at the beginning of the year, this took up much time. Although the burden of interviewing was shared by a number of the partners, the ultimate decision was largely influenced by me as managing partner. In retrospect, we probably spent more time than was necessary on the entire process – not because the process wasn't successful but because (as has happened since) it could have been more streamlined and professional, and should have been outsourced to experts.

The Smurfit Group had a legacy business in assembly and distribution of brown electrical goods; in 1989, it entered into a joint venture with my client Nokia Limited, a Finnish company that had been a timber products and paper manufacturer before switching to consumer electronics goods and then to mobile phones. I was asked by Nokia to sit on the board of the joint venture company, Nokia Smurfit Limited, to represent its interests. Later in the year Nokia Group, which was expanding its electronic business worldwide very rapidly, established a captive reinsurance company under the IFSC tax regime, North European Reinsurance Company. I became involved in this later, becoming its chairman (and chairman of a sister company) and retaining my involvement with them for more than twenty years.

WELL ESTABLISHED AND REACHING 50: LIFE AND SOLICITOR'S PRACTICE, 1990s

In early 1990, I met a lawyer from Paris and I worked with him on the establishment and administration of three aircraft leasing companies owned by Aerospatiale, the French state-owned aerospace manufacturer that built both civilian and military aircraft, including Concorde, rockets and satellites. It was a predecessor of Airbus, which is now a joint French and German manufacturer. We worked on some other transactions over the next fifteen years, and his French firm became part of a multinational firm with whom I also worked on a few occasions.

When Sunbeam Wolsey, the well-known Cork manufacturer, collapsed, I was asked to advise the purchasers. They bought it from the liquidator with a view to continuing the business – which now required only a fraction of the site on which it stood – and developing it as an industrial estate with the IDA. Sunbeam was iconic in Cork; although my clients were not the owners who had allowed it to be closed down, the fact that they were from Dublin resulted in a fairly hostile environment when they first got involved. It required all their charm to get established there.

I had had to deal with a second partner removal in GSOB in early 1990. Word must have travelled that I had achieved this successfully, as later that year one of the largest architect firms in the country engaged me when they had a similar problem; in the next year or so, I was engaged in similar situations in a firm of loss adjusters and an accountancy partnership. The partner who had left GSOB to join a financial services company in 1987 found that, two years later, that company was taken over by Woodchester Investments plc; he was now the internal legal adviser in a much larger company. He engaged me to assist in some of the legal work for his new employer, including the acquisition of Mercantile Credit Company Ireland. He rejoined us as a partner from the beginning of 1991, which was a particular relief to me and meant that I could shift back out of the banking work.

Other work included an increasing involvement in CRH and its subsidiaries; advising Coyle Hamilton Group, one of the largest insurance brokers in Ireland, on a variety of corporate issues; advising on more BES investments; advising Pat Donohoe on the sale of his company, Donohoe Engineering Lift Systems, to Schindler and a management buyout in another of his companies, Kes Security Systems; and advising on the acquisition of Irish Ropes, a public owned company.

Despite being busy, and although not a soccer fan, I managed to go to Italia '90 World Cup twice. The first was a day trip for the Ireland v Romania game in Genoa; I brought Shane and went with two of the GSOB partners, one of whom brought their own son. The other one, David Anderson, did not have a ticket for the game in Genoa, as he was supposed to be sailing around Ireland in the Round Ireland Yacht Race and had not intended to go. Nonetheless, as the yacht that he was on was demasted on the second day, that race was over for him, so we got him on the flight to Genoa. I contacted one of my friends from Fiat Trattori in Modena, Guido Alvera, and he arranged a ticket for us at short notice.

Later that week I went with Mary and some others – including David and his wife, Rosemary – to the quarter final game against Italy. Shortly after returning from that trip, which had not been planned until two days beforehand, I went on holidays with my family for nearly four weeks to New York, Seattle, Port Townsend, Vancouver Island, Vancouver and San Francisco. I then went to Atlanta in September for a golfing trip in Chateau Elan with three friends. It was an Irish American competition sponsored by Don Panoz, who had founded Elan Corporation and then invested in a golf resort and winery in Georgia. We didn't win a prize for golf, but we did secure a special prize for the team who seemed to have the most fun over the few days. Later that year, in November, Mary and I went to an AEPPC (European Insolvency Practitioners) conference in Vilamoura in the Algarve. The latter two were largely business development trips, but nonetheless relaxing and enjoyable.

On New Year's Day, 1991, I had to attend – in my capacity as legal adviser to the hospital – the inauguration of Dr Peter Boylan as master of Holles Street Maternity Hospital for a seven-year term and his signing of his contract. It was unusual for me to work on New Year's Day, but as it transpired the year 1991 ended unusually also, as I was in court – at a vacation sitting of the High Court – dealing with a spurious claim of contempt of court against me and the Minister for Industry and Commerce, Des O'Malley, by Dermot Desmond.

1991 was the twenty-fifth anniversary of our leaving St Paul's College, and a committee was formed to arrange a reunion. I was one of those who were asked to join the committee, and we had a number of informal meetings before the reunion dinner in Sutton Castle Hotel at the end of May. I was stunned to be told by one of my former classmates that he was already a grandfather – that probably made me feel old for the first time. Like most groups of the same vintage, there were a few divorces, and unfortunately there had also been a few deaths.

One of the clients that I had worked with for a few years was Hummingbird Productions, which was the trading name of Browbell Enterprises Limited and was led by Philip King, a musician, and his partner, Nuala O'Connor. I was a director of the company, representing BES shareholders, along with Pat Trundle, who had experience in the music business, and Kieran Corrigan, their financial adviser. The company had a contract with BBC and RTÉ to produce a five-part television series, *Bringing It All Back Home*, based on the connection between Irish music and songs and that of the USA. As a solicitor, I had very little to do after the initial contract was signed.

As a director, I had little to contribute other than trying to ensure corporate governance and that we had regular structured meetings. I guessed that Philip and Nuala found it a little frustrating, as the role of the board largely consisted in trying to rein in production costs and receive updated reports while the two of them put together the series, a book and a vinyl record and tape. They had got some well-known Irish musicians, such as Donal Lunny, Hothouse Flowers, Sharon Shannon, Mícheál Ó Súilleabháin, Liam O'Flynn and my namesakes – Paddy, Seamus and Kevin Glackin – to participate, along with Americans such as Emmylou Harris, Ricky Skaggs and the Everly Brothers.

The story, narrated by Philip, told of how dance music left Ireland with the emigrants and influenced diverse traditions in America, such as bluegrass, country and rock, and then fed its way back to Ireland. He managed to secure interviews with many music stars; some of them agreed to appear talking on the programme, but their record company wouldn't agree to allow them to perform for the album. The series commenced broadcasting on RTÉ on 7 April 1990, and on the BBC a few weeks later.

A launch party was held in Kitty O'Shea's in Dublin, and many of the artists featured in the TV series attended and performed; there was a great sense of achievement in getting it all produced and packaged. Our focus was then to commercialise what had been produced so far. There were only a few shareholders involved other than Philip and Nuala, who were the majority shareholders and controlled the company, and those few were friends of the directors. I personally got a lot of satisfaction from my limited role in the company; other than advising a writer on publishing contracts – and despite my one-time career ambition to be a playwright – I had had no previous involvement with the arts.

Early in 1991, I was introduced to Chris Slattery, a hotelier in County Meath who had an option – through a company, Irish Canadian Securities – to purchase Killeen Castle in Dunsany, County Meath and surrounding lands. The castle had been burned down in 1981. Chris was being advised by CFG, a corporate finance advice firm operated by Aidan Barry and Michael Goggins – each of whom I had known for many years. I visited Killeen Castle on a few occasions with Chris, who had a great vision for the grounds, including a golf course and major equestrian centre. He also sought to develop the castle as a hotel and build luxury houses around the estate.

Chris needed a major partner to undertake the entire development with him, and in August I joined him in Newport Beach, California as he entered negotiations with Marriott Corporation. I was travelling to Atlanta for the American Bar Association annual meeting, so I took in the extra trip to California for a few days. As it transpired, Chris wasn't able to put a deal together – the option lapsed, and it was ultimately developed many years later by an Irish property development company. A very good golf course designed by Jack Nicklaus was included.

Another transaction that took place early in 1991 was the sale of Classic Meats Group (formerly Master Meats) to Goodman International. Classic

Meats was owned by an Anstalt, a Liechtenstein form of trust. My instructions at all times came from Laurence Crowley, who had a power of attorney from the Anstalt. Prior to it being transferred to Goodman International, there was a major dispute between the person who fronted Master Meats in Ireland, Pascal Phelan, and his partner, a Mr Taher, who had owned a majority share through the Lichtenstein Anstalt. I was involved in this by virtue of advising Laurence Crowley and David Coyle, the latter being another accountant who had been appointed by the Anstalt to act as finance director. Pascal Phelan had been effectively ousted from management, even though he was still a significant shareholder.

This was a few months before the TV programme that made allegations against the Goodman meat processing companies, and which led to the Beef Tribunal. Although not directly implicated in the issues that gave rise to the Beef Tribunal, Master Meats was referred to on a number of occasions during the course of that tribunal, which was chaired by Liam Hamilton, the president of the High Court. This tribunal, which ran from May 1991 to August 1994, overlapped with the Telecom Inquiry – and as I outline later, also had other influences on the latter.

Late in the afternoon of 8 October 1991, I received a telephone call from Seán Dorgan, the secretary general of the Department of Industry and Commerce; I didn't know him at the time, but I got to know him over the next couple of years. He asked me if I was free to call over to the department immediately and meet the minister, Des O'Malley. I said that I could make it within an hour.

I anticipated that the minister was going to ask me to meet some new international visitor who might be considering investing in Ireland. Nevertheless, I wondered why he might suggest me, as our last meeting a few years earlier, regarding the Progressive Democrats (which will be related later), had not ended well, and since then he had not recognised me on the few occasions when I bumped into him in bars in Connemara. I walked around St Stephen's Green, was brought up to the minister's office and was greeted by him as if we had never met previously. He asked me if I knew anything about Chestvale Properties Limited and Hoddle Investments. I replied that I knew there had been some departmental investigation during the summer, and that, while at an insolvency practitioners' conference in Nice the previous week, I had heard that Laurence Shields had been appointed by the minister as an inspector, under the Companies Act 1990, to the companies.

Mr O'Malley explained that there was a problem with that appointment, as Dermot Desmond – who was allegedly centrally involved in the companies – had complained at Laurence acting as inspector. According to Desmond, Laurence had advised him on the making of a will some years previously, and he was thereby conflicted. As the minister did not want such a trivial complaint to detract from the speedy conduct of the inspectorship, he and Laurence had agreed that Laurence should resign – and that he would do so later that evening, if I would accept the appointment in his place. He told me that Laurence had recommended me and he, the minister, was happy to accept that recommendation.

He explained the commitment he would need from me: three weeks' full-time priority. He said it should be completed in that time, and before the October bank holiday weekend. I told him that I would have to talk to some partners about it and would call him later that night. By the time that I got back to my office, most of the partners had left for the night – I spoke initially to Frank Plunkett Dillon, who was still in his office.

Frank advised that I should accept the appointment and promised that he and other partners would cover for me with my other clients for that three-week period. I managed to get one other partner on the telephone, and he agreed with Frank. I had no real idea of what I was getting into, but being ambitious and adventurous, I called the minister and told him that I would accept. He told me that he would have the necessary papers prepared for signing on the following morning and that he would be arranging a press release for that same morning.

I sometimes wonder whether I would have undertaken the role if I knew then what I learned since: that the three-week commitment I gave to the minister would end up being more than twenty months; that my final report would be given to a new minister, Ruairi Quinn, as Des O'Malley had resigned and taken the Progressive Democrats out of the coalition government with Fianna Fáil over a dispute with the Taoiseach, Albert Reynolds, relating to the Beef Tribunal. I'm not sure of the answer, but I do know that some things in my life changed in the next couple of years – whether they would have changed anyway is not certain.

The Warrant of Appointment, signed by the minister, was in the following terms:

> The Minister for Industry and Commerce, Mr. Desmond J. O'Malley, T.D. in exercise of the powers conferred on him by section 14 of the Companies Act, 1990, being of the opinion that there are circumstances suggesting that it is necessary in the public interest, hereby appoints Mr. John A. Glackin as Inspector under the said section to investigate and report on the membership of Chestvale Properties Ltd. and Hoddle Investments Ltd. and otherwise with respect to these companies for the purposes of determining the true persons who are or have been financially interested in the success or failure (real or apparent) of these companies or able to control or materially to influence the policy of these companies. Without prejudice to the generality of the foregoing, the investigation shall extend to the investigation of any circumstances suggesting the existence of an arrangement or understanding which, though not legally binding, is or was observed or likely to be observed in practice and which is relevant to the purposes of the investigation.

The investigation arose out of the acquisition by Telecom Éireann, in May 1990, of a site at Ballsbridge, Dublin 4 for a corporate headquarters. Telecom had paid the sum of £9,400,000 for the site, which up to a short time beforehand had been the site of the Johnston, Mooney & O'Brien bakery and distribution centre. Johnston, Mooney & O'Brien's liquidator had sold the site to a company, Chestvale Properties, on 11 August 1989 for £4,000,000; this was pursuant to a contract entered into on 24 November 1988 between Johnston, Mooney & O'Brien and another company, United Property Holdings (UPH), for the sale of the site for £4,400,000. The site was then the subject of a series of transactions involving UPH, Chestvale, Hoddle Investments and Delion Investment Dealings Limited (a Cypriot registered company) between June 1989 and April 1990, before ending up with Telecom Éireann.

The government's interest in these transactions (the details of which only became known after they started their inquiries) had to do with the fact that Telecom Éireann was a state-owned company, and its chairman – Michael Smurfit, a Dublin businessman who was also chairman and chief executive of the Smurfit Group – according to newspaper reports, seemed to be a shareholder in UPH. Smurfit had been effectively removed as chairman of Telecom Éireann a few days prior to my appointment by Charlie Haughey, the then Taoiseach, and he resigned pending the results of the report of the inspector, Laurence Shields, who had just been appointed. Little was it known that the inspector himself would have to resign within a couple of days – and as I said, this led immediately to my appointment. In addition, at the same time Dermot Desmond had to resign as chairman of Aer Rianta, a government appointment, and stand aside as executive chairman of his stockbroking company, NCB.

Needless to say, these few issues alone created somewhat of a frenzy among the media, and I was caught right in the middle. One of the Sunday newspapers, when presenting a profile of me on the weekend after my appointment, described me as a 'soft carpet lawyer'. I hadn't heard of the term before and didn't know whether it was an insult or an acclamation. I learned when I went into my office on the following Monday that it merely meant that I was used to working in an office and not on the hard tile floors of the Four Courts as a litigator. I did not engage a public relations firm or adviser to deal with the media – who were regularly on to my secretary seeking information and interviews – even though I knew that Desmond did and assumed that Smurfit did.

Over the course of the next couple of years, I had many dealings with journalists, many of whom were relatively unknown at the time but became successful later. Some of them I trusted as independent, but some I quickly learned were effectively under Desmond's influence and merely served as his mouthpiece. One in particular, who has since gone on to national recognition and who trades on his impartiality, was at the time anything but. The media attention was not something that I was used to, or welcomed, but I knew that I had to live with it, as the inquiry was a public interest issue.

The publicity increased as the court cases increased. Most of the work involved could be, and was, done in private in my office. But any applications to and hearings in court were in public, and if the media didn't know about them beforehand, they learned very quickly. On some occasions it seemed that they received tip-offs from Desmond or his advisers when he was about to make an *ex parte* application to the High Court; on these occasions the media knew before I did and then contacted me for a comment. In these and many other instances, I learned more from the media than they learned from me.

Desmond tried, in many different ways, to intimidate me, embarrass me, block me or at least disrupt me. If he had any common sense, however, he would have learned a little about me first – that his tactics merely made me more resolute and determined to finish. If he had been honest and forthcoming *ab initio*, he would have saved himself and many of his friends, unnecessary publicity about their lives and businesses – attention that they naturally disliked. Desmond was clever in some ways, but not as clever as he himself thought. I believe that his own sense of being untouchable led him to adopt a stupid strategy.

At the end of July 1992, nearly ten months after my appointment, I presented an interim report to the minister, Des O'Malley, comprising 322 pages and twenty-four appendices encompassing another 156 pages. I had at that stage interviewed formally at least sixty persons in at least eighty interviews; the interview transcripts exceeded two thousand seven hundred pages. Nevertheless, because of obstruction by – or orchestrated by – some of the persons involved in the inquiry, I was not in a position to present a final report until 7 July 1993, almost twenty-one months after my appointment.

This final report comprised 121 pages and more than twenty pages of appendices. In the interim, I was involved in eight cases in the High Court, some of which were appealed to the Supreme Court, and most of which involved multiple hearings and motions. Some of the cases were instituted by me, to enforce my statutory powers, and some were instituted by involved parties seeking an injunction to restrain my investigations. In all cases, I was successful and was awarded legal costs – but those were the costs of the lawyers assisting me in court rather than my costs, as I was considered the client.

My investigations were based on following the money, and this led to inquiries around the world – through Cyprus, Guernsey, the Isle of Man, Jersey, Switzerland, the Cayman Islands, the Bahamas, the USA, the UK and Ireland. I traced the vast majority of the money, but the last part was thwarted by the banking secrecy laws of Switzerland; in respect of that part, I used other evidence to make the relevant conclusions. Although it was not the purpose of my investigations, the Irish Revenue Commissioners followed up and received very significant monies that would probably otherwise have been unknown to them.

One of the interviews that I undertook was in the remand cells of Lavender Hill Courthouse near Battersea in London; one of the parties involved was attending a remand hearing there on charges of fraud. It was the first time that I had been in a cell since my days in FLAC, back in the early 1970s, when I had to attend Mountjoy Prison to interview and advise one of the inmates. I'm sure that prison conditions everywhere had improved in the intervening twenty years, but there was no comparison between the remand cell conditions in that UK courthouse and what I remembered of the squalid interview room in Mountjoy. This interview in London was arranged by the anti-fraud section of the London Metropolitan Police, through the UK Department of Trade and Industry. My role wasn't to make findings of wrongdoing but merely to find out who the beneficiaries of the transactions were. Nevertheless, to help me in my role, I was entitled to avail of the assistance of those institutions that were within my authority to approach.

In addition to the formal interviews, I also met and talked to many other persons who I understood might have information that would be of assistance to my inquiries. On top of this, many interesting persons contacted me to offer information that they thought might be of assistance, including a stockbroker, an estate agent, a mining magnate and racehorse owner, a politician and an accountant friend of Smurfit. The last of these was a well-regarded former partner of KPMG with whom I had many meetings in the past; he told me that Smurfit was very worried about the matter, and he tried to persuade me that Smurfit was fully innocent and was being framed by three of the persons involved (who he named to me), and that he was being intimidated by them. I listened to the emissary and told him that I would bear in mind what he had said, but I was highly sceptical of it and felt that he must have been put under considerable pressure by Smurfit – for whatever reason – if he was approaching me in the way that he did.

As the investigation came towards its conclusion, I needed the assistance of the Attorney General, Harry Whelehan, to authorise the relevant bodies in the UK, Jersey and Switzerland to release information to me regarding bank accounts. There was resistance in Jersey and Switzerland, and it would have taken considerable time to overcome that.

I was able to get around the Jersey problem, as I had noted that AIB in the UK had been involved in the transactions with AIB in Jersey; I was able to persuade the anti-fraud section of the UK Department of Trade and Industry to oblige the AIB subsidiary in the UK to give me whatever information they had relating to the transactions as AIB in Ireland refused on the basis that the UK subsidiary was subject to UK law and it had no power to order the UK subsidiary to disclose the required information to me. This was before the subsequent revelations about Irish banks facilitating the opening of offshore bank accounts for its Irish customers. Together with other information that I had obtained informally from the bank in Jersey, that was sufficient to enable me to make the conclusions that I did in relation to the beneficial owner of the Jersey bank account, which had been in the name of Dr J. and N. McMahon.

In relation to Switzerland, I informed the minister, who by this stage was Ruairi Quinn, that it would take considerable time and expense to follow up the trail that led there and await a result; I added that in the end it might not be successful, as the Swiss were extraordinarily protective of their banks' secrecy laws and practice. I was anxious to conclude, and the minister informed me that the budget for the investigation had been cut by the government – that there were no additional funds that could be paid. In fact, I didn't receive any fees for the last two months of my work; I wrote the final report free of charge, but that did not compromise me in any way and I knew that I had gone as far as I could.

I wasn't sure if the budget cut was the result of pressure being applied by some of those involved in the transactions through their Fianna Fáil connections, as a last resort to prevent me from publishing my conclusions. But if it was, it misfired. I am commercial-minded and dislike working for nothing – but even more than that, I am obstinate, and I was determined to finalise my report even if the government did not now want it.

The political background had changed. Des O'Malley had anticipated – and had mentioned to me on a few occasions in the early stages of my inquiry – that he could be effectively forced to resign as minister. This happened in early November 1992 over issues arising in the Beef Tribunal, where he had made serious allegations about another minister, Albert Reynolds. The latter had become Taoiseach in February 1992, when Charlie Haughey was forced to resign over a phone-tapping scandal involving journalists some years previously. O'Malley refused to withdraw the allegations about Reynolds. When Reynolds later gave evidence before the same Beef Tribunal, he called O'Malley dishonest, which nobody believed.

When O'Malley resigned, he took the Progressive Democrats out of the coalition government, which then collapsed. A general election ensued, and no party was successful in getting a majority.

An alternative coalition with Labour was arranged by Fianna Fáil, the majority partner, and on 12 January 1993, Ruairi Quinn was appointed as Minister for Enterprise and Employment, which took over the former departments of Industry and Commerce, and Labour. In fact, Ruairi Quinn was supportive of me and did accept my request to get the Attorney General involved in the requests to the foreign governments. Nevertheless, he didn't seem to have the same power or leverage in this matter as Des O'Malley, hence the cutting-off of funding.

I drafted the final report in June and early July 1993, submitted it to any person and company against whom I had included any adverse comments and asked them to respond within ten days with any remarks or reactions that they might have. Most of the relevant parties did reply, and a few pointed out what they perceived as errors of fact or reasoning. I studied those responses, and where I considered it appropriate, I made corrections to the draft.

Nonetheless, the response from Dermot Desmond, through his solicitors, was that there was not enough time to respond. I refused to extend the time, partly because I wanted to be finished and partly because I knew from media reports that Mr Desmond was not dealing with the draft report at all – that he was playing golf in the Pro–Am before the Irish Open in Mount Juliet Golf Club and then attending the tournament.

I was also aware that political pressure was being applied to delay the publication of my conclusions, and Mr Quinn told me that the Attorney General, Harry Whelehan, had asked him to request me to extend the time. I guessed that Mr Desmond was intending to commence a further legal action to injunct me from finalising my conclusions and was using the Attorney General to buy time.

An article appeared in the *Sunday Independent* on 4 July 1993 that seemed to be based on leaks to the reporter by some of those persons to whom I had sent draft extracts of the final report. To me, it was blatant manipulation, as I was the only person who knew everything that was in the draft report. The article asked:

> Is it all over too soon? After two years, £850,000 and the public airing of scandalous accusations against Irish business, is the Glackin Report about to prove itself another damp squib? John Glackin [...] has, it would appear, run out of funds. His investigation, now expected to yield inconclusive results when its findings are published, has been financially capped. His efforts to uncover crucial facts – pertinent evidence about who actually made money from the transaction – are complete. Thanks to State thrift we may never learn the full story.
>
> The findings of Mr. Glackin's report are still under wraps, but sufficient material has been leaked – from the copies he has handed to the principal players in the affair – for us to learn a fair amount about the claims the document will make.
>
> Michael Smurfit will be cleared of any business malpractice in the affair. What's more Glackin will fall short of alleging that any fraud whatsoever was perpetrated – by anyone – against Telecom.
>
> He will be critical of Dermot Desmond, the broker who steered the site purchase through the mysterious waters of international finance towards its luckess recipient, but he too will be acquitted on any count of conflicting interests.
>
> No wrongdoing, no conflict of interest. Just a simple, everyday business deal of labyrinthine complexity.

This article surprised me, demonstrating that information that I understood was confidential – between me and the minister, regarding the cap on fees – was disclosed to some of the parties, probably because the party who applied pressure on the Minister for Finance to have the inspection terminated had been told that capping the fees was the best way to do so. The £850,000 mentioned included all the fees incurred by my retaining junior and senior counsel in the numerous High and Supreme Court cases, most of which had to be paid by the persons who lost the various cases, so the reporter's using that figure was a little disingenuous to say the least. It also represented an effort to manipulate the facts by some of the persons involved, and anticipated that the actual report would not see the light of day.

When the minister told me that I should delay signing and furnishing him with the report, I told him, as politely as I could, that he did not have power to so instruct me and that I intended to sign it on the following morning and deliver it to him. That was my right, and indeed my obligation, but I added that what he did with it was his decision. If, having received it from me, he did not want to publish it, then that was absolutely his right. But regardless of what his decision might be, I said that I was signing and delivering it.

That caused a little panic. The minister then got his officials to quickly read it, and they asked me to make a couple of minor typographical edits. By this time, the civil servants that I had been dealing with had changed; Seán Dorgan, the secretary general who arranged my first meeting with Des O'Malley, had moved to another department, and the person that I was primarily liaising with was now a different senior civil servant. After a brief discussion with the new person, I accepted some of the edits, incorporated them in the final draft, signed it and submitted it to the minister.

In fact, the minister did publish my report immediately, having had it printed by Iris Oifigiúil on the night that I presented it to him. That concluded that saga, or so I thought. Mr Desmond responded publicly that the report was totally incorrect and that he would publish the real report. I can't say that I'm still waiting for it, but no such 'real' report has ensued in the subsequent twenty-eight years. Some of the relevant persons involved and some media persons, from time to time, jokingly ask me if I have heard anything more about Mr Desmond's 'real' report, and I have to disappoint them and tell them that I haven't.

On the Sunday after the publication of the final report – Sunday, 11 July – the *Sunday Independent* gallantly ate humble pie for its article the previous week; in the course of very extensive coverage of the report, it published what was effectively an apology. It read:

> In an article in last Sunday's issue headed 'Who reaped the profits on this golden sale?' reference was made to Mr. John A. Glackin, Solicitor, who was appointed by the Minister for Industry and Commerce to investigate the 'Telecom Affair'.
>
> This article anticipated the findings of Mr. Glackin and suggested that because of lack of funds he was issuing a final report without the benefit

> of certain information, which action on his part would have been a serious breach of his warrant of appointment.
>
> We now accept that this was not the case and that the impression given in our article was unwarranted and unfounded. We accept that Mr. Glackin has carried out his investigation fully and professionally and has not been restricted in any way by the moneys available to him. We wish to apologise to Mr. Glackin for any contrary impression given in last week's article.

This apology was prompted by a gentle communication to the editor from a solicitor friend of mine, who I had consulted after I signed off the final report; he was an expert in such media matters, and was the adviser to one of the daily newspapers.

Some of the rest of the coverage was effusive and very flattering. One article written by the Business Editor read:

> The Glackin Report is more than an event; even more than a Page One sensation. It is the beginning of the end of an era. It represents either the advent of a new climate of business candour or it signals the end of a period of unacceptable 'nudge and the wink'.
>
> It is still too early to say which, but either way it is a good thing.
>
> During the past 20 months of the most intense investigation, helped by new legislation and an informed public opinion that has railed at the notion of a 'magic circle' and a business elite which shamelessly indulges itself, a great deal has been done to clear the air and focus on business priorities in Ireland.
>
> Before Glackin, no one could see Glackin ever happening. No one anticipated that a closed and protected business environment could have allowed the sort of laser show that John Glackin was able to stage at Telecom.
>
> The controversy arose out of the perception of business greed that followed the Greencore scandal and the overriding feeling that business was creaming off money at the expense of the rest of the community and especially the taxpayer.
>
> Glackin ended up demonstrating that the system does not have to work in the flyboys favour; and if it is manipulated to help people who wish to avoid tax and skirt around the system, they do not necessarily have to get away with it.

> The legacy of Glackin is that intelligent, serious people with determination and singlemindedness can get to grips with arcane, convoluted and maze-like situations.

However, in case I might develop notions about myself, the article then changed course a little, and there followed some criticism:

> There was one serious disappointment with the Glackin Report for those who read the same Inspectors Interim Report.
>
> In the previous document, which wound leisurely over the creation of the various companies, Chestvale, Hoddle and Delion, which were part of the JMOB [Johnston, Mooney & O'Brien] saga, the inspector apparently took the broadest possible view.
>
> He could look at what happened to various companies, ponder motivations and wonder if there was anything outside his strict remit which should be examined.
>
> [...] This time Glackin has been considerably more restrictive and stuck more closely to tight terms of reference. This time he examined only the deal and the tax avoidance measures and the companies involved in the complicated arrangements. Last week's report mainly featured Dermot Desmond. Some of his golfing cronies were mentioned but the Glackin Report is a Desmond spectacular and he has ended up being the tenor, baritone, soprano and contralto in the distinctly unmusical JMOB grand opera.
>
> He is also the only one of the main characters lying on the stage at the end of the last act.
>
> [...] To some extent it is an enormous pity that John Glackin or someone else was not in a position to look at the shameful waste that the JMOB site represented and perhaps at other waste in the State company system.

The criticism wasn't really justified, as the interim report referred to was intended to, and did, describe for the minister – the person for whom it was written – the background, the complications and the strands of coincidences and connections that I had encountered up to that point. The minister had insisted on my producing the interim report – and indeed had wanted it earlier, but I had to await the outcome of a Supreme Court decision that allowed me to present it. The final report was more focussed, because it was my obligation, under the warrant of my appointment, to determine who were the beneficiaries and the controllers. It was not my role to make findings about the peculiar decision-making process within Telecom, but I thought that I had sufficiently described the situation to enable further investigation of that company if that was considered necessary.

As Smurfit had been removed as chairman and was not reinstated, it was probably felt that it was not necessary to take it further, but I knew that I wasn't going to do any more inspections or investigations. I had done my bit.

In the interim report, I had recommended that a restriction under section 16 of the Companies Act 1990 be placed on the shareholding of Joe Lewis in UPH, as he had not co-operated in replying to my requests for information. Having managed to get his mobile phone number, I had actually spoken to him on one occasion while he was on his yacht in the Caribbean. But other than expressing amazement at my managing to get him on the telephone, and admitting that he had received the letter and reminder that I had written to him, he said little more and failed subsequently to reply to those letters.

Sometime after the publication of my final report, Lewis – or somebody on his behalf – wrote to the minister and furnished some information regarding his involvement. The minister asked me if I was satisfied that the restriction placed by Mr O'Malley be lifted. I had forgotten about it, as it was insignificant in the overall scheme of things. UPH or its liquidator probably wanted to pay a dividend or some other distribution to him, and I confirmed that I had no objection – that the minister should lift the restriction. Joe Lewis has reputedly since become a billionaire, mainly from currency trading, but he is probably best known as the majority owner of Tottenham Hotspur soccer club. At one stage he was also a major shareholder in Glasgow Rangers, while his friend Dermot Desmond became a major shareholder in Glasgow Celtic.

A mutual friend of Desmond's and mine had some weeks earlier invited both of us to the international cricket match in Castle Avenue on 10 July between Ireland and Australia. He hoped to mediate informally between us, not realising that I was nearly ready to complete my report. I was delighted to attend, but needless to say, Desmond did not turn up; the report had been published and he was now taking it very seriously. That was the day that the great Australian batsman Allan Border hit five successive sixes in one over but miscued his shot while going for a sixth, only getting two runs off the last ball. I enjoyed a lovely lunch and sporting day, despite missing Mr Desmond's company.

The principal interviewees during my investigation were Michael Smurfit, Noel Smyth and Dermot Desmond, as their names had appeared most often in the voluminous relevant documents that I had recovered from the various banks and professional firms involved. Naturally, I formed my own personal impressions of these individuals but did not allow those impressions to influence the findings of fact that I had to make in my report.

Smurfit was arrogant and did not readily accept that he was the subject of a corporate investigation. He thought that he could control the investigation, but I soon got through to him that he couldn't do so with me. He then thought that he could do so through the minister, but the minister reported to me on such attempts, quickly accepting that I wasn't going to do what Smurfit demanded – and he too stood up to Smurfit. Smurfit was used to getting his own way and what he wanted; he didn't take kindly to having what he said being queried by me. I thought that under his arrogant exterior he was quite insecure, personally. Observing him from a distance since that time has not changed my initial thoughts. He seemed to me to be unduly egotistical, but this may have been a psychological protection against whatever caused his insecurity. He had a high reputation as CEO and chairman of the Smurfit Group, but his involvement in Telecom indicated to me that his reputation was perhaps undeserved. He is obviously very wealthy, but I don't think that is the most important measure of a person.

Noel Smyth, I had known since our college days. We were not friends, but I respected him and I think he respected me. He was very bright and successful as a tax reduction lawyer and a property investor. I remember his being exasperated at me as he tried to explain the complexities of the property transfers, offshore companies and tax reduction measures that he had been involved in devising for use in these transactions; I had difficulty in grasping them at first, needing a little time to study. He was caught in a bit of a bind in the investigation, as he seemed to want to cooperate with me. He understood that I was operating with statutory powers and in accordance with my legal powers, but he was very concerned at the threat of being sued or otherwise damaged by his clients if he did so.

Desmond was involved at all levels of the transactions; he tried very hard to thwart the investigation, first by getting rid of the first inspector and then by trying to get rid of me. I found him to be totally unreliable in his actions and words, and I didn't believe that I could trust him. I think he underestimated me and my determination to complete the role that the minister had given me. Some would call it my stubbornness, but he didn't realise that I, like him, was a tough Dublin northsider. I still wouldn't trust him, but I readily acknowledge that many people have done so – and he has made a lot of money in business transactions since then, to add to what he made from the Telecom site sale.

I also interviewed J.P. McManus, who at the time was reasonably well known as a successful gambler and racehorse owner. His success seems to have continued since then; he has diversified his investment interests and, according to media reports, would now appear to be very wealthy. I have never trusted the integrity of the horse-racing business but have no reason to suspect that McManus is untrustworthy in that regard. I found him a likeable character, and wondered why he was so reluctant to be upfront and direct about his involvement in the Telecom site sale. Perhaps he was acting on advice from a friend that I would be got rid of and there would be no report; in doing so, however, I think he was misguided and brought unnecessary adverse publicity on himself for what was probably for him a simple property investment.

This entire saga – Telecom Éireann's purchase of the Johnston, Mooney & O'Brien site in Ballsbridge, my subsequent investigation and Mr Desmond's attempted blocks by High Court injunctions – justify a separate volume, and this may follow.

It was difficult for me to take on new work while the inspectorate was going on, at least in the early stage, due to the time commitment that I had promised to the minister. Even so, there were a number of ongoing matters that I had to try to deal with. Where I was a director or adviser, I continued to attend board meetings – this obligation included Browbell, Nokia Smurfit, Perigord, Oglesby & Butler, the National Maternity Hospital and Lark. I continued to go to client functions, whether golf outings or receptions, when I was available. One that I had to miss was a *Bringing it All Back Home* concert in the Olympia Theatre, but that was because my two daughters, Louisa and Sinéad, were performing on the same night in *Alice in Wonderland* in Sutton with their drama class.

As 1993 came, although I was still not finished with the inspectorate, the pressure had eased a little. I wasn't working on it all day every day, so I had the opportunity to undertake client work to a greater extent than in the previous fifteen months. One of the first new transactions from this period commenced with a meeting on 8 January; it involved my client Jamont NV – a joint venture of Nokia Corporation, at that time still with a paper manufacturing division, Gruppo Ferruzzi of Italy, and James River Corporation, a US company – which had decided to acquire Handipak Distributors Limited. The transaction was eventually completed in June.

Soon after that, I was involved with Unidare plc, which planned a new acquisition with the assistance of Riada Stockbrokers; later in the year, I was involved with IWP plc in its proposed acquisition of the Netherlands-based company Van Zil, which owned a range of businesses with the Van Zil brand name. I was also involved with Cigna (the US insurance conglomerate) and all its lawyers in Europe as it set about a corporate reorganisation; this involved a few days meeting in Frankfurt to get the matter started and co-ordinated. Nokia Smurfit convened board meetings in London in the early part of the year, and I had to attend those. Conveniently, however, I was able to include some other meetings with the anti-fraud section of the UK Department of Trade and Industry in London while I was there.

I was looking to the future and trying to assess whether we had enough space in Hainault House to continue to grow, as I knew that our lease was due to expire within a few years and wanted to see what our options were other than simply renewing it. One option that I did look at seriously was the upper floors of the new Irish Life development on George's Quay, but for various reasons I didn't proceed with it – soon after, it was leased by Ulster Bank as their headquarters.

Irish Life was prepared to deal with me, but in reality, they were hoping for a tenant to take a full block and I did not need that much space. The double rent deduction for tax purposes, as well as the location, was an attraction, although most of my partners would have had a longer commute than the existing one to St Stephen's Green. In the end, having analysed it with surveyors, architects and tax advisers, we did not pursue it and stayed where we were.

A group of managing partners of five of the six largest commercial law firms had informal meetings a few times each year; on these occasions, one or other would host a lunch for the others. We were very wary of falling foul of the new Competition Act and being accused of price fixing, so the question of hourly rates – while sometimes discussed – was never agreed or even attempted. One of the topics discussed was the issue of professional indemnity insurance, as the scheme arranged by the Incorporated Law Society was not considered adequate for the size of the transactions that we were dealing with, and we called ourselves the 'insurance group'. Each of the firms had indemnity cover levels of a multiple of that arranged by the Law Society, and we were able to negotiate favourable terms by doing so on a group basis with the same insurance broker.

During Easter 1993 I took my family by ferry to Scotland for a week; we stayed in Kinross, which was very convenient for visits to Edinburgh, St Andrews, Perth and Inverness. The hotel had a golf course beside it, as well as an ice skating and curling rink. My daughters would have happily stayed skating all day rather than see some of the sights; in fact, having been bored in St Andrews, it was only the prospect of seeing the Loch Ness monster that persuaded them to come with us on the following day to Inverness. It was a very pleasant trip and a welcome break for Mary and me, as we saw some of the places that we had visited on our honeymoon almost sixteen years previously.

I had one more enjoyable trip before I sat to finalise the report to the minister. Some friends and I travelled in early June to Riga, ostensibly to see the Irish soccer team play a World Cup game against Latvia – but as much to experience a country just emerging from behind the Iron Curtain. The standard of living, food, hotel buildings and general ambience was depressing; it was an eye-opener for all of us, and when we got home we complained a little less about the recession that Ireland was experiencing at the time.

Shortly before that, I met Mario Soares, the president of Portugal, at a Portuguese embassy reception to celebrate his first presidential visit to Ireland. Mr Soares was the first elected head of state in Portugal in sixty years and had become the first constitutionally elected prime minister, in

1976, after the revolution in 1974 that had overthrown the military dictatorship of Salazar and his successor.

After the revolution, many right-wing millionaires who feared retribution if they stayed in Portugal left and went to Brazil, one of Portugal's former colonies. When they realised that Soares and his successors were more interested in developing the Portuguese economy than seeking retribution, many of them returned and resumed their businesses, which had not been confiscated as they had feared. Portugal was a relatively poor country despite its colonies in South America, Africa and Asia – the reality was that only a limited number of its citizens benefitted from exploitation of the colonies. Portugal has progressed significantly in many ways, but its economic advancement since the mid-1980s, when it joined the EU, is of particular note.

On 24 July, after the finalisation and publication of the final report into the Telecom and Johnston, Mooney & O'Brien affair, the family and I went on holidays to Woodstown in County Waterford. We were joined by Mary's brother, Jim McCarron, and his family from the USA, along with Mary's parents, Jim and Ellen; they all stayed in a separate house in the complex. Ellen had been unwell for some time beforehand but was delighted to have all her family gathered together; she died peacefully while on holiday on 29 July. I remember my son Shane, who was 14 years old at the time, sitting beside her bed on the morning of the day she died, playing his guitar and singing 'Knock, knock, knocking on heaven's door' for her, although by that stage she was unconscious. After the funeral in Kilworth, County Cork, we came back to Woodstown for the last week of our holiday, as Ellen would have wished and maybe planned, and then I headed back to work.

Frank Plunkett Dillon retired as a partner in February 1992, on reaching the age of 65. It wasn't a rule that we had introduced, but Frank wanted to take life easier; he was happier to become a consultant in the firm, without the commitment of spending five days a week from morning to evening in the office. Nonetheless, he stayed as the principal legal adviser to CRH plc, our biggest client. On 2 June 1993, he and I were invited to lunch in Belgard Castle, the CRH headquarters, by Tony Barry, the CEO of CRH.

I was not aware of the purpose of the lunch in advance, but it was effectively an interview to satisfy Tony that I could be trusted to take over Frank's role as principal adviser. Tony also wanted to know when my final report on the Telecom investigation would be finalised; I had to be a little vague because although I was already writing the first draft, I couldn't disclose that. There was a little banter about some of the individuals involved, but I had to be careful not to react.

In any event, I must have sufficiently satisfied him: shortly after I returned from the holiday that I had taken in Woodstown after finalising the Telecom report, I was summoned to a meeting by one of the senior executives of CRH, the managing director of Irish Cement Limited. He asked me to take over the case involving Irish Cement Limited and the European Commission from one of the junior partners, who had been handling it since the end of 1992, when it first arose. I confirmed that I would take responsibility for it, then took over the file from my colleague and started work on it. Indeed, I was still doing some work on it many years later, as it transpired to be a long-drawn-out case.

The European Commission had alleged that there was an illegal agreement between many of the large European cement companies. It claimed that this agreement was a market-sharing cartel designed to prevent transhipments of cement from one EU country or region to another in the early 1980s, ten years previously – an infringement of EU law – and so had filed a statement of objections.

There was a limited time to respond to the commission's statement of objections, which had resulted from a commission investigation following a dawn raid on the offices of Cembureau, the European Cement Association – a representative organisation based in Brussels – some years previously. It was imperative that I looked into the file, the facts and the relevant law and procedures – with great urgency – before drafting the formal response.

This was the first time I was involved in a European competition law case, and I had to learn quickly. Following meetings with relevant people both within the company and outside it to gather more factual background, as my clients were not au fait with all the case alleged by the commission, I worked on a draft response; when I had a good, comprehensive draft ready, I engaged John Cooke SC to settle it. As we were dealing with Europe and not the Irish courts, it wasn't necessary to engage junior counsel. We filed our response in due time and then awaited the outcome.

Irish Cement's involvement arose after low-cost producers in Eastern Europe started dumping low-quality cement into Ireland in the early 1980s.

Irish Cement notified the European Commission at the time, in accordance with European law, and sought its assistance to prevent the illegal dumping. The commission prevaricated, and Irish Cement then sought the advice and assistance of Cembureau.

In the dawn raid, the commission seized documents from Cembureau; these included minutes of meetings regarding the illegal dumping that had taken place in other jurisdictions also. From these minutes, the commission extrapolated that there was a cartel operating to prevent the export of cement across borders with the intention of restricting competition.

In November 1994, the European Commission announced that it did not accept our defence and explanation – nor, indeed, that of many of the other respondents. Its decision was to fine the thirty three cement companies a total of €248 million; of this amount, €3.5 million was imposed on Irish Cement Limited. On studying the commission's decision, I advised the client that it had good grounds to lodge an appeal to the European Court of First Instance in Luxembourg, and this they agreed to do.

If I had not agreed to take the European Commission case in 1993, my life since would have been different and I would not have been involved in the expansion of CRH plc throughout Europe and beyond. It was another example of being lucky to take the right road when two diverged 'in a yellow wood'.

One of my other clients, Pat Donohoe, for whom I had acted for many years, had recently started a new venture in nanotechnology through Yale Securities Limited. The company, which had a number of different investors, was financing research in Moscow led by Valery Dyatlov. The dynamics in the company were strange; Pat Donohoe had a lot of trust in me, but one of the investors wanted to get rid of me as adviser for personal reasons. He didn't have enough control to achieve that. Pat also initially had a lot of trust in Dyatlov, but that waned over the following couple of years. Dyatlov expressed lack of trust in his research partners in the Mendeleev University in Moscow, where he was conducting research, and the investor who wanted to get rid of me was very wary of Dyatlov.

My impression of Dyatlov was that he was very nervous of lots of things in Russia. It was only many years later – when reading about business and politics in Russia, and the involvement of the Russian mafia and oligarchs in both after the fall of the Soviet Union in the early 1990s – that I realised why he was nervous: it was an almost lawless business environment. I met him on a couple of occasions, when he came to Dublin for meetings and negotiations; I was impressed with him but could see that he was a scientist and not a businessman, and that he was very uneasy.

On one occasion, he had another Russian with him, a Viktor Maleev, who I think was another scientist. The synergy between the two of them was strange; I wasn't sure whether they were colleagues or not. Pat had met Dyatlov on a few occasions in Moscow, and Pat, while liking him, was very uncomfortable in the environment there; he believed that he was being spied on at meetings and in his hotel.

As matters transpired, Dyatlov became almost impossible to contact from mid-1995, and this caused much agitation for Pat. The venture had almost ground to a halt, at least from my point of view, at the time of Pat's sudden death in March 1996. I don't think that Pat had re-established contact with Dyatlov before his death, but I since learned that Dyatlov had continued his researches and filed a series of patents with research colleagues in the field of nanotechnology over the next few years. I don't know if any of the patents were commercialised since. I found the saga interesting for a few reasons, but mainly because I had never heard of nanotechnology before my first meeting on the matter in November 1993. I learned a little about it then, and have remained fascinated since about how little any of us know about the world and what it's made up of.

In Autumn 1993, I visited the USA twice on leisure trips: the first, to Chateau Elan, near Atlanta, to play golf; the second, to New York, when I was delighted to take my mother there for the first time for her seventy-fifth birthday, which had fallen in April but was at a time when neither she nor I could make the trip. My sister Bernie also came with us, it being her first trip to New York as well. Both holidays were very enjoyable, albeit very different – Atlanta being sport, and New York being culture and sightseeing.

I had been advising parts of the CRH group since shortly after I qualified and started practising law back in 1973. Initially, I was dealing with matters such as road traffic charges against some of the Roadstone lorry drivers and licensing advice and court applications for the Roadstone Sports and Social Club. From 1975, when Bryan O'Flaherty had the road accident and I had to take over much of his work, I advised on the continuation of a major land, quarry and stone reserve acquisition programme by Roadstone in many parts of the country. This work continued over the ten years that followed.

The lands acquired included Cheeverstown, Lansdowne Valley, Feltrim, Belgard and Huntstown in County Dublin; Bunratty in County Clare; Arklow, Fasaroe, Blessington, Callary and Kilquade in County Wicklow; Trim and Slane in County Meath; Castlemine and Boyle in County Roscommon; Partry, near Castlebar, in County Mayo; Clane, Kerdiffstown and Kill in County Kildare; and Longpavement in County Limerick.

I had also advised on some claims against Roadstone for damage allegedly caused by blasting in quarries; however, I passed these cases to the litigation department if they could not be settled readily and seemed to be going to court. There were various other matters that arose over the previous twenty years relating to the CRH group, but from 1993 onwards the variety and value of the matters in which I was involved increased significantly, and the vast majority of my professional time was spent on CRH matters.

As CRH plc prepared for the annual general meeting (AGM) to be held in May 1994 – and which was usually a relatively quiet occasion – it became known that the Green Party, led by Roger Garland TD, intended to use the AGM to protest against various environmental issues that arose from time to time in a business such as that of the CRH subsidiaries. Although I had been in attendance on a couple of occasions at previous AGMs, as backup to Frank Plunkett Dillon, on this occasion I was the main adviser. Des Traynor was the non-executive chairman of the company and sought my advice on the handling of the meeting.

Tension was high at the meeting; the protests did take place and were recorded on film by some media persons. Nevertheless, despite the disruption caused at the meeting, Des coped with the situation and managed to have the business of the meeting transacted. Unfortunately, the tension and stress may have been too much for him, as he died suddenly in his sleep a week later.

The sudden death of Des Traynor came as a huge shock, as does any sudden death – the immediate effect in CRH being the appointment of the existing chief executive as interim chairman. He shortly afterwards retired as chief executive and was appointed as chairman, a position he held for many years. He was succeeded as chief executive by Don Godson. Don had been chief executive of Oldcastle Inc., the US subsidiary of CRH, and came back to Ireland when he received this latest appointment; Liam O Mahony, who was later to succeed Don as group chief executive, became chief executive of Oldcastle Inc. in his stead.

During the summer of 1994, the Ireland soccer team had qualified again for the World Cup. I had been invited to the game against Italy in the Giants Stadium in New York, but I declined the invitation as Shane was due to be sitting his junior certificate examinations at the time. As he was more interested in soccer than me, I felt that it would be unfair on him, and inconsistent with my encouragement of his studying, for me to go to the Giants Stadium.

I missed a great occasion, but I arranged to take the family to Orlando for the last round-of-sixteen game against Holland, and we went via New York. Shane had been to both New York and Orlando previously, but it was Louisa and Sinéad's first visit, and they enjoyed that part of the holiday. I had arranged with a lawyer friend in Dallas to go there with Shane if Ireland defeated Holland, as the quarter final was to be played there, with the victor facing Brazil. Mary and the girls were to go to Port Townsend, near Seattle, where her brother, Jim, lived with his family. As matters transpired, Holland beat Ireland in the sweltering heat of Orlando, so after spending a few days in Disney World, we all went to Port Townsend and continued our holiday there and in Vancouver.

During the rest of 1994, I became involved in advising on many new matters for a variety of clients, including AGB Scientific Limited, an Irish manufacturer of laboratory equipment; Tedcastle McCormick, which was originally a major coal importer but was trying to diversify and was interested in acquiring the business of Xtra-vision (which had gone into insolvency); Unidare, which was also diversifying and restructuring; the Institute of Women's Health, which had been set up within the National Maternity Hospital on Holles Street; and Oglesby & Butler Limited, which was considering the acquisition of a related company. I also advised Connie Dempsey on the sale of her 50 per cent shareholding in Professional Contract Cleaners Limited to her business partner, and Riada Stockbrokers as stock exchange sponsors on the flotation of Tullow Oil.

On 4 January 1995, Shane was interviewed for RTÉ News about his and a friend's project in the Young Scientists Exhibition. Later that same day, he appeared on TV on the schools quiz programme, *Blackboard Jungle*, hosted by Ray D'Arcy, for his school, St Michael's College. This had been recorded the previous August and marked the first of Shane's many appearances on the programme over three years – this first recording was just after he completed the junior certificate. Ray D'Arcy told Shane on one occasion, in 1997, in his third series of appearances, that he must have had a record number.

On 18 January, I gave a lunchtime talk to the partners and some friends of Simpson Xavier Chartered Accountants on directors' duties and responsibilities. It was fairly straightforward, but I had the impression that they had hoped to get more inside information on the proceedings of the Telecom inspectorate and my views on some of the individuals involved. It was a little too close to its completion, however, and I was not inclined to be forthcoming at that time – or, indeed, until now.

In addition to the many different CRH-related matters that were going on, some new business arose from other clients. Anglo Irish Bank had become involved as a lender to a company, Countyglen Limited, which was run by John Carway. The bank realised after some time that Countyglen was not what it seemed, and I was retained by Anglo to assist it in recovering its money. This led to a long saga in the High Court; the fraud squad also became involved after Frank Clarke SC, a High Court inspector (and subsequently the Chief Justice), found that Countyglen Limited was the subject of potential criminal deception. When I appeared before Clarke, who had acted as senior counsel in one of the many court proceedings against me in the Telecom affair, he commented, 'Mr Glackin, I hope that you won't be as hard on me now as I was with you recently in the Telecom case.'

In early 1995, I was informed that CRH was considering an investment in Poland; I was asked to become involved and to advise. The target company was Ozarow, a cement manufacturer. It had been a state-owned company, as most businesses in Poland were under the communist regime, and had then undergone a form of privatisation. But the principal shareholder was still a state-related company, Elektrim. Other shares were owned by investment funds that had bought up shares allocated to individual citizens upon privatisation, and still more belonged to provincial governments or councils, so the structure was complicated.

Ozarow needed major capital investment, but its shareholders were not in a position to provide this. CRH was interested in providing capital but had certain minimum requirements. Polish law had certain restrictions on inward foreign investment, and considerable ingenuity and drafting skills were required to achieve the various requirements of the different parties, as Elektrim and the other shareholders had differing ambitions.

Getting off first base was in itself a difficult task, as it required the appointment of Polish lawyers, and tax, financial and investment advisers. The investment banks that we were accustomed to were not active in Poland at the time, so there was quite a bit of learning as we went along.

The law firm that was appointed was Wardynski and Partners. One of the lawyers dealing with the case for us was an Irishman, and as I learned later, Mr Wardynski, the principal of the firm, had at one time been married to the daughter of one of my former senior partners. Unfortunately that marriage did not last, but I recollected that partner driving across Europe one horrible winter for his daughter's wedding, as his son-in-law and the Wardynski family could not get out of Poland to come to the wedding if it was to be held in Ireland. He spoke of how grim a place Poland was at the time, in the mid-1970s, behind the Iron Curtain and before the Solidarity movement commenced in the Gdansk shipyards. These connections to Ireland, although welcome, did not make a huge difference to the difficulties I faced in trying to get to grips with the new but evolving Polish company and commercial law and business practice.

Preliminary negotiations commenced in early 1995. The first agreement eventually signed was with the investment adviser, and everything accelerated after that. I spent fifteen days' vacation with my family in Renvyle, Connemara in late June and early July 1995; we had rented a house close to Renvyle House Hotel. There was a fax machine in the hotel, but not in our holiday house, and as voluminous draft documents were being prepared in Warsaw, they were being faxed to me at the hotel. The fax operated on a roll rather than separate sheets of paper, and there were occasions during the fifteen days when the rolls of paper were spreading across the foyer of the hotel as they spilled over the reception counter where the fax machine was kept.

There were so many documents sent to me, or by me, that I was relying on the hotel fax almost every day of my vacation. It is difficult to envisage now in the era of smartphones, emails, scanners and video conference calls, but the fairly constant flow of faxes – that seriously disrupted the hotel reception and telephone lines – was as advanced a technology as was possible in Connemara at the time.

Progress seemed to be made with the documents, and on 23 July I flew to Warsaw to meet two CRH executives, the Polish lawyers, the investment adviser and the other parties. As with any first-time journey from an airport to a city, I had no sense of the direction we were heading – the road twisted and turned, crossed over at least one bridge and then seemed to double back as it joined a motorway. I was fascinated at the buildings and their drabness. It was only six years since the fall of the Iron Curtain, and I had been in Riga, Latvia a couple of years previously, so it was not the first time that I had seen such a city. Nevertheless, it felt like something from a 1950s Soviet newsreel.

This was accentuated when we got to the Marriott Hotel, where I was to meet my clients. The hotel itself was modern, but it was facing a large ugly building, which I learned was the Palace of Culture and Science, originaly known as Josef Stalin's palace of Culture and Science. The Stalin name was dropped when he became persona non grata; the Soviets had built the palace as a gift to Poland between 1952 and 1955, at a time when he still ruled the Soviet Union and effectively controlled all of Eastern Europe. I thought that it was the ugliest big building that I had ever seen, and in many visits to Warsaw over the next fifteen years, I didn't change my opinion – or meet anyone who disagreed with me.

We had some meetings in the hotel on Sunday night, and on Monday we went to meet our local Polish lawyers. A meeting had been arranged with Elektrim on Tuesday morning at its offices, Elektrim being the principal party with which we were entering into a complex set of agreements.

I have never been blessed with much patience, and found the approach adopted by the Elektrim executives difficult to understand and accept. They seemed to be going back on some basic issues that I thought had been agreed already. After some initial tense discussions, agreement on the outstanding issues with Elektrim was reached quickly; we could now proceed to develop the draft legal documents and start meetings on the approvals that were needed. The rest of the week was taken up with meetings, and for me it was principally in the lawyers' offices. On a couple of evenings, we walked from our hotel to the old town and had dinner in one of the many fine restaurants there. On this visit, I didn't see much of Warsaw other than what I could see on this walk, which included the monument of the Tomb of the Unknown Soldier, constantly lit by a permanent flame. I later read a little about Poland's history over the past few centuries and realised that we in Ireland may complain about our ancestors' difficulties, but at least since 1923 there has been peace and relative prosperity here. In Poland, peace didn't begin until 1989, and relative prosperity only came after Poland was admitted to the Europen Union in 2004.

Progress was made during the various meetings, and I returned to Dublin at the weekend. Further discussions and drafting of documents continued with the various parties over the next six or seven weeks; on 18 September I went back to Warsaw for the final round of negotiations and the signing of the various necessary agreements. It was the first of many investments by CRH in the cement industry around the world; many more were to be made over the subsequent twenty years. This first one was conducted through Irish Cement Limited, but soon afterwards, a new division – CRH Europe Materials – was formed, and it got its own offices, management structure and personnel.

Some other new clients from this time included Liz Claiborne and Serco Services Limited, both of which subsequently grew to be significant companies.

In July 1995, I was asked to meet a representative of an international telecommunications company. It was explained to me that this company, which was the largest mobile phone company in one of the European countries, had been asked to join a new consortium to enter a bid in a competition for the second Irish mobile licence, and I was asked to advise it. Its partners were to be Southwestern Bell (a US telecommunications company), Deutsche Telekom and three Irish businessmen. I was asked to advise the three Irish businessmen as well.

The consortium was led by Southwestern Bell, which had been a partner of Denis O'Brien's company Esat Telecom in the first competition that year; it was the most advanced of the partners in its analysis and study of the market in Ireland. This first competition was aborted when challenged by one of the participants, and a second competition was ordered.

When I met Jack Kirwan, the Irish lawyer for Southwestern Bell, to commence negotiation of a consortium agreement, he told me that Southwestern Bell considered itself totally incompatible with Denis O'Brien and his approach, did not want to stay as part of his consortium, and therefore had set about finding new partners after the second competition was announced. The matter was very urgent; a strict deadline had been set by the government, which stated that it was unhappy with the delay caused by the first competition being aborted.

After meeting the Irish clients and Jack Kirwan, I flew to Bonn in Germany for a meeting with my clients and Deutsche Telekom, as they had a common interest; I was asked to advise the German company as well. Nevertheless, the drafting of the bid documents was led by Southwestern Bell and its lawyer. It shared its acquired knowledge with its new consortium partners, as it was not possible to conduct a completely new due diligence for the licence terms in the short time involved. For this reason, the agreement between the consortium partners was more complicated than might otherwise have been the case.

There followed fairly intensive work over a relatively short period, with the clients and with Jack, and the bid was delivered on time. Irish Mobicall, the name adopted by the consortium, was very confident of success; when the result was announced and the Denis O'Brien consortium won, there was shock and disbelief. Irish Mobicall was adjudged to have come third, and its representatives were naturally disappointed as well as stunned.

Following on from some revelations made shortly afterwards, very serious corruption allegations about the competition and the result were subsequently made and upheld in a government tribunal of inquiry, known as the Moriarty Tribunal. These allegations have been repeatedly denied by Mr O'Brien and his partners, and some litigation is still going on in the Irish courts twenty-five years later. I don't think any of Irish Mobicall's foreign partners have done any business in Ireland since then, such was their distaste for the process.

A further matter that arose late in 1995 was a major row in another small but successful firm of solicitors – one that led to a split in the firm. The company was well established and respected, and included two brothers among its partners. The principal dispute was between the brothers, and I was asked to advise one of them. I must have developed a reputation for dealing with major feuds and splits in professional and business partnerships, as I had earlier dealt with similar situations in firms of chartered accountants, architects and insurance assessors – as well, of course, as in my own firm.

In none of these had I come across the level of bitterness and intransigence that I did in this case between the two brothers. Most of the other partners had stayed in the firm when my client left, and they were caught in the crossfire. Although I dealt with this difficult situation reasonably well, it reminded me of the decision that I had made back in my FLAC days, in 1972, not to get involved in family law disputes. And even though the circumstances of this matter were quite different, many of the emotions involved were similar, and I did not enjoy it.

When researching these memoirs, I have relied on my memory, assisted by my old diaries. It has taken only a reference to a name or place to jog my memory and remind me of meetings, court cases, clients and their businesses. There were only two names that did not ring a bell for me, and which I did not remember – one of which was a company. I noted from my diaries a couple of mentions of each, in mid-1995 in relation to two lunches. Intrigued by the fact that I could not remember either, I was amazed when I checked both on Google and read a November 2010 article published in *Paris Match* titled 'Karachi. Boivin, celui, qui fait trembler la République' that tied the two together.

The article informed me that the individual with whom I had the lunches was an employee of DCNI (Direction des Constructions Navales Internationale) and had used an Irish company, the company mentioned in my diary, as part of his activities. That did ring vague bells in my subconscious, but what the article was stating was that my lunch companion had a web of offshore companies in Luxembourg, the Isle of Man, Switzerland, Malta, Mauritius, the Bahamas, the British Virgin Islands and the Cayman Islands, all of which were allegedly used to pay 'commissions occultes' (kickbacks) to government officials in different parts of the world – specifically Pakistan and Libya – to buy French-made submarines manufactured by DCNI, which was owned by the French government. I was intrigued at this and searched further on Google.

Another two articles appeared in *Asia Sentinel*, a web-based Asian regional publication, on 7 and 13 June 2012. The first article was headed 'Malaysia Sub Scandal Spreads to Malta' and stated that Malaysia's long-running submarine scandal appeared to have spread to Malta, where an opposition MP alleged that a French-owned, Malta-based financial consultancy, Gifen, was being investigated for its role in the Malaysian government's controversial US$1 billion purchase of the boats. The article added that a Luxembourg company was being investigated by French officials over allegations that part of a €114 million commission paid to a company owned by a close associate of the Malaysian prime minister had been laundered through Malta.

It stated that Gifen, which had been founded in 2001, was well connected with the French secret services and had close ties with both former French president Nicholas Sarkozy and former French prime minister Dominique de Villepin, and that after France signed the UN Convention against Corruption in December 2003, my lunch companion allegedly began to operate through different channels – setting up the above-mentioned offshore companies.

I don't know if the company mentioned in my diary was the Irish company that was being referred to, as I had no further involvement with it after October 1995; as far as I remember, a firm of accountants and financial advisers took over its company secretarial work, which is what we had been doing. There was no obvious substantive legal work forthcoming from DCNI, as I had originally anticipated, so there was no role for me, and I suppose that was the reason that I forgot about it.

As I read the *Asia Sentinel* articles further, I realised that what was involved in this saga was very political and dark. Reference was made to a connection with Sarkozy and bribes having been promised to Pakistani generals for the purchase of SSK Scorpene submarines from Armoris, a unit of Direction des Constructions Navales (DCNS), a French defence contractor. Eleven French technicians were blown up by a car bomb that was first blamed on Al-Qaeda, but subsequent stories in France about the scandal, called 'L'Affaire Karachi', alleged that Pakistani generals blew up the van in retaliation for the cancellation by then French president Jacques Chirac of kickbacks promised in the sale of the vessels.

Sarkozy denied the allegations, and it is unclear whether this was followed up. The second article in *Asia Sentinel*, titled 'The Man Who Keeps the Secrets', stated that the man I lunched with:

> according to a plethora of news stories in France and Luxembourg, is at the heart of a scandal that stretches across half the earth to Pakistan, Taiwan, Malaysia, India and untold numbers of other countries whose defense ministries bought armaments from the French defense giant DCNS around the turn of the century. At least three of those sales have been dogged with stories of bribery and the murder or unexplained deaths of 19 people.

The article goes on with further allegations and references that would make for a great TV series or at least documentary. I didn't realise that I was so close to such excitement and international intrigue – and perhaps I wasn't, but at least someone I met on a few occasions seemed to have been.

Reverting to the early part of 1996, I was asked to advise one of my best friends, Paul McLaughlin, who was an executive director and significant shareholder of ILP Packaging Limited, which had decided to float on the London Stock Exchange and later took an Irish listing. It changed its name, at that time, to Iretex Group plc. Some time later, a dispute arose at board level and Paul became managing director; the previous managing director and founder of the company left the board but remained a shareholder. Later still, Iretex issued new shares to raise funds, and I bought shares in the company. In 2001, the original managing director and founder launched a bid to acquire all the shares in the company; this was accepted on advice of the financial advisers and brokers of ILP, and I made a handsome profit, which enabled me to pay a deposit on a property in France and thus began another part of my saga.

As we in GSOB had had a successful year in 1995, I invited the partners and senior associates to a dinner on 2 February in the private dining room of Patrick Guilbaud's restaurant. We had a very pleasant evening, which was enhanced by Guilbaud's own celebrations – it had been announced that day that his restaurant had been awarded a second Michelin star, the first Irish restaurant to gain that achievement. Indeed, he has retained that second star every year since, but as this was the first occasion, he had the good wine and champagne flowing for his staff and best customers. It was purely fortuitous that we were there that night; as even though I did go there on special occasions, I would not have been considered a regular.

I didn't realise it at the time, but there weren't many more occasions for the GSOB partners to celebrate. In the next couple of years, some partners either left voluntarily or had to be persuaded to leave.

On the following day, I had the pleasure as a proud father to attend the National Concert Hall and watch and listen to my two daughters playing violin in a concert by their orchestra.

One of my favourite clients was Lir Chocolates Limited, founded and operated by Connie Doody and Mary White in Connie's kitchen at home. At the time, they were very innovative and their chocolates very sophisticated for Irish tastes, but their business was growing rapidly. They moved to new premises at the IDA Enterprise Centre on East Wall and were ultimately bought by an international confectioner; they subsequently moved out of Dublin, and the company is now one of the largest confectionery companies in Ireland. When I was involved with them in the early days, I was always delighted to go to a meeting in their small premises, with the office almost in the kitchens where their chocolates were being made by hand. I was always offered some specials; they must have believed that I would be a good advertisement for their products.

In mid-October I travelled again to the Chateau Elan golf tournament near Atlanta, as I had done on three or four occasions previously with friends and clients. During the trip I was approached by Seán Fitzpatrick, the then chief executive of Anglo Irish Bank. He said to me that his two favourite law firms were GSOB and another firm – the official solicitors to the bank – but that each of the firms would be much improved by merging, as each was not large enough on their own and would complement the other in many facets. I was intrigued at his observations, which came out of the blue; while I didn't disagree that we weren't large enough, and I had been thinking of a merger as a growth platform, I didn't immediately see the compatibility with this other firm.

He tried to persuade me to talk informally to the managing partner of that firm, who was on the same golf trip. Without my agreeing to it, Seanie must have spoken to the managing partner – during the flight home, he came down to my seat from his own in business class and opened a conversation. I knew him well for more than twenty years, but had not met him for a few years prior to this encounter.

I told him that an aeroplane was not an appropriate place to have such a conversation, which should be of the utmost confidentiality. He asked if he could call me when we got back to Dublin, and I agreed. We met a week or so later and discussions commenced, lasting for a few months. I had told my partners in GSOB of the approach, and they approved my continuing discussions. By a coincidence, around this time one of my partners, who I knew did not like the person I was talking to, informed me that he intended to leave – this being his second occasion to do so – and was joining another firm. On the previous occasion, he moved to a client company; on this occasion, he informed me that he was joining a rival firm of solicitors.

He, in fact, was closer to Seanie Fitzpatrick than I was. Although I never asked, my guess is that Seanie had spoken to him before he spoke to me, and that he was unhappy about the prospects of such a merger. Having said that, the same individual only stayed a few years at his new firm before changing to another; he stayed there for a few years before he had to retire with serious early onset dementia. He, unfortunately, never seemed happy with his lot, and although very intelligent and able, I always found him a little complicated.

The resignation of this partner, who was in our commercial department and in charge of banking and financial services, changed the balance a little between GSOB and the other firm that I was talking to; the latter considered it a loss to us, and to the plan that they envisaged. As the discussions proceeded, I was more and more surprised at the scathing criticism that my counterpart made of many of his partners – some of whom were my contemporaries and had been in that firm for much longer than he had. He strongly praised the younger partners, whom he took credit for recruiting, and argued that he had succeeded in changing the ethos of his firm from being an old-fashioned establishment firm to a young, dynamic, business-oriented one. He may well have been correct, but I did not like his attitude.

Over time, and as our discussions progressed – which was relatively slowly, as there was no urgency from either side – he was equally scathing about some of my partners. In the end, he tried to persuade me to leave on my own and join his firm, as I was the only one that he considered compatible with what he wanted. These discussions had changed radically over the few months. I reported back to my colleagues on the progress, or lack of it, but I had no interest in what he was proposing.

Nevertheless, I did find the process personally unsettling, and it gave me an insight into what other firms thought of us. I did not necessarily accept what he had said to me; however, I did begin to look at the future in a slightly different way. I realised that I enjoyed being a solicitor, and the work that I was doing, but no longer wanted to continue as managing partner – a role that I had performed for more than ten years.

I gave the matter considerable thought over the 1996/97 Xmas holiday and decided, as a first step, to stand down as managing partner. I announced on 14 January 1997 that I was resigning, and two days later Bryan Strahan was elected as my successor. Although I remained head of the commercial department, resigning as managing partner was like the lifting of a weight off my back. Bryan then became directly involved with me in the merger discussions, but he didn't have much enthusiasm for it; later in the year, discussions terminated.

Other CRH-related matters that I was involved in during the mid to late 1990s included a bond issue in conjunction with UBS, the investment bank; a joint venture with Viridian, a Northern Ireland electricity producer, to form Huntstown Power; lengthy negotiations in relation to an investment in Ukraine; the acquisition of a company in Finland and another in Estonia; the acquisition of Ibstock plc, a UK listed company; and further add-on acquisitions in Ireland and Europe.

Most of these transactions involved travel; on many occasions, I had to go to different parts of Europe, either with CRH executives or to meet them or to meet other lawyers. What struck me again on these trips – as it had on many previous occasions, on business or on holidays – was the proliferation of the English language, and the facility with which so many Europeans could do business in English. Equally striking was the antipathy of so many Europeans to the English. England had never conquered much of Europe, so the antipathy was not the remnants of a past imperial domination; I sometimes wondered why there was such dislike shown towards its people in so many different countries and cultures.

I remained as busy as ever with existing cases and clients, and I continued to get referrals to new accounts on a wide variety of issues. New clients included Accor Hotels, the French hotel group, which was looking for investment opportunities in Ireland (and was looking in particular at three existing hotels); ICS Building Society, which planned to acquire the mortgage business and loan book of Royal Liver Assurance Company; and Lilly Industries, which was seeking to establish its new Irish business and contracts with the IDA. I also advised on the restructuring of a very successful business in the clothing industry in Donegal, and guided my old friend Cormac Hughes in acquiring a Ford dealership in south Dublin.

As a consequence of the Telecom inspectorate, or so I presume, the media regularly contacted me for my views on business matters where there was some element or allegation of fraud or corporate wrongdoing. I was interviewed on RTÉ by Ursula Halligan and Gerry Barry (who I knew from my time long ago in the L&H in UCD), and later by David Nally and Mike Mellotte. Indeed, I was invited to give a lecture at the Listowel Writers' Week, presumably on the basis that I had recently had two lengthy reports published, but I felt that I should decline and I haven't been invited back since.

In the meantime, Shane's TV appearances on *Blackboard Jungle* continued, and he successfully completed his leaving certificate, starting his first-choice subjects of politics and philosophy in Trinity College.

As we entered 1998, I was approached by the managing partner of another firm that was a little smaller than us but which, at first glance, might have fitted well. Discussions took place between him and me, with the approval of my other partners. This dialogue went on for a couple of months, but I realised that this merger would not solve the problem that I perceived; while they had some good partners with a good following, they also had a few that did not impress me. Therefore, I recommended to my partners that we cease those discussions.

Another tribunal, established in 1997, was the Tribunal of Inquiry into Certain Planning Matters and Payments, better known as the Planning Tribunal, chaired initially by Judge Flood and later by Judge Mahon. Over the next couple of years, I was asked to advise and accompany many persons who were called for preliminary examination by the counsel for the tribunal and subsequently to give evidence before the tribunal chairman. These were mostly bankers from Anglo Irish Bank whose clients were being investigated by the tribunal, but there were also others who had a tangential connection with the matters being investigated. Some persons had found themselves in a compromised position, even though their actions were ordinary business transactions – in these cases, the counterparties were acting in a manner that gave rise to subsequent queries which were of interest to the tribunal.

Around this time, I also advised Anglo Irish Bank on a number of other matters, including separate disputes with Jyske Bank (a Danish bank) and

Ormond Inns, the company that was operating the Ormond Hotel in Dublin.

Arthur Andersen was conducting an internal investigation into some aspects of the National Irish Bank, and I advised on some issues that arose. This was separate from a later investigation by inspectors appointed by the Director of Corporate Enforcement, which took place a few years afterwards.

IWP International, an investment holding company quoted on the stock exchange, continued to expand and acquire new businesses, and in 1998 it acquired Jeyes Ireland. I advised on this acquisition.

Accor continued its investment programme in the Irish hotel industry, and some other clients were either interested in acquiring new businesses, selling off some of their assets, or in dispute with partners or shareholders, so I was kept busy while I ruminated on my future.

Towards the end of October, a partner in our property department left suddenly to become a District Court judge. In some regards, it was not a surprise; he had become disaffected with the other partners and vice versa. He was friendly with the Attorney General, so when he wanted an exit from the practice, he did not have any difficulty in being appointed. Although he had not spent much time in the courts during his career as a solicitor, he developed a good reputation as a judge. Unfortunately, he died in 2014 after a long illness, having retired just two years previously.

Shortly after his resignation from the firm, we were approached by the managing partner of another firm, who asked us to consider a merger. Discussions in this case went on from December 1998 to the end of May 1999. They were very nearly consummated, but at the last minute I decided that I didn't want to proceed – and even though some other partners were happy to do so, the merger wasn't going to proceed if I wasn't going to be part of it. These discussions developed into negotiations and became more and more serious, involving many meetings at different levels and detailed planning for the future.

Unfortunately, in the course of the negotiations, two of our partners left the firm – one involuntarily and the other voluntarily – so that the balance between the two firms was changed, and the other firm tried to take advantage of that. That was unacceptable to me, but I also realised that there wasn't enough strength in depth in the other firm. Even though we were now weaker, with the loss of two partners in addition to the resignation of a partner from our property department a few months earlier, my assessment was that we would be better not to proceed with this merger.

I made the relevant senior executives of CRH aware of the discussions, as CRH and its subsidiaries provided the major part of my work during this period. While their principal interest was to be satisfied that I, as their main legal adviser, had appropriate backup and support to ensure that they would not be left without a trusted adviser, they believed, as I did, that we needed to be bigger and that organic growth would not suffice. Whatever the case, they were not trying to influence me one way or the other. I did learn afterwards, however, that they were very happy with my decision not to pursue this particular merger.

The decision not to proceed resulted in the resignation of another partner at the end of June 1999. We were now quite a different firm than we had been twelve months earlier, and vulnerable to the loss of clients. Nevertheless, most of our important clients stayed with us, and we promoted new, young partners who were ready to step up. We also recruited more assistant solicitors so that we were able to continue with the same level of service – or if not, an enhanced level.

One of my busiest clients for a few years had been Coyle Hamilton, a large insurance broker. It had become very dynamic under the leadership of Ronan Fearon and Hugh Governey in particular, but it also had other very good senior executives. The company had continued to expand, and in early 1999 it instructed me in relation to the acquisition of a substantial part of the business of Inbro Citygate, a Lloyds brokerage in London. Negotiations and due diligence continued for a few months, involving a series of meetings in London and Dublin before eventually being completed in London.

Another very successful and busy client was in the mushroom and compost business. I had acted for him since he commenced his business many years earlier. He had continued to expand through acquisitions, joint ventures and new investments in Ireland and in the UK, becoming one of the top two or three mushroom suppliers to the UK. He decided to restructure his companies, and I worked with NCB Corporate Finance and Arthur Andersen, tax advisers, to achieve a structure that met his requirements. This took more time and meetings than I had anticipated but we eventually completed the restructuring.

In mid-May 1999, the Trinity scholars for that year were announced. Shane was one of those awarded a scholarship, which, *inter alia*, gave him right of residence on the university campus for up to five years. The downside of this, as it transpired, was that from October we saw less of him than ever; he effectively moved out from home, using up the five-year right of residence in Trinity while he finished his primary degree and then an MPhil. After that, he left for the University of Leeds to undertake a PhD. Nevertheless, at the time of his scholarship – before the drawback of his absence became apparent – we were delighted and indeed very proud of his achievement. Later in the year, Louisa completed her secondary education at Loreto College, St Stephen's Green, sat her leaving certificate, was very successful, and earned sufficient points to enter the medical school in Trinity College. She was awarded a Trinity scholarship three years after Shane; she also availed of residence rights in Trinity until her graduation, together with the usual other perks.

In early June, Bryan Strahan approached another firm about the possibility of a merger. Discussions continued for a few weeks before he realised, as I had from the beginning, that this other firm would not be a good fit for us. A different firm approached Bryan, through an intermediary, seeking to discuss a possible merger. Bryan and I met them, and although the firm was very successful in property transactions and very ambitious, we realised immediately that we would not fit together. We informed them of that without much delay.

In the meantime, I received a phone call from a partner and former managing partner of KPMG whom I had known for many years. I had worked with him on some large transactions in the past – in some cases, where KPMG Corporate Finance were on the same side as me; in others, where they were in opposition. I assumed that he wanted to refer me to another transaction, but he asked me if I would meet some of his partners; they were considering the establishment of a law firm as part of KPMG and thought that I might be interested. I wasn't aware that this might be possible under Law Society regulations, but he told me that this had been considered, and in the UK it had become possible.

I was intrigued. I felt it might be a sufficient challenge – something out of the ordinary that could regenerate my enthusiasm for management.

I agreed to meet him again with another partner who I had also known for many years, and we did so within a week. Over the next four months, there was a series of meetings about future plans with a group of the KPMG partners. I had insisted from an early stage that any discussions would have to be on the basis that the new firm would provide, as well as company and commercial services, litigation and property services. This was understood by all parties, as I was not willing to leave the other partners in GSOB who worked in those areas. In early August I was to meet the managing partner of Fidal, the French law firm established by KPMG, to discuss his experience of a law firm within an auditing and financial services firm, but this meeting fell through, as he had another urgent meeting and was then going on vacation.

A couple of days later, I travelled to London with some of the KPMG partners. We met the partners of K Legal, the law firm affiliated to KPMG, and I was impressed with those that I met. Due to holiday commitments, there was a gap of a couple of weeks before we resumed discussions; I then met two more KPMG partners in Ireland, including the managing partner. In early October I learned, at a meeting with the managing partner, that the issue of litigation and property departments becoming part of the new firm was a potential problem for KPMG, as they did not see them fitting into the new firm.

A series of five meetings ensued to discuss how we could resolve the problems – whether there was any solution that would meet their requirements and mine – but on 22 October, we eventually agreed that the proposed deal was off. This was probably the first occasion in the various merger discussions that we had held over the previous couple of years – and, indeed, including preliminary and tentative dialogues some years earlier – when I was disappointed at the breakdown. But I didn't get much time to dwell on my disappointment: while this last series of meetings was going on, I had become immersed in a crisis for a client that quickly developed and involved my full-time attention for months afterwards.

When I look back at the mid-1990s, I remember that I was not achieving the same level of job satisfaction that I had up to then. Perhaps it was the onset of manopause or some equivalent syndrome, but I was no longer enjoying the office – and in particular, being managing partner. There were tensions among some of the partners; some of the older ones who remained after the retirement of the original senior partners seemed to resent the progress of some younger female partners who were seeking a greater say in the operation of the firm and a greater share in the profits.

While I had considerable sympathy with the female partners, I was anxious not to unduly upset the older male partners. Trying to reconcile these conflicts caused me more stress than I recognised at the time, and it did not occur to me to seek advice from external experts. In the end, I saw that the solution would be to merge with another firm, making us larger; in my mind, any individual partners would then have less influence and impact. It might also allow the opportunity for an alternative managing partner, as I did not see most of my existing partners as suitable to replace me, and any that were suitable were not interested. As it transpired, those older male partners left anyway. Subsequent to their departures, I knew that we were less attractive as a merger participant, and the process was more difficult.

In late September 1999, a major news story broke. It was disclosed – during an application by Mary Harney, the Minister for Enterprise, Trade and Employment, to the High Court for the appointment of inspectors into the affairs of Ansbacher Cayman Limited – that Des Traynor, the former non-executive chairman, had allegedly operated an unlicensed bank from the CRH registered office at 42 Fitzwilliam Square in Dublin city centre. What's more, according to the news story, a number of former CRH directors seemed to have had accounts at this bank.

This application had a fairly long and circuitous genesis. It arose indirectly from a family dispute in Dunnes Stores Limited, one of Ireland's largest companies and the largest retailer in the country. Ben Dunne had hit the headlines a few years previously, arising from a cocaine binge in Florida that culminated in his sister, Anne Heffernan, trying to oust him from the company. Legal proceedings commenced between the siblings. In the course of this, Ben Dunne averred, in an affidavit, that he and Dunnes Stores had made large payments to Charlie Haughey, the former Taoiseach. This information became public, although it could have been kept confidential; Haughey was forced to comment on it and denied the assertion.

Nonetheless, there was a media call for a formal inquiry into the alleged payments to Charlie Haughey, and Judge Brian McCracken, a High Court judge, was appointed to head the tribunal, which was set up by the government in February 1997 and became known as the McCracken (Dunnes Payments) Tribunal. It set about its task mainly in private, soon making a breakthrough in discovering the involvement of relevant accounts of Dunnes Stores with connections to Haughey. This, in turn, led the tribunal to Ansbacher Cayman, a seemingly offshore bank connected with Guinness Mahon Bank.

The puzzle unravelled, the tribunal got the names of persons connected with the matter, and Haughey – when confronted with incontrovertible evidence – admitted receipt of money from Ben Dunne, or Dunnes Stores. The McCracken Tribunal reported in August 1997 that Dunne had given more than £1 million to Haughey; that Des Traynor had been contacting wealthy people and asking them for money for Haughey; that Traynor had been looking after Haughey's finances since the 1960s; that Traynor had run a secret offshore banking system from Dublin that was used by many well-known Irish business people; that Haughey had an Ansbacher account; and that Michael Lowry, or a company owned by him, had received payments from Dunnes. The role of the McCracken Tribunal was quite limited in its terms of reference, however, and it did not proceed further.

A new tribunal, the Moriarty (Payments to Politicians) Tribunal was established in September 1997 for the purpose of investigating payments to Haughey and Lowry and any others that were referred to it. Lowry was a former Fine Gael Minister for Communications who was also suspected of receiving bribery payments in relation to the award of a mobile phone licence a couple of years previously. The tribunal also inquired into whether any other politicians had money in Ansbacher Cayman deposits.

Interestingly, it found that there were two such politicians – Hugh Coveney, a Cork businessman and Fine Gael politician, and Denis Foley, a Kerry businessman and Fianna Fáil politician – but there was no finding of any illegal activity by either of them, other than perhaps non-payment of tax. These two politicians are the fathers of two government ministers in the 2020 coalition government of Fine Gael, Fianna Fáil and the Green Party.

As the Moriarty Tribunal revealed these accounts in the course of taking evidence in public, a media-led curiosity developed – people wanted to know the names of all the Ansbacher Cayman account holders. But such disclosure was resisted politically, at least in public. Without much public notice, Mary Harney, the relevant minister, had appointed a civil servant, Gerry Ryan, as an authorised officer to investigate the affairs of Celtic Helicopters Limited (a company associated with Haughey through his son) and Garuda Limited (a company associated with Lowry and Ben Dunne), both of which had been mentioned in the McCracken report as having had connections with Ansbacher Cayman.

Ryan advised that he was stymied in his investigations unless he could get access to accounts in Guinness Mahon Bank and in Irish Intercontinental Bank, both of which – according to him – appeared to have been in breach of some aspects of company law. For this reason, Minister Harney appointed Ryan to investigate certain aspects of the business of those banks; shortly afterwards, she had him investigate Ansbacher Cayman and a related company, Hamilton Ross.

Ryan presumably reported regularly to Harney, and as he ran into some roadblocks in his investigation – mainly in the Cayman Islands – he advised her to apply to the High Court in Dublin for the appointment of inspectors. This she did in September 1999, and the application was grounded on an affidavit, sworn by Ryan, that set out what he had discovered so far in his investigations. When the affidavit was opened to the court, the media were present and the weekend newspapers were full of the details reported.

Eight former directors of CRH were among those named as having had Ansbacher Cayman accounts in the past. However, that was less damaging than the description of Traynor: how, upon his retirement from Guinness Mahon, he transferred the operation of the 'offshore' Ansbacher Cayman business from his former workplace to the office that he was allocated as chairman in the CRH registered office, initially at 19 Lower Pembroke Street and later at 42 Fitzwilliam Square; how he used junior CRH staff to assist him; and how he gave his assistant, Padraig Collery, access to the CRH office despite the fact that he had no connection to the company or any of its subsidiaries. There was no indication or suggestion that any of the CRH directors other than Des Traynor himself had done anything illegal, but premature assumptions were made and everyone became tarnished with the same brush.

Traynor had died more than five years earlier, and CRH had continued to expand after his death – many persons now involved had no knowledge of him. The CRH board had travelled to the USA for their annual board meeting there. CRH executives who were still in Dublin had got some inkling through the media that a major story was about to break relating to Des Traynor but not much more. That changed when the Ryan affidavit was opened in the court and the media demanded explanations and formal company statements.

Bankers and investors were applying pressure and wanted to know more, but the senior executives knew nothing more than they read in the newspapers, which got their information from the Ryan affidavit.

I was asked to fly to Atlanta, Georgia, where the board was meeting. I was joined by Fintan Drury, their communications adviser, and James O'Dwyer of Arthur Cox, as the independent non-executive board members also wanted advice from an independent lawyer. There were a series of board meetings and caucus meetings over the next few days to consider how best to deal with the situation, as the corporate governance of the company was being questioned.

A course of action was agreed on, an independent firm of chartered accountants was appointed to advise the company on its corporate governance practices (which had always been considered to be of the highest standard), and an internal investigation was arranged to ascertain all the relevant facts regarding Traynor's interaction with the company and its facilities and staff. This investigation was not only for the board but also constituted preparation for dealing with the anticipated examination by the recently appointed High Court inspectors.

A NEW MILLENIUM AND A NEW CENTURY: SOME CHANGES AT HOME AND AT WORK

Mary's father, Jim, died on 11 January 2000. She maintained that he hung on to see if the new millennium would be any different, and having satisfied his curiosity, he was happy to go. But it was a sad start for the rest of us as we brought him back from Dublin, where he died, to his old home in Kilworth, County Cork for his burial. Sinéad went to Le Mans in France that day on a student exchange and was very lonely and disappointed to miss the funeral, but we decided that it was better that she proceed with her plans. Mary and I visited her there at the beginning of February for a weekend.

In the meantime, life in the office continued as we prepared for the Ansbachers inspectors interviews. In January, the inspectors started to interview those CRH directors who had relevant accounts and were still alive. In their subsequent report, published in July 2002, they accepted that the directors always believed that their deposit accounts were in Guinness Mahon Bank and that they knew nothing of Ansbacher Cayman.

Over the next couple of years, the inspectors also interviewed the senior executives of the company and those members of staff who had any interaction with Traynor in his office, which was remote from the operational offices of the group. They sought to ascertain whether CRH was responsible for Traynor's carrying on of an illegal banking business in the chairman's office, but in July 2002, after lengthy legal submissions based on the facts as elicited in the investigations, the inspectors concluded that CRH was not responsible.

This saga took the board, the senior executives and the professional advisers an enormous amount of time to deal with. Yet everybody felt it incumbent on them to protect the integrity and hard-earned international reputation of the company. It was a very difficult period of almost three years, but it did not slow down the expansion of the group within Ireland or internationally – it continued to grow rapidly.

New work continued to come in, from CRH and other existing clients, and also from new clients. This provided the variety that I welcomed. Some of these were new indigenous companies in the technology sector, and some were international companies that wished to establish subsidiaries in Ireland or to acquire existing Irish companies.

In the summer of 2001, our daughter Louisa was in Santa Barbara in California on a J1 visa, so Mary and I decided to visit her and have a holiday in California at the same time. We drove from Santa Monica to Santa Barbara and stayed there for a few days; we then drove to the Carmel peninsula, also spending a few days there before driving back to Los Angeles and flying home. Louisa finished her trip a few weeks later and flew home, arriving just before 9/11. Some of her friends had stayed on or gone to visit New York, and were caught up in the travel chaos that followed. Thankfully, we were home by then. I was in my office when the Twin Towers collapsed, watching it incredulously on my computer screen after someone had alerted me to do so. I was very relieved to be home after my recent trips abroad.

I had left Lark Developments in 1997, sold my shares to my partner and resigned as a director. The company thrived over the next few years, and in addition to its housebuilding, became involved in developing industrial estates and a business park. However, it ran into cash flow difficulties towards the end of 2001, arising largely from its redevelopment of Johnstown Hotel and Spa. I subsequently advised it on an examinership; when it sold the hotel, it survived and continued successfully for a number of years.

I was on two committees of the Irish Stock Exchange – as an independent outsider, chairing one of them – and although this did not keep me busy, when an issue arose, it did have to be dealt with as a matter of urgency. There were a few such issues in the early noughties.

CRH had a significant business in Ireland through its subsidiaries and joint ventures in cement manufacture, concrete and concrete product manufacture, contracting, lime manufacture, roofing tile manufacture, brick manufacture and other related construction products. Competition was strong, and competition law issues were regularly raised with me, as the executives were very conscious of their responsibilities in that regard. These issues took up much of the executives' and my time, as we checked regularly with economists, both academics and consultants, to ensure that the companies were compliant with best practice, and to be ready to deal with complaints from competitors, who sometimes saw CRH's public company status as a vulnerability to be attacked.

Environmental law compliance was becoming an increasingly significant matter for CRH and its businesses in and outside Ireland. As its businesses directly affected the environment, CRH paid more than lip service to its obligatons on this issue, which it took very seriously; there were a number of environmental advisory and compliance officers in the group who had considerable influence. Therefore, when the Glending illegal dumping issue arose, it caused anger and embarrassment for the management.

A public outcry had arisen when it was discovered that a substantial amount of waste material had been dumped in an old disused quarry of Roadstone in Glending near Blessington, and that it potentially contaminated water in the locality. Investigations by the company and the Gardaí revealed that one of the waste collection operators for south Dublin had, unknown to the company, been dumping waste he collected on a regular basis for a number of years.

Nobody with authority in the company had been asked for permission for such dumping, or granted it. Nor was anyone aware of it until it was discovered. The only persons prosecuted were the owner of the waste disposal company and his son. Their company went into insolvent liquidation, and Roadstone, the owner of the land, was unable to recoup the costs incurred by it in removing all the illegally dumped waste, having it sorted and treated when necessary and then legally disposing of it.

The Oireachtas Joint Committee on the Environment and Local Govenment had invited senior CRH executives to appear before it in early February 2003, to explain the company's position and to answer questions. I accompanied the executives to the hearing in Leinster House, where they answered the questions put to them by the committee members as best they could.

We satisfied the committee chairman that we had disclosed everything that we could at that stage. We promised to return if we were invited to return when more information became available. In fact we were never asked to return.

My mother celebrated her eighty-fifth birthday in April 2003 with a big family party in the Four Seasons Hotel. We didn't realise it at the time, but she soon became ill. Despite fighting cheerfully and courageously, she was to pass away three years later, just before her eighty-eighth birthday. All deaths affect us in some way, but my mother's death made clear to me that my generation was next; that I should try to ensure that when my time came, I wouldn't have regrets about how I spent my time. It helped me to be more determined to retire relatively young and do something different for whatever time I had left. As somebody once said, you seldom hear anybody on their deathbed saying they should have spent more time in their office.

A significant outcome of the Ansbacher Cayman saga for me personally, however, was my getting to know James O'Dwyer, the senior partner of Arthur Cox, better than I did previously, and vice versa. I realised that Arthur Cox was a firm that I could be very comfortable in, and James realised that the business and expertise that we in Gerrard, Scallan & O'Brien could bring would be a welcome addition. Although ten or twelve years earlier, the firms were somewhat similar in size – albeit Arthur Cox was larger – it had grown significantly in that period, and we had shrunk. Given this disparity in size, a merger of equals was never contemplated.

Discussions between James and I started tentatively, but with goodwill, in late 2002 – and they progressed over the months that followed despite a few major disagreements. At an early stage, I had told the CEO of CRH that discussions had commenced with Arthur Cox, and he was pleased with that. Prior to my telling him that, he had suggested the possibility of my joining CRH as an internal legal adviser; in this capacity, I would be a full-time employee of CRH and would manage and co-ordinate their legal affairs around the world. I was fairly close to doing that job already, but he felt that if I were to join full time, it would give them more comfort and I could then engage other law firms as I needed. I gave this considerable thought but saw some disadvantages – and in the meantime, the Arthur Cox talks had commenced, and I thought this was a better solution.

At the end of July 2003, after we dealt with the junior partners and those employees who didn't want to transfer to Arthur Cox with us, the balance of GSOB joined with Arthur Cox. The merger had the blessing of Frank Plunkett Dillon, the surviving member of the original firms that formed GSOB in 1968, and this was important to me, even though Frank had retired as a partner in 1992. Frank had informed me many years previously of an interesting historical connection between Arthur Cox and GSOB.

John L. Scallan and Company, one of the constituent firms of GSOB – and which was owned by Frank's maternal grandfather – had employed Arthur Cox as a young solicitor for a few years, up to 1920. Indeed, Arthur had been apprenticed to one of the partners in the firm. After he qualified in 1915, he remained as an assistant solicitor in their office at 25 Suffolk Street in Dublin. Eugene McCague, who was, at one time, a managing partner and later a chairman of Arthur Cox, in his biography of the firm's founder, writes of the death of John L. Scallan in 1920: 'In the same year, Arthur, at the age of twenty nine, decided to leave the practice and establish his own firm. His decision was greatly influenced by the suggestion that another assistant solicitor, more closely related to the Scallans, would be offered partnership.'

That other assistant solicitor was Frank's father, John Plunkett Dillon, who had recently married the daughter of John L. Scallan. It was obviously a career-enhancing move, and it did not endear him to Arthur. John Plunkett Dillon quickly became the principal of the firm on the death of his father-in-law, and he and Arthur – who developed his new practice quickly – did not speak socially again for nearly thirty years, although they would have had to have had business discussions.

Nonetheless, Frank himself was friendly with Arthur until the latter's death in 1965 – after his retirement as a solicitor and ordination as a priest. Both firms were very successful over the next eighty years, albeit John L. Scallan merged with another firm, Ryan and O'Brien, in the early 1960s to become Ryan, Scallan & O'Brien; it merged again with Thomas Gerrard and Company to become Gerrard, Scallan & O'Brien. Arthur Cox, on the other hand, retained the same name until the present time.

The merger in 2003, therefore, represented the coming together again of a separation that took place eighty-three years beforehand. I had intended to retire from practice by age 60, and although I didn't announce that at the time, I knew that this merger would allow me to do that without leaving any clients in difficulties. Even though I worked very hard for the next five years, and thoroughly enjoyed the new experience in a larger firm, I did succeed in retiring from full-time practice a week before my sixtieth birthday.

On 28 July 2003, I moved to Arthur Cox, whose offices were on Earlsfort Terrace. It was just around the corner from Hainault House on St Stephens Green, where my office had been since 1968. On the previous day, I had injured my knee while playing golf with some friends; it was a ligament strain and quite painful, so for my first day in Arthur Cox, I was using a crutch to get around. I'm sure some of the younger lawyers in Arthur Cox were wondering what old crock had now joined them. Thankfully, with some physiotherapy sessions over the next few weeks, my knee recovered and I was able to discard my crutch.

One of the aspects that I enjoyed most was not being obliged to be directly involved in the management of the firm. The administration platform in Arthur Cox was impressive, and beyond what we had experienced previously. The information technology, library, marketing, human resources, archiving, post and accounts departments were all well resourced, and it was easier to concentrate on client requirements without having to be concerned with how the administration was performing.

For the first four months of 2004, I spent much time in Lisbon while CRH negotiated and eventually entered into a joint venture with a local conglomerate holding company, Semapa, which had owned 100 per cent of Secil, a Portuguese cement and ready-mixed concrete manufacturing company; the latter also held interests outside Portugal, mainly in North Africa. My involvement commenced with a visit to Lisbon, for two days, on 15 and 16 January. There I met CRH's local lawyer and had preliminary meetings with Semapa's advisers. I was back in Lisbon for three days the following week, and I had two further three-day visits in February. In the interim periods, and in the following couple of weeks, there was a series of conference calls among ourselves and our Portuguese lawyer while we continued to work on draft documents for the share purchase and the subsequent joint venture.

I was back in Lisbon again on 17 March with three senior executives of the CRH Europe Materials division, to finalise the negotiations and sign the agreements. Late on Friday, 19 March, however, negotiations had not been finalised, as Pedro Queiroz Perreira, known as PQP, who controlled Semapa, sought to renegotiate some issues that had been agreed.

It seemed for a while that the deal was not going to happen. Agreement was reached a couple of hours later, however, and the necessary documents were signed, providing for the purchase of 49 per cent of Secil, subject only to regulatory approvals and satisfactory due diligence, which were to be completed within a short time.

The due diligence was conducted by the Portuguese advisers and reported back to us. The relevant regulatory approvals were obtained in Portugal, and we went back to Lisbon on 2 May to complete the purchase, returning to Dublin on 3 May.

On 2 September, Mary and I headed off on a holiday to China and Japan. We went first to Hong Kong and stayed in a Shangri-La hotel in Kowloon. After a few days we flew to Shanghai and got a taxi from the airport to our hotel. As we got out of the taxi, it was being hailed by someone emerging from the hotel. To my amazement, I recognised that it was one of the CRH executives. He had recommended that particular hotel to me some weeks earlier, but I didn't realise that he would be in China at the same time. I don't know how many people there were in Shanghai that day – the resident population exceeded sixteen million – and I thought it was an amazing coincidence to bump into someone we knew as soon as we arrived. He was on his way to meetings, but we did meet up later that night for dinner, when he was also joined by another of his CRH colleagues.

They were scouting for investment opportunities in China at the time; as it transpired, I was back in China for meetings on many occasions over the next few years as their scouting came to fruition. I didn't know this at the time, so Mary and I saw as much as reasonably possible of Shanghai and Beijing over the next week, before we flew to Japan. I almost expected to meet someone I knew at each of our next destinations – Tokyo, Osaka and Hiroshima. That didn't happen, but we had a very pleasant holiday, with plenty of sightseeing and interesting experiences.

A major transaction involving another client of mine took place in 2004 when Willis Group, a US-owned but multinational insurance firm, agreed to acquire Coyle Hamilton in a quite complex deal. Although I was very involved in the early stages of the deal, I had to bring in some of my colleagues to do much of the finalisation work, as I was spending so much time in Portugal. I had titled this transaction Project Trinity, because the Coyle Hamilton offices overlooked the Trinity College sports grounds at College Park.

I commenced 2005 with a skiing holiday in the south of France. After Xmas, we had gone to the apartment that we then owned near Nice and had driven up to Isola 2000, a ski resort. I had a few awkward falls on the slopes, twisting my knee and injuring my shoulder; as it turned out, this was the last occasion on which I went skiing.

Early in March, I was informed of CRH's intention to attempt to acquire the share capital of Uniland SA – a Spanish cement manufacturer, based mainly in Catalonia, that had its headquarters in Barcelona. As project names were assigned to potential deals with a view to preserving some level of confidentiality, I christened this as Project Belfield. We engaged the services of a Barcelona law firm as our advisers, and I started to work with two of that firm's partners. I had only been in Barcelona on one occasion previously, and that was a transiting single-night visit, but over the next few years – and particularly during the next fifteen months – I spent quite a bit of time there at meetings. I was very impressed with the city and most of the persons that I met there.

Uniland was the result of a merger, thirty years previously, of two family-owned cement manufacturing companies. It was a privately held company, and not listed on a stock exchange. Those families had operated harmoniously, even though the shares had become spread among many family members; in 2005, it had eighty shareholders. CRH was alerted to the fact that this harmony had broken down – that some shareholders wanted to sell their shares and were very unhappy at the price being offered by the members who wished to stay. The position was quite complicated; some shareholders held their shares through entities based in Switzerland and other jurisdictions, so I had to take trips to Geneva and Zug to meet Swiss lawyers who were involved.

Progress seemed slow despite numerous meetings and conference calls, but on 23 December there seemed to be a breakthrough.

There was a series of conference calls over the next five days, which disrupted Xmas for all of us involved. Draft documents went back and forth over the few days, and late in the evening of 27 December, we accepted that there was sufficient progress in the discussions to justify going to Barcelona to try to finalise the deal, so we got a flight there the next day. I was supposed to go with my family to Nice that day for a week's holiday, so the family proceeded without me.

On 28 and 29 December, there were intense negotiations and two tranches of shares were acquired, but that was as far as we got. This led to litigation initially in Barcelona and later in Madrid; this lasted for many years, and I had to go to both cities for meetings and court hearings on many occasions over the next few years. CRH did not succeed in acquiring the balance of the shares, but it had a harmonious relationship with the Spanish group that acquired them and eventually sold its shares to that co-shareholder in 2013 on terms that suited it.

In 2005, my mother went to our apartment in Nice for a holiday with her usual travelling companions – cousins of hers. A couple of days after her return, she went into hospital for an operation. Although she did travel again in Ireland, that trip to Nice was the last of her foreign holidays. On 17 May my mother, along with me, Mary and her sister, Auntie Teenie, celebrated Louisa's graduation in medicine from Trinity College and Shane's graduation with an MPhil. We had a very enjoyable lunch in L'Ecrivain and were joined by Louisa's then boyfriend, Lee. That night Mary and I were in attendance at Louisa's graduation class dinner and ball with all the other new doctors' proud parents.

Later that year Sinéad celebrated her twenty-first birthday with a party at home, and my mother and Teenie were there also. Unfortunately there weren't very many more parties for her, but we did have a big family gathering at our home on Christmas Day in 2005. My mother died in April 2006, a few days before her eighty-eighth birthday.

I travelled to Beijing on two occasions, and Hong Kong once, for meetings in the middle of the decade. I had previously been involved with deals in many parts of the world – East and West, North and South – but have to admit that I was not quite prepared for the Chinese.

I probably should have prepared better – studying their negotiation tactics and principles, their legal system, their business hierarchies and their general business philosophy in advance – but I didn't. And even though I was well advised and assisted by an American lawyer who had settled in China, I found the transactions quite difficult, and have huge admiration for my clients who persevered and finalised two very good deals in that period. The negotiations took a long time; in addition to my trips there, I had numerous conference calls and meetings with the lawyers and financial advisers involved in the transactions, and had a sense of satisfaction when the deals were completed.

My final trip was in 2007. Beijing had changed significantly in the three years since my first visit on holidays – driven largely by the preparations for the Olympic Games in 2008 but also by the new capital, both domestic and foreign, that was pouring into the city, and indeed other cities in China. On our first visit, we had visited the hutongs, which were old narrow streets or alleys with small one- or two-storey residential shacks on either side. On my last visit, while out for a stroll one evening, I noted that these had been demolished, and construction was ongoing on high-level apartment blocks. This was inevitable, as the amount of city centre space was very limited and the only way to accommodate the millions that wanted to move there was to build upwards, as most cities do.

Nearer home, in mid-March 2007, CRH completed the acquisition of 50 per cent of the shareholding of an integrated cement and ready-mixed concrete business based in Denizli, on the Aegean coast of Turkey. It was acquired from a privately owned industrial holding group, and CRH entered into a joint venture agreement with that company such that CRH would have joint management control and responsibility.

As part of the negotiations, I travelled to Istanbul with one of the CRH executives, for meetings in early November 2006. We went from Dublin via Frankfurt, and there I had one of the few scary moments I have experienced while flying. As we came into land, the landing wheels lowered and the ground was very close; however, the plane suddenly lifted up again and went into a circling pattern before eventually landing fifteen minutes later. A small plane had left an adjacent runway and come straight across and into the landing path of our flight. We only saw it when looking behind us to find out what had happened when our plane ascended; the pilot must have seen it very late, or assumed that the other plane would stop. There was no storm or lack of visibility, but human error nearly caused disaster.

We were on a very tight flight connection as it was, and the delay meant we missed that connection. The first flight to Istanbul that we could get was from Dusseldorf, so we had to get a train there overnight and get a very early morning flight onwards; nevertheless, we succeeded and arrived safely. I had pleasant memories of Istanbul, as I had been there seventeen months earlier when Liverpool had the miraculous comeback victory against AC Milan in the Champions League.

We met our local lawyer, who had been recommended to me by two of my colleagues in Arthur Cox; they had been in class with her in Harvard Law School some years previously. Another classmate was Barack Obama, who by this time was a US senator and was being mentioned as a possible candidate in the Democratic Party presidential primaries. She was a very pleasant lawyer and introduced us to one of her colleagues; we worked closely with them over the next few months and completed the deal without my having to go back to Istanbul.

Poland came back on my radar again in 2006. A few matters had arisen in the previous ten years that had required my involvement there: firstly, when CRH acquired the balance of the Ozarow shares, and then when Ozarow acquired other companies, expanding its business in Poland, and CRH expanded into Ukraine.

In 2006 some issues arose in Poland that required my involvement over the next few years; I had to travel there on a number of occasions so that I could advise the CRH executives there and back in Dublin. The physical changes in Warsaw since my first visit in 1995 were amazing; like Ireland, Poland quickly benefitted – to a major extent – from its EU membership, having joined in 2004. Even before that, through its pre-accession alignment process, there were considerable developments since its application to join in 1994. New apartment blocks, new hotels and new office blocks were being built all around the city, and the traffic, which was reasonable ten years earlier, was now constantly gridlocked – an obvious sign of increasing prosperity.

Another deal that I was involved in between 2006 and 2008 was a proposed joint venture in India. I never had to travel to India, but for a time it looked like I would; I obtained a visa to travel there in mid-2006. A few different possible transactions were being considered, and negotiations were slow, so it wasn't considered necessary for me to travel to India immediately. I had mixed views in the sense that I would have liked to see some of India, but at the same time I had heard many stories of persons getting ill while there. Accordingly, I had my reservations about travelling.

Progress was being made during 2007, and towards the end of that year I was requested to have a series of innoculations in preparation for a visit in early 2008. That visit was postponed and eventually cancelled, as it was possible for me to work on the deal remotely through conference calls to the lawyers in India and meetings back in Dublin with the CRH executives who were spending time in India.

One of the senior CRH executives became very ill while there and almost lost his life. Despite scrupulously observing hygiene advice, avoiding any water-based product and staying in the best hotels, he was struck by a very malevolent form of 'delhi belly', which it was believed had been contracted while on a train journey to Hyderabad. Any ambivalence that I had about travelling to India disappeared; the transaction, which was the acquisition of 50 per cent of an Indian cement company and the formation of a 50-50 joint venture, thankfully got completed without my attendance, and CRH proceeded to a long-term investment in India. I initially resented the fact that I had gone to the trouble of getting the series of innoculations, some of which were quite painful, but I quickly appreciated that the pain involved was minimal compared to what I might have suffered if I had been with my client on that train.

My brother-in-law was killed tragically in a work-related accident in County Kerry in February 2007. This, coming so shortly after my mothers's death, reinforced my sense of mortality, as I could see that family members of my own generation were now passing. This sense was exacerbated a couple of months later when our son, Shane, became very ill in Leeds, where he was researching and writing for his PhD at the University of Leeds. He developed empyema after a bout of pneumonia and gave us some very worrying weeks before he recovered. He had initially been detained in Leeds General Infirmary and effectively became imprisoned in a ward there because of an outbreak of MRSA. For this reason he couldn't be moved out for the necessary surgery.

I was helpless, which is not a state in which I feel comfortable or accustomed to, but there was nothing that I could do. After what seemed an eternity – but in reality was just thirteen days – he was moved out to St James's University Hospital, and a few days late he underwent four and a half hours surgery on his lung, which thankfully was successful. He was discharged eleven days later with a lung drain; this, in turn, was removed ten days later, and he commenced his recuperation. Nevertheless, as he could not travel for some time, his recuperation was in his apartment in Leeds. Accordingly, Mary – and I to a lesser extent – travelled regularly to Leeds over the course of a few months, until he was able to return to Howth to continue his recuperation at home. Indeed, Mary had spent much of her time in Leeds when he was ill – both before he went into hospital and while he was there – and was undoubtedly of enormous assistance to Shane during this difficult period. Other than delaying the completion of his doctoral thesis, and consequently the award of his PhD, by approximately a year, it doesn't seem to have had any adverse long-term effect on him. All the same, it was a very worrying and stressful time for us.

On 14 February 2008, I was called to a meeting in Cabinteely, County Dublin, in the then offices of CRH Europe Materials, the division of the group that managed the various CRH investments outside the USA and Ireland in building materials such as cement and concrete. A major issue had arisen in Secil, the Portuguese joint venture that CRH had entered into in 2004.

Matters had proceeded reasonably well with the venture. In late 2007, however, a major split in the joint venture with Semapa occurred, arising from a proposed investment that PQP wanted to have effected by Secil. This resulted in a series of meetings and conference calls as the crisis developed and PQP persuaded his nominees to the board to support him. The dispute escalated, and during the following period, relationships deteriorated between the two corporate partners. At Secil's AGM in Lisbon on 14 April 2009, which I attended with one of the CRH executives, there was open hostility. This hostility continued to the extent that, despite the best efforts of the professional managers, the ongoing operation of the joint venture company was compromised. I had a series of meetings in Lisbon and in Dublin over many months. Not long after this, Semapa served notice of termination of the joint venture with a claim to buy back, for a ridiculously low price, the shares sold to CRH in 2004.

Settlement negotiations ensued, but without success. In November 2009, CRH referred the dispute to the International Chamber of Commerce in Paris for arbitration, in accordance with those terms of the joint venture agreement that dealt with dispute resolution. There then followed more than eighteen months of intense preparation for the hearing, which took place over a period of two weeks in May 2011 in Paris.

I was supposed to be retired at this stage, but with this – and other work in relation to parts of the CRH business around the world – as well as other work that I had not anticipated, I was working as long and hard as at any time in my career. My plans to hand over my CRH responsibilities to some of my partners in Arthur Cox were put on the back foot, although to be fair, they did start to deal with any new matters that arose and were helping me with the current work – to that extent, I was slowly making my exit.

The arbitration result was strange. It held that Semapa was entitled to serve notice of termination of the joint venture, as there were obviously irreconcilable differences between the parties, but it ordered Semapa to pay a price that exceeded our expectations – particularly as by the time of the decision, most of the world economy had collapsed, and nowhere more than in Portugal.

CRH wasn't unhappy at the outcome of the arbitration, and Semapa was devastated at their pyrrhic victory. They appealed but eventually withdrew, as they realised that they had no chance of success.

After I retired as a full-time partner in August 2008, just before my sixtieth birthday, I went with Mary to our home in France for a long holiday; shortly after New Year 2009, we went on a holiday to Australia, visiting Sydney, Melbourne and Hobart, as well as much of the countryside between. I realised quickly that if I had gone to Australia when I was in my twenties, I would probably have stayed. I wasn't to know, though, as we returned from that trip, that over the next ten years I would visit Australia many more times for family reasons.

On my return from that first trip to Australia, the financial sector of the economy was unravelling rapidly. I became involved in the legal aspects of some interesting projects. Many of Arthur Cox's partners were heavily involved in various aspects of the government rescue of the financial sector and in the establishment of NAMA. It was a particularly busy time for Arthur Cox, and its partners played a very important role in advising the government on the stabilisation of the economy. This followed in the tradition of Arthur Cox himself, who had played a very important role in advising the first government of the state and the introduction of the first constitution.

As I explain later, I had taken on rugby administration roles in Clontarf and Leinster in anticipation of having little else to do after my retirement in 2008; however, I now found that I had to combine them with the extension of my professional life. On reflection, I think that I was very lucky at the way that matters transpired for me. Although I had planned for retirement at age 60 – and had wanted to retire – it would have been too early, and the work over the following few years after formal retirement was good for me and helped the transition. It was only after I retired as a partner and became a consultant – not working full time or every day – that I succeeded in finally transitioning my client base to other partners in Arthur Cox, thus achieving the target that I had set when I first joined that firm.

I still remained involved in the firm and sat on its conflicts and compliance committee until I finally left at the end of 2015. For the previous few years I had been attending the office only sporadically, so when I finally left, there was no yawning chasm in my life, and I believe that I was very lucky in how I managed my winding down. This coincided with when I slowed down my involvement with the Leinster Rugby management committee and left me totally free to travel the world and visit family and grandchildren.

As these reminiscences show, my law career was very different from most other lawyers in Ireland – and particularly in the last twenty years of it, I dealt with far more foreign lawyers than Irish ones. From my early dealings with the Wall Street lawyers in New York in 1983 – when I initially felt a little intimidated by their reputation – to the later dealings with European, Asian and American lawyers, I realised that Irish lawyers were well enough trained to practise successfully anywhere in the world, and thankfully many do so.

In June 2008, Louisa became engaged to Lee and set her wedding date for early June 2010. On Friday, 13 June 2008, Mary and I, along with Louisa and Lee, went to the Leonard Cohen concert in the Royal Hospital grounds in Kilmainham, which overlooked the River Liffey. Here, I enjoyed what was probably the best live concert that I have ever attended. The evening was balmy, the attending crowd were all in great form, and the music, singing and general presentation were exceptional. It was hard to believe that the great economic crash of 2008 was just around the corner.

On the following evening, Louisa and Lee hosted an engagement party in the penthouse area of Odessa, an entertainment venue in Dublin city centre. It was a fantastic evening, but towards the end, the staff started to cordon off part of the area; they apologised but told us that a celebrity VIP group was about to arrive and so they had to provide some privacy. That didn't cause any real inconvenience to us, as the area was fairly extensive anyway and some of Louisa's guests had already left.

It transpired that the celebrity group was Leonard Cohen's entourage – including his band and singers, his producer and his manager – who had just completed another performance in the Royal Hospital grounds. The cordons were quickly removed, and we mingled with, bought drinks for and chatted to Sharon Williams, the Gibb sisters, Javier Mas, Bob Metzger and the rest of the band until well into the morning; when we asked if L.C. himself would be coming, we were informed that he was already gone back to his hotel bed, completely exhausted. This completed a fabulous few days of celebrations for Louisa and Lee; one of my nephews, Eoin, himself a popular singer-songwriter, assumed that I had arranged the presence of Cohen's entourage at Louisa's party.

I hadn't, but when Louisa and Lee got married in June 2010, they had their wedding reception in a marquee in our garden. I had engaged Neil McMahon and Friends, a well-known jazz group, to play in the garden during the reception. Neil, who is the father of our next-door neighbour Lorraine, was himself famous and had played with the Jazz Coasters back in the 1970s. I was amazed when I realised that Neil had Louis Stewart as his guitarist for the afternoon; I considered Louis to be the best jazz guitarist in the world at the time. It was pure luck on my part that Neil had invited Louis to play with him that day, but I felt like a big-time concert impresario – and Eoin, my nephew, was now convinced that I was.

In the interim, I celebrated my sixtieth birthday. Mary and I hosted a birthday party in our garden a week after I retired as a partner, during which week I had a few retirement dinners and receptions with colleagues and clients. I had asked my namesake, the well-known traditional fiddler Paddy Glackin – who is not related to me but who I knew through my brother – if he would play with some of his friends at my birthday party. Paddy wasn't free that day, but he put me in touch with John Regan, another traditional musician, and John and his group played in a small marquee in our garden for a few hours. I also arranged that my friend Pat Trundle, one of my favourite entertainers, and his pal, the late Liam O'Farrell, would continue to entertain us afterwards, which they did for many hours that evening. This very enjoyable party helped me to face confidently into my seventh decade.

When my second daughter, Sinéad, got married in October 2013, to Alan, I did actually act as an impresario. A few weeks before the wedding, at a dinner for Sinéad, Alan, Declan and Kathleen (Alan's parents) and Mary and me in Carton House, where the wedding reception was to be held, I noted that Paul Harrington was playing the piano and singing in the dining room. I knew that Charlie McGettigan would be coming to the wedding as a friend and neighbour of Alan's parents, so I approached Paul, explained the position to him, and asked him if he would come down to the wedding reception after he finished his performance in the dining room on the night of the wedding. He and Charlie had won the Eurovision Song Contest in 1994 with their song 'Rock 'n' Roll Kids', and I hoped that he would perform it in a duet with Charlie on the night. He agreed after a little persuasion. On the night I explained to Charlie what I had arranged; he was surprised but agreed. When I brought Paul down and got both of them on the stage together – performing what is probably one of the greatest Eurovision songs – I felt that I could nearly charge the wedding guests an admission fee.

In March 2008, Shane was awarded his PhD for his research and thesis on 'The Role of the Fact/Value Distinction in Modern Moral Life'. I cannot say that I understood much of his thesis, but I recognised the quality of research and thinking that went into it. Nevertheless, I took great pride in reading it and felt the same way subsequently when we attended the graduation ceremony later that year and he was conferred with his degree.

In August 2012, Louisa went to Perth in Western Australia with Josh, her son, and was soon followed by Lee, her husband, to do her fellowship training in the Perth Children's Hospital. She was not long there when it was proposed to her that she become engaged in a research project with a view to preparing a thesis for a PhD. She agreed to do so and enrolled in the University of Western Australia School of Paediatrics and Child Medicine; her research and study was part time, as she continued her fellowship training, became a mother for a second time – with the birth of Lexi, her daughter – finished her training and was awarded a Certificate of Satisfactory Completion of Specialised Training (CSCST) by the Royal College of Physicians of Ireland, as well as her fellowship to the Royal Australasian College of Physicians. In this time, she also moved to Sydney to take up a position as a consultant paediatrician in respiratory medicine in Sydney Children's Hospital in Randwick. Nevertheless she persevered with her research and in the writing of her thesis, which she completed in July 2018, and was awarded her PhD. The thesis was titled 'The impact of *in utero* and early life factors on the respiratory health of young adults - 24 year review of the Perth Infant Asthma Follow-up study'.

Again, I was very impressed and proud to read the thesis and to attend the conferring ceremony in Perth in December 2019 – the conferring having been postponed, as Louisa had her third child, Cody, in summer 2019. I was even prouder when, at the conferring ceremony, Louisa's key finding was specifically acknowledged by the university vice chancellor in his address to the large crowd in attendance; he gave it as an example of the significant contribution to medicine that can be made by first class research. The finding was that the structure of the child's airways is laid down in the antenatal period and that this structure remains relatively stable throughout childhood, whereas postnatal lung growth may be more vulnerable to influence by external factors.

Sinéad also obtained her CSCST from the Royal College of Physicians of Ireland, having spent two years training in BC Children's Hospital in Vancouver, British Columbia, where she was awarded her fellowship. She has attained a postgraduate masters degree in science from the University of East Midlands in England and has published important research papers in paediatric endocrinology in Canada and in Ireland. She, too, is a consultant paediatrician, but unlike Louisa, who specialises in respiratory medicine, Sinéad specialises in endocrinology, which includes diabetes.

While I am very proud of each of my family, I can take little credit for their academic achievements. It was Mary who helped them with their homework from an early age while I was still at work; it was Mary who read to them at night, thus fostering a love of reading and study. I suppose that I did contribute in the sense that they will have realised from my example that hard work and ambition is needed to achieve success in a chosen field. I did consider myself as relatively intelligent, but I have no doubt that Shane, Louisa and Sinéad have an intelligence level well above mine. Nonetheless, it is their apparent happiness rather than their success per se that gives me more satisfaction than mere pride.

Life isn't all sweet-smelling roses, however, and no matter how well it seems to be proceeding, tragedy can strike from anywhere. The death, on 17 November 2011, of my nephew Colm – who was Mary's and my godson – in an accident near Manchester had a strange effect on me. Colm, who was a medical student in the University of Manchester, was cycling that morning from his apartment to Wythenshawe Hospital, where he was undertaking part of the usual medical student training, when he was killed in a collision with an articulated truck. His mother, Vee, received the news from the police while she was at work in her hospital in London; she called me at my office, assuming that I would be there. Margaret, my secretary, contacted me, briefly told me about the call from Vee and asked me to call her. I did, and at her request I called a policeman in Manchester whose name she had been given; Vee did not want to believe what she had been told, so she asked me to get the confirmation. Unfortunately, the policeman did confirm that it was Colm in the accident and that he was dead. I confirmed that to Vee, telling her that I would get to London that afternoon and come to her. She asked me to tell Gerry, her ex-husband and Colm's father, who had remarried and was then living in Melbourne.

I called Melbourne, where the time was almost midnight, and had to tell Gerry – my youngest brother – that Colm had been killed. Those two telephone calls with Vee and then Gerry were the two hardest calls that I have ever had to make, and I hope that I never have to do anything like that again.

I got the first flight that I could to London and went to Vee's house in West Acton. We were both in a state of shock; when I hugged her, Vee told me that it was supposed to be Colm hugging her at that time, as he was due to come home for a few days' break that evening. Unfortunately it was me and not Colm who arrived. I went by train to Manchester on the following day with Vee, a cousin of hers and a friend of Colm's to identify the body. I had heard of persons having to identify a body after an accident but had no real idea how traumatic that was, and I wouldn't wish it on anyone. We then went to see the location where the accident occured. I arranged a substitute for a function I was due to attend that night as president of Clontarf Rugby, stayed overnight in Manchester while Vee and the others went back to London, and on the following day I met Gerry and his family, who had flown from Melbourne on the first available flight after getting my news. I went back to the mortuary with them, then out to the accident location, and then flew home at 7.30 p.m. for a dinner in Howth connected to Mary's captaincy of Sutton Golf Club.

The time between a death and a funeral tends to be more drawn out in England than in Ireland, and particularly when a post-mortem has to be conducted. Over the next couple of weeks, I spent quite a lot of time in London, where Colm's body was brought, but came home on a few occasions, as life went on whether I was involved in it or not. It was a very difficult time for everyone; Colm was a particularly popular young man, and my family and the wider Glackin clan found it difficult to come to terms with the situation. I slept very little during those couple of weeks, and one night, while lying awake, I started composing a song for Colm. I had never before written a song, or even a poem, but I stuck with the task, got it down on paper, made a few adjustments and started humming the words to a few different compositions until I found something that sounded right.

On the evening that Colm was taken to church for an all-night vigil, I stood up and sang the song. It wasn't going to win any awards, but writing the song, expressing how I remembered Colm and then singing it in public was very good for me and my stress level. As the effective *paterfamilias* of the Glackins, which is a large extended family, but having never had to consider that role beforehand, I undertook more responsibility than perhaps I should have. Nonetheless, my inclination has always been to step into a breach if I see something that should be done, and on this occasion, it was as much to help me as to help Colm's immediate family.

Since then, other tragedies have shaken me and the confidence I had in my apparently charmed life. In particular, there was my first cousin Aidan Donnelly's diagnosis of dementia at a relatively young age; he died from Covid in a nursing home in early 2021, where he contracted the disease on the day he was due to be vaccinated. His younger brother, Kierie, was diagnosed with motor neurone disease a few years after Aidan's diagnosis and died recently, in December 2021. Another first cousin, Marcella – one of the McManus family from Enniscrone – was diagnosed with lung cancer a couple of years ago and recently died. I think I have learned not to take anything in life for granted or to assume that the good things in life will continue for ever. As I reflect, however, I'm not sure that this realisation has changed my approach to life – other, perhaps, than to live each day as if it is my last.

MALAHIDE, SUTTON, BAILY, CAP DE NICE AND OTHER PROPERTY INVOLVEMENTS

As I stated earlier, I agreed to buy my first house – 126 Millview Lawns, Malahide – within a few days of first seeing it in 1975 – and, indeed, within a couple of weeks of deciding that I wanted to buy a house. I probably looked at two or three other houses before I saw this one and decided that it would suit me perfectly. I bought a couple of beds, a sitting room suite and a fridge, all new, and then bought a kitchen table and chairs secondhand from one of my solicitor partners; all this, along with the other kitchen equipment that was sold with the house, and I was ready to move in.

Malahide was a charming, small village at the time, situated about 10 miles from the city centre. It was served by train and bus but I don't remember ever using either. My house was a ten-to-fifteen-minute walk from the village, but other than using Hogan's Supermarket or Mahon's, the newsagent at the Diamond, or visiting one of the pubs in the village – usually Gibney's, before it became very trendy – I didn't tend to go to the village. Malahide in the mid-1970s was very different from the Malahide now. The village was surrounded by farmland, most of which has since been built on, and although it was growing and had increased significantly in size in the previous ten years, it was still an old-fashioned village with more pubs than restaurants; it also had two small hotels.

I was working very hard in my office, with regular late nights; I sometimes worked weekends, in the office or from home. I did a little gardening if I was at home, but that really consisted of cutting the grass in the generous front and back gardens, and trying to control some of the shrubs that had come with the garden when I bought it. I didn't regularly cook dinner at home, and if I did, it tended to be out of a packet. Initially, after I moved to Malahide, I was either dining out with clients or more often calling home to Seafield Avenue and indulging in my mother's cooking. Later, with Mary, I would call to her apartment in Rathgar.

I don't know what my Malahide neighbours thought of me, but I didn't try to integrate myself into the community; most of them were young married couples with young children, and I was a young freewheeling bachelor. I did have very good neighbours on both sides of me, but as my house was the first semi-detached house after a few detached houses and bungalows with large gardens, I seldom saw the neighbours on that side. On the other side – the other half of my semi-detached – a young married couple lived. They were maybe a year or two older than me, but they were more settled and had two young sons.

Even though it was my bachelor pad, I didn't have too many all-night parties, and don't think that I played music too loud, so we had a harmonious relationship. On one occasion, in summer 1976, when I had been away for three weeks on my first long holiday with Mary, I returned home expecting to find my gardens had turned into meadows, as I had not had time to cut the grass for a few weeks before I left. Instead, I found that the front lawn had been cut and was looking better than I had ever managed with it.

I was puzzled, and when chatting to my neighbourhe next day about the 'For Sale' sign recently put up outside his house, he told me that he had taken the liberty of cutting my lawn, as he thought it would make his house more attractive to potential buyers than if his neighbour's garden looked scruffy and untended. He apologised, but I assured him that I had no objection – that if he ever wanted to come in and cut it again, he would be very welcome. He didn't need to do so again, as he sold his house and moved to another bigger house elsewhere in Malahide.

Even before Mary and I got married in June 1977, we had started to look at other houses. Mary liked the house in Malahide, but I wanted to move. Over a period of six months, we looked at quite a lot of houses in different parts of Dublin. One of our principal criteria was to be near the sea – as, indeed, I was in Malahide – or in the mountains, so we looked at houses from Portrane to Shankill and up to Enniskerry and Kilternan. We very nearly bought a very nice house in Shankill overlooking the sea, but after deciding to buy, I discovered that there was an old right of way that interfered with the property, reducing its privacy at the very least, so we pulled out. Shortly afterwards, we found the house at 56 Offington Lawn in Sutton, which we both loved; once we viewed it, we quickly decided to purchase it. It had been owned by an Arthur Cummings, who had died, so the sale was by the executors.

On the night that we moved in, in November 1977, I noticed that an English-registered car and caravan had parked across the road from our house. I didn't pay much attention to it, and it was gone by the following night. A neighbour informed me that the caravan had been parked in the driveway of our new house for many nights before we moved in; that it was owned by a son of Mr Cummings, who was upset that his father hadn't left the house to him in his will and the executors hadn't allowed him in there. He added that the son was quite strange, normally lived in England, and they presumed that he would go back there.

We didn't pay any more heed to the matter, and I had totally forgotten about it until a Dominic Cummings began to achieve media prominence in England as an adviser to the Prime Minister, Boris Johnson. The name was unusual, and it reminded me of the incident; I wondered if there was any connection. By a coincidence that we didn't become aware of until we had moved from Offington to Baily in 1986, that same Arthur Cummings had lived in the house immediately behind our new house before he moved to the house in Offington.

Offington Lawn was a very pleasant neighbourhood. It was part of the Offington Estate, the building of which had commenced in the early 1960s – by the Gough Brothers – on lands that were originally part of the Howth Castle Estate. Offington consisted of four or five avenues, on each of which were bungalows – on plots of approximately a third of an acre each – at different angles, so that there was a sense of space throughout. The design and layout were reputedly based on a residential estate in Florida that the Goughs had either worked on or had visited. It was situated at the foot of Howth Hill, which we could see from the front of the house, and was less than a ten-minute walk from the sea, so it was ideal and met our requirements.

There were gardens at front and back, and on this occasion I took more interest; unlike Millview Lawns, I envisaged staying here for a long time.

Our next-door neighbours, when we moved there in 1977, were in number 55 – Sandy Sorensen and his wife, who were both from the USA – and in number 57 – John Fanning and his wife and family. Across the road were the Langfords, Askeys, Quinns, Keoghs, Garveys, Mentons and Kavanaghs. Within a couple of years, the Sorensens sold and went back to the USA, and they were replaced by the O'Connells; the Fannings sold and were replaced by the Crawfords.

Shopping was done mainly at Sutton Cross, where Superquinn, Keogh's newsagents and Higgins butchers were situated. The old Superquinn, which had previously been a cinema before Feargal Quinn had converted it into a supermarket, was burned down in the early 1980s; it was replaced by a modern Superquinn and a shopping centre with a variety of retail shops and services. Up until that point, shopping facilities were very limited. The Marine Hotel, which is still there, was the local pub for many people who lived in Sutton; other than Suttonians Rugby Club near the railway station or the tennis club, there was no other watering hole between the Elphin on Baldoyle Road and Howth Harbour, and that remains the case still. Opposite the Superquinn shop, on the other corner on the Howth side of Sutton Cross, was a vacant site. It remained this way for many years while its owner tried to get planning permission to develop it. He did eventually do so, and a smaller shopping centre – Sutton Cross Centre – was added, so that Sutton Cross became a reasonably sized and serviced shopping hub. A new Chinese restaurant, the Pagoda, was also opened; it was the only restaurant in the area other than the hotel.

Sutton was well serviced with sports facilities, accommodating rugby, tennis, squash, golf, sailing and water-based sports. Sutton Cross is at the entrance to the Howth peninsula; it has sea inlets on both sides, a few hundred metres apart, so is itself effectively an isthmus. There were warnings back in 1977 that Howth could become an island within thirty years if the sea level rose by a relatively small amount. Forty-three years later, the same dire warnings are still being made, and I suppose if they are repeated every forty years for a few hundred years, they will eventually become reality.

Although we were very happy with our home in Offington Lawn, I developed an ambition to have a bigger house further up Howth Hill. Mary and I looked at a few houses that were of interest, but none justified making a move. Joe Kelly, a local auctioneer who knew that I was looking for a new property, called me one day and asked if I would be interested in a site as distinct from a house. Building a new house wasn't on my radar, but I agreed to look at it.

He explained the background: that the original owner had carved the site out of a large field, had applied for planning permission and had eventually received permission from the Minister for Local Government on appeal, it being prior to the introduction of An Bord Pleanála. He further explained that the original owner had agreed to sell the site to a lady who had applied for a revised planning permission and had received permission for a slightly larger house, but again after an appeal. He told me that the lady had changed her mind and no longer wanted to build a new house, hence she was selling on the site with the benefit of the planning permissions. He added that if I wasn't satisfied with the plans for the new house, I could apply to change it. He explained to me where it was, and I went to see it that evening. As I stated earlier, I fell in love with the site as soon as I saw it. In fact, I fell in love with the view from the approach road even before I saw the site.

I then showed it to Mary and persuaded her that we should pursue it. That was in late 1982. There followed negotiations with Joe on the price, which we eventually agreed – subject to a condition that an agreement had to be subject to my getting planning permission for a house that we wanted, as the house for which the previous planning permission had been obtained would not meet our requirements. Eventually all was agreed, and planning permission was obtained in late 1984 from An Bord Pleanála, which had rejected an appeal by a neighbour – the same neighbour who had objected to the earlier planning permissions. Interestingly this person who objected was living in the house previously lived in by Arthur Cummings, who had been our predecessor in Offington.

I then paid the purchase price and completed the purchase, and the plans were put out to tender. The successful tender, as recommended by my architect Jackie Reynolds, was about to be accepted, but that builder became insolvent and we were left slightly stranded. At that stage, Tony Murray, the managing director of Lark Developments, suggested that Lark could take over the tender and undertake the contract if he could have the company's quantity surveyor examine the details. Having examined it and satisfied himself on its feasibility, he was comfortable to proceed at the price that had won the tender. I was a little wary: being a director and shareholder of Lark, I didn't want to become involved in a conflict of interest. But after discussing it further with Tony and with my architect, I agreed to proceed. The builders went on site in November 1985, and we moved into the new house in August 1986.

When we started considering the design of the new house, the world was deep in the Cold War; Ronald Reagan was talking about Star Wars against the USSR, which was pre-perostroika and glasnost at that stage. A nuclear war was often mentioned as a possibility if matters between the USA and the USSR got out of control. As I had the space and was at an early stage of planning, I instructed the architect to provide for a nuclear shelter beside the garage, so the early drawings did include plans for this. Thankfully, the political situation was changing in the USSR. Gorbachev came to power, which quickly de-escalated tensions, and the USA responded in similar fashion. Consequently, in a short space of time the threat of nuclear war seemed to diminish and I never proceeded with the shelter.

Shortly after we moved to our new house, Hurricane Charlie – a major storm by Irish standards – struck, and we seemed to be right in the teeth of it. I remember thinking that the roof was going to fly off the house that night; indeed, we did lose some roof tiles, but the house stayed standing and passed its first test for us – as well as for the architect, Jackie, and the structural engineers who had designed it. The roof, or roofs, had been designed by Joe O'Donovan, an old Clontarf friend who later, as the motorway network was developed, achieved major professional recognition as the designer of bridges across the country; this included the beautiful new bridge over the river Boyne, now called the Mary McAleese Bridge. We have experienced many violent storms since then – as we are very exposed to the south and south-west – but we have the confidence now that the house will not fall down, something of which I was doubtful in the middle of that first storm.

Many of our neighbours, when we moved into our new home, were older than us; nevertheless, they were very friendly, and we settled in quickly. Indeed, Mary and I were the youngest couple on the road at that time, and for many years later. We hosted a garden party for our neighbours a couple of years after we moved in, but unfortunately most of the men who attended the party died within a dozen years of that gathering. The first was John Guinness, who died tragically in a fall on Snowdonia in Wales.

Two of our neighbours who were closest to us in age have since moved to homes elsewhere in Howth, so our neighbourhood has changed significantly and we are now the elders. Our immediate neighbours were a very delightful couple: Brian and Mary Boydell, who lived in Derlamogue. Brian was a composer and emeritus professor of music in Trinity College, and Mary was a world-renowned expert on glass and an adviser of Sotheby's in Ireland. We always enjoyed their company, and they were particularly good neighbours to us, but both Brian and Mary are dead for many years.

Thankfully, we are still living there in the same house – although it is only Mary and me there now, our three children having moved on. Arguably, the house and gardens are too big for just the two of us, but it has served us very well for nearly half of our lives and neither of us has lived anywhere else for a longer time.

I have enjoyed living on the Howth peninsula since 1977 – firstly in Sutton, and since 1986 in Baily. I have enjoyed it even more since my retirement, as I have been better able to enjoy its natural amenities and beauty. There is a myriad of great walks on the peninsula, including the cliff path, upper and lower; the Howth Castle grounds; Shielmartin Hill; the Ben of Howth; and Howth Harbour, the village and the two piers. These along with its sporting amenities – sailing, golf, tennis and various football pitches – readily lend the area to an outdoor life. This is facilitated by the fact that it is virtually the driest part of Ireland, largely caused by the rain shadow effect of the Dublin Mountains across Dublin Bay.

Howth is a very old part of Dublin, with connections to the Viking era – and, indeed, beforehand, as witnessed by the old monastic ruins. In fact, the earliest mention of the Howth peninsula may be that on a map attributed to Ptolemy in the second century, when it is referred to as 'Edri Deserta' and portrayed as an island. As the Romans are not reputed to have landed in Ireland – and accordingly, Ptolemy was observing it from a ship – one can readily understand why he thought it was a deserted island. There is evidence of human habitation on Howth peninsula as far back as 2200 BC.

Howth Castle dates back to Norman times, and the same St Laurence family resided there until recently. In the eighteenth and early nineteenth century, Howth Harbour was the main embarkation point for shipping to

England. The building of the Bull Wall by Captain Bligh had an adverse effect on Howth due to changes in sandbars, and although it remains the main fishing port in Dublin and has a large marina for recreation sailing, it lost its role as an embarkation port for England and Wales many years ago.

King George IV, when visiting Ireland in 1821, landed in Howth en route to Dublin city; his footprints were recorded in concrete at the time, and are still preserved there on the west pier. Interestingly, it was very close to the spot where the Howth gun-running took place in 1914, when the *Asgard* unloaded 1,500 rifles to members of Fianna Éireann; many of these guns, which were reputedly used originally in the Franco-Prussian War of 1870–71, were used by the Irish Volunteers in the attack on the GPO, which commenced the Easter week rebellion in 1916.

James Joyce, in *Ulysses*, used Howth Hill as the location for part of Molly Bloom's imaginative and erotic musings during her famous soliloquy. What's more, Howth is referred to in some of the old Irish myths about Fionn Mac Cumhaill, the Fianna and Diarmuid and Gráinne.

Being situated on a peninsula and on a hill, there are many spectacular views from different parts of Howth Hill and from the houses dotted around it. On the north and east sides, there are great views of Ireland's Eye, Lambay Island, St Patrick's Island and up the coast as far as the Mourne Mountains. From some parts of the hill, which at its highest is 171 metres, it is possible to see the Welsh coast and Snowdonia, although admittedly that is on rare occasions and only when the light is perfect. Other parts have great views of the Baily Lighthouse, the approach to Dublin Bay and as far down the coast as Wicklow Head. From our house, we can see from Wicklow Head right up past Bray Head, Killiney and Dalkey to Dún Laoghaire and along the coast up to the mouth of the Liffey and around the north side of Dublin Bay and the Bull Island. It may not be unique in the world to have such a scenic facility so close to a capital city, but it isn't common, and it is a great privilege to be able to enjoy it.

Mary and I had considered, on a number of occasions, buying a holiday home. We had looked at homes in many parts of Ireland, and in other countries, but without ever being serious about it. Around 2000 or 2001, however, we focussed on buying in France and then wondered where in France we would look at. I was initially attracted to the Biarritz area, but having spent a holiday there, I soon changed my mind. I had been to Nice and the Côte d'Azur on a few occasions on short holidays or business, and we decided to look in that area. In fact, it was the first place that I had gone on holidays with Mary, in 1976; although not imagining then that I would ever be in a position to buy a property there, when the opportunity came later, I thought that it would be a nice location. I had recently realised a little capital when Iretex Group plc, the company of which my pal, Paul McLaughlin, was chief executive; was taken over, and I had made a nice profit.

We looked at a few properties in Nice, Cannes and Èze, and finally decided to buy two adjoining apartments in a new development at Palais de la Méditerranée, just behind the Promenade des Anglais in Nice. I acquired two, as there were no three-bedroom apartments in the development; I envisaged knocking the wall between the two apartments, which had two bedrooms and one bedroom respectively. We bought the apartments off the plans, paid the deposit with the profit I had recently made on the Iretex shares, and waited for the building to be completed. I arranged a mortgage in France for the balance of the purchase price, and in 2003 we took possession of the apartments. I didn't say anything about merging the two apartments until some time after I had paid the deposits; I was told that it wasn't possible to do what I had planned, so I ended up with two separate apartments.

Nice is itself a beautiful city, and is the capital of the Côte d'Azur. It is a pleasant size, with all the cultural amenities that one expects to find in a city – lots of museums, art galleries, theatres, concert halls, shopping areas – as well as the amenities of a beach side town, where a beach runs for 7 kilometres along the Promenade des Anglais, the southern perimeter of the city. At the same time, it is at the foot of the Alpes-Maritimes, and within fifteen minutes you can get from the city centre into magnificent mountains and valleys. It has easy access to Monte Carlo and the Ligurian region of Italy, as well, of course, as the more westerly parts of the French Riviera, such as Antibes, St Paul de Vence, Juan-les-Pins and Cannes.

We enjoyed some holidays there over a few years, and I was delighted that my mother and some of her regular travelling companions were able to stay there for a holiday in the year before she died. Nevertheless, I wasn't satisfied with the apartments. I could hear the sea and the waves crashing on the shore, but I couldn't see them – the views from the apartments were limited to other buildings and a glimpse of the mountains behind Nice. I realised that I had made a mistake in relation to those apartments; even though we loved Nice, its buildings, its restaurants, the sea and its proximity to many amenities, including ski slopes, I had – from an early stage after taking possession – started looking at alternatives.

Being used to having beautiful views at home, which I always found relaxing, it was an essential for me to have views in a holiday home. Having looked at many alternatives and left my name with many estate agents, I eventually found what I was looking for in an apartment in a relatively small complex at Cap de Nice, which is right on the sea at the bottom of Mt Boron. It had three bedrooms, a shared swimming pool and the convenience of lovely walks along the sea and in Mt Boron forest; it was also close to Nice city centre and within walking distance of Villefranche, a beautiful village by the sea. But most of all it had magnificent views of the Mediterranean Sea and the Baie des Anges – a bay that spans from Cap Ferrat to Cap d'Antibes – over to the Alpes-Maritime and back along the coast to the centre of Nice. The French have a word for the views: *époustouflante*, which most closely translates as 'breathtaking'. This is the term that the estate agent used when first describing it to me. In many respects, the area around Cap de Nice is very similar to the Baily area of Dublin, but with more sun.

Although Mary and I often travel to different parts of the world on holidays and to visit family, Cap de Nice is our favourite holiday destination; we go there regularly, but perhaps not as often as I originally envisaged. Mary goes more often than I, and at least once a year she goes with her old college friends, who now call themselves the Nice girls.

Most of my other involvements with property were through Lark Developments and its subsidiaries, which developed and built housing estates in the Greater Dublin area, including Crestwood, Ashbourne; Beaufield, Maynooth; Ballyowen, Lucan; St John's Wood, Clontarf; St Helier's Copse, Stillorgan; Kenmare House, North Great Georges Street (in the city centre); Westminster Hall and The Hedgerows, Foxrock; The Maltings, Bray. They also undertook renovation projects on existing houses and commenced industrial estate development at Ballycoolin, County

Dublin. I left the company in the late 1990s and sold my shareholding to Tony Murray, some of whose children joined him in the building business. Nevertheless, for nearly twenty years I took an active part in the company as a shareholder and director, and I remain very proud of the developments that were carried out.

TRAVELS IN IRELAND AND AROUND THE WORLD

I have referred to some of my travels as they arose in the earlier chapters of this memoir, but as travel has become a significant part of my life, I decided to describe some of my trips in more detail. Most of my travels in Ireland have been by train or car, although we travelled to my grandparents' home in Strokestown for the first twelve years of my life mostly by bus – until my father bought his first car, a Standard Triumph, registration number LYI 440. Not particularly big, but big enough to carry nine of us. I don't remember much of those early car journeys, but I do remember that my father bought a larger car a couple of years later, a Ford Cortina Estate, registration number XZE 366. It had a rear compartment, or boot, where two or three of us would sit or lie in relative comfort.

The roads then, and until recent times, were very different from the motorway system that we now enjoy around the country. The road trip that I most often undertook after I got married was to Kilworth in north Cork, to visit Mary's parents, Jim and Nell. After driving through Dublin city to get to the start of the Naas dual carriageway, which in itself could be an ordeal, the road passed through Naas, Newbridge, Kildare, Monasterevin, Ballybrittas, Portlaoise, Abbeyleix, Durrow, Cullahill, Johnstown, Urlingford, Littleton, Horse and Jockey, Cashel, New Inn, Cahir, Kilbehenny and Mitchelstown; after that, a couple of miles before Fermoy, there was a turn off to Kilworth. Many of these towns had traffic lights and road junctions that caused traffic tailbacks and delays. Now I can go from the roundabout where the M1 meets the M50 to the turnoff for Kilworth and Fermoy – and, indeed, on to the Dunkettle Exchange roundabout just outside Cork – without a traffic light or stop, with merely a slowdown for two toll booths. The change, which happened gradually at first, with some towns initially getting a bypass, accelerated in the 1990s and early 2000s, and has made travelling around much easier – but perhaps not as interesting, until one gets off the motorways and encounters the local winding roads again.

As I have indicated, after my trip to Holyhead when I was 4 or 5 years old, I didn't leave Ireland again until I was 18 or 19. My mother's brother, Tommy, lived in Liverpool, and her aunt and cousins lived in Wallasey, so I went to Liverpool by boat on a couple of occasions and stayed with them for a few days. On my second visit I went from Liverpool to Llangollen in North Wales for the Eisteddfod, travelling initially by bus and most of the way by hitchhiking. I had been at a Fleadh Cheoil in Enniscorthy a few months earlier and thought that the Eisteddfod might be similar, but in fact it was quite different. It was mainly choirs rather than folk groups – choirs being more common in Wales. I did enjoy myself, but as I was on my own and had no understanding whatsoever of the Welsh language, which was being used everywhere, I did not stay overnight; instead, I hitchhiked back to Liverpool that evening. The Eisteddfod seemed more serious than the Fleadh Cheoil, with less fun and craic, but perhaps this reflected the difference between the typical Irish and Welsh character. I have been back in Liverpool on many occasions since, to visit family or to watch Liverpool at Anfield, but that was the one and only time that I hitchhiked.

I was in London for the first time in the following summer, when I had to sleep rough at a tube station for a night. I have been back in London on numerous occasions since then, for business, family or sporting visits, but have never had to repeat my first night's experience. Despite my many visits, I have never really got to know London, and would still be confused if I was dropped in the centre and asked to find my way on foot to Buckingham Palace, St Paul's Cathedral or Hyde Park. For many years I tended to stay in the Knightsbridge or Kensington areas; my favourite Italian restaurant anywhere was Verbanella on Beauchamp Place, until I found Giambelli 50th in New York. I like London as a city to visit, but I cannot imagine feeling at home there.

Wales is the nearest part of Britain to Dublin; I have been in different parts of Wales on many occasions, but it has never really impressed me. I have found Cardiff and Swansea dull and uninteresting. Though Cardiff has the magnificent Millenium Stadium, where I have been lucky enough to see some great rugby games, it is not enough to enliven the rest of the city. Neither Holyhead nor Pembroke, where the ferries from Ireland tend to go, seem welcoming or interesting, and even though I have been in both ports on many occasions, I have never stayed there longer than a few minutes, unless queueing for a delayed ferry. In early March 2020, just before Covid 19 restrictions, we stayed for a night in Llangennith, on the Gower Peninsula; we were on our way back from Thorverton in Devon, where Shane lives, to Pembroke, where we embarked on the ferry back to Ireland. The Gower Peninsula is interesting and Llangennith picturesque, but one night was enough.

The part of Britain that I most enjoy is Scotland. My first visit to Scotland was on my honeymoon, and I have been back on numerous occasions since. Edinburgh is a beautiful city – my favourite in Britain. I have always loved the city centre, with Princes Street overlooked by the imposing Edinburgh Castle, as well as the Royal Mile in the Old Town. There are also the lovely Georgian buildings and squares, such as St Andrew Square and St George's Square in the New Town, which was built in the eighteenth and early nineteenth centuries.

Scotland is renowned for its scenery, its islands and – more importantly for me – its many superb golf links. My first visit was in 1977, and when I next returned in 1983, the Sabbath obversance laws had been repealed and a Scottish Sunday seemed more like home, where Sunday is for leisure rather than strictly for worship and prayer. I have had some great fun in different parts of Scotland and hope to get back again soon.

My first trip to the USA was in 1980, when we went to visit Mary's brother and his wife in Port Townsend in Washington State, north-west of Seattle. During our holiday we drove around the Olympic Peninsula and then over to eastern Washington. On the Olympic Peninsula, we visited Lake Quinault and came close to Cape Flattery, the most north-western point of mainland USA. While walking through thick woodland near Lake Quinault and going off beaten paths, it occurred to me that it was probably the first time that I had stepped somewhere that perhaps nobody had walked previously. It was very remote and spectacularly beautiful, and the Lake Quinault Lodge, where we stayed overnight, had magnificent views.

When we went to eastern Washington, we visited Leavenworth, a small town in the Cascade Mountains that is modelled on an Alpine village; we then went to Winthrop, which is an Old West town with western-style store fronts, wooden boardwalks and swinging half doors into the local bar or saloon. The first home in Winthrop was built in 1891, and it had been less than one hundred years since the first permanent white settlers had arrived in the area in search of gold. We then went to see the Grand Coulee Dam on the Columbia River, which is one of the largest structures built by mankind. It required 12 million cubic yards of concrete in its construction, sufficient to build a highway from Seattle to Miami – 3,300 miles. It was very impressive; it was 550 feet high and nearly a mile long. We had a Gordon Lightfoot tape playing in the 'suburban', as Jim called it – or SUV, as it would now be called – while we drove for a couple of days. Any time that I now hear Gordon Lightfoot, my memory brings me back to those rolling roads through the Cascades.

Before returning home, Mary, Shane and I visited San Francisco and had a lovely stay there, seeing many of the city sights. We went out to Alcatraz Island, the former federal prison, by boat, which took us around San Francisco Harbour and under the bridges.

When I first visited New York and Boston a few months later and was talking to some locals, they were very surprised that I had been to the west coast and explained that only a small percentage of Americans had been to both coasts. When I was next in Port Townsend, in 1990, having been in many parts of the USA in the interim years, including Florida, Washington, DC, New York and Cape Cod, I got the same reaction from the west coasters, very few of whom had been to the east coast. I was less surprised this time; I had read in the meantime that only a small percentage of US citizens had a passport, as they never envisaged themselves leaving the US for any reason. I thought that they might have travelled around the USA, but it seems that the majority never leave their own state, whatever about travelling from coast to coast. This strange fact was borne out again recently in surveys taken during the 2020 US presidential elections; these showed that supporters of Trump were more unlikely to leave their own state than those who intended to vote for Biden. Travel broadens the mind and shows the traveller that the world isn't all the same as home – that people in places away from home are not all the same. If more US citizens travelled around the world, the USA – and the world – might be a better place.

Since those early trips to the USA, I have been lucky to visit the country on many more occasions. I have been in Florida; New Orleans in Louisiana;

Atlanta in Georgia; Los Angeles, Orange County, Santa Barbara, Carmel, the Napa Valley and Yosemite in California; Greenwich in Connecticut; Crestwood in New Jersey; Nashville in Tennessee; and Chicago in Illinois. This is not to mention the various occasions I've visited New York, San Francisco and Seattle. The USA is a vast country, but I find it perplexing. In lots of ways, I do not understand why it is still called the United States – in reality, it is very divided. For example, citizens in South Dakota have little or nothing in common with those in Manhattan or San Francisco. Yet it survives, and perhaps its diversity is a strength, even though it doesn't seem so at election times.

Would I have travelled as much as I have if I had not met Mary? When I did meet her in 1975, I had not been further than London, and was perfectly content taking my holidays and leisure breaks in different parts of Ireland. I particularly loved the west coast, from Donegal down to Kerry, through Sligo, Mayo, Galway and Connemara, and on to Clare. I remember a friend telling me in the mid-1970s about a great trip to Paris. When I asked him what was great about it, he explained that he and his friends had found a great pub on the first night that served lovely pints of Guinness, so they spent their time there. My reaction was to think, 'regardless of how lovely the pints were in that Paris pub, they could not have been nicer than the pints in hundreds of pubs around Ireland, so why go to the trouble of going to Paris for pints.' That didn't make sense to me.

Mary had travelled a lot before she met me, having interrailed in Europe and worked as an au pair in France while in college, then living for two years in British Honduras (since renamed Belize) in Central America while working as a volunteer teacher. She had availed of the opportunity, travelling regularly to Mexico and then around much of South America. Shortly after I met her, she went on a month's trip to the Greek Islands with a friend. I quickly realised that if I wanted to impress her and be part of her life, I was going to have to be more adventurous – to be prepared to travel beyond the west coast of Ireland and London.

Thankfully, I have since had the opportunity to travel extensively to most parts of the world. I have had some great experiences and some not so great. There are still many places that I would like to visit, and some that I have already visited but would like to go back to. We had planned to visit Vietnam and Cambodia with four friends in March 2020, but this was cancelled because of the outbreak of Covid 19. I have been fascinated by Vietnam since the war of the 1960s and early 1970s, even though – other than reports in newspapers at the time of the war – I did not read much about the country until recently. The more I've read, the more determined I've become to see the country and meet more of its people.

New Zealand wasn't high on my wish list of countries to visit, but having spent a few days in Auckland on our way from Los Angeles to Sydney a few years ago, I moved it up my list. I now know that I would love to visit again and see much more of the north island, as well as the south. My grandson Josh, who travelled to Los Angeles from Sydney via Auckland on Air New Zealand, informed me that the staff on this flight were the nicest people he had met on flights anywhere in the world – and though only 7 years old at the time, he was a very experienced traveller. He, his sister Lexi and his parents, Louisa and Lee, were on the same flight as us on their return leg, and again he expressed the same. My experience of the flight was no different, and I was delighted to note that the people we met in and around Auckland were all very friendly and welcoming.

I have been in Warsaw on many occasions, on business trips, but have not travelled around Poland to see more of the country. It is on my list to do so with Mary, and to show her Warsaw also.

Istanbul is a very interesting city that I have visited twice: once on business, and once to see Liverpool defeat AC Milan in the European Champions League final. Istanbul was originally known as Constantinople, and only became Istanbul in 1930. As Constantinople, it was the capital city of the Roman–Byzantine Empire and then the Ottoman Empire; it has existed as a city for nearly 1,700 years. My opportunities to sightsee while there were limited, but anything I did see was definitely worth a revisit.

One of the few package holidays that I have gone on, other than skiing trips, was in 1978 to Rhodes. The lasting memories I have of that holiday were firstly the heat of the sand on the beach near our hotel, which was unbearable on bare feet, and secondly the unquenchable thirst I experienced. The latter caused me to suffer from dehydration; I had never previously experienced it, and I tried all sorts of drinks to quench the thirst, including water, unusual fruit juices, Metaxa brandy, retsina wine, Coca-Cola and 7 Up, but nothing worked for a few days. One evening after dinner, Mary and I were in a bar with some others we had met on our holiday; it was there that I spotted some bottles of Guinness. I disliked bottles of Guinness, but because it was in Rhodes, I decided to try one. It was horrible, but I persisted and finished it. Amazingly, it gave me the first relief from dehydration that I had in those few days. I knew that Guinness had medicinal qualities and was often prescribed to nursing mothers, but I hadn't realised how effective it was as a remedy for my ailment. I didn't need to keep taking it once my dehydration was resolved, but I ensured that I never got as thirsty again.

The other package holidays that we went on were to Gran Canaria. We went on a few occasions over the winter in the early 1980s, staying in an apartment complex in Puerto Rico de Gran Canaria. There wasn't much to do there other than swim in the pool or lie on the artificial beach and soak up the sun, but that is what we wanted; it was a welcome break in the middle of winter. On the second occasion, there was a scare on the outward flight, an hour or so into our journey. The plane lost height very suddenly and seemed to plummet out of control. Mary had fallen asleep and didn't notice it, but I was sipping a drink and noticed when the glass shot up and over me. It probably lasted less than a couple of minutes, but it seemed a long time before the drop ended and the plane levelled out.

One of the air hostesses went up the cabin to the cockpit and emerged a couple of minutes later. She tried to explain over the intercom that the air pressure system had failed and the pilot had to take the plane down immediately, but she was out of breath from the lack of pressure; in gasping for air as she spoke, she caused panic among some passengers, who thought that she was nervous and frightened. The pilot then came on the intercom and explained what had happened – that he had to return and fly low over the sea but would try to land in Cork in less than an hour. The speed of the plane reduced significantly; we seemed to be limping back over the Atlantic. As we approached land, he updated us and said that he was going to try to get back to Dublin, as there was some problem preventing his landing in Cork. He eventually got us back to where we took off from, and we disembarked.

Aer Lingus were very apologetic, offering three alternatives to the passengers: firstly, they could have a flight later that day to anywhere on the Aer Lingus schedule; secondly, they could have a full refund, take their luggage and go home; or thirdly they could wait for an hour or so as the plane was checked and the faulty part replaced, then fly out to Gran Canaria as originally planned. Mary and I quickly decided that we weren't going home, as we had a babysitter in place and had been looking forward to getting away for a week. We then decided to go ahead with the flight to Gran Canaria, which we did. The vast majority of the passengers on the original flight seemed to opt to take their luggage and go home, a few seemed to go for an alternative destination, and the remainder joined us in going to Gran Canaria. This second flight had a new crew, as the crew of the first flight were still quite upset. Nevertheless, I had reckoned that Aer Lingus would not send the plane out again unless their mechanics were absolutely certain that everything was in order.

I have mentioned the USA, but I have also been to Canada on a number of occasions – most often to Vancouver in British Columbia. Vancouver is one of my favourite cities in the world, and my favourite in North America. It is largely because of its location, with the mountain backdrop dominating most parts; however, it is also the manner in which the city has developed to take advantage of its closeness to the mountains and the sea, the latter coming right up through the city and providing beautiful walks along the seawall. Its highrise apartment blocks never seem to dominate the landscape, as they themselves are dominated by the mountains.

Mary and I spent Xmas 2016 there with Sinéad and Alan, and their son Charlie, and Shane joined us for a week from Devon. Nonetheless, I have mostly been there in summer or autumn. Mary and I took a forty-minute trip on a seaplane. It took off from the water using the sea as the runway and then took us over the city, up into the snow-clad mountains and over Vancouver Island, and then landed back on the sea and taxied to its berth. I found the entire trip fascinating and even a little scary; the tiny plane flew through valleys towards the mountains, only seeming to climb over or curve away at the last second. Nausea did set in for the last few minutes of the trip; if I was to do it again, I would book a shorter flight.

I have also been lucky enough to see part of Central America and South America. In 1998, we had a family holiday in Central America, staying in Playa del Carmen on the Yucatan Peninsula. It was a relatively quiet resort at the time, but in the subsequent twenty years it has developed rapidly and is now well known. While there, we took a trip to Cozumel, which is a small island in the Caribbean Sea, off the coast of Mexico. I tried snorkelling, which was fascinating – the seabed seemed to be coral, and it was full of tropical multicoloured fish. I didn't have the courage to swim into the caves to join Shane, Louisa and Sinéad, however; they were much better swimmers than me, and much braver.

We also hired an air taxi to take us from Playa del Carmen to Chetumal, a small town on the border with Belize – a trip of about 300 kilometres. Once there, I hired a car to take us to Corozal in Belize, which was about 25 kilometres away. The car was at least forty years old, an old American Dodge. I asked if it had air conditioning, as the outside temperature was very high; I was informed that it was not necessary, as the car didn't have windows. It couldn't go faster than 40 kilometres an hour. It was just as well, as it was falling apart; it didn't seem to have any suspension system, so it rattled constantly. We reached our destination, and Mary showed us where she had lived for two years in the early 1970s. We stayed overnight in a motel owned by the son of the lady that she used to board with, and with some difficulty found a restaurant or cafe for dinner. On the following day, I went for a drive into the countryside; I didn't go far, however, as I didn't trust the car, and the road was poor. Instead, we went on a boat trip to an offshore island, where we spent a short time. We did have a pleasant couple of days, but Louisa felt miserable and was later diagnosed with glandular fever.

On our return via the air taxi, we stayed another few days in Playa del Carmen. We then flew to Cancun, where we spent another week before returning home.

I have been to Argentina on two occasions with Mary. On the first, we visited Buenos Aires and Iguaza Falls, which is actually situated where three countries meet – Argentina, Brazil and Paraguay. It is one of the wonders of the world; I have never met anyone who has been there and was not impressed. On our second trip, we visited Buenos Aires again, but also Patagonia, the Pampas and Tierra del Fuego; two of my sisters, Bernie and Thérèse, joined us.

Argentina is another of the places I have been to that I would like to revisit. It is vast, and each region has its own many attractions. On our first visit to Buenos Aires, we came across the protest by the Madres de la Plaza de Mayo. At first, we did not know what it was, but we noted its dignity and the white headcoverings the protestors wore. When we were told what it was, I remembered reading about the protest some years beforehand. They were the mothers of the disappeared – the mothers of those who were arrested or kidnapped by the military junta that ruled Argentina from 1976 to 1983, were never heard of again, and were erased from public records. Most of the disappeared were young students, and when any bodies were found afterwards, it was realised that they had been tortured before being murdered. In fact, only a small number of the thousands who had disappeared were found, and evidence was subsequently given that many were killed by being taken in military aircraft and thrown into the ocean.

On our second visit to Buenos Aires, in 2018, we attended a St Patrick's Day celebration in Plaza del Mayo. The event had been recommended to me by Sandra Gutrejde of BA Travel Guides, and we met her there with her husband. A large crowd was addressed by Eoghan Murphy, then an Irish government minister, from a stage that was being used for a concert of Irish music and dancing. Eoghan was very impressive, speaking in fluent Spanish. I spoke to him briefly afterwards; he told me that later that evening, he was meeting for dinner with a fourth or fifth cousin who lived in Buenos Aires and had contacted him, Eoghan's great great grandfather having emigrated to Argentina in the nineteenth century. I told Eoghan that I was in Argentina to try to find where my great grandfather had lived and worked in the 1860s, but that I had no known relations still in Argentina.

The folk group on the stage sang many well-known Irish songs, and when they sang 'In Dublin's Fair City', I joined in heartily. The man standing beside me commented that it was great to be able to celebrate St Patrick's Day so far from home. I agreed with him and learned in our subsequent chat that the man lived in Clontarf, on Castle Avenue, opposite the rugby grounds. He was on a sightseeing holiday in South America and by chance happened to come across the concert as he walked around Buenos Aires. I was surprised at the coincidence, and called over my sisters and Mary, introducing them to the man and explaining to them that he lived on Castle Avenue. Just then, four ladies were passing through the crowd, and one of them turned and said, 'Did I hear you say Castle Avenue, Clontarf?' I replied that she did; she said that she grew up on Stiles Road, Clontarf, which is about three hundred yards at most away from Castle Avenue. She added that she left there when she finished school in the early 1960s. We didn't get to chat further, as she was rushing to catch up with her friends, who had continued walking on. Neither I nor any of us there could believe the double coincidence and the randomness of the meeting in Plaza del Mayo.

In the year 2000, I went on a trip to Bahrain with a group from Clontarf Rugby. Two teams, management, physios, doctors and a large contingent of supporters made the trip. It was my first visit to the Middle East, and although I have since been in the airports at Doha, Dubai and Abu Dhabi, I have never stayed in any of those locations. Bahrain was interesting, and we were treated very well by our hosts in Bahrain rugby club, many of whom were Irish ex-patriates who worked for Aer Lingus or Aer Rianta (the latter operating the duty-free shop in the airport). Most lived in a compound or enclosed estate, and I got the impression from them that they seldom socialised or associated with the locals; instead they stuck to other Irish or ex-patriates from other countries, including Britain, Australia and New Zealand. I played golf at Awali Golf Club, which is the oldest golf course in the Gulf area, having been founded in 1957. What I remember most are the bunkers, which seemed to be at least a hundred yards long, and the greens, which were actually 'browns' – but that wasn't too surprising, as the course was built in the desert.

On the Friday night, there was a large influx of men in our hotel bar wearing the traditional Saudi attire – a long white robe and red headdress. It was explained to us that these men were from Saudi Arabia, which was linked by a bridge to Bahrain, and that they were a small representation of a large group that came every weekend to drink and chase women, alcohol being illegal in Saudi Arabia.

On one occasion we went into the centre of Manama, the capital city of Bahrain, to shop and experience the traditional bazaar; it was great fun, as I wasn't used to shopping on my own and haggling over prices. Many of us bought jewellery for wives and daughters from a gold merchant who had been recommended to us by some of our hosts. We seemed to be getting bargains, but I never checked back in Dublin whether or not this was actually the case.

On another occasion, I had reason to go to Israel. I travelled through Amsterdam on KLM, as there were no direct flights from Dublin to Tel Aviv. At Amsterdam, I learned that the flight to Tel Aviv was delayed. That in itself did not concern me, as it often occurred when a trip had multiple stops; however, as often happens, the delay was underestimated, and it was late in the evening when we departed. We were a few hours into the flight when we were informed by the pilot that the plane would be diverting to Malta. The explanation given was that because of the delay, the flight would have arrived in Tel Aviv at a time that would force the crew to stay there overnight due to the limit on their duty hours. As the second intifada had broken out in Israel, the KLM crew were not prepared to overnight there. By stopping in Malta, they would not have to go to Tel Aviv; another plane would take us to Tel Aviv and then immediately return to Malta. I knew before I left home that there was an intifada in Israel, but I didn't pay too much attention to it and it didn't unduly bother me.

The extra delay meant that it was nearly 4 a.m. local time when I got to my hotel room, and I knew that I had to be up fairly early in the morning. After meeting some people in Tel Aviv, I went on a tour to Acre – or Akko, as it is known locally. It is situated on the Mediterranean Sea, approximately 115 kilometres north of Tel Aviv and about 15 kilometres south of the Lebanese border. The route took me close to Nazareth, the Golan Heights and the Sea of Galilee, but I didn't actually see them. Acre is a walled port city and amongst the longest continuously inhabited settlements on Earth, having been occupied since the Middle Bronze Age. It was the last city held by the Crusaders in the Middle East before it was captured by the Muslims in AD 1291. I went down to the old citadel, which is well preserved and overlooks the fishing port – not unlike citadels on the northern shore of the Mediterranean, with which I was more familiar.

While there and looking at the citadel, one of the sightseers with me received a call from home, wondering if we were safe. Apparently a bomb had been detonated in Jerusalem; there were casualties, which had led to riots and arrests. One of the Israelis with me then made a call and confirmed what we had heard. I didn't know how far Jerusalem was from Tel Aviv; I was told that it was 67 kilometres – much the same as the distance between Dublin and Newry – so I didn't feel any more endangered than I did by the bombing in Newry and surrounding areas over the previous years.

On the way back from Acre, I stopped outside Haifa, the largest port in Israel, the city of which is built on tiers up the side of Mount Carmel. There is a magnificent view from the top, over the landscaped terraces of the Baha'i gardens down to the gold-domed Shrine of the Báb, but we didn't stay there for long. I then went back to my hotel in Tel Aviv and out for dinner in a nearby restaurant. Tel Aviv seemed very lively that Friday night – not unlike any cosmopolitan city at a weekend.

On the following morning, I headed to the airport for the flight home, this time via London. There was a heavy army presence at the airport, and I had considerable difficulty getting through security. I was questioned by three different soldiers about where I had been, who I had met and why I was going home via London, having arrived from Amsterdam. The fact that I was Irish seemed to exacerbate the situation – the first time in my travels that being Irish seemed to be a disadvantage – but I was eventually waved through. I ran to get to the departure gate, as I was late and didn't want to miss the plane, possibly having to go through the same interrogation again after spending another night there.

Some of the most spectacular landscapes that I have seen were in South Africa. Mary and I went there in 2010, with a group, to play golf and to see part of the country. We started our trip with a few days in Cape Town, where we did the usual tourist things: visiting the V&A Waterfront, close to where our hotel was; taking a tour bus around Cape Town city; and taking a boat trip to Robben Island to see the prison where Nelson Mandela had spent eighteen years of his imprisonment. We then went to Arabella, a golf resort that's a ninety minutes drive away from Cape Town. We also saw Stellenbosch, Paarl, and Hermanus with the group before hiring a car and heading off ourselves. We visited Sanbona Wildlife Reserve for two days of safari; here, we saw many species of bird and animal, including four of the 'big five' – the Elephant, Lion, Cape Buffalo and Rhino. We then went along the Garden Route, a magnificent stretch of coastline, over to Knysna and Plettenberg.

On our way back to Cape Town, we went to Cape Agulhas, the most southerly point of Africa, and got a cable car up part of Table Mountain, continuing to the top on foot. Despite warnings not to do so, we drove by the Khayelitsha Township in taking a short cut to the south of Cape Town. Once arrived, we stayed for the last night of our trip in Hout Bay.

My abiding memory of that trip is the sight of the townships outside every town or city. The townships were equivalent to a suburb but contained poor quality housing; during the time of apartheid, only black people lived there. Many of the dwellings looked like shacks and mobile homes. We knew by the sight of the townships that we were near another city or town, and this was confirmed on each occasion. The map that we were using for navigation did not show the townships, and each one seemed more dilapidated than the previous one. On the main road close to any township, there were always long lines of persons; I learned that these people were queuing for a bus, as the buses did not go through the townships, and as very few persons had cars. The only way to get to the city or town, or wherever they wished to go, was by bus.

I have considered going back to South Africa on a few occasions, as I know that I only saw a small part of it; I have not been to Durban, Johannesburg, Pretoria or many other areas in between. Nevertheless, I'm not sure that I will do so.

I have been to China, or at least Hong Kong, Shanghai and Beijing, and perhaps would like to see and experience more of its vastness, but again I'm not sure that I will do so. What I did see on my few trips was fascinating, and I would strongly recommend to others taking a trip there – the culture is so different to what we are used to, and worth experiencing. The Great Wall of China (which is best accessible from Beijing), the Summer Palace and the Temple of Heaven alone make Beijing worthwhile as a place to visit, demonstrating to any doubters that ancient Chinese civilisations were as advanced as ancient Western civilisations, if not more so. Having said that, the twentieth century was a very difficult period in Chinese history; the country's occupation by Japanese forces during the Second World War, the Communist Revolution, Mao's 'Great Leap Forward' and the Cultural Revolution caused enormous unhappiness for the vast majority of the Chinese people.

On our first visit to Beijing, we engaged a private tour guide for a couple of days, as had been recommended to us. The guide was very knowledgable and interesting, and told us harrowing stories of his childhood. He was taken from his parents, who were doctors that were banished to the remote rural regions, and he was put in the equivalent of an orphanage; here he was effectively starved, resulting in his being particularly small, even as an adult. When talking openly to us, he was always very careful that he was alone and that his driver, who also accompanied us, was not in hearing range.

While travelling in the car to the Great Wall, I spoke on my mobile phone to Shane, who was in England at the time. In the course of our conversation, I told him that we had been in Tiananmen Square on the previous afternoon and that we saw the large crowds around the memorial to Mao. Shane asked me jokingly if there was a memorial to the students who were massacred there in 1989. I was replying to him when my phone went dead. This surprised me, as mobile telephone reception had been excellent in each city that we had visited. I mentioned it to the guide, who did not respond at the time but later told me that my phone may have been monitored; he speculated that when the conversation turned to criticism or sarcasm about the Tiananmen massacre, coverage was cut. I didn't know whether to believe him, but I do know that I couldn't re-establish contact with Shane, nor he with me, although I was able to make other calls soon afterwards. It was a little spooky.

I have also been to Japan and Malaysia with Mary, and to South Korea with my friend Paul. Each is very different from the other, but all are even more different from Ireland and Europe. The bullet train from Tokyo to Osaka, around the base of Mount Fuji, is probably the highlight, but the view from the KL Tower in Kuala Lumpur, over the city and the dense surrounding rainforest, is well worth seeing also. Each of these countries probably deserves another visit, to see more than I did on these short visits, but they have to join a long list of possible future trips.

When I first visited Australia in early 2009, I was just past my sixtieth birthday. I have been lucky to visit again on many occasions and, as mentioned, have the distinct feeling that I would have stayed and lived there, had I first visited in my twenties. I'm not exactly sure what it is that attracts me to such an extent. It has so many amazing, varied landscapes and physically attractive cities, but I suppose that it has to do with the lifestyle of the people, who seem to take a more relaxed approach to life and enjoy a much better work–life balance than most of us do in Ireland and Europe generally. The climate probably helps them to live so much of their life outdoors, and they do avail of that opportunity.

I have been lucky to have visited Perth, Freemantle and Margaret River in Western Australia; Hobart and Port Arthur in Tasmania; Melbourne and the Great Ocean Road in Victoria; Sydney, Woolongong and the Blue Mountains in New South Wales; Brisbane in Queensland; Corowa on the Murray River, the border between Victoria and New South Wales; and the Snowy River and Kosciuszko National Parks near Canberra. That still leaves the vast majority of Australia to visit and see; perhaps I'll get the opportunity to see some more in the future, but as my daughter Louisa and her husband, Lee, live near Sydney with their family, I guess any further visits to Australia will be centred on Sydney, a city that I have loved from the first time that I saw Sydney Harbour back in January 2009.

I have been to many countries in Europe, and in some countries – particularly France, Italy, Spain and Portugal – to many parts, but I have not yet been to Norway or what are termed the Balkans – Serbia, Croatia, Montenegro, Kosovo, North Macedonia and Albania – nor to much of Eastern Europe. Even though I was and still am fairly knowledgeable on world geography, I often confuse the seas that surround the Balkans and Baltic Sea. I have been in most of the Baltic countries, albeit some were very short visits. For example, I visited Russia and Estonia, but they were only day visits from a cruise ship that went from Stockholm as far as St Petersburg via Tallinn, sailing at night and arriving at a different port each morning.

St Petersburg seemed worth a longer visit, as we spent most of our visit in the Hermitage Museum. The Hermitage was interesting; we had a very knowledgeable guide, who was articulate and spoke clear English, but the museum is vast and has more than three million pieces in its collection, so what we saw was a minute fraction of what was there. St Petersburg was the imperial capital of the Russian Empire for two hundred years; it is still the cultural centre of Russia, even though the political capital has for many years been Moscow. For that reason, it would be interesting to compare its buildings and monuments with those of Paris and London, which were imperial capitals at the same time.

In summary, I have seen a lot, but much more remains to be seen. Whether I enjoy the health and energy to continue my travels cannot be certain, but at least I do have great memories of my travels to date; I am thankful that I had the opportunities to travel and that I availed of those opportunities. Even in 2019, before the world changed due to Covid 19 restrictions, I visited Argentina, the USA, France and Italy on a few occasions, as well as Australia. Indeed, Mary was in Australia twice that year – once for the birth of Cody, and then with me for a holiday in Sydney and to attend the awarding of Louisa's PhD in Perth. I hope that such travels can resume soon.

Wedding photograph at Aherlow House Hotel, June 1977.

Left: Author's father and mother at author's wedding to Mary in June 1977.

Below: Wedding photograph with Mary, her parents Jim and Ellen, and author's, Joe and Isabel, 1977.

First Communions and Confirmations.

Author's family growing up.

Some family holidays.

Above: Author with family in JB Carr room, Sutton GC after Mary's drive-in, January 2011.

Below: Author as President Clontarf Rugby and Mary, Lady Captain Sutton GC, 2011.

Left: Author as President of Leinster Rugby, 2014–2015.

Below: Author speaking from the rostrum at the House of Lords before Leinster Schools Cup Draw for 2015. *Photo courtesy of Sportsfile.*

Above: Josh Owens, author's eldest grandson, at RDS as Leinster team mascot, December 2014 with family group.

Below: Author as President of Leinster Rugby with Leinster Senior Squad 2014–2015. *Photo courtesy of Sportsfile.*

Opposite: Author presenting Leinster Rugby Academy Graduation certificates to three future Irish internationals, Tadhg Furlong, Luke McGrath and James Tracey. *Photos courtesy of Sportsfile.*

Above: Author addressing spectators at RDS before presentation of Leinster Schools Senior Cup to Cistercian College Roscrea. *Photo courtesy of Sportsfile.*

Below: Author presenting Leinster Senior Cup to Clontarf Captain and team, 2015.

Above: Two Presidents and one Captain – author with Pat McHale, President Clontarf Rugby and Sam Cronin, captain, with Leinster Senior Cup 2015.

Right: Author with Mary, at Leinster Rugby Awards Ball, 2015. *Photo courtesy of Sportsfile.*

Above: The Royal Dublin JB Carr golf team 2018 with club captain, caddies and club professional (author in centre of middle row). *Photo courtesy of Owen O'Connor Photography.*

Below: Last pre-Covid family Reunion December 2018.

SPORT AND MY INVOLVEMENT

Sport has played an integral role in my life from an early age. Between participating, spectating and administering, it has probably taken up more of my life than anything else other than sleep and work. One of my early memories is kicking a ball with my grandfather in Fairview Park. I don't remember him having any great interest in sport, but I know that my father did – particularly in Gaelic football.

He played in Tyrone and Dublin. In the mid-1950s, he became involved in the Tyrone Men's Association in Dublin, which was a group that supported and assisted in funding for the Tyrone football team when they qualified for All-Ireland semi-finals. He subsequently became one of the founder members of Clontarf GAA Club – as he had years earlier with Edendork in Tyrone – and was a team manager and committee member for many years after that.

My first experience of watching sport – other than seeing boys and men playing football in Fairview Park as I went from Nottingham Street to visit my grandparents in Marino – was probably the All-Ireland football final in 1955, when Dublin were defeated by Kerry. I can't say that it meant much to me – other than being told that the Freaney brothers, Ollie and Cyril, who were stars of the Dublin team, lived near us in Clontarf, on Vernon Avenue. In the following two summers, Tyrone twice reached the All-Ireland semi-final. Because of my father's excitement at this development, this Tyrone team did mean a lot to me, and I can still remember the names of some of those players: Thady Turbett, Jim Devlin (who had two brothers also on the team), Jody O'Neill, Frankie Donnelly and Iggy Jones.

I remember Frankie Donnelly being nearly bald and wondering how a man as old as that could be playing with the younger men. I also remember the speed of Iggy Jones and his toe-to-hand solo running, subsequently learning that he was considered the best in Ireland at it. The reason that this team meant so much to me, however, was probably the fact that my father took me with him into the dressing room after one of those two semi-finals. I can't remember if that was in 1956 or 1957, but I do remember the smell of wintergreen and being introduced by my father to Iggy Jones and a few of the other players, who shook my hand. That was probably my first sporting thrill.

What is it about sport that I and millions of others find so emotional, so infectious and so obsessive? It probably starts off with the ambition of emulating heroes and the awakening of a competitive spirit which is innate in most humans but, in the modern era, can be enjoyed without the likelihood of death or serious injury, as would have been the case in earlier times. That competitive spirit brings on adrenaline flows and excitement. And then there is the social aspect: if we are not competing, we like to watch others doing so, and to talk about it and reminisce about the days of our own exploits.

In 1998, while on a holiday in Mexico and Belize, I visited a Mayan temple and village, Chichen Itza, and was intrigued to read that the Mayans had a ball game which was a cross between basketball and soccer. It seemed to be a difficult game, and one score was usually sufficient to win. The game had a religious flavour, with rituals and the presence of religious and political leaders. The winners were heroes, but the captain of the losing team was usually sacrificed to the gods in the hope that the gods would ensure the health and prosperity of the survivors. That reminded me of the well-known saying attributed to Bill Shankly, the legendary manager of Liverpool FC: 'Football isn't just a matter of life and death. It's much more important than that.' I suppose the same could be said about gladiators fighting at a sporting spectacle in Roman times or Mongol youths doing battle with swords and lances to impress Genghis Khan, gaining some favour by killing or maiming their opponent.

Thankfully, the sports that I participated in, and watch now, are not so dangerous – although the excitement that it generates may not be advantageous to good health. I recently had to wear a blood pressure monitor for twenty-four hours and try to occupy the time as normally as possible, to enable my cardiologist to assess what was causing raised blood pressure. I gave the monitor back to my GP on a Saturday morning, when the time was completed, and I received a phone call from her a few days later. She wanted to know what I was doing at 8.30 p.m. on the Friday. I couldn't remember immediately, but when she told me that the monitor reading had literally gone off the chart at that time, I recalled that I was watching an All-Ireland League rugby game between Clontarf and Terenure College; that I had got very annoyed when a Clontarf player missed two successive easy tackles towards the end of the first half, leading to a score for Terenure. My doctor's advice was that watching rugby games was very dangerous for me, but as she knew that I was unlikely to change my habits, she advised that I do something about my blood pressure.

When I was 9 or 10 years old, I suffered a serious laceration on my forehead when playing hurling in St Anne's Park, where I often went with the other boys from Seafield Avenue to play and practise. We could play football and hurling on the street, but it was frowned on by some neighbours, and the Gardaí were often called to stop us; Tom O'Connell and I got caught once and received a summons for the District Court. So the alternative was to go to St Anne's Park, which was a ten-to-fifteen-minute walk for us, or a three-to-four-minute cycle. Tom – or Mossy, as he was known – was originally from Kilkenny, and his father was from Cork, so he took his hurling very seriously and had a metal band around the 'bas' of his hurl, copying the inter-county hurlers. Anyway, on this occasion, for some reason, the band had broken; when he swung across my head, the jagged edge of the metal hit my forehead and it bled profusely.

One of the other boys, Frank, grabbed a bicycle and rode as fast as he could back home to Seafield Avenue, where my mother and Mossy's were chatting at the side of the road. Frank shouted that they had better go up to St Anne's Park, as I was dying and Mossy had killed me. I can only imagine what the mothers felt, but Mossy's mother stayed calm enough to ask for more detail, and when they learned that I was standing and walking, they were obviously relieved.

They came to collect me, I was brought into the emergency department of Temple Street Children's Hospital for the first of many visits in the ensuing fifty years, and I had seven or eight stitches inserted. I still have the mark on my forehead more than sixty years later, so I don't think the doctor doing the stitching was too worried about my facial looks. I wore the scar as a badge of honour for some time after that. Mossy later became an economist and was assistant director general and chief economist of the Central Bank of Ireland from 2005 to 2009.

The other experience that Mossy and I had – when we were caught by the Gardaí – happened around the same time. It was a little scary, but also amusing. We played football and hurling on the avenue regularly but knew that certain neighbours were unhappy with that – particularly those who had nice gardens but no children and didn't want us entering their gardens to retrieve balls that had gone astray. On a few occasions, the Gardaí were called by telephone. We were never caught, as somebody usually spotted them and told us, or we saw them on their bicycles and could run faster than they could cycle, or we had stopped playing and merely received a warning. Indeed, on one of these occasions where we were playing hurling but had stopped by the time law enforcement arrived, the garda turned out to be Terry Kelly, who was also an All-Ireland medal winner with Cork. He saw the hurley sticks on the side of the road and proceeded to chat to us about hurling, giving us some coaching before he got on his bicycle and left.

On one occasion, however, a local garda – Garda Foley – sneaked up on us behind a bus and saw us playing football before we stopped to allow the bus to pass. We were about to resume, as we hadn't seen him, when he roared at us to come over to him. All five or six of us scattered and ran, and I went into a neighbour's garden and hid behind a bush.

He must have seen which garden I ran into, as he followed me after he caught Mossy and was shouting and roaring at me to come out. I didn't move, hoping he wouldn't find me, but I was quite scared. We often played hide and seek; this was a little like that, but this time it was real and not a game. He kept searching until I was found and taken out onto the avenue by the scruff of my neck. Garda Foley took our names, addresses and the names of our respective fathers; at the same time, I could see some of the others who had been playing with us looking out from windows in their houses.

Mossy and I, and our respective fathers, were served a few weeks later with a summons to the District Court for playing football on the road, which apparently was against the law. Neither Mossy nor I had to go to court, but we were found guilty and then given the benefit of the Probation Act.

I'm not sure whether Mossy could have advanced as far as he did in his economist career, and I could have qualified as a solicitor, if not for being granted probation, but that was moot anyway. It didn't stop us playing on the avenue, but we were more careful to keep someone as a lookout. Mr and Mrs Evans, the suspected culprits for calling the police, soon sold their house and left to go back to the UK; Mr Evans, who worked for the British and Irish Steam Packet Company, was posted back to Wales.

As I explained earlier, I had captained the Belgrove National School under twelves team that won a schools football competition in Croke Park in March 1961. As our team was doing well that season, there were regular match reports in the *Evening Press*, which allocated very good coverage of the schools games. The paper had a feature each week in which they published two team photographs and a portrait photograph of each team captain, writing a profile of the captain after an interview. The feature was titled 'Stars of the Future'.

I was featured in early 1961, and in the course of the interview, when asked what was my sporting ambition, I replied that second only to leading Clontarf to winning the cup, I wanted to see the establishment of a GAA club in Clontarf for juveniles. This was a slightly unexpected answer for the journalist, but he reported it accurately. I know that my comment stimulated my father and some of his friends, who proceeded to establish and register the club within a few months. The new club entered the north Dublin under thirteens hurling league at the beginning of the summer and actually won. I was delighted to be part of that team, and so won another medal in 1961.

As mentioned earlier, Clontarf is on the edge of St Anne's Park, which was owned by Dublin Corporation. There were many different sports pitches in the park, and these were leased to various clubs as their home pitch. Belgrove soccer club had their grounds near the top of Seafield Avenue; the farthest boundary of the grounds adjoined St Anne's Park, but I'm not sure if they rented them from the corporation. Although I went to see games there on a few occasions, I never found it interesting and soon stopped going.

In the 1950s, one of the best Gaelic football teams in Dublin was Sean McDermotts; they played in the Dublin senior competitions and were comprised almost exclusively of players from outside Dublin who worked in the county. Most of them were inter-county players, many of them well known. One of the football pitches in St Anne's was known to us as Sean McDermotts pitch, as it was their home pitch. I remember, in the late 1950s, going with friends to see games in which at least half of the players were inter-county – particularly when Sean McDermotts played St Vincents, who always had a large cohort of the Dublin team playing for them.

It was like having Croke Park in our back garden. Formally, this pitch was known as pitch 35. I'm not sure how it transpired, but this pitch became Clontarf's from summer 1961. I have a vague recollection that one of my father's friends – a co-founder of the new club – worked in the parks department of Dublin Corporation and used his influence and inside knowledge to arrange the allocation of the pitch to Clontarf. It was the prime pitch in St Anne's Park: it had direct road frontage and was closest to the concrete-built changing rooms that serviced a few of the nearby pitches.

This under thirteens hurling team played at under fifteens level for the next two years, and as minor or under eighteens for the three years that followed, albeit having been joined by some players who were closer to the age limit. The club also entered under thirteens and under fifteens teams in Gaelic football from 1961 onwards, and I played on those teams as I got progressively older – while I was still playing rugby at school. The GAA's famous 'ban' on foreign sports was in force at the time, but it didn't apply to school sports. It was abolished for all in 1971, but for the few previous years it was honoured more in the breach than in compliance for the ordinary player who wasn't likely to find his name in newspaper reports of rugby or soccer games – or if he was, he played under an assumed name.

I took pride, from an early stage, in the fact that voicing my wishes in the newspaper interview led almost immediately to the establishment of the club. I still do, as Clontarf GAA Club has grown from that seed in 1961 to be one of the biggest GAA clubs in Dublin. I ceased playing myself by the late 1960s, save for an odd game over the next year or so, as I became involved in many other different sports. But by then my football future was behind me, as was my 'stardom'. I enjoyed playing Gaelic football and hurling during my teens – and I still retain an interest, at least when it comes close to the time of All-Ireland finals.

One of my most emotional moments in sport – and there have been many – was when Tyrone won their first All-Ireland final in September

2003, defeating their close neighbours Armagh in the final. A friend of mine had a corporate box in the Hogan Stand and invited me to it for the day. There were twelve of us there, but there was sufficient privacy for me to weep copiously, remembering my father – all he had done to encourage my love of sport. He would have loved to have been there for the occasion, but unfortunately it was more than twenty-one years too late for him.

I don't know how he would have felt if he had seen his grandson, Tadhg Morley, playing for Kerry against Tyrone in recent years. He never knew Tadhg, but I'm sure that some of his footballing genes have been passed on to another generation. Indeed, all his grandsons have played one or other code of football competitively, and they are all sports enthusiasists, as are his many granddaughters. I know that my father would have been proud of that.

In 1966, after leaving school and starting work in Irish Life, I probably realised that I was not going to be brilliant at any one sport. That is not necessarily the reason why I tried so many different sports afterwards; however, trying so many probably did ensure that I wouldn't excel or be a star at any.

Irish Life had a large hall or social area that served as a restaurant during the day. Various activities took place there in the evenings, one of which was table tennis, or ping-pong. Although I had played table tennis at home since I was very young, it was on an extended dining room table and I had seldom played on a full-size table. I quickly realised that guys who had been to boarding school – where table tennis was one of the principal after-study activities – were far better than I was. Nevertheless, I was enthusiastic, partly because there were mixed teams, and I managed to get on the team that competed in the Dublin Business Houses League.

I had played on the cricket team at school once but never developed a serious interest in the game. However I do sometimes enjoy watching the shorter forms of professional cricket – 50 overs or 20 overs and on my first trip to Australia in 2009, I went to see Australia play against South Africa in an evening game at the famous Melbourne Cricket Ground. I also started playing hockey in Irish Life, learning quickly from some colleagues who played senior hockey at club level. I also played Gaelic football, hurling, tennis, seven-a-side rugby and cricket for Irish Life in inter-office competitions. At one stage, on a trip to Killaloe with a group from Irish Life, I tried waterskiing; I found it really exciting but also discovered that I wasn't very good at it. Perhaps I should have been more patient and tried it again a few times, but because I found it difficult to stay upright and jump over the wake – leaving me in the lake too often and too soon – I gave up on it. This was probably another example of my lack of patience.

At the same time, I played basketball at senior league level for the St Paul's past pupils team. Even though I was relatively small for a basketball player, I was reasonably good; rather than depend on winning rebounds off the backboard against guys who were six or more inches taller than me, I relied on good, accurate shooting and terrier-like defencing. That team seemed to break up after my first season with them out of school, or at least, I stopped playing competitively – I can't remember.

The only other sport that I played at senior level was hockey. When I went to UCD in 1968, I stopped at the hockey club stand at the freshers' exhibition and was chatting to a very attractive girl. When she learned that I had played the game previously, she invited me to a mixed hockey tournament in Belfield on the following Sunday. I turned up, had a great time – with barbeque and a few drinks – scored a few goals and was asked by the captain of the men's hockey team if I was interested in trialling for their senior team. I went for it and was picked as centre-forward for the first match, holding my place for the rest of the season.

We didn't win many games, but we won enough to avoid relegation. There were two separate clubs, men's and women's, but they were very close and socialised together regularly. The highlight of the season was the inter-varsity competition for the Mauritius Cup, which was to be held in January 1969 and was hosted by Queen's University in Belfast. UCD, Dublin University, Queen's and the Royal College of Surgeons were the participants. I was selected for the UCD team and, by playing against Dublin University, earned my 'colours'. Queen's, who won the tournament, had two future Great Britain internationals on their team; they were in a different class to the rest of us.

I resumed at the start of the next season, but in the first match I tried a manoeuvre that I had seen one of the Queen's players do in Belfast. Lifting the hockey stick above shoulder level was prohibited, but by jumping, keeping the stick at shoulder level and parallel to the ground and striking the ball, one could get an advantage for a head-height ball. But it required practice. I tried it without practice, misjudged the height of a ball struck from a long corner, misjudged the timing of my jump and managed to hit the ball with my head. That wasn't a sensible thing to do, as the ball was very hard, and I definitely came off worst. I was stunned, probably concussed, and quickly developed a big bruise on my forehead. I took a break for a few weeks and then discovered that our practice sessions were clashing with Law Society lectures for the second solicitors' exam, so I never actually went back to playing.

I had initially learned to swim in the Clontarf baths; after that, I swam in the Tara Street baths, where Belgrove National School had arranged classes on a Saturday morning. I was never a very stylish swimmer, but I was reasonably competent and swam regularly off the Bull Wall or on Dollymount Strand. I can't remember the exact year when I last swam off the Bull Wall, but it was probably 1967 or 1968. What stopped me was seeing a dog's severed and bloody head floating in the water just below where I was about to dive in. When I mentioned it to some friends, I was amazed that they weren't shocked; they indicated that they had seen something similar in the past. It was certainly unusual for me, and it put me off swimming in Dublin Bay.

The advantage of swimming off the Bull Wall was that one could dive straight into the water when the tide was in rather than having to wade in off the beach as the cold water slowly lapped up to the delicate nether regions. Over the next fifty years, I often swam in seas and oceans around the world – but often I remember that incident off the Bull Wall, which was my local venue.

There were probably only two occasions when I felt in danger while swimming or in the sea. The first was in Coominole, near Slea Head in west Kerry, a beautiful beach looking out to the Blasket Islands that had a treacherous undercurrent. I was there one bank holiday weekend in the early 1970s, swimming and playing around with a beach ball in the water with a few friends.

Someone noticed that another guy – who was part of a different group doing much the same – had got into difficulties, was being dragged out and was struggling to stay above water. One of his friends, or someone else standing nearby, caught him; a few of us then went to assist. We formed a chain to try to get him back to the beach, passing him from one to the other. There was a severe current, and whatever happened, the guy in difficulties dragged me down. For a few moments, I too was in difficulty. Someone else then grabbed me, got me free from the other guy, and I started floating again. We all got to the shore safely and without further mishap. I recovered quickly, but the other guy needed resuscitation from a lifeguard before he too recovered. What was most frightening was the speed with which I went from being in control to being in difficulty; even though it was only for a short time, I got quite a scare.

The second and only other time that I can remember getting into trouble was on a surf beach in Cronulla, south of Sydney in New South Wales. Mary and I were visiting my daughter Louisa, her husband, Lee, and our grandchildren. There were other stretches of Cronulla beach that were more suitable for swimming – it is a very long beach with a wide variation of beach slopes and directions, so there is a wide variation of conditions – but I thought that it would be good fun to try bodysurfing in the breaking surf. I grossly underestimated the force of the waves.

It wasn't that I had swum far out from the edge of the water. I guess I wasn't more than ten to twelve yards out – most of which I walked, as the water wasn't up to my knees – but before I realised it, a quick series of large breaking waves lifted me off my feet, tumbled me as if I was in a washing machine and dumped me head first onto the sand. I was stunned – probably even concussed, as I was seeing stars for a few minutes – and I hurt my shoulder and back, which were sore for at least a week after the incident. I was in my late sixties when that happened, and I was surprised at my own stupidity in thinking that I could master the waves at that age.

I had tried boogieboarding a few years earlier. I was on a beach at Inverloch on the Victoria coast, south of Melbourne, and I managed it well, instructed by my brother, Gerry, who lived outside Melbourne and had a holiday home there. The only problem I had then was that it exhausted me; when I came back to the beach, I lay down on the sand, fell asleep and got burned by the Australian sun. But at least I had been a surfing beach bum for a few hours.

Surfing is definitely one of those sports that should be started young in life. My daughter Sinéad, who was active in many different sporting activities, became a surfing fan; during one of her medical postings in Sligo Hospital, she lived for a while beside the beach at Strandhill – which is one of the most well-known surfing beaches on the west coast of Ireland – and surfed almost every day. Her son Charlie got a boogieboard for his fourth birthday, and as he lives in Sligo, I expect that surfing will be one of his hobbies.

Many years after my attempts at waterskiing, I tried windsurfing with approximately the same level of success. I remember the first occasion that I saw windsurfing: it was off a beach in the South of France in 1976 during my holiday there with Mary. It seemed idyllic, but when I tried it back in Ireland, it was quite different. Besides it being much colder than in the South of France, I realised that I couldn't master the balance, ending up in the cold waters of Malahide Estuary too often for my comfort.

Even though I had always lived near the sea, I had never tried sailing or fishing. It wasn't until 1980, when visiting my brother-in-law Jim McCarron in Port Townsend, Washington State, that I first sailed on a yacht. I then went fishing for salmon with him and some of his friends in the sea between Puget Sound and the Strait of San Juan de Fuca – between the USA and Vancouver Island in Canada. Jim was a very enthusiastic fisherman and hunter – and still is – although salmon fishing in that region is now limited to the Native Americans, who asserted their traditional rights and were granted them. I went out on three occasions with him and his friends, and none of us had any success on the first two days; even though the company was good fun, I wondered what the purpose or excitement was.

On the third evening, Jim and his friends had caught a salmon. When the next one was hooked, I was given the rod and allowed to reel it in and land it. I was surprised at how thrilling it was to battle with the 'running' fish as it tried desperately to shake off the hook, swimming out and back, then under the boat and out the other side; I was holding on to the rod for dear life, as it had come out of the rod holder on the deck while I was trying to reel in the fish. Thankfully, the salmon tired before I did, and we got it on board. I got some understanding of the thrill involved in landing a fish like that – why it is such a popular pastime for many. I have never tried it again, but I still remember how sore my shoulders and arms were from the 'battle'.

Soon after I returned from that trip, I was invited out on a sailing trip on Dublin Bay by one of my law partners. David was an experienced offshore sailor, and we had a very enjoyable afternoon on the bay. A couple of years later, another friend and solicitor, John Gore Grimes – who was a world-renowned sailor and had undertaken some epic journeys from Howth to Disko Bay in Greenland and the Arctic – invited me for a trip on his boat, *Shardana*. We sailed up to and around Lambay Island, and again I thoroughly enjoyed it.

Later that year, autumn 1983, another friend – also a solicitor – invited me to sail with him as crew on his folkboat, a twenty-four-foot sailing yacht that he raced regularly. I completed that autumn series with him, joined the Howth Yacht Club and crewed regularly with him over the next few years. My friend was a very competitive sailor when in a race, and still is, but he probably preferred cruising in a bigger yacht in the Med or further afield. I wouldn't have been his first call when he needed crew – and I wasn't always available when he did call – but I did sail quite a lot with him, and was delighted to be used as a regular substitute.

When I mention that my friend was competitive, one particular occasion illustrates that. It occurred in May 1984; I think it was the day of the Lambay race from Howth, and he was determined to win. As high winds and rough seas were expected, he, as skipper, wanted a full crew on board and I got the call.

Earlier that week, I had been on a trip to the USA with Mary and two friends – a mixture of leisure and business in New York and Washington, DC. We had flown from Aldergrove Airport in Belfast on an inaugural flight by Olympic Airlines, which was being subsidised by the European Commission to use Belfast as a staging post between Athens, Greece and New York.

Before we left, there was a reception in the airport for a couple of hours. It was attended by many Northern Ireland dignitaries and representatives of all the political parties, including Austin Currie of the SDLP and Ian Paisley of the Democratic Unionists, as well as business leaders. The latter were all delighted to support this initiative for business in Northern Ireland, as there weren't many initiatives at that time, in 1984. Champagne and alcohol flowed freely, and the general ambience was exacerbated by a ninety-minute delay of the flight – during which delay, the party continued. Ian Paisley, even though he wasn't drinking, was very affable; he met and shook hands with most of those present, but he couldn't understand why such an occasion had to have four 'southerners' present – me, Mary, my friend Hugh Cooney and his wife, Nuala. The explanation was complicated. It involved a friend who had a senior political position in Brussels and was the original guest on the trip; he and his wife weren't free to travel, so they offered four tickets to another friend – that friend couldn't travel either, so we were invited to take their place. We didn't try to explain all this to Paisley.

The rest of the trip continued in the same vein, and when we arrived back in Aldergrove Airport on the Friday morning, facing a drive back to Dublin, there was a serious sleep deficit. That deficit wasn't recovered that night, as our children were excited to have us home and didn't allow me to go to bed immediately, as I would have needed.

The next day was the day of the race. As expected, the sea was very rough on the Saturday morning and there was a lot to do. After more than three quarters of the way through the race, we were leading and all the crew were in good form. I must have dozed off, as when the skipper called 'prepare to gybe' and the crew replied 'ready', I didn't react; when the boom swung around fast, I was caught on the forehead and knocked out of the boat, which was accelerating away from the previous mark.

I'm not sure how I managed it, as I was momentarily knocked unconscious, but my survival instincts kicked in, I grabbed the side rail of the boat and hung on, although most of my body was in the water. One of my fellow crew members told the skipper who hadn't seen what happened; he was concentrating on getting the boat to speed up again. He had to stop the boat while I was hauled in, but two or three other boats passed us and we never got back in front again.

For weeks afterwards, he cursed me for losing him the race. He probably had a bet on it, but more importantly, he lost bragging rights. He told me that it wasn't him who wanted to stop the boat for me; that it was his first mate, a very pleasant gentleman, who insisted on him stopping. I'm not implying that my friend would have let me drown, but if he could, he would have dragged me along outside the boat until I got myself back on board. That didn't stop me sailing, but for various reasons I sailed very little for the rest of that summer and didn't resume regular sailing until the autumn series in Howth.

A couple of years later, I decided to buy a sail boat with a friend, Tom Duffy. We wanted to buy a Shipman, which was a twenty-eight-foot yacht with four berths, as we were both crewing on that boat class at the time in Howth and knew that there was a large and competitive fleet of them in the

Dublin area. We sourced a suitable boat in Kinsale, County Cork. I called to inspect it on my way back from holidays in Kerry, did a deal with the owner and arranged a survey of its seaworthiness. The surveyor advised us to proceed, which we did. The money was then paid over, we arranged a berth on the marina in Howth Yacht Club, and Tom and I got two friends – more experienced sailors than us – to join our crew for the trip home from Kinsale. We flew to Cork to collect the boat on a Friday evening, with the intention of sailing her back to Howth by Sunday night; ten days later, we eventually got her home.

That was a long saga. Our problems commenced when we tried to start the engine but it wouldn't respond; as there was nothing else we could do at the time, we set sail from Kinsale later than planned, only making it to Dunmore East Yacht Club by Saturday night. We headed off again on Sunday morning and hit a very severe storm, with winds and tides against us, a heavy swell on the sea and me very seasick for much of the day. I had never been seasick before then, albeit I had sometimes felt a little queasy, but this was definitely the worst I had ever felt on land or sea by quite a margin. I had heard previously that when one gets bad seasickness, you just want to die. I didn't believe it when I had heard it, but I could now vouch for it. It was unbelievably bad; I wanted to give up, throw myself over the rails and let myself drown.

One of the friends helping us to get the boat home – and who was skippering the boat on the trip – tied me to the railing of the boat to prevent me being washed overboard or jumping in myself. He encouraged me to stick with it – that ultimately I would feel better. He was right, but it took about three or four hours of misery before I felt well enough to start helping the others crew the boat. We had to go out towards the Welsh coast before turning up the Irish coast towards home. We only got as far as Wicklow by Monday morning, so we berthed the boat there and got the train home, as we had to get to work later that afternoon. On the following Saturday we got the train back to Wicklow, with a slightly different crew, and sailed the boat back to Howth by that night.

We arranged to have the engine repaired over the next few weeks and then had our children choose a name for her, as neither of us liked the existing name, *Wayfarer*. She was eventually named *Bilbo* after Bilbo Baggins of Lord of the Rings, and we proceeded to have great fun over the next few years – with ourselves and friends racing, and with our families on cruising trips. When racing, I don't think we ever finished in the top half of the fleet, and I realised after a few years that I was really a landlubber, got out of the habit of sailing regularly and sold my share of the boat to Tom, who still owns it. Thus, I ended my sailing career, but I had the satisfaction of introducing sailing to my three children – and even though they no longer sail regularly, they each greatly enjoyed their own sailing careers, and two of them qualified as sailing instructors.

Another sport that I tried was rallying: when I navigated, on a few occasions, for my friend Jimmy Cahill in evening rallies, on closed roads, in the early 1970s. We only had one serious crash, which was in our – or at least my – final race. We demolished a wall, and the wall more or less demolished Jimmy's car. Jimmy's father owned one of the largest car dealerships in north Dublin, with related workshops for customer car repair, so after a few months Jimmy was back on the rallying circuit – but by mutual agreement, I was no longer his navigator. It wasn't that I was being blamed for the crash, but I didn't have the time to practice and Jimmy wanted to go more often.

Squash racquets became a very popular indoors game in Ireland in the 1970s, and I played regularly for a few years – never very successfully, but always enthusiastically. I initially played at Squash Ireland on the Howth Road in Clontarf; later, I played in the Kildare Street and University Club on St Stephen's Green in the city centre.

I had played tennis regularly as a teenager although I wasn't then a member of a club. I was even on the school senior tennis team in my last year in St.Pauls and was on tennis teams in Irish Life and later for GSOB in solicitors inter office competitions. I later joined Sutton LTC and for many years played once or twice a week. However I eventually realised that my knees and ankles were not up the strength standards that my ambitions to chase and return every wide, long or short ball required and as I was beginning to suffer soft tissue injuries, I stopped playing in my early fifties

I went skiing for the first time in 1994, with my family. We went to Soldeu in Andorra, and all of us thoroughly enjoyed it. We knew that our friends – the Reynolds family – would be there, and they had four children, three of whom were the same age as our three, so they had ready-made skiing mates and progressed quickly while I was stuck on the learner slopes for a few days. On the third day, and still on beginner exercises with some timid ladies and awkward men, I knocked down a line of about eight persons, who ended up lying on top of me. When the instructor pulled them off, I asked him 'where is the nearest f—ing golf course'. He replied that it was about 10 kilometers away – but it was under snow and would be for the next few months.

I had a few more drinks than normal that night, and when the morning call came from the children, who wanted to be on the slopes as soon as the lifts started to operate, I told them to go ahead without me – that I was staying in bed. All the same, I did get up after half an hour, made my way to the lift, went up the mountain and started to ski down. For whatever reason – perhaps being more relaxed – I could then do it. Much to my amazement, I progressed quickly over the next three days, to the extent that I was sorry to have to go home. I realised that it was a little like learning to ride a bicycle or to swim: one moment you can't do it, the next moment you can. We went skiing once a year for a number of years; and even when the children wouldn't come on summer holidays with Mary and me, they would always come on a skiing trip. Eventually, when my skiing ability peaked at the intermediate level, I realised that my technique was never great. It began to hurt my knees in particular, so I stopped skiing – although I still love to go up the mountain, to the base of the ski slopes, and feel the cold air and see the fun that people are having.

Although soccer is the football game played and watched by more people around the world than any other, it doesn't hold this position in Ireland, where Gaelic football is the number one football game. I never played soccer competitively, but like most other boys, I played a form of it. Compared with rugby or Gaelic, it was easier to play on the road or on a beach – the ball was kept lower and therefore was less likely to be kicked too far away. 'Three and in' was the usual way we played; only one set of goalposts or markers was required, and whoever scored three goals first became the goalkeeper – this process being repeated.

I did go to Belgrove Park – which was at the top of Seafield Avenue, where we lived – to see Belgrove Soccer Club play. But this was only on a few occasions, and more because a few others wanted to go. I found it fairly boring; indeed, I still find most of the soccer on television boring. I do like watching highlights, if there are any, but I can't sit through ninety minutes of a full game unless, perhaps, it is Liverpool that is playing. For some reason or other, I still get excited or depressed when watching Liverpool, depending on how they are performing. I have been a fan now for more then sixty years.

Perhaps the reason that I find much of it boring is my lack of patience at the slow build up and scarcity of scoring, but perhaps it's because I don't fully understand the tactics. That doesn't prevent me from expressing my opinion and criticising. There was one occasion, in 2006, when returning on a flight from Lisbon to London – on my way home from a few days of business meetings – that I found myself sitting behind Sven-Göran Eriksson, the then England soccer team manager; he was in the first row, on his own. I didn't pay too much attention to him, as I was working on a document, but I did notice that he had two or three big files on the table in front of him. Halfway into the flight, a person in the seat across the aisle from me got up to go to the bathroom; as he returned to his seat, he spoke to Sven. From the tone of the conversation, they obviously knew each other. They were discussing a European Champions League game that they had both attended on the previous night in Lisbon. I recognised the voice of Jim Beglin, who was a regular television commentator, having been a great Liverpool and Ireland player previously.

I took a break from working on my document, joining in the conversation with the two experts after introducing myself. I didn't try to pretend that I was an authority, but I enjoyed the chat, which turned to Liverpool's win in Istanbul the previous June; I had been lucky enough to attend, and we exchanged a few anecdotes about that night. After the conversation finished and we all resumed what we were doing previously, I put aside my document and handwrote a memo for Sven on how I thought he could lead England to World Cup victory in a few months' time.

The memo stated that he needed to build his team around a spine consisting of Jamie Carragher at the back, regardless of whoever else he chose beside him, Stevie Gerrard in midfield, and Peter Crouch as the striker, and I gave him three alternative selections for the team. I also wrote a few notes on strategy. I added that, as Ireland had failed to qualify, I hoped that England would go on to win – as it would at least get the English to stop talking about their win in 1966. I didn't tell him that I had never played the game, other than a few matches for GSOB again in Dublin solicitors inter office competitions in recent years, but as we got off the plane, he thanked me and said he found my notes very interesting. England didn't win the World Cup that year, but I don't think I can be blamed, as Sven didn't follow my advice as closely as necessary.

I was lucky to attend three world cups, or at least one game in each of the three, starting with Italy in 1990, then Orlando, Florida in 1994 and finally Seoul in 2002, when I went with my pal Paul McLaughlin for the weekend. I also attended international games in Wembley and Latvia, and two or three in Lansdowne Road, but I have never attended a domestic senior soccer game in Ireland. My obsession with Liverpool still puzzles me, considering I have so little interest in the game of soccer generally, but perhaps it is another example of the old Shakespeare adage 'the child is father of the man.'

Golf is the game that I play now, and I have done so for many years – again more enthusiastically than successfully. Nevertheless, my regular golf partners Brendan, Tom, Eddie and Brendan would maintain that I'm too successful in our friendly games – that I too often win the few euros bet that we play for. I first started with a few golf clubs when in my teens: a five iron, an eight iron and putter that I bought in Clerys on O'Connell Street. I should have got lessons before I started playing regularly, or shortly afterwards, as I now know that I treated the golf swing as a mix of hurling, hockey and squash, so I never really mastered the tempo necessary for the game. I initially joined Howth Golf Club in 1979, which was the nearest course to my then home. I enjoyed the time that I played there but thought that it would be too hilly for playing as I got older and less agile.

Accordingly, I applied to and joined the Royal Dublin Golf Club on the Bull Island in Dublin Bay, which is a classic links course and very different from the course at Howth Golf Club. Royal Dublin was formed in 1885 and has had an illustrious golfing history, having hosted many important championships since then. One of its many claims to fame is its association with Christy O'Connor, who was the club professional and who played on ten successive Britain and Ireland Ryder Cup teams.

The club professional when I joined Royal Dublin Golf Club was Leonard Owens, the father of my son-in-law, Lee Owens, who was also a golf professional but is now involved in the business aspect of the game in Australia. Both of them are excellent golfers and a delight to play with. Louisa, who is married to Lee, was not a golf enthusiast before she started going out with him, but in 1993, when she was 12 years old, she did play with me on a Par Three course near Woodstown, County Waterford, where we were on vacation. She had a hole in one at the first hole – her first time to swing a golf club – and when I high-fived her and got excited, she shrugged her shoulders as if to say, 'Why are you so excited, isn't that what you're supposed to do?' She was a gymnast and succeeded in performing in a flying trapeze show while in Club Med in Metaponto, Italy a couple of years before that.

One of the aspects of golf that I most enjoy is the fact that I can go out and play with golfers who are much better than me – even professionals – and be competitive against them, because of the handicap system. The reason is that we are not so much playing against each other (as in tennis or squash) but against the course. In fact, I very much enjoy playing with such players, and tend to play better than if playing with others of my own standard. Besides the exercise benefits that it provides – particularly if walking rather than riding in a buggy – its main benefit is the social interaction that takes place during the game and in the bar afterwards.

I have been lucky to play golf in many parts of the world, both Northern and Southern Hemispheres, including in Tierra del Fuego Golf Club, which is the most southerly golf course on earth. Asia is the only continent where I haven't played. One of the best aspects of golf, which I realised early, is that courses throughout the world tend to be built on beautiful parts of the land, with magnificent landscapes and stunning views – so even if the golf isn't good, one can enjoy a few hours in a lovely outdoors setting, admiring the scenery.

Despite often being frustrated by my own bad shots, I love to play and keep my competitive spirit alive and well. One of my sporting thrills was winning a parent-and-child annual competition in Howth Golf Club with Shane when he was about 14 years old. I have won many competitions since, albeit no majors, and have had the good fortune to have had two holes in one: one in France, in St Donat Golf Club near Grasse; one at home, in Royal Dublin. Having done so, and having barely missed many others, I know that a hole in one requires as much good luck as skill. Considering my good luck in other respects, perhaps I should have had more.

Since 1985, and almost every two years since then, I have gone to Edinburgh for the Ireland–Scotland international rugby match and to play golf on the west coast and on some of the Edinburgh and East Lothian courses. A core group has been involved in most of these trips; many others have been on a few before falling by the wayside, and others, for various reasons, have only been able to come once. In addition to one or more games among ourselves, we play a match against a group of Edinburgh golfers who call themselves the London Reunion Club (or the LRC for short) for the Stephenson Quaich, a trophy put up for competition by one of the Scots – a replica of the trophy that Ireland and Scotland play for every year. This match is usually played at Luffness New Golf Club in Longniddry, about 20 miles east of Edinburgh centre. Initially we had a return match in Ireland when Scotland were playing in Dublin, but that fell away many years ago, as the Scots who travelled preferred to carouse.

On one of our early trips, we stopped in Kilspindie House Hotel on our way back to Edinburgh for a few drinks and a sing-song. We realised that the name of the hotel bar was the Addicts Bar, so we promptly named ourselves the Addicts. I noticed that the hotel had an unusual tie for sale at the hotel reception area; it was a navy tie, with a crest showing a syringe on top of a golf ball. On enquiry, I learned that they had a few of them, so we promptly bought their entire stock – one for each new member, and a few extras – and now considered ourselves as a fully fledged and very exclusive touring golf society. The Addicts survives, even though some of its members – and some of the LRC members – have died in the meantime. But the golfing and rugby trip is still looked forward to, even though it has been a little more civilised in recent times.

It was only in 2018 that I had the honour of being picked for a Royal Dublin golf team for the first time. This was the J.B. Carr trophy team, a scotch foursomes team competition for over sixties. I was the oldest on the team and had the highest handicap, but my style of play suited being paired with a lower handicap player; I thoroughly enjoyed the experience. We won a number of matches, firstly in the north Dublin section, then in the Dublin final, and then in a few games against other county winners in Leinster. We were eventually defeated on a home and away basis in the Leinster final by the K Club, which represented County Kildare.

I wasn't picked for the team for the first round in 2019, but they were defeated in that first round and I didn't get an opportunity to regain a place for further rounds. Nevertheless, in 2019 I qualified for the Super 70s, a competition for those aged 70 and over who were involved in some clubs in north Dublin and Louth that had links courses. Although the team was not as successful as the previous year, I again enjoyed the team aspect of competition and look forward to contending for my place again in future.

Even though golf is the only sport that I continue to play, I watch other sports, both on television and in person. I have been lucky enough to see many great sporting events, in Ireland and abroad, and of these, three stand out in particular. In my mind, they epitomise the incredible excitement that arises – emotions swinging from despair to absolute exhilaration; seeing the unthinkable and seemingly impossible actually occur.

Interestingly, these were in three different football sports. The first was in soccer – in 2005, in Istanbul – when Liverpool defeated AC Milan in the Champions League final after a magnificent second half comeback and penalty shoot out. The second was in rugby, in May 2011, when Leinster defeated Northampton in the Millenium Stadium in Cardiff to win the European Heineken Cup – again after a spectacular second half comeback. The third was in Gaelic football, later that year, when Dublin defeated Kerry in the All-Ireland final, this time in a glorious last-ten-minutes comeback.

It is impossible to explain the shifts in emotions that occurred in these games. Or, for that matter, in other sports that I watched on television, such as the Ryder Cup in 2012, when Europe defeated the USA in Medinah Country Club, Illinois. I'm sure that it doesn't help one's health, psychological or physical, to undergo such emotional swings – such dramatic bursts of adrenaline – but I wouldn't want to trade these excitements for a more staid life where everything is predictable. That, I suppose, is the reason why I enjoy sport so much – why it has been such a significant part of my life to date.

CLONTARF RUGBY, 1996–2005

In 1996, Paul McLaughlin, one of my closest friends for many years, was appointed manager of the Clontarf Rugby senior team that was playing in Division 2 of the All-Ireland League (AIL). Although I wasn't a regular supporter of the club's games at the time, I had been a regular in the mid-1960s and again in the mid-1970s, and had trained a bit in the club. For various reasons, however, I had never played on a Tarf team. I usually attended a few games each season, either in Castle Avenue, their home ground, or for an away Leinster Senior Cup game. In fact, I more frequently attended when they played mid-week games in Anglesea Road in the Smithwicks Old Belvedere Floodlit Cup, which – as the name implies – were held under floodlights.

I had remained a regular attendee of Ireland's international games; I attended the home games and usually made at least one away game each season. I first bought ten-year season tickets in the early 1980s, when the IRFU redeveloped the East Stand and called it the Triple Crown stand. I also attended some of Leinster's games in Donnybrook before the game went professional, when there were seldom a thousand spectators there – unless playing against Munster, which tended, even then, to get a reasonably good attendance. I also attended a few Leinster Schools Cup games each season, which were held on mid-week afternoons. I found them very refreshing, particularly when I was working under a lot of pressure. This may seem counter-intuitive, but for me it was like a break, and I usually skipped lunch or had a sandwich in Kiely's, Donnybrook on the way there.

With Paul – or Locks, as he is better known – as manager, I started to go to a few more games in Castle Avenue, and then more away games. Clontarf were doing well that season and ultimately won their division, which gained them promotion to Division 1. In 1997, the Celtic Cup – which later became the Guinness PRO14 – had not commenced, and was not even thought of, so Division 1 of the AIL was effectively the next tier of Irish rugby below the internationals; many of the established international players were involved each week, playing for their clubs.

To some extent, it was a professional league: the game had accepted professionalism since 1996, and the IRFU wanted to have their international-level players playing in Ireland rather than in England or Wales, so they introduced the concept of central contracting. The IRFU could then direct the players to play club rugby in Ireland, the incentive being that if a player rejected that and went to play abroad, he would not be selected for the international team. Given how matters transpired over the next twenty years, this concept proved very successful. It showed remarkable foresight by Tom Kiernan and Syd Millar, the two leaders of the IRFU to which this policy was attributed.

There had been some professionalism, even before 1996, in Irish rugby, particularly when clubs brought in foreign players and paid them a moderate salary – although sometimes not much more than accommodation and food (and beer money). These were usually young players who wanted to travel a little in the Northern Hemisphere before settling at home in South Africa, New Zealand or Australia. One of these, Gary Teichman – perhaps the best ever foreign player to join an Irish club – joined Clontarf at the age of 20 in 1990. He played for a season before returning to South Africa, and although he missed out on the South Africa team that won the World Cup in 1995, he went on to have a long career with the Springboks and captained them from 1996 to 1999, on thirty-nine occasions.

Another foreign player to come to Ireland was Brent Pope, who joined St Mary's College as a player-coach in 1991 and was recruited by Clontarf as their coach in 1995. He quickly made an impact. In the following season, 1996/97, his team were comfortable winners of Division 2, as Clontarf Rugby began to climb to the top of Irish club rugby.

From the commencement of the new season in autumn 1997, I became a regular attender and supporter of the team. I particularly remember their very first game after their promotion to Division 1. It was in the Leinster Senior League, and they were at home playing against County Carlow, which had just been promoted to senior status at the end of the previous season. County Carlow were obviously very excited, bringing a couple of bus-loads to Castle Avenue. This wasn't unusual in the AIL, but it was unheard of at Leinster League level. Clontarf were quite complacent, and perhaps condescending, but that didn't last long – their bubble was soon burst and County Carlow won the game. It didn't matter much, but it was the last time that season that Clontarf were complacent about a game, so a good lesson was learned at little cost.

As I became more evidently interested, and was fairly well known to many of the club officers, I was persuaded to get more involved. Over the next few seasons, I arranged executive buses for supporters to travel to away games in Cork, Limerick, Galway, Ballymena and Dungannon. I also got involved in some fundraising events and talked to potential new sponsors, and I arranged funding to complete a refurbishment of a bar in the clubhouse. Some potential new players were also seeking jobs; I assisted in recruiting them by helping to arrange interviews and introductions to clients or business contacts for them. The rapidly expanding IFSC proved particularly helpful in this regard.

In mid-January 1999, a couple of days after watching a particularly inept performance by Clontarf against Galwegians in Galway, I wrote a very strong and undiluted letter to the then president of the club, Dave Kennedy, asking him to take radical action to rescue what was beginning to look like a slippery slope back to Division 2 – and as I said, 'God knows where from there.' The letter was critical of many things, but I also attempted to be encouraging, and finished by stating, 'Please excuse the liberty I am taking in writing this to you but I would prefer to express these views openly than behind your back – my views, I know, reflect those of most if not all those who watched the game on Saturday.' Nothing was ever said to me about the letter.

Thankfully, the team did improve, and in the last league game of the season they had a dramatic injury-time win with a four-try bonus point at Terenure College grounds in Lakelands Park. This had the effect of sending Blackrock College, who had just won their last game at the same time, down to Division 2. When the Blackrock game finished, Clontarf were losing, but matters changed in the midst of the former's celebrations. Alan Lewis, who refereed that game in Lakelands Park, had had the courage to play seven or eight minutes of injury time – which was absolutely correct, as there had been a series of stoppages during the second half. Somebody suggested that Alan should be elected an honorary life member of the club, and he himself has joked that he expected to see his statue in the grounds. That didn't happen, but he has always been welcomed in Castle Avenue since that day – and even been forgiven for many subsequent decisions that went against Tarf. He went on to become one of the best referees in world rugby, with forty-five major international test matches to his credit.

David Kennedy, the president whom I had sent the letter to, became the first chairman of the club at the end of that 1998/99 season. On Easter Monday in 2000, I received a telephone call, totally out of the blue, from Dave. He informed me that he was resigning as chairman from the end of that season and asked if I would be prepared to accept his nomination to succeed him. This was an absolute shock to me, as I had never served on any of the club's formal committees previously; it was only later that I realised that the letter I had written fifteen months earlier had struck a chord and perhaps had had unforeseen consequences.

I initially refused, but after some explanations and persuasion, I agreed to at least think about it. Dave explained that the chairman's position was essential, even though it was new. He said he was spending too much time in the UK on business and didn't have time to continue – and that in any event, some persons in the club resented what he was doing and were planning to oppose his re-election, which would be terribly divisive for the club. He wanted to nominate someone who wouldn't be identified with any existing factions. I asked for liberty to consult with two or three friends who were highly regarded in the club, and Dave agreed that I could, on a strictly confidential basis.

I was exceptionally busy work-wise over the next few weeks, and was out of the country at meetings on a couple of occasions, but I did eventually get the opportunity to chat with those I wanted to and trusted. I decided that I could do the job well and would find the time to do so, but it would have to be subject to some conditions. I spoke to Dave, explained that to him, and he agreed that what I required was feasible. Word then got out that Dave was going to resign and that I was going to be the executive committee's nominee to succeed him.

There was initial opposition from some quarters, but I met and spoke to those who had indicated some unhappiness. I outlined some of the changes that I intended to implement and persuaded them to allow me the opportunity to make these changes. Eventually, at the AGM on 27 June 2000, I was elected chairman of the club and thus a new chapter in my life began.

Clontarf Rugby was formally known as Clontarf Football Club and informally as Tarf. It was founded in 1876, achieving senior status in 1901. Although it had many successes at junior and under-age level, its senior successes were limited to winning the Leinster Senior Cup – which was the premier club competition in Leinster for more than a century – in 1936 and then in 1999. The club had also won the Smithwicks Old Belvedere Floodlit Cup in 1989, 1997 and 1998, as well as the All-Ireland Floodlit Cup in 1990.

The AIL had started in 1990, but Tarf didn't compete in it until 1991, when it qualified for the old Division 2. They were relegated in 1993 but quickly got promoted back to Division 2 and, as mentioned earlier, won Division 2 honours in 1997 and qualified for Division 1. For the first few seasons in Division 1, Tarf struggled, and as in 1999, mentioned earlier, the 1999/2000 season went to the last game, in May 2000, which was the second leg of a playoff with UCD, who were endeavouring to gain promotion from Division 2. Nonetheless, Tarf survived. Thus, when I became chairman in June 2000, Tarf had been a Division 1 team for three seasons – but they were not yet firmly established there.

The club, which is situated in the centre of Clontarf, a middle-class suburb, was the only Division 1 club on the north side of Dublin. It had enormous potential, but in my opinion, it hadn't realised that potential. In Autumn 1999, Alex 'Grizz' Wylie had been appointed coach of the senior team, as Brent Pope had left and ended up back in St Mary's College. Grizz was also from New Zealand; he was a well-known former All Black and had coached Canterbury, then the All Blacks, then in South Africa, England and Argentina, and in the 1999 World Cup he had coached Argentina in their famous win against Ireland in Lens, France in a quarter-final playoff.

Grizz had met one of Tarf's stalwarts, the late Ollie Byrne, at a pre-World Cup function in Dublin. In chatting to Grizz, Ollie learned that Grizz didn't have any plans post World Cup but also didn't think he was ready to return to his farm in New Zealand just yet. Ollie asked Grizz if he would be interested in coaching Tarf, and although he had probably never heard of it previously, Ollie and a few others persuaded him to get on board. When he arrived in Clontarf after Argentina were eventually defeated in the quarter-final, he immediately set about introducing professional rugby standards to Tarf, particularly in relation to the backup management personnel, and training, fitness and conditioning roles – as he was accustomed to international level standards from both – but also in coaching the players and improving their skills and game plans.

Although he didn't achieve success for the club during his two years as coach, he did lay the foundations for its later success and development into one of the leading Irish clubs over the subsequent twenty years. Everyone in the club who was involved in the coaching and management of rugby teams learned from Grizz. I enjoyed working with him, and although we did have a falling out towards the end, I admired him and what he did for the club, and I still do.

When Ollie Byrne persuaded him to join us, he didn't pay any attention to the costs that would be involved, which were considerable. Although Grizz wasn't responsible for it, by the time that I became chairman eight months later, our finances were in trouble. In fact, a new club honorary treasurer, who was elected at the same time as me, resigned less than three months later, when he realised the state of the finances and that his role was more than just keeping an eye on the incoming cash.

In some respects, his resignation was a blessing in disguise, as I was then able to co-opt my own choice as treasurer, Pat Mullen. Pat – who was, and still is, a great friend of my brother and had his own accountancy practice in another north Dublin suburb – took over the position at my request, at short notice, and agreed to do the job until the next AGM at the end of the season. Pat was still in the position fourteen years later, with only one short break of less than a season in the interim.

One of the first tasks we had to tackle was the restructuring of the club finances, as it quickly became obvious that we were spending more than we were taking in; our bank manager was putting us under pressure and we faced considerable capital expenditure on the clubhouse, which was not optional. As I thought that I would be able to leave day-to-day rugby issues to others, I was able to concentrate on the overall administrative structure of the club and the overall rugby organisation in the club.

I reviewed the role of the executive committee and the various subcommittees, and the roles of the members of those committees, which allowed me to more clearly define each of them. It was difficult to cut expenditure immediately, but we could soon get more information on its details and forecast outgoings for the rest of the season; in this way we could then focus on raising more funds, satisfying the bank that we were in control of the overall position while also dealing with the fairly precarious situation that prevailed.

Even though Tarf was primarily a rugby club, probably less than 20 per cent of the members were still active rugby players; the membership was mainly composed of former players and persons who lived in or near Clontarf, or had sons playing there. For many it was a social centre, with a reasonably good bar trade for six months a year. Still, it was obvious to me that the bar's potential was not being maximised for various reasons. One of the executive committee, Derry Kealy, who was himself a successful publican, recommended that we employ a professional bar manager on a full-time basis. We took that advice and employed Paul Fallon, who is still doing the job and has made a fantastic success of this aspect of the club, with the bar being open seven nights a week and during the daytime at weekends.

Shortly after I became chairman, Grizz Wylie had said to me that to succeed, the club would have to decide whether it was a rugby club or a drinking club. I replied that we wanted to be both, as one would not succeed without the other. We wanted success on the pitch, but we also wanted to maintain the reputation and reality of the club as a fun place – a venue where one could come to relax, have a few drinks with friends or acquaintances, maybe watch a game, chat about sport and the world in general, and avoid getting involved in petty personal hassle and disputes. That became our mission.

It was a club with huge membership numbers: more than a hundred adult playing members and three to four hundred mini and youth playing members. It was also a busy bar business, with other social functions, including pre-home match lunches for up to one hundred and fifty persons. I perceived that this whole operation, and the general regulatory and administrative issues that came with it, could be – and needed to be – made more efficient. I realised very quickly that in order to keep all these matters up to date, we needed to have somebody working in the club every day rather than relying on part-time volunteers.

The volunteers who had managed all these administrative matters had done a superb job, but it was unfair on them – and unwieldy for us – to continue if I wanted to increase our efficiency and be in a position to be demanding of those charged with these functions. We needed someone in the office every day to help the administration.

This was one of my pre-conditions, and so I appointed Mary Walsh as secretary-manager. Mary was married to Peter, the manager of the senior team, and a daughter-in-law of Billy, a former honorary secretary and past president of the club and the past presidents' representative on the executive committee. Mary wasn't appointed because of these connections, however; she was appointed because she was the most impressive of those who presented for interview.

We created an office for Mary in what had been an old storage area, bringing all the club records and accounts back there. Soon Mary was running the day-to-day operations of the club in conjunction with Paul Fallon and Pat Mullen. Mary continued to do so for more than ten years, until she died suddenly on 27 December 2011. In her own quiet but firm manner, she set the tone and standards for a well-run club. She worked officially from 9.30 a.m. to 1.30 p.m. each day, but she was always on hand on other occasions, when the need arose.

With these persons in place, and with the help of the other members of the executive committee, we were in a position to drive forward and start to realise the full potential of the club. I wanted to extend the club catchment area – to have the club as the centre of an expansion of rugby in the northern suburbs of Dublin. Looking back now, I know that we didn't succeed. It was beginning to move that way, but then Leinster Rugby took off in the early 2000s with the introduction of the Celtic League, the hyping of the Heineken Cup – ironically by the success of Munster Rugby – and the development of its stadium at Donnybrook, followed soon after by it's move to the RDS.

As Leinster Rugby began to realise its potential and expanded its footprint beyond its traditional Dublin 4 base, it effectively took the rugby fan base in north Dublin that I had envisaged could be harnessed by Clontarf. As Leinster Rugby has gone from strength to strength, the club has struggled to attract what might be termed the 'floating' fan; this has been the case for all the other clubs in Leinster, and indeed those in the other provinces. That does not mean that the club is in difficulty or has not been successful, but it has thwarted the ambition to extend its sphere of influence beyond Clontarf and the adjoining suburbs.

One of the more unusual tasks that I had to perform in my first few months as chairman was to liaise with a university in New Zealand. One of its final-year students was to come to Clontarf for a couple of years, but he – Gerard – had to be in the country before the end of October 2000 to comply with the IRFU's eligibility regulations. He was a very good rugby player, and Grizz Wylie had recruited him as our outhalf for the season, not being fully enamoured of the existing outhalf – one of the Clontarf heroes, Richie Murphy, who incidentally has progressed from being one of the Ireland assistant coaches to being the Head Coach of the Ireland U20 team. Gerard hadn't completed his final year degree examinations before he came to Ireland, and I persuaded the dean of the university that if he made special allowance, I would personally supervise Gerard's sitting of the exam, in my law office, as close as possible in time to when he should be sitting the exam at home.

This was agreed to, the two exam papers were couriered to me, and Gerard arrived into my office. He had been up all night cramming for the first paper, which as far as I remember was in English literature. As soon as he opened the paper, I could see the look of terror on his face; his head went down, and he was almost in tears. When I asked him what the problem was, he told me that he thought that the English exam was on the following day – that he had been cramming for the geography exam, which he thought was first.

I looked again at what I had to certify for the university dean, seeing a loophole that would enable me to switch the papers so that Gerard could do geography on the first day and English on the second. When I told him that I would allow him do the papers in the order that he had been expecting, the look of relief on his face was amazing; he proceeded to pass his exams and graduate with his degree.

Unfortunately for Gerard, rugby in Clontarf didn't work out as well for him – mainly because another future legend of the club appeared out of nowhere, asking to join us after he had heard that we might need a second row forward. This was the giant Ben Gissing, another New Zealander. As we could have only one foreign professional player, and as Grizz began to accept Richie Murphy, Ben was chosen and Gerard had to play the season on our seconds. In the following season, he moved to Italy and played professionally as an outhalf for many years, including in the Heineken Cup. Gerard was a very likeable young man; I was delighted that his career took off professionally, despite his disappointment with us.

In my five years as chairman, I worked with five different presidents: Gerry Costello, Robin Brophy, Andy Meldrum, Trevor Merrey and Vinny Higgins. Each of them was very different in personality and in approach to their role. Nevertheless, each of them did a great job for the club, and I developed a good personal relationship with them during their respective years in office. Unfortunately, Gerry Costello and Andy Meldrum died within a short time of completing their presidencies; however, the other three still retain a close involvement with the club, and I meet them regularly at Tarf games and other club functions.

We had the same honorary secretary, Geoff Blake, for the five years that I was chairman, and Geoff did a superb job as secretary during that time. As I wrote earlier, Pat Mullen was honorary treasurer; he outlasted me and served the club wonderfully. There were a number of others who served in different roles on the executive committee during that five-year period, for a year or more, and each of them was very supportive of me in my role. I had told Dave Kennedy when I agreed to take on the role that I would commit for a year. Halfway through that first year, I agreed to extend my commitment for another two years.

As many office holders in Tarf – and, indeed, in other clubs – have found, it is very hard to resign. Partly because it is difficult to find someone willing to take over, but also because the role becomes a bit of a habit, which – like many habits – is ultimately self-indulgent. I was persuaded to continue for each of the next two years, and I considered it a personal compliment that I was allowed to do so. All the same, I announced early in the fifth year that I was definitely not continuing beyond that season. I believe that in leadership roles like that, a change is advisable after a few years, as it is too easy to become set in one's ways and not recognise quickly enough the benefit – if not the need – for doing things a little differently.

I don't want to give the impression that it was always sweetness and roses – it wasn't, and there were many occasions when there were significant disagreements on issues of policy and of detail at executive committee level. Nevertheless, we ultimately reached agreement in the best interests of the club, as we perceived it. In some ways my role was similar to my role as managing partner in Gerrard, Scallan & O'Brien: encouraging those working with me to play their roles efficiently, and if they were not doing so, trying to rectify the problem and get them to discuss the issue with me before bringing it to the executive committee; introducing new initiatives and considering – and if applicable, promoting – those suggested by others; questioning all customs and conventions that were taken for granted to see if they were still appropriate; trying to achieve consensus at meetings when issues of difference arose and, where necessary, taking a decision when consensus was not possible; and generally providing leadership when needed.

One of the most difficult issues that I had to deal with was when someone underperformed in their role. This was usually caused by their taking on a position and then not having sufficient time to deal with their duties. I sometimes had to consider whether to ask that person to relinquish their role, or to cover for them and persuade them not to go for re-election at the end of the season. I was conscious that these were all volunteers – that they all had the best interests of the club at heart – and that perhaps I was too demanding and impatient, but I had a vision of where we needed to be, and how to get there, and felt that I had a responsibility to ensure that the club was best served.

My daughter Sinéad, who has ultimately become a consultant paediatrician in Sligo University Hospital, didn't start studying medicine immediately upon leaving school, although she had qualified to do so. She chose instead to study sports science in the University of Limerick; she was as much a sports fanatic as I was, and thought that a career in that field would be what she wanted. As it transpired, she changed her mind after completing first year in May 2003, coming back to Dublin to study medicine in UCD.

While in Limerick, she started playing rugby with the university team and the associated club team, UL Bohemians, and did so successfully, learning quickly and playing on a superb team, many of whom later played for the Irish International team. Sinéad was selected to play for Munster U19s, won the women's AIL with UL Bohs, and won the Irish and European inter-university competition with University of Limerick.

It was some consolation for me that she and another Clontarf girl, Fiona Coghlan, won AIL medals in 2003 even though Clontarf were defeated in the final of the men's competition later that season. When Sinéad came back to Dublin, she played rugby with UCD and was selected for Leinster U20s. Women's rugby in UCD was not as well organised, as in UL as UCD only competed in inter-varsity competitions, which didn't match her ambitions or expectations, so she also played AIL rugby with Old Belvedere for a season. She had suggested to me that Clontarf start a women's team; she said she would join if we did. Having checked with a few committee members, we eventually agreed to do so. Sinéad moved over to play with Tarf but had to retire soon after, as she suffered a broken ankle and then a couple of ankle sprains, which were interfering with her medical training.

She had also developed the habit of having her nose broken; by the time she stopped playing, she had broken it four times, three of those while playing rugby. Women's rugby in Clontarf lasted for only a few years at that time, but it has been resurrected again in recent years and seems to have established better roots now.

When I eventually resigned as chairman, I thanked all those that I had worked with but gave special mention to Terry Browne, who served as chairman of the rugby committee for the previous four years. That role is in some ways the most important in a rugby club, and Terry did a fantastic job while at the same time continuing to progress his successful banking career. In the subsequent fifteen years, Terry has had at least two more spells in that role. Given that he also played for the club for nearly twenty years – mainly on the senior team – his contribution to the club is unsurpassed.

Nonetheless, before Terry was elected, two significant changes were made. Firstly, I found it necessary to change our senior coach, Alex Wylie, at the end of the 2000/01 season. Although Grizz had done a great job as our senior coach, and had advanced the rugby standards in the club, I had learned that his relationship with many of the most experienced and best players in our senior squad was poor; they were considering leaving the club if his contract with us was renewed, as they knew he wasn't going to change his ways and personality.

My relationship with Grizz had been businesslike. Although we weren't close, we did spend quite a bit of time together, and I think we respected each other. That relationship began to sour in the third quarter of the season, when I tried to raise the subject of his relationship with the players. That wasn't really my role, but the then chairman of the rugby committee was very busy in his business and was not able to spend as much time in his club role as was needed. I had to raise the matter myself.

While Grizz may have respected me generally, he didn't accept any views that I expressed on the team or the rugby, even though he knew that I wasn't expressing views that were solely my own. When it became obvious that Grizz wasn't prepared to change, a decision was made not to renew his contract. The chairman of the rugby committee was the one who notified him, but I was the one that he blamed. He didn't take it well, and at one stage said to me that I was 'the first f— who had ever sacked me in my career'. When I made a presentation to him at the end of the season, he refused to shake my hand, which I thought was unlike him and not in keeping with rugby traditions. Even though it wasn't a happy parting, it didn't adversely affect my high regard for what he did for us.

We then had to set about recruiting a successor coach for the senior squad. Some very good candidates were considered, including one well known international player who was coming to the end of his playing career. Shortly after our first meeting, while we were getting down to some detail, he was – unexpectedly to him – offered a one-year extension to his international contract by the IRFU. He called me to say that he was backing out of the process and that maybe we could talk in twelve months' time.

We conducted a fairly extensive interview process with potential coaches and eventually appointed Philip Werahiko, who showed us at interviews that he had the vision and ambition to match our own. This was the second change referred to. Happily, we made the right appointment. With Phil as our senior coach, we continued the development that had started with Brent Pope and then Grizz Wylie. Even though I stayed in touch with the Irish international player, I didn't talk to him again about his coaching us, as matters had moved on in the intervening twelve months.

By the end of that season, 2001/02, we had reached the semi-final stage of the AIL and had played that semi-final against Shannon in Thomond Park. Even though we were then in our 125th year as a club – and Shannon was nearly ten years younger, and much younger as a senior club – they considered us as new kids on the block. They had already won the AIL on four occasions and knew that this was our first time to get this far. We were defeated and Shannon went on to win the final. Although disappointed, we had a great day and were all immensely proud of our team and our work in getting the team to that stage. In the following season, we were top of the league, which entitled us to a home semi-final. This was an amazing occasion, with a marquee, a big crowd of supporters for both sides, and – on this occasion – victory, resulting in our reaching the final in Lansdowne Road against Ballymena.

We had already defeated Ballymena in the league, but the team that faced us in that final was completely different. The vast majority of the Ballymena team that played the final were regular Ulster professional players – some were internationals and had won the Heineken Cup with Ulster a few seasons previously. We were ultimately defeated after a magnificent display against the odds, but we weren't the only ones who felt aggrieved at what Ballymena had done – discarding most of the players who had played for them all season and bringing in all their professionals.

The rules of the competition were changed for the following season, preventing a club doing what Ballymena did – and with some tweaking since then, this new rule has remained in place. The circumstances have changed, and there is also a limit on the number of professional players that can play at any one time in an AIL game, but it was very hard to accept the defeat at the time, as we were the outstanding team throughout the season and deserved to win outright.

The day of that final will live in the memory of all those who were there for as long as they live; the incredible excitement in Castle Avenue when the supporters gathered to wish the team well as they set out with a Garda Síochána escort to Lansdowne Road; the excitement of a close game that Clontarf should have won, even against the odds; the fantastic reception that the team got from the supporters back in Castle Avenue when the team arrived in their bus. The night was such fun that we wondered how we would have coped if we had actually won – or how we would cope if we won in the future. We had to wait eleven years to find out.

We were defeated in two more finals – in 2006 and 2009 – by Shannon, the first in Lansdowne Road, the second in Thomond Park. In 2006 we were well beaten, but that latter final of 2009 ended in a draw, as did the extra time played. We both scored the same number of tries, which was the next tie-breaker, but much to the amazement of most of the spectators, Shannon was deemed the winner because they had scored first. It was a silly rule, and was changed for future seasons, but even if the supporters didn't know of it, the team and management did and never tried to use it as an excuse for the defeat.

The behaviour of many of the Shannon supporters towards the Clontarf supporters after that game was deplorable; it didn't involve physical violence, but I don't remember seeing such reprehensible behaviour by winning supporters in any rugby competition previously or since. It was obvious to me then that Shannon, at the time, had supporters that were totally lacking in any traditions of the game; I knew that Shannon were in trouble as a club, despite their having many fine rugby men involved. That has transpired to be true. Although they have won the AIL on nine occasions in total – more than any other club – they have not come close to winning it since that day in 2009, spending most of the next decade struggling in Division 2.

From soon after the time that professional rugby was introduced – and the Irish provinces and the IRFU contracted the best players – the clubs became concerned that their status was reduced at the expense of the professional teams. Their primary concern was that their top competition – the AIL, which had quickly become very successful when introduced in the early 1990s, and was important to the clubs – was effectively downgraded. The AIL clubs formed their own associations in the late 1990s, with separate associations for the first, second and third divisions, as they did not believe that the long-established provincial branch committees were capable of representing the clubs regarding the AIL – the provinces now being direct competitors of the clubs.

Clontarf, as a first division club, had a representative in the First Division Clubs Association, who later became its secretary. There were very few rules governing the operation of the association, but one was that the club that provided the secretary could have another representative; I proposed myself, and was appointed with the approval of our club rugby committee, as we found that our representative, the secretary, wasn't reporting back to us on the meetings. The secretary's role was to take minutes of the meetings, circulate them for approval, prepare an agenda for the next meeting with the chairman – circulating it in advance – and arrange the subsequent meeting with the hotel at Dublin Airport, where the meetings were usually held.

On a couple of occasions, our representative was unable to attend, and I was asked to temporarily act as secretary. I was then informed by a few of the other club representatives, and the chairman, that they were very unhappy with the performance – or lack thereof – of the existing secretary, and I was asked to continue with the role. I resisted for a while but soon realised that the service by my colleague was well short of what was required – I had to ask him to stand aside. Around this time, the IRFU embarked on a review of the AIL; it became clear that the intention was to downgrade the competition. Their plan, as we were led to believe, would adversely affect each division differently, and some of us perceived a divide and conquer strategy.

We convened a joint meeting of the three divisional associations, agreeing to establish a working party to consider a unitary association. I was one of the representatives of the Division 1 clubs and attended a few meetings before we established what I christened as AISRCA, an acronym for 'All Ireland Senior Rugby Clubs Association', and I was appointed its first secretary. This new association was active for many years. It played an important role in ensuring the continued development of the AIL, but I'm not sure if it still exists or indeed whether the individual divisional associations, which continued to exist alongside the combined grouping, are still active.

AISCRA was perceived as a threat by the provincial branches, but it was never intended that way. It saw its role as being limited to the promotion and development of the AIL. It was happy to work in conjunction with the branches, but it wanted a direct line of communication to the IRFU on this issue. In this regard, it was successful. Interestingly, many of the original club representatives on AISRCA later became officers in their respective branches, and in the IRFU, showing that they weren't in opposition to the original organs but rather were complementary.

My time in AISRCA ended when I retired as chairman of Clontarf, and although I didn't anticipate it at the time, it did provide some training for when I later served as the Clontarf representative on the Leinster Branch. But that was a few years into the future.

CLONTARF EXECUTIVE COMMITTEE AND PRESIDENCY AND LEINSTER BRANCH EXECUTIVE COMMITTEE, 2009–2016

In May 2007, I was asked by my successor as chairman of Clontarf Rugby if I would be prepared to accept a nomination at the forthcoming AGM to be a junior vice president. The position would involve me becoming president in June 2011, for the 2011/12 season. I was highly honoured to accept, and I did. Nevertheless, I stated that I reserved the right to change my mind over the next couple of years, as I knew that my life was likely to change when I retired.

I had been thinking of retiring as a partner in Arthur Cox and thought that an appropriate time would be around my sixtieth birthday. One of the retirement presents that I bought for myself was a pair of ten-year tickets for the new Thomond Stadium. I envisaged going fairly regularly, to see Munster play, while getting in a round of golf in Ballybunion or Lahinch. I didn't know what I was going to do after retirement; having bought a very pleasant holiday home near Nice in France, I thought there was a possibility that I might be spending so much time there that I wouldn't be in a position to fulfil the role of club president.

I did retire as a partner at the end of August 2008, becoming a consultant – which was not intended to be full time. Although I went to Nice twice in the next couple of months, spending about five weeks there, I realised that there was so much going on at home that I wasn't going to move there with such permanency that it would prevent me from serving as president.

Therefore I confirmed to the club chairman, in early 2009, that I would be taking up the position of president in 2011, as planned.

Shortly after that, Finbarr Crowley – who was the Clontarf representative on the Leinster Branch of the IRFU and a member of the executive committee of the IRFU – told me that he was going to be appointed as chairman of the management committee of the IRFU, which would mean that he would have to stand down from his role in the Leinster Branch. He asked if I would take over from him. I hesitated again, as I had to consider whether I was the right person to take that role in representing Clontarf, and whether I would have the time to do so. It transpired that, as a consultant in Arthur Cox, I was much busier than I had anticipated; what's more, I wanted to travel more with Mary around the world.

Finbarr urged me to take the role and got others, including the club chairman and secretary, to try to persuade me. In the course of these discussions, it became clear to me that whoever was to be the Clontarf representative on the Leinster Branch would also become the president of Leinster Rugby in 2011/12 or 2012/13. I indicated that becoming president of Clontarf was my priority, and that I would therefore have to turn down becoming the Clontarf representative. I suggested two or three other Clontarf members who I thought would be more appropriate. One of those I suggested had, unknown to me, recently been diagnosed with a serious illness and wouldn't consider it. Another two turned it down because they were too busy with their profession or business.

In the meantime, Finbarr had approached some of the officers of the Leinster Branch; he explained the dilemma and agreed with them that Clontarf's right to nominate the president of Leinster would be postponed for two or three years if I was to be the nominee, so that I could undertake both offices. It wouldn't have been feasible to do both together, or even in successive years. I can't say that I was left with no alternative, but when presented with this plan – and having the opportunity to consider it over a week or so – I decided that I would go along with it. I realised that my retirement years were going to be full, albeit not in the manner that I had originally anticipated.

My purchase of the Thomond Stadium tickets didn't work out as good value for me. I went to the opening game, when Munster defeated New Zealand in November 2008, and probably used the tickets ten or twelve times over the ten years, lending them to friends and relations a few times as well. Leinster, however, got priority. While I loved to see Munster doing well, it was never at the expense of Leinster, and I was overjoyed when Leinster defeated Munster in the Heineken Cup semi-final, in Croke Park, in 2009; it was a major milestone in the development of the Leinster success in the next eleven years.

By becoming the club representative on the executive committee of the Leinster Branch, I also became an *ex officio* member of the executive committee of Clontarf Rugby. Thus began another spell on that committee – one that was actually longer than the first five years. When I joined the Leinster Branch, Leinster had just won the Heineken Cup for the first time, so a very upbeat attitude prevailed – a sense that the tide had turned in favour of Leinster and against Munster, who had dominated the noughties until then.

The Leinster Branch consisted of a number of committees who worked in conjunction with the administrative staff of the branch. The largest of these was the executive committee, on which each senior club was entitled to a representative. There were also representatives for each of the five junior club areas, along with representatives for the referees, women, youths and schools sections. Also present on the committee was the secretary of junior rugby.

The most powerful committee was the management committee, which consisted of the chief executive, the president, the senior vice president, the immediate past president, the honorary treasurer, the honorary secretary and the chairpersons of the five standing committees – professional game; domestic rugby; finance; premises and administration; and marketing and commercial. All decisions of the standing committees were referred to the management committee, supposedly discussed there and – where appropriate – approved and reported to the executive committee for formal ratification. Each of these standing committees had a number of subcommittees; some were long-standing, others were *ad hoc*.

There was an unwritten objective: to try to ensure that each member of the executive committee had a role on at least one of the standing committees or subcommittees, where most of the work was done. Most did, but in the seven years that I spent there, I noted that there were one or two who seemed happy to just come along to the executive committee meetings, which largely rubber-stamped decisions made earlier. In other words, they weren't contributing to any of the other work that had to be done. The executive committee was unwieldy, as it was too large, but it did comprise persons who had done or were doing important work for their clubs or sections; and they were all very capable. Whether the committee structure got the maximum benefit from their experience is debatable.

Having said that, some interesting issues were raised for the first time at the executive committee meetings; they were outside the ambit of the other committees, and more general in nature while still relating to the sport. One example was the issue of concussions, which was raised and discussed before it became a major public issue. Addressing this and other matters meant that the relevant persons in Leinster Rugby were at least familiar with the issues when they arose publicly in the media.

A major weakness of the representative committee system was the tendency to groupthink, which was anathema to me. In fact, as I realised over the next few years, the same applied at management committee level. And from my limited experience of interactions with the IRFU, it applied there also. I became conscious after a few years of the extent to which this tendency applied at the Leinster Rugby finance committee, which was dominated by its chairman, who was also the honorary treasurer. I wasn't on this committee for the first few years, and understood that it was a finance oversight committee; however, when I did go on the committee, I realised that it wasn't what I thought – a form of checks and balance – and in fact it had a very limited role. I tried to introduce a change that would have seen a separate chairman introduced to the committee, to ensure that all power did not reside in one person. This resulted in a major confrontation with the incumbent treasurer just before I was elected president. He threatened a major row over the issue, and I decided, perhaps foolishly, to back down for an easier life. But this was a few years in the future.

In my first year as the Clontarf representative in Leinster Rugby, I was nominated to the rugby committee as the representative of the senior clubs. My main role was to chair a subcommittee to review the AIL. This was in line with the IRFU's decision to review the league; they delegated to each of the provinces the task of canvassing the views of the clubs on its future structure. I was entitled to choose the members to sit with me; we had a very hard-working group that was representative of the different divisions of the AIL and of the city and outside city senior clubs. This subcommittee had a number of meetings, and we reported regularly on our general progress to the rugby committee. I devised questionnaires and, when agreed to by the other subcommittee members, submitted them to each club secretary, to each director of rugby or head coach and to the players.

I also had a meeting with the Leinster head coach, Michael Cheika, to canvas his views on the benefits or otherwise of the AIL, enquiring how it could be made more relevant and could connect more to the professional game. I had been told by others that Cheika didn't respect or care about the AIL, but I found that to be untrue – I found that he was very knowledgeable about it and supportive of maintaining close links between the Division 1 clubs and the professional team generally. He considered that these links could be maintained and strengthened by the provision of coaching, fitness and conditioning, and nutritional advice and assistance by the Leinster professional staff to these clubs, which he perceived were acting as feeders to his professional team.

Having received a reasonably good amount of returned questionnaires with responses, we set about writing our report, submitting it to the rugby committee and upwards to the executive committee via the management committee. At each level, it was slightly improved; it was then submitted to the IRFU as the Leinster Branch position. By the time the IRFU completed their review and published their report a few months later, our Leinster report was hardly recognisable in it. Nonetheless, as I knew from previous dealings with the IRFU, this result was not unusual. I also recognised from their report that it represented a series of compromises of different aspirations and requirements between clubs in different provinces and clubs in different divisions. These differences were not going to be reconciled easily, to provide a long-term solution for the structure of the AIL – and so it has transpired to be, as the AIL has changed a few times since and is still not acceptable to all clubs.

In September 2009, shortly after I joined the Leinster executive committee, the Leinster team – as European champions and holders of the Heineken Cup – were invited to Nice on the Côte d'Azur, as part of their pre-season training, to play a friendly game against the rugby club of Nice. It was an opportunity to train in the sun, play a game that wasn't unduly strenuous and have a relaxing break. As I had a holiday home outside Nice,

I arranged to meet Mick Dawson, the chief executive, Des Lamont, the recently elected president, Pat Fitzgerald, the chairman of the commercial and marketing committee, and Richie Boucher, chief executive of Bank of Ireland (the main sponsor of Leinster), all of whom had travelled over with the team. We had a beachside lunch before joining the players and going on to the stadium for the match. It was a very enjoyable day, and I learned much about the inner workings of Leinster Rugby in the general chat.

On the following evening, Michael Cheika and many of the senior players were invited to a reception on a yacht in Monte Carlo by a former Irish business executive who was in his early seventies and had moved to Monaco. I was informed by some of the guests on the following day that it was very embarrassing, as the host paraded what were obviously a number of Russian ladies and indicated that some of them were regular friends of his. As well as embarrassed, some were disgusted and insulted by the sleazy reception. The information did not unduly surprise me – it conformed to what I had been told many years previously in relation to the same person.

In early June of that year, 2010, I was asked to play for the Clontarf Rugby Club golf team in the annual Lorcan Sherlock Trophy for senior rugby clubs; it is organised by the Leinster Branch and takes place in Grange Golf Club. Each club is represented by four pairs in a scotch foursomes format – the best three cards, when aggregated, count as the team score, with one card discarded.

Although the card that was discarded was that of John Pardy and me, we didn't mind as Clontarf won the trophy for the first time since 1944. We were each presented with a pewter tankard and the team trophy by the Leinster president in what tends to be his first official duty of the season. We won it twice more in the next three years, and I was on the team in each instance. Our victory in June 2014 was just after I myself was elected as president, so I managed to present myself with a tankard. Thankfully, my card wasn't discarded on those next two occasions.

I had a private visit to the new Aviva Stadium in December 2009 and was delighted to attend the first game played there on 31 July 2010. Nonetheless, despite having attended very many games there over the next ten years – in a wide variety of seats and levels – I still consider it a very poor sports stadium, when compared with equivalent stadiums around the world. It seemed particularly so after moving back from Croke Park, where the rugby internationals had been played since 2007 – and where Leinster had their famous win against Munster in the 2009 Heineken cup semi-final, watched by a world-record crowd for a club game. That game was followed by their victory against Leicester in the final at Murrayfield.

Croke Park had further resonance for me. In addition to having played there as a young boy in 1961, I had experienced the emotional rush of watching Ireland play and defeat England there in 2007. On that occasion, Mary and I were seated beside Peter Mooney, better known as Pete St John, who broke down with emotion when the entire crowd of Irish supporters – and I guess many English supporters – sang his best-known song, 'The Fields of Athenry'. Neither the old Lansdowne Road stadium nor the new Aviva Stadium had the physical attributes to allow the same atmosphere to be repeated in the crowd, regardless of the excitement being generated on the field.

In April 2010, Leinster played Clermont-Auvergne in the RDS in the quarter-final of the Heineken Cup. Leinster won that game, albeit Clermont should have won – their kicker, Brock James, had a very bad day. I was in the committee box with my son, Shane; behind us were a recent past president of the IRFU and a friend of his, another member of the IRFU executive committee. At some stage, the Clermont assistant coach stood up from where he was sitting, just inside the touchline and in front of the committee box. The IRFU past president (who was there on a freebie) verbally abused and shouted at him for blocking his view.

Shane turned to the gentleman and politely told him to calm down – that the person in question was Joe Schmidt, who had very recently been announced as the new Leinster coach. Joe continued standing, trying to read the game and coach his team – doing what he was being paid for, and what he then did for Leinster and Ireland for the next nine years. When he finished what he had stood up for on that occasion, he looked behind him at the committee box and smiled wryly, realising that coming to Leinster was going to give him new experiences.

Leinster went on to play and lose to Toulouse, in Toulouse, in the semi-final. Shane and I attended, and we then drove to San Sebastian to watch Munster losing to Biarritz in the other semi-final. The reason that this stands out in my memory is that Shane and I drove back to Marseille to get a flight home only to find that the ash from an Icelandic volcano had recently erupted and caused the cancellation of the flight – and most flights in Europe. Instead, we made our way home by train and ferry, firstly via TGV from Marseille to Paris, then by Eurostar to London, then by train to Holyhead, and by ferry home to Dublin. We arrived home at 6 a.m. a day later, but I was still in time for the CRH AGM scheduled for 11 a.m. in Dún Laoghaire – a meeting that I was expected to attend in an advisory capacity – and Shane was in time to give a scheduled tutorial in Trinity.

The IRFU had a list of persons who were selected to sit on panels that adjudicated on disciplinary issues. By this point, I had been invited to join this list. I sat on panels to review red cards and other offences referred by citing officers, who reviewed videos of games afterwards to find foul play that the on-field referee may have missed. I commenced with AIL club-level games, then graduated to Magners League games and eventually Heineken Cup games. I never proceeded to international level, although some of those who sat on panels with me did so. I was on a long list for the World Cup in 2009 but never got further than that. As I became more involved in Leinster committee work, I felt – because of potential conflicts of interest – that I shouldn't continue, so I stood down from the IRFU disciplinary panel.

At the end of that season, 2009/10, Clontarf were in difficulty and were demoted to the newly created Division 1B, which was a variation of the old Division 2 but with the new provision that the winner of Division 1B would qualify with the top three teams of Division 1A for the semi-final playoffs. Clontarf had changed their coach at the end of the previous season, and this had been very divisive within the club. Andy Wood – who had joined the club with Phil Werahiko in 2001 as a player, and who had taken over as first team coach from Phil when the latter had departed for an English club in 2006 – was very popular and highly regarded by most in the club, and particularly by the players.

Nevertheless, the team had had a run of defeats during the season 2008/2009 – some persons panicked a little, including me. At that time, Bernard Jackman made it known that he was interested in coaching Clontarf. He himself had played for the club before getting a professional contract with Connacht and then with Leinster, and he had since got a few international caps. Talks took place with Bernard, and he was told that he would be appointed from summer 2009; Andy Wood was told that his contract would not be renewed.

Ironically, the team recovered after Andy was told he was being let go; they got to third position in the league, which earned them a semi-final against Cork Constitution in Cork. They duly won – despite a great display by a 19-year-old Peter O'Mahony – and reached the final against Shannon in Thomond Park. This was the final that ended in a draw even after extra time, and was decided against Clontarf on the basis that Shannon had scored the first try – having won the toss and played with the advantage of a strong wind in the first half. If we could have rolled back the clock by a few months at that stage, Andy Wood wouldn't have been let go, but the die was cast.

Bernard came in July 2009, tried to change things unnecessarily – and without a proper review – and recruited new players who weren't near the appropriate standard. This turned out to be a disaster and we were relegated in his first year. At the end of that first year, there was a player rebellion and a number of long-standing players threatened to leave the club if Bernard was staying. I was back on Clontarf's committee at this stage and was centrally involved in trying to settle the problem with the players.

The committee had decided that the recruitment of players had to be taken out of Bernard's hands, as most of those that he had recruited didn't match up to his description – or our expectation. There were a number of players living in Cork and Limerick who were considering moving to Dublin for work or postgraduate studies, and they were consequently put in touch with us. They had heard negatives about Bernard, but we convinced them that he would be successful; when we introduced them to him, he impressed them. We also got Ben Gissing back to play for us. Ben had joined the club back in 2000 and had played in the game against Ballymena in 2003; he had subsequently become a professional with Leinster, Treviso and finally Glasgow. When his contract wasn't renewed, he rejoined us – we had a very strong team for Bernard's second year as coach.

As it transpired, Clontarf won Division 1B. As well as being promoted back to Division 1A, we reached the semi-final by virtue of the compromise in the creation of Division 1B, playing Old Belvedere in their home ground in Anglesea Road. We were winning until the last minute, when a terrible unforced error resulted in a breakaway try and conversion by Old

Belvedere. Even before this game, the players' rebellion that we had quelled the previous year had erupted again.

We were called to a meeting with a players' committee two days after the semi-final. As the incoming president, I was invited to attend. I did, thinking that their success in achieving promotion and nearly getting to a final again would have satisfied the players; however, we were given an ultimatum: more than half of the team that played in the semi-final said they would leave the club to play elsewhere if Bernard was to stay on. The committee was left with no alternative but to tell Bernard that his contract wasn't going to be renewed. It was very unfortunate for Bernard, but it was a practical solution for the club. The players were needed, and I supported the decision on the basis that the unity of the club was more important than any one individual; having experienced difficulties with players in each of the previous two years, we couldn't afford to do so again.

I was extremely busy at that time. I was making final preparations for a major commercial arbitration case in Paris, which necessitated staying there. This resulted in my absence for the following three weeks. I had had a good personal relationship with Bernard since he rejoined Clontarf in 2002, having moved from Sale in England. I was upset with myself that I didn't take the time to meet him before I went away. I did contact him on my return and arranged to meet; the damage had been done to our personal relationship by then, however, and it was a cold meeting. I did wish him the best of luck in his career, and there is no doubt that his coaching career took off after he left Clontarf – going to Grenoble and quickly becoming the head coach there. He is now a very successful and popular rugby pundit on various media. By the time I got back from Paris, the committee had conducted a series of interviews for his replacement, and Andy Wood was reappointed.

Thus began my term of presidency in early June 2011. It was already transpiring to be a strange year for me personally, and my responsibilities for Clontarf and Leinster were particularly time-consuming. The end of the year, 2011, was a very sad period. My nephew and godson Colm, as I mentioned earlier, was killed in a road accident on 17 November; Mary Walsh, the secretary-manager of Clontarf Rugby and a good friend, died suddenly on the night of 27 December.

The year had commenced with my wife, Mary, becoming Lady Captain of Sutton Golf Club in January 2011, and our sporting year had started with her drive in (a tradition in which an incoming captain drives off a tee box near the clubhouse, watched by family, friends and club members, before retiring to the clubhouse for a celebration, indicating the start of their captaincy and the start of the new golfing year) on Sunday, 2 January. Although our terms of office as captain and president of our respective clubs only overlapped for seven months, we had a very busy sporting year between us.

My first trip abroad that year was when I went to Paris on 20 January for the Heineken Cup fixture against Racing Metro 92. Mary wasn't free to travel with me, as she was busy in her new role. Leinster won the game comfortably in Racing's old stadium, Yves-du-Manoir, and the members of the Leinster executive committee who travelled to Paris with the team met Jackie Lorenzetti, who had recently bought the club. He told us of his ambitious plans to build a new stadium and entertainment complex just outside Paris, in La Défense. He eventually succeeded, and the new stadium opened in 2017.

On 18 March 2011, I awoke at 3.00 a.m. in excruciating pain but had no idea what was causing it. I went downstairs and rolled around the floor for a few hours in agony trying unsuccessfully to find a position where the pain might alleviate. When Mary awoke and came downstairs, she got a fright when she saw me. She brought me down to our local GP, and I was seen before the surgery opened. I was advised to go to an emergency department; not wanting to have to wait too long, Mary drove me to the Blackrock Clinic Emergency Department. We were just ahead of the busy morning commuter traffic and quickly got to Blackrock.

I was seen immediately by a nurse and emergency registrar, got various medications – including painkillers – and was eventually told that I had a gallstone which had dislodged and got stuck in a duct. The pain eased sufficiently for me to be allowed home, but I knew that I didn't want to suffer that pain again. When my consultant gastroenterologist, told me a couple of weeks later that the best way to ensure that I didn't have a repeat was to have my gallbladder removed, I readily agreed to this. However, as I had a few major appointments coming up in the next few months – personal, rugby and business – we fixed a date for 3 June, which would be after the AIL final (if we reached it), after the long arbitration case in Paris (fixed for early May) and after I was elected president of Clontarf on 2 June. I went into hospital early on the morning after that election and was operated on for a cholosystectomy, which thankfully has worked – at least to the extent that I have not had a recurrence of that particular pain.

My first grandchild, Joshua, was born on 6 March of that year. Wanting to see and to babysit him added to the time constraints arising from preparation for the Paris arbitration case, other work in Arthur Cox, additional committee work that I had assumed in Leinster and disciplinary committee cases that I was involved in – in Leinster, AIL and Europe. All of this meant that I was as busy as I had been before I retired. This was exacerbated further when I became president of Clontarf, but there was some respite during the summer for a couple of weeks in which I got a chance to recover from the surgery and got back on the golf course, which I had missed for various reasons.

At this stage, Leinster was progressing rapidly with the building of their new headquarters at Newstead Building in Belfield, UCD, near the Clonskeagh entrance. The development had been arranged by Mick Dawson and financed largely by a benefactor through UCD; it comprised new offices, meeting rooms for the administrative staff, rugby coaches, backroom staff and playing squad, and an ultra-modern gym. This was a very exciting development for Leinster Rugby, reflecting more superb foresight and planning by Mick Dawson, who was a very effective chief executive.

In July, on a site visit with the architect, the management committee got its first viewing of the work in progress. We were all suitably impressed. On 22 August, I collected my Clontarf president's blazer from Jim Markey Mans Shop in Drumcondra, and on the following day I collected my Leinster management committee blazer from Best Menswear in Dundrum, so I was properly kitted out for all the social occasions that were to follow in the two capacities.

As well as the rugby standing committee and the management committee in Leinster, I was also appointed to the facilities and administration committee. I was on some subcommittees for the latter standing committee, including the grounds and premises subcommittee and what was called the consultative committee, which had been established to manage the operation and maintenance of the Leinster grounds in Donnybrook, which were also occupied by two tenant clubs, Old Wesley RFC and Bective Rangers FC. I was also on a subcommittee reviewing the branch bye-laws and regulations and another reviewing the disciplinary procedures to be applied when there was a red card or a player or official was cited at a Leinster Branch-organised game, as these had to be conformable to changes being made by the International Rugby Board.

At the end of September, I attended the Clontarf Cricket Club annual dinner as a special guest, it being our sister club, and later that night I attended the latter part of a dinner for the past captains of the St Paul's College SCTs, it being the 50th anniversary of opening of the school. I wasn't a past captain but was invited as the president of Clontarf Rugby, which had been closely associated with St Paul's since the first past pupils started leaving there in the mid-1950s.

On 3 October, I had a photoshoot for the Clontarf programme and website at 4.30 p.m., and then a photoshoot with the Leinster management committee in Anglesea Road at 5.30 p.m.

Traditionally in Leinster, each senior club has an annual dinner to which all the other club presidents are invited. This was known as the club dinner circuit, and it starts off each year with a reception hosted by the president of Dublin University Football Club in the Pavilion in College Park. In 2011, this took place on 13 October, and for the first time in its long history, the Dublin University club president was a woman, Kay Bowen, a very pleasant lady and a great representative of her club during the season.

On 15 October, Clontarf had an AIL away game against Garryowen; we narrowly won, and I drove home soon after its end, as I had to go to the St Anne's Golf Club annual dinner that evening. In addition to the Leister rugby clubs' annual dinners, the Clontarf president was invited to the annual dinners of the three local golf clubs (Royal Dublin, St Anne's and Clontarf); the cricket club, as I mentioned above; and the local tennis, GAA, hockey and yacht clubs. Added to this were other *ad hoc* dinners and receptions. These alone – without all the rugby games I attended at all levels – would have kept me occupied, but I thoroughly enjoyed the rugby and social aspects of the office and was very honoured to be able to represent my club on so many occasions.

Each dinner involved a number of speeches by club members and guests. For my own club's annual dinner, I had invited Eugene McCague, one of my former partners in Arthur Cox, as a guest speaker. I knew that Eugene was a superb after-dinner speaker; this dinner was no exception, and he entertained the guests to a very witty and self-deprecating speech about his sporting exploits. When I was president of Leinster Rugby in 2014, Eugene also accepted my request to speak at one of the major pre-match functions and again was superbly entertaining.

Clontarf had a very strong team that season; coming to the end of the season in April 2012, they were on top of the league. As a consequence of the IRFU further tinkering with the AIL, playoffs had been abolished and whoever topped the league at the end of the season would win the league. With two games to go, Clontarf were on top of the league. The penultimate game was at home to St Mary's College, who – if they defeated Clontarf and then Young Munster on the last day – were the only team that could pass out Clontarf.

If Clontarf defeated St Mary's then they had won the league. In fact, the IRFU had sent the trophy to Castle Avenue that afternoon on the assumption that Clontarf would succeed, facilitating an immediate presentation. Unfortunately, the game didn't work out in the manner that we had hoped and the IRFU had expected. St Mary's scored a couple of tries that were too easily allowed, but it was the loss of two critical players – Barry O'Mahony and Killian Lett – to injury during the second half of the game that ultimately lost the game for us; they were our two best line-breakers and those most likely to get, or create, the score that we needed. St Mary's had defeated us with a last-minute penalty when we played away to them earlier in the season, so on that basis they deserved to win the league. But more excitement was to come on the following Saturday, when we played Lansdowne on the main pitch in the Aviva and St Mary's hosted Young Munster in Templeville Road.

We defeated Lansdowne that day and had to wait for the result of the St Mary's game, because it was running a few minutes late. Young Munster had a player incorrectly sent off with a red card early in the first half, but when our game finished and I went out on the pitch to be with the players and managers, Young Munster were still leading. It was too early to celebrate, but for a couple of minutes, the tension was palpable – the despair and disappointment of the previous week was lifted as we realised that we were back in the race.

There wasn't a fairytale ending for us, but there was for St Mary's. They scored in the last minute of injury time, winning the game and the AIL. It was very disappointing, but the reality was that we had done our grieving and teeth-gnashing after the previous weekend's defeat; if we had won the AIL, we probably would have been too shocked to celebrate. It did demonstrate, however, the highs and lows that sport produces, and the truism that a game isn't won or lost until the final whistle blows. I have no doubt that if there had been playoffs that season – as there had been previously (and which were reintroduced two or three years later) – we would have won, but there weren't and we didn't win the critical game at home.

Thankfully, Leinster didn't let me down that season and provided some consolation for Clontarf's failure to win the AIL. I had flown to Bath in December 2011 for the Leinster v Bath Heineken Cup game, which was won easily by Leinster. It was my first time in Bath and in their ground, the Rec, which is almost in the centre of the city. There we met Bruce Craig, who had recently bought Bath Rugby Club; I took a fairly instant dislike of him and his attitude to us.

Later, as a member of the Leinster management committee, I got to accompany the team to London for the final of the Heineken Cup against Ulster in Twickenham. I travelled with Mary, who had also gone with me to the two previous finals that Leinster had contested and won – the first in 2009, at Murrayfield in Edinburgh, when they defeated Leicester; the next in 2011, at the Millenium Stadium in Cardiff, when they had the miraculous second-half comeback against Northampton. In both of those games, Leinster weren't hot favourites to win – this was not the case in 2012.

We had lunch in Twickenham, and it was probably one of the worst lunches I have had before a rugby game, anywhere in the world. It wasn't necessarily the fault of the caterers – as I had had two very pleasant lunches there before the Cambridge v Oxford University games a few years previously – but this lunch was appalling. Nevertheless, I witnessed something that I found very uplifting, which was the presence of Peter Robinson, the First Minister of Northern Ireland and a member of the Democratic Unionists, and Martin McGuinness, the Deputy First Minister and a member of Sinn Féin, sitting beside each other at a guest table; they were clearly at ease in each other's company, laughing and joking together. It was an indication to me that the world had changed since I had been involved in politics in 1986, and I was delighted to see it. They weren't laughing and joking after the game, however, as Leinster easily won. So although I had been very disappointed at the end of the AIL, I was cheered at the end of the Heineken Cup.

Clontarf won a record number of Leinster Branch pennants for successes at junior, youths and minis rugby in that season, 2011/12, so while we didn't win the most important competition, I was very proud to be present for each of those victories, and it was deemed to be a successful season for the club. At the AGM in June 2012, I handed over office to my successor, Terry Browne. Although I stayed closely involved in Clontarf's committees, my focus had to shift towards Leinster, as I was elected junior vice president at the Leinster Rugby AGM a couple of weeks before the Clontarf meeting.

During the season, while I was president of Clontarf Rugby, I suggested to my fellow committee members that we should consider arranging some big event for the millennium of the Battle of Clontarf in 2014. I jokingly said that we should invite the Barbarians to play in Clontarf or organise a Leinster v Munster game in Castle Avenue – as the battle had been as much a clash between the kings of those two provinces as it was one between Brian Boru and the Vikings. I wasn't aware that my idea had been adopted until many months later, when I was asked by Philip Orr – who was the Irish representative on the Barbarians committee – if I knew anything about a letter written by someone in Clontarf Rugby inviting the Barbarians to a game in Clontarf.

The secretary of the Barbarians remembered receiving the letter but had mislaid it; when he mentioned it to his committee as they were planning their season for 2013/14, they asked him to follow it up. I soon discovered that Shane Harnett, who was chairman of the commercial and marketing subcommittee of Clontarf Rugby, had taken the initiative to write to the Barbarians but hadn't told us. I followed up the issue with Philip Orr, who confirmed that there was interest in the event, and a good possibility that it could be arranged.

As the 2011/12 season came to an end, there was a presentation on Saturday, 26 May to the Tarf U17s, who had won the Leinster Youths Cup. I had arranged to collect the Heineken Cup for the weekend so that it was present for the U17s; I also organised for Cian Healy and Mike Ross to attend and present the medals to the youths. I was chatting to Mike Ross, who was affiliated to Clontarf, and he asked me if Tarf had any other young prop forwards like Cian coming along.

I told him that he should keep a watch out for a young under 20 named Tadhg Furlong – that I thought he was going to be really top class. Mike said that he would look out for him and help him if he could, but neither he nor I realised that Tadhg would replace him on the Leinster and Ireland teams within four years, quickly becoming the best tighthead prop in the world. I know that Mike did act as one of Tadhg's mentors, but I don't claim responsibility for that, as Mike was happy to help anyone who was interested in the science of front-row play.

On the following day, Leinster was surprisingly defeated by Ospreys in the PRO12 final in the RDS. Just before that, however, I was to give the Heineken Cup back to a Leinster Rugby employee. He wasn't where I was supposed to meet him, in the foyer of the Four Seasons Hotel, so I went into the room where the pre-match reception was to be held and put the cup on a plinth, which looked as though it was dressed for it. That caused a diplomatic incident for some of the organisers, as it had been reserved for the PRO12 trophy, which had a different sponsor, Rabobank. I had to remove the Heineken Cup and place it in the boot of my car, where it remained for the next few hours – until I located the person who was to take it from me. Incidentally, Leinster didn't win the competition again until 2018, when it had become the European Champions Cup.

During the second half of the 2011/12 season in Leinster, the honorary secretary, Des Kavanagh, indicated to the management committee that he intended to retire at the end of the season; he had been elected at the end of the previous season as a Leinster Branch representative to the IRFU and believed that he couldn't maintain the two positions.

The senior vice president, Ben Gormley, was anxious to ensure that an appropriate person was in office when he took over as president, as Des and his predecessor were very efficient and capable administrators – all their documentation was always accurate and available promptly for meetings. It was unanimously agreed that a subcommittee selected by the management committee – comprising me, Des Lamont (a past president) and Ray Ryan (the incumbent honorary treasurer) – should interview those interested in the position, with the objective of recommending the most appropriate person to the executive committee. The latter would then make the appointment, as set out in the branch regulations.

Three candidates completed the detailed application forms, which set out the criteria we were looking for and which had been approved by the management committee. We were looking for someone with proven experience in rugby administration, and who had general administrative, secretarial and word processing abilities. The three applicants then presented for interview, which was very thoroughly prepared for by the interview panel, all of us being experienced in the process.

We were then informed that the then president of Leinster was proposing himself for the position and did not believe that he should have to submit himself to the interview process. As he was a member of the management committee, which had approved the process, this shocked all of us. Of the three persons who applied for the position, two were very competent – they would have been very satisfactory in the role. The third, however, was outstanding, and was our clear choice as the recommended candidate. When we reported back to the management committee, our recommendation was readily accepted; however, the president indicated that he wasn't prepared to accept the recommendation and would insist on his right to have an election at the executive committee meeting.

He was a popular person, 'hail fellow, well met', but wouldn't have ranked among the top three candidates if assessed by the criteria that the interview panel had agreed and used. At the ensuing election, the president won, having canvassed extensively behind the backs of the management committee. His subsequent performance as honorary secretary unfortunately matched our expectations, but his popularity has kept him in position. His *bonhomie* and very friendly nature is a bonus to the Leinster Branch but, in my opinion, more is required.

It was embarrassing for the favoured candidate, who was effectively put up for election against the president; he wasn't on the executive committee at the time, wasn't extensively known and wouldn't have been made aware of such an election at the time that he applied. Thankfully, he overcame the incident, later becoming a member of the executive committee and, in 2017/18, a very successful and popular president of Leinster Rugby – so in the end, he eventually emerged well out of the process and is now the incoming chairman of the IRFU management committee.

The 2011–12 season ended without much more controversy and a new season commenced. After a management committee meeting on 14 August, I headed for Perth in Western Australia. My daughter Louisa had moved there a few weeks earlier with her son, Joshua, and Mary had gone with her to help her settle. Louisa moved there to commence her respiratory paediatrics fellowship, and was followed shortly afterwards by Lee – once he managed his exit from his club professional position in Killiney Golf Club.

I stayed for three and a half weeks, but Louisa and Lee have stayed in Australia since – albeit they have moved to Sydney, and Joshua has been joined by Lexi and Cody. I arrived back on 9 September. On 11 September I had a consultative committee meeting, a special management committee meeting and an executive committee meeting; on 13 and 14 September, I had meetings with the IRFU regarding the Clubs Strategic Plan and its working party, played in the golf outing for the 2011/12 club presidents in Greystones Golf Club and then represented the president at a Leinster U20s game in Donnybrook. So I was back quickly into active mode.

On the following Sunday, 23 September, I travelled with some of the Leinster playing squad and committee to Ravenhill for a memorial service for the late Nevin Spence, an Ulster player who had died tragically a few days previously. Isaac Boss, who was with us, had played with Nevin before he himself moved to Leinster; he seemed particularly upset in spite of his usual bubbly, gregarious self. It was the first of a few visits to Ravenhill for me over the next few years; despite the very good atmosphere usually generated there, I never warmed to it.

Even though we had been using it for a few months, the official opening of the new Leinster Rugby headquarters took place on 26 September. It was followed by a lunch hosted by the president of UCD and a very pleasant afternoon in Ashtons. Pleasant to the extent that I had to cancel, at short notice, a meeting of the facilitiies and administration committee – which, as chairman, I had foolishly convened for that evening. As some of its members were with me and it suited most of the others not to have to come over to Clonskeagh, no problems ensued.

Two days later, most of the management committee travelled in a minibus to Galway to see Leinster being well defeated by Connacht. Having arrived back late from Galway, I then travelled by train to Cork early on Saturday morning. There I saw Clontarf being narrowly defeated by

Cork Con, who scored in the last second of the game for a two-point win. The sporting weekend, which seemed a disaster, was rescued by Europe's remarkable and really exciting comeback win in the Ryder Cup golf match at Medinah Golf Club near Chicago.

Over the next few weeks, I had to chair a series of meetings regarding the introduction of consistent bye-laws for the various junior areas. I also had to chair IT and internal communications subcommittees, and board meetings for Nokatus and Nerco, as well as attend and contribute to other committee meetings for Clontarf, Leinster, the IRFU, St Michael's House golf and Arthur Cox. Between meetings, watching rugby games, playing golf fairly regularly and travelling – both within Ireland and further afield – my life for the next couple of years was mapped out.

It may seem boring, but I have to admit that I enjoyed most of it; it was a good transition between my full-time working life, which ended in 2008, and my full-time retirement in summer 2016. On 18 March 2013, Blackrock defeated St Michael's College in a very entertaining Schools Senior Cup final. Some stars of the future played in this final, including James Ryan for St Michael's and Garry Ringrose for Blackrock. Garry was the place-kicker and missed only one place kick during the final. This was his first miss in the four rounds they played, achieving twenty-seven out of twenty-eight kicks – a remarkable record. He doesn't seem to have been asked to kick regularly for Leinster or for Ireland in his career since, which is a surprise. I had always enjoyed watching a few schoolboy games in the Senior Cup and identifying future stars; in my few years on the Leinster management committee, I went to watch more than usual, seeing many of the Leinster and Ireland teams of the 2017–21 era coming through at that age.

On 5 April, a few of us from the management committee flew to Luton and got a taxi to High Wycombe to watch Leinster defeat Wasps in the quarter-final of the Amlin Cup, the forerunner of the European Challenge Cup, at Adams Park Stadium, the then home ground of Wasps. Mick Dawson has been to most towns and cities where Leinster has played over the years; he knows a good restaurant and bar in each place, but he was caught out by High Wycombe. We did get something to eat and drink in Zizzi, but it was no surprise to us when we learned soon after then that Wasps were moving from there to Coventry.

On 17 May, Leinster defeated Stade Français in the Amlin Cup final; on the same day, Leinster A team defeated Newcastle in the B&I Cup final; and on 25 May, Leinster defeated Ulster in the final of the Rabo PRO12. It was a very successful season for Leinster, albeit they had been knocked out of the Heineken Cup at the qualifying stage.

On the following Thursday, 30 May, the Leinster Branch AGM was held. Paul Deering from NUIM Barnhall was elected president, and I was elected senior vice president, all of which had been arranged as far back as 2009, when I first joined the Leinster Branch executive committee.

At the pre-match lunch before the Amlin Cup final, I fortuitously met Mark Dennis, one of the Clontarf stalwarts. I had just shortly before that received confirmation from Philip Orr that the Barbarians would come and play Clontarf on 23 April 2014, the millennium anniversary of the Battle of Clontarf. I mentioned this to Mark, asking if he would be prepared to help in organising the day, and his response was an enthusiastic positive. So when I told the Clontarf executive of the forthcoming event and they wondered how they could organise it, I was able to tell them that I had recruited Mark to help. That immediately took a weight off their shoulders, as Mark was known to be capable and trustworthy. Preparations commenced almost immediately.

On 2 June, Mary and I travelled to Perth to visit Louisa, Lee and Josh. This coincided with the Lions' tour to Australia; we attended the first game of the tour, in Perth, against Western Australia, which the Lions won easily. Unfortunately, Cian Healy, who was the first Clontarf member to be selected for the Lions(if one disregards Brian O'Driscoll, who played up to U17s with Tarf) injured his ankle in this game and was unable to continue the tour. It was very disappointing for him and his family, but also for his many fans back in Clontarf.

Louisa, who was working in the Perth Children's Hospital, had to conduct a clinic in Broome once every two months. Broome is a town in Western Australia more than 2,200 kilometres north of Perth and situated on the coast. One of these engagements arose while we were there; it involved a two and a half hour flight north in the morning and then back in the evening, as there was no children's hospital nearer than Perth. She explained that some of the children she treated had travelled up to six hundred kilometres to meet her and that this could have taken them the best part of a week, travelling there and back, depending on their mode of transport or lack of it. It gave me a good perspective regarding the vastness of Australia, to an extent that I hadn't realised in earlier visits. It brought back memories of a 1960s television programme called *The Flying Doctors*.

I flew to Melbourne and visited my brother, Gerry, before going to see the second Lions test against the Qantas Wallabies – as Australia were called – in the Etihad Stadium, where the Lions were defeated by a point. I was amazed by the number of people from Dublin that I met before and after the game, including two contingents of Clontarf members. The Lions won the third and last test in Sydney on the following Saturday, winning the series, but I was back in Perth by then and starting to plan our return home – which we did on the following Thursday, 11 July, after nearly six weeks away.

The new season, 2013/14, started with a management committee meeting on Monday, 15 July. The season continued as before, but I was even more involved; I could see that it was building up to a very busy year as president in the following season, 2014/15. Some of the additional tasks included subbing for the president where he had clashing appointments, but I knew that I would have equivalent support for the following year. One of the new issues that arose around this time was a proposal to develop the grounds at Donnybrook, building apartments and a new clubhouse for Bective Rangers, whose existing clubhouse was almost dilapidated but stood where a proposed development might fit. Meetings ensued with estate agents and the tenant clubs, but intransigence and lack of foresight by Bective saw this proposal ultimately fail.

My second daughter, Sinéad, who was also a paediatrician, got married at the end of October, so that was my main focus for the second half of the month. Louisa, Lee and Joshua came home for the wedding, as did Shane – who at this stage was lecturing in philosophy in Exeter University – and Mary's brother and his family from Washington State. But if there was a brief respite from meetings and rugby activities, they soon resumed.

I was also managing to see many of Clontarf's AIL games, both at home and away, and they were doing well – winning seven of their first eight games, losing only to Old Belvedere in the first game. Leinster were also doing well in the Heineken Cup, but in early December, having won easily against Northampton in Franklin Gardens, they lost to them the following weekend in the Aviva. This was a major surprise and was still referenced many years later by Leo Cullen, the Leinster coach, when trying to dampen expectations.

I ended 2013 by falling on ice when on a long walk around the Howth peninsula – a trek that included the cliff path and the Claremont and Burrow beaches in Sutton. I cut the side of my face and injured my hand, wrist and upper arm. I walked back up Howth Hill, not realising that my face was covered in blood and wondering why people passing looked strangely at me. As my arm was still painful on the following day, New Year's Eve, I went to Blackrock Clinic, had X-rays taken, had a support or splint put on my left forearm and started 2014 as a semi-invalid. Mary had fallen in Grafton Street shortly before Xmas, also injuring her arm. On 3 January, a fracture was confirmed and she had a cast put on her arm. So the year did not start promisingly, but thankfully matters improved – we ended up having a great year.

On January 11, we went to Castres for a Heineken Cup game. Leinster won, restoring their winning run. Castres, which we visited on a couple of occasions with Leinster, is a very pleasant old city near Toulouse, and we had a good night and day there.

Meetings of various Leinster committees resumed, and at a management committee meeting, I indicated that I wanted to change the Leinster tie. It may seem strange to those who know me well that I would have an interest in such a matter, as I had ceased wearing a tie in August 2008, when I retired. I felt that having worn one for more than thirty-five years, I wasn't going to continue doing so unless I had to. Despite court appearances, board meetings, weddings, funerals and any other occasion when I might have been expected to wear one, I had only worn either a Clontarf or Leinster Rugby tie since retirement – and only for rugby functions.

I made exceptions for these rugby functions on the basis that I was representing others rather than myself. It was part of the uniform that was expected. In any event, I had decided that if I had to do so – and I knew that I would have to do so on a few occasions every week as Leinster president – I would wear a tie that I liked and that clearly represented the Leinster colours. Before raising it at the meeting, I had consulted with the two vice presidents who would be succeeding me; they agreed with me, so when Mick Dawson objected to my proposal on the basis that there couldn't be a situation where every president could choose his own tie, I was able to reply that there wouldn't have to be a change for at least three years. Mick relented, and we proceeded to get the new design agreed and manufactured. Having done so, I can confidently say that I won't undertake such a task again; I didn't realise the number of options that can go into the design of something as mundane as a tie, but my consolation is that the design has basically remained the same since.

In early April, Leinster played Toulon, in Toulon, in the quarter-final of the Heineken Cup. I had gone to Nice earlier in the week with Mary and some friends, and we got the train from Nice to Toulon on the morning of the game. At the pre-match lunch, I was sitting with the wife of the owner, Mourad Boudjellal, and I asked her why he wasn't joining us for the lunch. She told me that he was so tense and nervous before a game that he couldn't eat or be civil with strangers, and so he didn't like to attend.

Later, shortly before the game, we saw him lead the Toulon team into the stadium, walking in front of them and a marching band, swinging a flag and behaving like an emperor, waving to the thousands of supporters who lined the road to the stadium entrance. It seemed bizarre to us, but obviously the Toulonnais loved it. It helped that he invested millions of euros into the club, signing many international stars. Toulon proceeded to defeat us and then went on to retain the Heineken Cup, which they had won for the first time in the Aviva in the previous year. We went back to Nice that night. We were disappointed, but I wasn't to realise that in twelve months' time, Toulon would cause me to suffer one of my most disappointing sports losses ever.

On 14 April 2014, at a special general meeting of Clontarf Rugby, a resolution was proposed and passed to borrow €500,000 on a twenty-year loan from a Dublin businessman, who was a friend of Mark Dennis. The money was intended to facilitate the redevelopment of our junior pitch, which – because of poor drainage and grass growth – was causing us a lot of problems each season. For the club, this was the first of three historic and crucially important events to take place over the course of nine days.

The second event was on Saturday, 19 April in the AIL. Clontarf were lying second to Old Belvedere, with just one game each to play. Clontarf were playing at home against Ballynahinch; Old Belvedere were playing away against Garryowen, who were already relegated. Old Belvedere only had to win that last game to become champions, and everyone assumed that they would, as Garryowen had nothing to play for except pride. Thankfully, self-pride is hugely important in sport, particularly when the opposition is overconfident.

Late in the Tarf game, they were losing to Ballynahinch and Old Belvedere were losing to Garryowen. Old Belvedere seemed as if they were going to win the AIL for the second time in three years, and at the expense of Tarf, who would be their oldest enemy – Old Belvedere was formed in 1935 by a breakaway group of Tarf players. Sport, however can sometimes be emotionally overpowering, and it was on this afternoon. Tarf scored again and defeated Ballynahinch; a few minutes later, word came through that Garryowen had won, which meant that Tarf had won the AIL for the first time.

The celebrations started slowly, as most of us were in shock, but when the reality sunk in, people who hadn't been in the Tarf grounds for years came along. Once they got going, there were magnificent celebrations that lasted all weekend and into the following week. The AIL trophy had gone to Dooradoyle for presentation to Old Belvedere by the president of the IRFU, but due to the foresight of Gordon Black – the experienced AIL administrator in the IRFU – a dummy trophy was brought to Castle Avenue and presented by Philip Orr, a member of the IRFU executive committee who had been deputed to attend just in case. I had often thought of what my reaction would be if we eventually won the AIL; I wondered if perhaps it might be an anti-climax. But I now knew that it wasn't. Having been near despair a few hours earlier, when Tarf were losing their game, I had swung to absolute elation – and, indeed, satisfaction – that the work that had been done by so many friends over many years was now rewarded.

The celebrations continued into Tuesday, when the Barbarians arrived. I arranged a golf game in Royal Dublin for those of their committee who wanted to play, and then a dinner that night for all involved, including the incredible Mickey Steele Bodger, president of the Barbarians. In the meantime, in Castle Avenue, Nigel Owens – who had agreed to referee the game, but who was also a TV personality and brilliant raconteur – was entertaining a large audience of Tarf supporters and friends in a huge marquee.

We eventually got home that night – which for many of us was the fourth consecutive night of celebration – while Mickey Steele Bodger and his committee went back to Clontarf Castle, where they were staying, and stayed up most of the night, as there was a big party there for the Battle of Clontarf Millenium celebrations.

On Wednesday, 23 April, we went back to Castle Avenue for a pre-match reception and lunch. This was followed by the game, which Tarf won by one point in what was probably the best game ever played in Castle Avenue: the Tarf team, still celebrating Saturday's big win, responded to the Barbarians' traditional style of open-running rugby with a fantastic display, throwing off the shackles of competitive rugby to demonstrate to everybody there just how high their skill standards were. The IRFU had rescued the original AIL trophy and medals from Limerick, and they were then formally presented to Ben Reilly, the Tarf captain, and his team. It was a magnificent finale to an unbelievable nine days and made everybody involved with the club incredibly proud.

The next day, Thursday, 24 April, saw me back to Leinster business, with a meeting regarding the building development in Donnybrook. On the following day, I attended a junior league final, where I had to present the trophy and medals; on the Saturday, I had to attend a junior inter-provincial game between the Leinster Juniors and Munster Juniors in Wexford, with a pre-match reception and post-match dinner. With due respect to these players, I eventually achieved a much-needed anti-climax and relaxation. Later that week, the Leinster management committee went to Belfast for the Leinster v Ulster PRO12 game, preceded by the official opening of the new Ravenhill Stadium. On the following evening, Mary and I attended the Leinster Rugby Awards Ball at the Mansion House, at which Brian O'Driscoll, Leo Cullen and a number of others were presented with official Leinster caps on either their retirement from rugby or their leaving Leinster.

From the latter part of 2012, it had become clear that there was a serious risk of the Heineken Cup not being continued. Its future was threatened by a dispute over who plays in the competition, how much those clubs are paid and who runs the competition. The then current European Rugby Club (ERC) accord was to run out at the end of the 2013/14 season, and unless renewed or replaced, that would have had a devastating effect on rugby in

Europe. Various parties were involved in the dispute: clubs and regions, leagues, unions, the ERC, the International Rugby Board (IRB) and the TV companies, which had the broadcast rights. The English and French clubs were unhappy that the PRO12 teams – which comprised teams from Ireland, Wales, Scotland and Italy – had significantly greater representation in the competition, that the share of the profits was skewed towards those PRO12 participants and that the English and French clubs didn't have as much say in the ERC as they believed they were entitled to. Many of these English and French clubs were privately owned, as hobbies, by wealthy businessmen; they wanted more control for themselves and less for the rugby authorities. They also wanted more money for their clubs. Prominent among the club owners causing difficulties were my old acquaintances Bruce Craig, Jackie Lorenzetti and Mourad Boudjellal, who believed that their money gave them the right to control the game in Europe.

The Irish, Welsh and Scottish rugby unions had insisted that their clubs wouldn't participate in any European competition unless it had the full approval of the IRB. The French clubs indicated, in November 2013, that they would participate in a tweaked ERC-run European tournament in 2014/15, which left the English clubs isolated. The Welsh regions then threatened to leave the PRO12 and join the English clubs in an Anglo-Welsh competition. The English clubs took no consolation from that, as it was not what they were trying to achieve – which was more control of a European competition – and anyway, the Welsh Rugby Union was not in support of their regions' proposal.

There was a series of meetings over many months, and apparently one of the IRFU representatives on the IRB was taking a different line to the IRFU itself, which was anxious to resolve the situation and was leading a move towards a compromise. This individual reputedly said that any compromise would be over his dead body. This was not the policy of the IRFU management committee and led to a dispute between that individual and the chairman of the management committee – a dispute that ended up with both of them being lost to rugby administration at the end of the 2014/15 season. This was undoubtedly a loss to Irish rugby, as both men had made significant contributions to its administration in the past, and were likely to do so in the future, but one pulled the other down, ensuring that they would both go down in flames together.

The IRFU were reviewing some of their rules and, on 20 May 2014, hosted a meeting with the Leinster representatives to brief them on what they had in mind. There was then a wider review meeting, with representatives of all the provinces, on 22 May. This was the precursor of a series of meetings during the following year that ended up with a rebellion by IRFU past presidents – who would lose influence and perks under the proposed new rules – and also to the downfall of the two gentlemen referred to above.

LEINSTER RUGBY PRESIDENCY, MAY 2014–MAY 2015

The Leinster AGM at which I was elected as president was held on 29 May 2014. My year of office commenced with storm clouds above me, although they weren't recognised as such until the end of my term. The first function after my election was the PRO12 final in the RDS, when Leinster were successful – for the second time in succession – in defeating Glasgow Warriors by a score of 34–12. Although I had been president since the previous Thursday, a custom had developed that the outgoing president presided for the final when it came a few days after his term of office had expired. This didn't diminish, to any degree, the excitement and pleasure of being associated with the victory. Although I had seen a selfie stick previously, it was the first time that I saw one up close and realised what their use was: Jimmy Gopperth ran off the pitch to the dressing rooms in the middle of the celebrations and re-emerged with it in hand, holding it up as the team celebrated and did a lap of honour around the stadium with the trophy.

Under the bye-laws, the officers of the Leinster Branch – which included the president and the senior vice president – were *ex officio* members of all standing committees; what's more, the president could, if desired, chair the management and executive committee meetings. I chose to do so – as, indeed, did all other presidents during my time there. On 5 June, I had a meeting with Marcus Ó Buachalla, the recently appointed communications and media manager at Leinster Rugby, when we discussed how he could assist me during the season. I would have to write articles for the Leinster Rugby website, club annual programmes and the official match programme produced for all Leinster home games at the different levels, and he offered to write those for me. I explained to Marcus that I welcomed his assistance but that I thought that I would write them myself. However, I would be happy to have him edit them.

He also offered to script the many speeches that I would have to make during the year; again I told him that I thought that I could do so myself but would welcome the opportunity to bounce ideas off him as time went on, recognising that by the end of the season I might have grown tired of this facet of the work. Marcus also arranged a photo session, so he and I would have a range of photographs to use for media purposes during the year. This took place on 11 June.

The next engagement, other than a few committee meetings and a meeting with the solicitors advising Leinster Rugby, was the Lorcan Sherlock golf competition; as I mentioned earlier, I played on the Clontarf team, which won again, and I made my first speech and trophy presentation of the season.

Leinster Rugby had been talking to the Royal Dublin Society for some time about the feasibility of being involved in a joint development of the sports arena in the RDS complex. We believed that we could, and should, have capacity for greater attendances and that the new facility should be state of the art, allowing also for premium seating and corporate entertainment facilities. We envisaged demolishing the Anglesea Stand – which was past its useful life – replacing it with a new stand and joining up that new stand with the existing uncovered North and South stands by using small corner stands, and possibly roofing those uncovered stands to achieve a stadium effect.

The RDS were in general agreement, as it would involve upgrading the show jumping arena for the annual Horse Show, and they were anxious to bring the facilities up to modern international standards. The details regarding funding, new lease terms and design possibilities had not been explored, but there was a broad understanding that the RDS would contribute most of the funding and that Leinster Rugby would attract some government and sponsorship funding, as well as pay higher rent. It was agreed that in order to enable progress, the design needed to be advanced and more or less agreed between all parties; accordingly, an architectural design competition was announced at a reception in the RDS on 11 July. This was attended by representatives of Leinster Rugby, the RDS and the Royal Institute of the Architects of Ireland – the latter being involved in the adjudication.

In the meantime, I had been to Nice for a short break and then to Manchester for the posthumous conferring of my late nephew Colm's degree – during his former fellow students' graduation ceremony – and the unveiling of a plaque in his memory in the gardens of the Stopford Building of the university.

The 2014 IRFU annual council meeting was held on 18 July in the Aviva Stadium. I had previously attended the meeting on a couple of occasions as one of the Leinster delegates. On my first occasion, I had treated it as I would the AGM of a public company: on reviewing the annual accounts when they were presented for approval, I dared to ask a question about an item in the accounts dealing with the apportionment of some fairly large expenses between the IRFU and the provinces that I didn't understand.

The honorary treasurer, who was presenting the accounts and proposed them for approval, asked if there were any questions, which I took at face value. The honorary treasurer didn't have the answer to my question readily to hand and passed it to the chief financial officer, who partially explained the issue – at least to the extent that I then understood it. I became aware from the glares at me from some of the regular attendees – past presidents of the IRFU – that my asking questions was delaying the meeting and their getting to the free bar; that asking questions was not normal; that everything presented was accepted as given and, in reality, the council meeting was merely a formality on the way to the bar and a very good dinner.

Tom Grace, who was the honorary treasurer, came up to me later in the evening, congratulated me on the question and apologised for not having an answer ready. Nonetheless, I had now learned the protocol for such meetings, and so this 2014 meeting was, for me, just a pleasant social occasion, where I had a few drinks with the presidents of the other provinces, each of whom I would be meeting regularly during the next year, including on our trip for that season on the goodship jolly international weekend circuit.

At this meeting, Louis Magee was elected as president of the IRFU; Martin O'Sullivan, from Munster, was elected as senior vice president; and Stephen Hilditch was elected as junior vice president. They were very fine and worthy appointments. Each of them had been nominated and agreed at the IRFU executive committee meeting a month or so earlier, as that committee would know, from their contributions and work, whether or not they deserved such an honour. The elections at the council meeting were intended as ratifications of the decisions made by those who knew best. Louis Magee had been president of Leinster Rugby some years earlier and was on the Leinster executive committee with me for a few years. I had found him a really sensible contributor on issues that arose. He was a diligent worker who always completed any task he had been given in due time, and as the rapporteur to the Leinster executive committee on IRFU matters, he was very clear and comprehensive while remaining discreet, not breaching his oath of confidentiality to the IRFU.

On 22 July, I had lunch with Mick Dawson, the chief executive of Leinster Rugby. We had a general chat about the year ahead and the issues that were likely to arise and might cause a problem; we also discussed our respective roles, ensuring there was no stepping on the toes of the other. Mick's advice to me was to enjoy the year – that if I stuck close to him, I'd never be too far from a pint of Smithwick's, which was my favourite tipple at the time. I had a high opinion of Mick from my experiences with him up to then. That only grew during the year, as we worked very well together; I found him to be great company on our many trips together, while at the same time very efficient yet calm. He was an excellent ambassador for Leinster Rugby and, indeed, for Irish rugby.

On 24 July, I travelled to Perth, where my first granddaughter, Lexi Owens, had been born two days earlier. Mary had already travelled there on 17 July to babysit Josh for Louisa and Lee. I had a great holiday in Perth and arrived home, refreshed and ready for the long season, on 19 August.

Later that day, I had a meeting with two former presidents, who were also members of the IRFU executive committee; they wished to chat to me about my new role and advised me to avoid being radical or controversial in comments that I might have to make during the season – comments that would be in the public domain. In the president's address for the website, which I had drafted and emailed to Marcus from Australia, I had strongly criticised those English and French clubs that had tried to hold all others to ransom over the European competitions to replace the Heineken Cup. They had been shown this in advance of publication, and hence the meeting. I was happy to accept the two former presidents' advice in general, and to curtail the criticism in such a public forum, but I did tell them not to expect me to remain anodyne for the entire year. We parted on good terms, and I met Marcus on the following day and amended that section of the address.

Commencing on 21 August, Leinster hosted an U18s tournament for Languedoc of southern France, Northampton, a Leinster Schools team and a Leinster Clubs team. On the first day, the Leinster Clubs team defeated Languedoc and the Leinster Schools team defeated Northampton, both games being played at the St Mary's College RFC grounds in Templeville Road. I then hosted a dinner for each team's management and officials in the Oar House in Howth, at which there were a few short speeches. Northampton had been defeated 39–0 that afternoon; their management excused themselves from the dinner, as they wanted to stay with their players and try to revive their confidence.

Two days later, I flew to Birmingham with Mick Dawson and Ben Underwood, the chairman of the professional game committee; we then went to Northampton, where the Leinster senior team had a pre-season friendly game against Northampton Saints. The Leinster team lost this game, which in itself wasn't important, as it was the first game of the season and the team that played was experimental. We didn't realise at the time, however, that it was an augury of the season to come.

We flew back that night with the team. On the following day, 24 August, I drove to Clongowes Wood College in Clane, County Kildare, which hosted the games between Leinster Schools and Leinster Clubs – narrowly won by the Leinster Schools team – and between Languedoc and Northampton. These games were followed by a reception for the parents and guests, and then a dinner with speeches – including a short one by me – and a presentation. On 27 August, Leinster Schools played Languedoc at the Wanderers FC pitch on Merrion Road; this again was followed by a dinner, speeches and a presentation.

On Thursday and Friday, 28 and 29 August, I drafted the address from the Leinster president for the official programmes of seven of the Leinster clubs that had requested it. The core of all these addresses was much the same, but the tops and tails all had to be specifically targeted for each club, so I was glad to get it finished before Mary arrived back from Perth. She was surprised to find that I had survived so well on my own for ten days, but I had to admit to her that that was helped by having four rugby-related and two golf-related dinners. We were still in pre-season, and since arriving back from Perth I had also attended five rugby-related meetings and watched seven games.

On Saturday, 30 August, the Leinster senior team had their second friendly game, on this occasion against Ulster. It was held in Tallaght Stadium after a pre-match reception hosted by South Dublin Council to celebrate Leinster's first game there. They were defeated again. The same was the case in their first competitive game of the season, the PRO12 game against Glasgow Warriors in Glasgow on Saturday, 6 September, which was played on Glasgow's new all-weather pitch at Scotstoun.

The season had started poorly, but thankfully other Leinster teams had commenced successfully. I had watched the U20s defeat Munster in Ashbourne on the Friday night, before travelling to Glasgow; while I was there, Robert McDermott, the senior vice president, watched the Leinster U19s defeat Munster in Dublin and Frank Doherty, the junior vice president, watched Leinster Women defeat Connacht in Galway. The game in Glasgow marked the first start for Tadhg Furlong for Leinster seniors; it was another step on his rapid rise to success, as I had foretold to Mike Ross just over three years earlier.

The season had really started now, and a series of meetings ensued. This commenced with a meeting on 8 September with the chairman and secretary of the schools committee. The officers of the schools committee had changed in the past year. The previous secretary had served for a long time; he had to be effectively moved on by one of my predecessors, as he was over 90 and insisted on staying. It is very difficult to have an officer removed from office, but my predecessor had set himself the task of ensuring that change was made. Unfortunately, the previous chairman had retired at the same time, because he had been appointed head master of his school and no longer had the time required to continue. Given this, the two new officers came to me with some issues that had arisen and on which they needed advice. We then went into a meeting of the schools committee, which proceeded to approve what they wanted.

On 11 September, I attended a meeting of the professional game committee at 8 a.m. Richie Murphy, one of the assistant coaches and responsible for skills development of the senior squad, gave a presentation to the committee about his role – about the level of development of some of the younger players and about how he envisaged their progress during the season. This was actually his first time to make a presentation to this committee. His presentatation was excellent, and one could see that Richie was going to progress well in his career. This was followed, later that day, by a golf competition in Milltown Golf Club for the past presidents and executive committee members; this, in turn, was followed by a dinner, a speech by me and a presentation of prizes.

On Saturday, 13 September, Leinster played against Scarlets from Llanelli, Wales in the PRO12. At last, we had a victory: 42–12. The U19s defeated Ulster in Belfast; the U18 Clubs team won in Dublin and the U18 Schools team tied their game in Dublin, both of which were also against Ulster. The U20s lost to Ulster and Leinster Women lost to Munster, so it was another mixed weekend. Nevertheless, a general sense of relief prevailed that the senior team had at last got their season going.

On Thursday, 18 September, the president of the IRFU hosted a golf competition for IRFU committee members and their wives; the presidents of the four provinces were also invited. Not everybody played golf, but all joined for the dinner and drinks reception. The great thing about this event, for me, was that I could totally relax as a guest; I didn't have to concern myself with speeches and presentations.

On the following day, I drove to Galway for the PRO12 game against Connacht. After a pre-match reception and dinner in the G Hotel, I watched Leinster lose again. I was amazed at the excitement of the Connacht supporters after the win; it was a narrow win, but they celebrated as if it was the final instead of being only the third round. I met with a group of the Official Leinster Supporters Club committee members in the Huntsman Inn after the game, and while chatting they spotted Robbie Henshaw and expressed their admiration of him. I couldn't tell them that we had reason to be talking to Robbie and were hopeful that he would transfer to Leinster within the next couple of seasons, which he did – but not before starring for Connacht in the PRO12 final at the end of the following season, in 2016.

I was fairly disappointed at the result in the game against Connacht, but my mood was lifted on the following day when I went back to the Galway Sportsground and watched Leinster U19s and U20s defeat Connacht comprehensively and heard that the U18 Clubs team also won in Naas, as did Leinster Women in Ashbourne. As Connacht didn't have an U18s schools team, we were denied a clean sweep on that Saturday. The captain of the Leinster U19s and the outstanding player was James Ryan, who has since gone on to fame and huge success. One of the Connacht mentors said to one of his colleagues in a serious tone, 'Do you see that James Ryan there, his mother is one of the Lynchs of Clonbur. If we had kept her in Clonbur, he'd be playing for us.'

Of that team, five others have become successful professional players for Leinster: Hugo Keenan, Jimmy O'Brien, Vakh Abdaladze, Will Connors and Max Deegan. Keenan, Connors and Deegan have gone on to gain international caps. The Leinster U20s team included ten players who are having successful professional careers: Conor O'Brien, Joey Carbery, Andrew Porter, Jeremy Loughman, David O'Connor, Josh Murphy, Conor Oliver, Nick Timoney, Eric O'Sullivan and Greg Jones. The Leinster U18 Clubs team had four players who are now successful at professional level – Ciaran Frawley, Jack Aungier, Jack Regan and Paul Boyle – and the U18 Schools team had Jordan Larmour, Caelan Doris and Hugh O'Sullivan. Some of these young players have also moved to Munster, Connacht and Ulster for game time.

All of this is evidence of the number of players that are coming through the underage system in Leinster – and of their quality. As I said at the time, and have repeated since, the identification of potential elite players by Leinster scouting staff and their subsequent development by Leinster coaching staff is what makes Leinster so strong and so different from most other professional rugby clubs, and great credit should go to them.

As the U19s had won their inter-provincial competition, they were invited, with their parents, to a pre-match reception and presentation before the next PRO12 game on Friday, 26 September against Cardiff – a game that Leinster thankfully won. I had been at the launch, at 6 p.m., of the Blue Room at the RDS, which was a new corporate hospitality area. After making a speech welcoming everyone there and congratulating the commercial and marketing committee for their initiative, I went over to the reception for the U19s in a different part of the RDS.

In my address to the boys and their parents, I said:

> Playing for Leinster and wearing that blue jersey at any level is a huge honour – only a limited number of talented players ever get to do so. I myself never

> did, but if somebody fifty years ago had asked me if I would prefer to play for Leinster or to become president, I would definitely have gone for the jersey rather than the blazer, and I still would, but after waiting those fifty years and not getting a call from the selectors, I decided to take what was offered as a consolation.

I added that 'Some of you will undoubtedly go on to play professional rugby for Leinster and for Ireland, and you will make new friends, but I'm sure you won't forget any of the guys sitting beside you now.' I encouraged them, saying that even if they didn't become professional players, they could still be a great club player, referee or coach. I strongly urged them not to give up their involvement in the game too early.

One of Leinster's major games of the season took place on the following Saturday, 4 October, when we hosted Munster in the Aviva. There was a big pre-match reception and dinner, and my friend Eugene McCague gave another brilliant speech after the dinner when he described the contrasting scenario between Donnybrook and Clontarf on Saturday, 19 April, when Old Belvedere expected to win the AIL but were foiled by Garryowen and Clontarf won the AIL from under their noses. Even the persons from Old Belvedere who were present thought it was very clever and amusing. Just as well, because the game that followed saw Leinster lose again to their greatest rival. The inconsistent season continued.

As rugby had failed in St Paul's College, to the dismay of many of its past pupils, another effort was under way to get it revived. Finbarr Crowley, as chairman of the IRFU, and I, as president of Leinster Rugby, wanted to lend our weight to those efforts, so a meeting was arranged with the new school principal and the head of sport for Monday, 6 October. In advance of that, Finbarr and I had a meeting to discuss our tactics; in the course of that, we chatted about Finbarr's future, as he was due to finish his term of office as chairman at the end of the season.

I assumed, as did many in Clontarf, that Finbarr would be nominated as junior vice president of the IRFU at the end of the season with a view to being elected president two years later. Finbarr told me at that meeting that, for various reasons, he wasn't sure that he wanted to become president. I tried to persuade him to go for it and said he deserved the honour – that it would also be a great honour for his club, Clontarf, and for St Paul's

College. He listened to me but didn't commit himself. We agreed that we would talk about it again, and he said he'd think about it further.

I had various meetings during the week, and on Friday, 10 October flew to Parma, Italy with the team for their PRO12 game against Zebre that weekend. Philip Orr travelled along with us as a member of the IRFU committee, as it wanted a report on the new training facility recently opened there by the Italian Rugby Federation. The Italians were delighted to meet Philip, as they remembered his playing for Ireland for many years.

At the pre-match reception, both of us were presented with a large chunk of Parmesan cheese. This was pursuant to a tradition in which the president of the host team gives a gift to the visiting president. It usually consists of alcohol, a plaque, a scarf or some memento, but this was unique and greatly appreciated by Mary when I returned home. The game was won fairly easily, and it was notable for the debut appearance of Josh van den Flier, who has gone on to make many appearances for Leinster and, indeed, for Ireland. His father, Dirk, travelled over for the game and was probably one of the few Leinster supporters there other than Philip and me, and of course the manager, coaches and medical staff.

On 14 October, we had a meeting of the premises subcommittee about the proposed development in the RDS, and then an executive committee meeting followed. On the following evening, Dublin University FC had their reception at the Pavilion; it was the start of the circuit of club dinners that I had experienced three years previously as president of Clontarf, only now I was repeating it as president of Leinster.

The following morning involved a photo session with the Leinster squad in the gym and I first met Ben Te'o; he had just arrived from Australia, where he had won the National Rugby League Championship playing for the South Sydney Rabbitohs. Matt O'Connor, the Leinster coach, knew him in Australia and believed that he could make the transition to rugby union quickly; indeed, he selected Ben after just three weeks in Leinster, but unfortunately Ben broke his arm in his first game.

Leinster never got the best of Ben, but Matt's vision for him was justified: Ben later became an established England international, getting his first English cap before playing for his new English club when he left Leinster in the summer of 2016; he also became a Lions player on the tour to New

Zealand in 2017. Ben was a very pleasant guy, but I think he found it difficult to settle in Leinster, as the season was well under way when he arrived, most of the others knew each other well and he then suffered the unfortunate fracture in his first game.

Later that day, on 16 October, I again met Finbarr Crowley to review our meeting with St Paul's College and discuss how to progress our outline plans. Before we finished, I again raised the issue of his seeking the presidency of the IRFU. He told me that a few of the IRFU committee had approached him on the same issue but that he understood that Philip Orr was also considering putting his name forward. Finbarr said to me that he wouldn't run if Philip was pursuing that, as he didn't think it appropriate for the IRFU to have a contest. I pointed out to him that he would have only one chance, as he would be out of the IRFU at the end of the season unless he was the junior vice president, whereas Philip would have more opportunities so long as he remained one of the Leinster representatives on the IRFU.

I wasn't anxious to interfere unduly but said that I might broach the subject sometime with Philip if I got an opportunity to do so. The following day saw Leinster A team play Jersey in the B&I Cup, which they won in appalling weather conditions, and on 19 October after a pre-match lunch in the RDS Concert Hall for supporters and guests, Leinster defeated Wasps in the first game of the 2014/15 European Rugby Champions Cup. This was the first game of the new competition, which had replaced the Heineken Cup, so it had that significance.

As we took our seats in the committee box before the game, I noticed that the seat beside me was vacant; word spread that there was a special guest to attend, and to my surprise and delight – and, indeed, Mary's – we were joined by Rory McIlroy. We chatted before the game and at half time. I learned that Rory was in Dublin for the weekend with a couple of pals; knowing that there was a game, he had appropriate enquiries made on his behalf, and Mick Dawson was able to accommodate him with a front-row seat. Rory was most gracious and generous in posing for photographs with many of those in the committee box, but he wisely left before the end of the game to avoid the crowds that would have descended on him as word spread of his presence.

It was only a couple of days later that I realised that he was in Dublin for meetings with his lawyers to try to settle the multimillion-euro legal dispute that he had with his former manager. I'm sure that the rugby game was a welcome break from meetings in lawyers' offices, and he did seem to enjoy himself.

I spent a few days in Devon with Shane in the following week. On Saturday, 25 October I travelled to Castres via Toulouse, with the team and some members of the management committee, for the European Rugby Champions Cup game against Castres, which was scheduled for Sunday afternoon. Leinster had a very good win, and before the game I was a guest at the opening of the new stand at the Stade Pierre-Antoine.

There were a few meetings on Tuesday, 28 October, including with the bye-laws review, finance and rugby committees. Two days later, I attended the funeral of Ken Mills, one of my predecessors as Leinster president. I had known him as a barrister rather than through rugby, and the past presidents who were in attendance formed a guard of honour with me.

Friday, 31 October was another busy day, commencing with a meeting of the commercial and marketing committee at 8 a.m. in the Newstead Building, as usual. I then attended a lunch in Royal Dublin Golf Club, where the guest of honour was Brian O'Driscoll, who did a Q&A with John Pardy; Brian was doing a favour for his father, Frank, who was fundraising for his favourite charity, Don Bosco Club. I then attended a reception at 6 p.m., in Bewley's Hotel, for the committee that had worked on and produced a report on junior rugby in the province; this was followed by a pre-match reception for the Edinburgh Rugby directors, and I then watched Leinster gain a much-needed PRO12 competition victory.

On the following day, I watched Clontarf lose an AIL game to Terenure College RFC and then attended the 40th Anniversary Gala Ball of Ashbourne RFC as one of their special guests, along with Joe Schmidt and Johnny Moloney – the latter a former Irish international scrum half who I had played against for St Paul's, when he played for St Mary's College, in our schooldays.

Johnny was one of the four or five best players that I had played against, and he was on one of the great school teams, which also included Henry Murphy and Shay Deering. That team defeated Newbridge College in the Schools Senior Cup final. The Newbridge team included another great player that I played against, Tom Grace, who – like Johnny – went on to play for Ireland and the British and Irish Lions on many occasions.

At the Ashbourne gala, I was delighted to be invited to stand in a photograph with Joe Schmidt and five sons of first cousins of mine who were all former playing members of Ashbourne. It was a very pleasant evening, with lots of reminiscing and catching up with cousins and friends.

The next month started with more meetings. On Saturday, 8 November, Ireland was playing against South Africa in the Aviva; Mary and I attended the pre-match lunch on the Presidents Terrace with the presidents of the other provinces and then had seats in the VIP section. Ireland had a very good win over South Africa, which augured well for the season ahead, and after the match, all the provincial presidents and wives went for dinner in Dax Restaurant on Pembroke Street, which is owned by a great rugby enthusiast from Dax in France.

Wednesday, 12 November was a significant occasion for Leinster Rugby, as the new all-weather pitches in the Donnybrook Stadium were formally opened. This was a project that had been supported *ab initio* by the grounds and premises committee and then steered through the consultative committee, which managed the Donnybrook Stadium. There was a formal ribbon cutting by Michael Ring, the Minister of State at the Department of Transport, Tourism and Sport, as the project had received significant grant support from the department. There was a series of photographs and then a lunch, a speech from the minister and a reply by me.

I thanked the government per the minister for their financial support and told the minister that he was the greatest 'Ring' in Irish sport since Christy. Being from Mayo, which is not a great hurling area, I'm not sure that he got the allusion.

The following weekend involved two more games: an international against Georgia and a club game, when Clontarf lost to Cork Con. There was a Monkstown RFC club dinner on Friday evening, a pre-match lunch in Castle Avenue on Saturday and a pre-international match reception on Sunday.

Next week, there was the Old Wesley RFC annual dinner on Friday night, and on Saturday, 22 November, while Ireland were defeating Australia in the Aviva, I was on my way to Treviso with the Leinster team for their PRO12 game the next day. Leinster managed to tie the game but scored four tries and got three points – it wasn't a disaster, but it was a disappointment.

In the next four days, I had five more committee meetings. On Saturday, 29 November, I watched Leinster A team defeat Carmarthen Quins – when two future British and Irish Lions, Tadhg Beirne and Josh Adams played against each other – went to the RDS for a pre-match reception for the Leinster U18 Club team and then watched Leinster defeat Ospreys in a PRO12 game. I had invited a group of five old friends to the game with me, and we sat in the front row of the committee box.

At one stage a ball kicked for touch was about to strike one of my friends, who didn't see it coming. He has Parkinson's disease and a damaged back, and I instinctively – and at the last second – stretched my hand over his head to catch the ball or at least divert it. I'm not sure that I was ever able to catch a high-flying ball in one hand, but I certainly didn't catch it on this occasion. Instead, it bent my hand back and bounced off, and I ended up early the following morning in the Blackrock Clinic. There, an X-ray revealed that the pain I suffered all night was caused by a hyperextended finger and wrist. I had an MRI scan the following week and was strapped up – I guess that I suffered a worse injury at that game than any of the players, but I felt quite foolish explaining my lack of skill.

On Friday, 5 December, Mary and I travelled to Jersey with the Leinster A team for a B&I Cup game against the local team. Robert McDermott, the senior vice president, and Philip Orr came with us. We had never been to Jersey, and thankfully got an opportunity to view much of the island on the Saturday morning when Bill Dempsey – an Irish expatriate and officer of the club – took us on a quick tour. We then went to a pre-match reception and met General Sir John McColl, the Lieutenant Governor of Jersey, and a few other Irish expatriates, enjoying a very narrow win over Jersey.

The visit was pleasant but short. On Sunday morning we flew to Gatwick airport and got a taxi to the Stoop – the Harlequins RFC ground, near Twickenham. Leinster proceeded to lose their European Rugby Champions Cup game against Harlequins but gained a useful losing bonus point – again, a disappointment but not a disaster. We then flew back with the team from Farnborough Airport.

During the weekend, I had the opportunity to chat with Philip about the presidency of the IRFU. He informed me that he had spoken to a number of persons who were on the IRFU committee with him, and to Finbarr, and that he wasn't going to contest an election against Finbarr this season. He added that, in fact, he would support Finbarr's candidacy but understood that he himself would be supported for the position in the following year. That settled the matter in my mind, and I understood that to be the end of the issue.

Monday, 8 December was the day for the Schools Cup Draw, and in recent years it was hosted by Bank of Ireland in the parliament building at College Green. I knew that the building was the first purpose-built bicameral parliament building in the world – that prior to the Act of Union of 1800, it was the home to both Houses of Parliament, the Lords and Commons. The then young Bank of Ireland bought the building, Parliament House, from the British government in 1803; it was no longer needed by the latter, because of the abolition of the Irish parliament by that Act of Union. Nevertheless, the sale was subject to the condition that it had to be modified so it could never again be used as a parliament. The House of Commons was divided up into the banking hall and various small rooms and offices, but the House of Lords remained more or less as it had been, being used as the bank's board room for more than one hundred and seventy years.

I had been in the House of Lords chamber on a few occasions previously, on social occasions, but had never had the opportunity to speak there. When the Schools Cup Draw was held there on 8 December, I relished the occasion. It definitely fed my ego, and I have kept a photograph of me addressing the attendance from a rostrum inscribed with 'House of Lords'.

After the addresses, the draw for the four school competitions, and a drinks reception, I left and changed into a tuxedo. I then went to the Irish Youth Foundation Sports Awards Gala Dinner in what used to be the Burlington Hotel. Arthur Cox had sponsored a table at this fundraising function, which was hosted by Padraig Harrington, and we were joined by two special guests: Nigel Carr, the former Irish rugby international who had been badly injured in a bombing incident at the border as he travelled to Dublin for a training session with the international team squad in 1987, and Mickey Harte, the Tyrone football manager. I had a good chat with both of them and was delighted to tell Mickey Harte that he had given me one of my most emotional sports moments, when Tyrone won their first All-Ireland final in 2003 – as I had wept for my father, who had died without seeing Tyrone win a final, partly for joy and partly for missing him. He replied that he was happy that his team's win had had such an emotional effect.

Saturday, 13 December was another of the busy days, with multiple events. It started with a pre-match reception at 1 p.m. in Donnybrook to entertain the officers of Plymouth Albion RFC; Plymouth was playing the Leinster A team in the B&I Cup at 2 p.m. After watching that game, which Leinster won, the other Leinster officers and I walked down to the Ballsbridge Hotel, where the Leinster Provincial Towns Cup Draw was to take place at 4.30 p.m. I had been told of it, but I didn't realise how big an occasion this draw was for the junior committee.

Fergus McFadden, the Leinster and Ireland player who was recovering from injury at the time, was to do the draw for the first round with Seán O'Brien, but Seán O'Brien couldn't get to the event, so Fergus had to do it with me. Before we started and went up to the rostrum, I asked Fergus how many international caps he had, and he told me he had twenty-eight. I then addressed the attendance, welcoming everybody there, and introduced Fergus by saying that I was particularly happy to have him make the draw with me, as between the two of us we had twenty-eight international caps.

Fergus smiled at having fed me the line, and we got on with the draw quickly, as I had to leave for the Aviva. There, I was to host another pre-match reception on the Presidents Terrace at 5 p.m., as Leinster was to play Harlequins at 7.45 p.m. This was the reverse of the game six days earlier, and as we had been well entertained in the Stoop, we wanted to reciprocate. Leinster won the game narrowly – hanging on in the second half, having built a lead in the first – and kept their European season alive.

On Friday, 19 December, my daughter Louisa arrived home from Australia with Lee, Josh and Lexi. It was Lexi's first visit to Ireland, and she was just five months old. Leinster was to play Connacht in the RDS that evening, and I had arranged that Josh would be a Leinster mascot. As he was under the regulation age, he could only do so if I went out with him – and it would have to be when the players went out for their warm-up rather than when both teams were going out to play.

There was a pre-match dinner for the Connacht president and his officers, and I made a shorter-than-usual address, as I wanted to get over to my family and allow Josh's run on. Unfortunately, the Connacht president didn't take the hint, having had a very liquid lunch earlier, and he proceeded to give a long, rambling and largely irrelevant speech. I was torn between being polite to him and getting over to the dressing rooms, where

Jamie Heaslip, the Leinster captain, was waiting with Josh. I was getting ever-more-urgent text messages from Marcus Ó Buachalla, who was the organiser of the mascot event and wanted it to proceed without delay.

I eventually left, as the Connacht man wasn't paying attention to my signals to quit and come back to his seat. I ran as fast as I could – which wasn't very fast, as I was wearing a big stadium jacket – and when I got to the dressing room entrance, my family were standing there absolutely frozen, having left the thirty-plus degrees of Perth's summer just thirty hours earlier to come to a particularly cold winter's day in Dublin.

Jamie had lost patience with me and gone out to his warm-up. This was perfectly in order with me – I know that many players have a very fixed routine, which they hate to have disrupted. When he came back in, he very graciously stood with us for photographs – as did Rob Kearney – and Josh got to go out onto the pitch with me, but he missed going out with Jamie. Leinster defeated Connacht, but Louisa and Lee had taken the children home before the game finished, as they were frozen and jet-lagged.

The next two weeks were to be family time. Nonetheless, I did take Josh to watch Leinster A against Ireland U20s in a trial game in Donnybrook on 23 December, and I travelled to Thomond Park on St Stephen's Day to watch Leinster play Munster in the PRO12 game. For the latter game, five others travelled with me on a mini bus. We all attended the pre-match lunch, where I met Andy Lee, who had recently become a world boxing champion; he is from Limerick and was a special guest of honour. Although I have no interest in boxing, and haven't had since the days of Muhammad Ali, I enjoyed the chat with Andy, who is a very pleasant guy. Unfortunately, Leinster lost again to Munster, 28–13, so the yoyo nature of the season results continued as we reached the end of 2014.

The Christmas break wasn't as quiet as I had hoped, as an issue arose, requiring a few unscheduled meetings and phone calls. It was known that Finbarr Crowley was to retire as chairman of the management committee of the IRFU, leaving a vacancy. Vacancies were also arising for chairman of the rugby committee and chairman of the professional game board. Leinster were very anxious that a Leinster person be appointed as chairman of the management committee, as it was perceived as an advantage for us – and the two previous chairmen were from Leinster.

The four Leinster representatives on the IRFU dealt with the matter themselves initially, agreeing that one of them would apply for chairman of the management committee and another would apply for chairman of the professional game board. The other two Leinster representatives didn't allow their names to be put forward for any position. We on the Leinster management committee understood that the selection was very process-driven, with a detailed guidance document and selection process for each position, although we hadn't seen those.

Though we weren't involved, we understood that the interviews took place in the first half of December, with two candidates for the management committee position – one from Munster, and our candidate from Leinster. There were three candidates for the professional game board position: a candidate, from Leinster; one from Munster; and one from Ulster. And two candidates for the rugby committee position: one from Munster and one from Ulster

We were informed by our representatives on the IRFU that the nominations subcommittee's recommendations would be made later in the season, but on 16 December we heard that a decision had been made: that neither of the Leinster candidates had been successful and that the only position filled was for the professional game board, where Gordon Hamilton, the former Irish international player – nearly a hero in the 1991 World Cup quarter-final against Australia – was successful.

We also heard that the competition was being reopened for the two committee positions and that they were not confined to members of the IRFU committee. This caused quite a bit of consternation in Leinster; I was asked to call Finbarr Crowley, who had gone on vacation to Lanzarote. He told me that there was to be a letter sent from Philip Browne, the chief executive of the IRFU, to each branch chief executive. He said that the letter would set out the position – that we should wait for it and not make any assumptions before reading it.

Finbarr said that he thought it had gone to each branch already, but I assured him that I had been talking to Mick Dawson earlier that day and it hadn't been received in any format. He said that the IRFU representatives from two provinces (including Leinster) had complained that they didn't know in time that non-IRFU committee persons could be considered. Munster did know and had put forward a very credible candidate for the professional game board position (although he was not successful). He added that if a province put forward a second person at this stage, it wouldn't reflect badly on the existing nominee from that province – that the panel would look objectively at all candidates. He suggested that we should look at the terms of reference and the criteria set out in the guidance document.

I reported back to those of the Leinster management committee who were available, and it was agreed that we should consider putting forward another candidate for the IRFU management committee position. My name was suggested, but I advised that we approach Paul McNaughton – a former international player and former manager of the Leinster team who subsequently became manager of Ireland and then interim chairman of European Professional Club Rugby – or alternatively Frank Sowman, who was on our professional game committee, had been a former manager of the Ireland team and was very experienced in rugby administration.

Mick Dawson felt that Paul couldn't take the position, as he was in a very delicate but critical position with European Professional Club Rugby. It was agreed that I would call Frank and ask him if he would accept a nomination, as – compared with me – he would be more likely as an acceptable candidate. I called Frank, discussed the situation and asked him to consider the proposal. Frank did consider it, but he called back within twenty-four hours to decline the offer, adding that he was very flattered but didn't want to put himself up for election. I tried to persuade him otherwise but didn't succeed. I was then asked to call the president of the IRFU, who was also chairman of the interview committee. I tried to get a sense of where matters lay, as we had received the letter from Philip Browne by then, but that letter had raised more questions than it had answered.

The president told me that the interview board had decided that they had to look beyond what they had seen. He said that one of the unsuccessful candidates had put his hand up for the rugby committee position – that if the Leinster candidate for the management committee position was interested in that position, he should apply for it now, as he would be reinterviewed for it. He added that that candidate was perceived to have a weakness in his lack of experience in dealing with the professional game – which was so important to them – but that he was still in the process.

He added, however, that there were three people that they were really interested in; and although he didn't specifically state it, I understood that Paul and Frank were among that three. He expressed disappointment at the approach taken by the Leinster Branch representatives in a recent vote at an IRFU committee meeting and said that there was a serious risk that there wouldn't be any Leinster representation at the management committee table for the next few seasons.

I again reported back and convened a special meeting of the Leinster management committee for Monday, 22 December. I also invited the Leinster representatives on the IRFU committee to attend. As I was still a potential candidate for the chairmanship of the IRFU management committee, Paul and Frank having been ruled out, I decided that it wouldn't be appropriate for me to chair this meeting – as I would normally do – and so I asked Ray Ryan, the long-serving honorary treasurer, to do so. This was agreed by everybody at the meeting.

In advance of the meeting, I had received a letter from the Leinster candidate for the IRFU management committee chairmanship, and I circulated this at the meeting. In it, he stated that he had spoken to the president of the IRFU and was assured that he remained in the frame, adding that if he was advised to the contrary, he would do the honourable thing and withdraw. At that meeting on 22 December, the letter from Philip Browne was discussed and it was agreed that Mick Dawson would contact Philip on the following morning to seek clarifications on a few ambiguities.

Ray Ryan asked for clarification on the procedures involved, and it was explained that a candidate successful in the interview had to be proposed and seconded by members of the IRFU committee and then be approved by that committee. The possibility of an outside chair of the IRFU management committee being appointed was then discussed. It was felt by our representatives that the IRFU committee wouldn't agree to this; it was stated that there had been a vote at the last IRFU committee meeting and that the motion had been carried by only one vote.

We on the Leinster management committee indicated that we hadn't heard of this issue being voted on previously. It was only later that we discovered that it was part of a general move by the officers of the IRFU to widen the field of candidates for all positions rather than confine them to a narrow group who were unlikely to be most qualified. I realised that this was the vote that the president had referred to in his earlier chat with me. This was to cause further difficulties later in the season, as the turkeys were not inclined to vote for Christmas.

As it appeared that the Leinster candidate wasn't excluded but was in a form of limbo, I decided that I wasn't going to allow my name to be put forward for a position that I didn't particularly want – a position that I was considering only because some on our management committee had asked me to put myself forward in an effort to ensure that a Leinster person got the position. As it later transpired, no outside candidate could be persuaded to go forward and the Munster candidate was selected and later elected by the IRFU committee. A new IRFU standing committee was created at the end of the season, and the unsuccessful Leinster candidate was appointed as chairman, which facilitated Leinster having some representation on the IRFU management committee. I believed that the entire process reflected poorly on the Leinster representatives to the IRFU. Nevertheless, life went on.

Louisa and Lee left for Perth with the children on Saturday morning, 2 January. On the same day, I headed back to the RDS for the next PRO12 game against Ulster. As she did on numerous occasions during the season, Mary came with me to the drinks reception and lunch before watching the game. Leinster won, getting 2015 off to a good start. The usual series of meetings ensued during the week, and on Friday, 9 January, I flew to Cardiff with the Leinster team for a PRO12 game on the following day.

Our flight was due to take off at 5.30 p.m. but was delayed for an hour due to high winds. There was a group of forty U12 players from Clontarf minis, along with their parents and managers, on the flight; they were on a weekend trip to play a local team and then come to watch the Leinster game. Once we got airborne, the flight was uneventful but the plane – which was relatively small – was buffeted a little in the wind. Just before we landed in Cardiff Airport, after a very bumpy and rocky approach, the pilot aborted the landing and lifted the plane again. Some of the senior players screamed in terror – notably two of the biggest and toughest foreign players in the squad – and anybody with a window seat was most likely to notice that the plane was bucking like a bronco as it came close to the ground.

I had been on a few scary flights previously and took a fairly resigned attitude to our predicament; the group of U12s, who were sitting behind me, thought it was great fun and that they were on a massive roller coaster. The pilot came on the speaker, explained that he was forced to abort because of the very dangerous winds on the runway, and said that he would go around and retry. This did nothing to reassure the nervous flyers at the front of the plane; when he came in for the second time, there was a very noticeable tension, with everyone now straining to see out the windows.

On this second occasion, it was even more bumpy, and at times the engine seemed to cut out, causing more screams. When the pilot aborted again, from very close to the ground, the group of U12s cheered, almost believing that he was putting on a special show for them. There was absolutely no panic from them, and I felt very proud of their behaviour. At the front, on the other hand, some of the players were panicking badly. The pilot then announced that he wasn't going to try a third time but had been told that he could land at Bristol airport, which he duly did. He got a round of applause as we disembarked, and he thoroughly deserved it.

The only problem was that we were now nearly 50 miles away from where we wanted to be. But Ronan O'Donnell, the operations manager of Leinster Rugby, swiftly took control; along with the representative of JWT, our travel agent, he arranged busses as quickly as possible to get us to Cardiff. We were about three hours later than scheduled, but nobody complained and it was a very quiet bus journey. I said goodbye to the Clontarf boys and their parents and didn't see them again until the airport on our return journey, although I did hear them cheering for Leinster at the Cardiff Arms Park – the former international ground, which is next door to its replacement, the Millenium Stadium.

Leinster won by 22–14 and gained a bonus point for four tries. To the delight of the Clontarf boys in attendance – and, indeed, mine – the first try was scored by Noel Reid and the fourth by Tadhg Furlong, two Clontarf players. The only other memorable moment from the game was Rob Kearney almost having his head taken off in a clothesline tackle, with the offending player receiving a red card and being sent off.

On the following Saturday, 17 January, I was again busy with multiple engagements. It started with the final of the Leinster Senior Shield, at 1 p.m., between Wanderers and Greystones. Wanderers won, and I presented the trophy and medals to the winning team. In the meantime, there was a pre-match reception at 2.15 p.m., before the final of the Leinster Senior

League Cup between Clontarf and UCD, which was to start at 3 p.m. I hosted the reception for a short time, before the presentation to the winners of the first game. I would have loved to watch the Clontarf game, but unfortunately I had another event to attend – a pre-match reception and dinner in the RDS, also at 3 p.m., for the Leinster v Castres European Champions Cup game.

I was kept on edge during the pre-match function, as I was getting regular text messages from Donnybrook to update me on what was a very close game. I had explained my dilemma to the Castres president, and in due course I excused myself and got a lift back up to Donnybrook. I was in time to see the last few minutes and was absolutely delighted to see Clontarf win, 32–28, and to then present medals to the Tarf team and the cup to Sam Cronin, the captain. Later, at the end of the season, I realised that that presentation was one of the highlights of the presidency for me – I treasure the memory of that occasion.

Nevertheless, I had to leave the celebrations, get my lift back to the function at the RDS and then go out to watch the game. Leinster had a very convincing 50–8 win, and after a post-match drink with the Castres officials, I went for dinner with Mary and Sinéad; later, on my way home, I called in to Castle Avenue to join in the Tarf celebrations.

On Friday, 23 January, the members of the Leinster management committee flew with the team to Birmingham and bussed on to Coventry for the final pool game of the European Champions Cup; it was against Wasps, who had just moved to the Ricoh Arena in Coventry from the atrocious Adams Park in High Wycombe, referred to earlier. We had a very pleasant dinner in an Italian restaurant; it was quite a few notches higher than the Italian restaurant where we had had lunch in High Wycombe on the previous occasion when we had gone away to play Wasps.

On Saturday, we were entertained before the game by the Wasps directors, led by Derek Richardson. He was from Dublin and was a former Wanderers player; he had bought Wasps and was the mastermind behind the move to the Ricoh Arena. It involved a complicated property deal with Coventry City Council, and as explained to us, it seemed a brave business move. Leinster and Wasps tied their game, 20–20, which was sufficient for Leinster to top their group and earn a home quarter-final against Bath. Wasps also qualified for the quarter-finals and an away tie against Toulon.

We flew home after the game. Mary collected me at the airport at 7 p.m. and brought me over to Templeville Road for the St Mary's College RFC annual dinner, and then collected me after that and brought me home. The Leinster Senior Schools Cup started on the following day, Sunday, 25 January, with a game between Blackrock College and Terenure College on the new all-weather pitch in Donnybrook. Before that game there was a reception for the family of Anne McInerney, who had been the administrator of schools rugby in Leinster for many years and had died a few weeks previously.

As I anticipated, and as has been borne out on numerous occasions since, the all-weather pitch was particularly advantageous for the schools competitions, allowing for fast open rugby, even when the weather was unkind – as it often is during the six or seven weeks of the competitions.

The following weekend was a little quieter. On Thursday night, 29 January, I attended the reunion dinner for the Leinster club presidents of 2011/12; on Friday night, I attended the Terenure College RFC annual dinner. On Saturday night, I was present at the Old Belvedere RFC annual dinner when my old acquaintance John Mahony – a former president of the club and larger-than-life character – in proposing the toast of the guests in his own inimitable and scurrilous manner, managed to get a good dig at me. But as someone once said, it's better to have people talking badly about you than not talking about you at all. Anyway, I knew that it's a long road that doesn't have a turn, and I was likely to get an opportunity at some stage for a riposte.

Earlier that week, the consultant hand surgeon had given me the all-clear on the injury I had suffered at the end of November – but I already knew that, as I had recommenced playing golf some weeks beforehand and had discarded the splint and support that he had put on it.

The Six Nations competition started on the first weekend in February, and we travelled with the IRFU party to Rome. I hadn't been in Rome since the first time that Ireland played Italy in the Six Nations back in 2001; I was looking forward to seeing it again. As events panned out, however, we didn't get to see as much as I had hoped – our flight to Rome being delayed, leaving only part of Friday afternoon and a little of Saturday morning for sightseeing.

Nevertheless, it was a great trip, and an opportunity to see how well the IRFU looked after its committee members, who probably deserved it, but also its past presidents. The provincial presidents and our wives piggy-backed on this as one of the perks of office, but in our case, it was for our year of office only, as one would have expected. Indeed, it should have been the case for the IRFU presidents also. In the game, which took place on Saturday afternoon, Ireland got off to a good start to the series of games, winning by 26–3.

On Friday, 13 February, there were three clashing dinners; colleagues in Leinster covered for me in two of them, while Mary and I dined with some of the other provincial and exiles presidents in the Oar House in Howth. On the following day, after the pre-match lunch, we watched Ireland defeat France, 18–11, and then attended the team dinner after the game, which included the two teams, the coaches and the managers, as well as the French union representatives. I had invited Pat McHale, the Clontarf club president, and his wife, Bernie, to join Mary and me.

These post-match dinners, as I learned, have a fairly standard format: speeches, an exchange of gifts, a presentation of caps to those getting their first cap, and a presentation of mementoes to those who have just gained a significant number, such as fifty or seventy-five. Another tradition is that new caps must sing a song of their own choice. In the old days, that might not have been too much of a problem, as players usually had a good few pints before the dinner. In the professional era, however, that wasn't acceptable, so young players had to get up and sing without the comfort blanket of the pints.

On the following day, Sunday 15 February, Leinster had a PRO12 game against Dragons, and after the pre-match drinks reception, we watched Leinster being surprisingly defeated. Leinster didn't have their international players available to them because of the Six Nations; nevertheless, the team seemed strong enough on paper to win. So it was a mixed weekend, but for me a very disappointing end.

The following week involved the Wanderers FC annual dinner on Shrove Tuesday, as was their long-standing custom. On Friday evening, 20 February, another customary occasion took place at the RDS: I, as president, hosted a dinner and a group photograph for all the Leinster past presidents before a PRO12 game – on this occasion against Zebre, which thankfully we won, continuing the yoyo results of the season.

I jokingly told the past presidents that a new protocol had been agreed when any of them died, as it was likely some would die in the next forty years, adding that three of their number had died already that year. We wanted to let everyone in the branch know if and when it happened, and I asked them to bring their smart phone with them in the coffin, wherever they were going – up or down – and let Mick Dawson, or whoever his successor was, know in case their family forgot to tell us.

On the following day, I watched Clontarf defeat Terenure College in the AIL. On Sunday, I went to Clondalkin RFC for a pre-match reception, then watched Clondalkin play Gorey in the Towns Cup and later conducted the draw for the second round. The next Saturday afternoon, after the usual three or four meetings during the week, I travelled to Swansea with Leinster via Cardiff for the PRO12 game. Thankfully there was no problem landing at Cardiff on this occasion, and Leinster tied the game, 9–9. Although not what I had hoped for, and a somewhat boring game, it was not a disaster.

We got home that evening, and on the following day, 28 February, I visited the strength and conditioning course conducted by the Leinster strength and conditioning team in Industries Hall, RDS. They ran the course on a commercial basis to help fund equipment for their work with Leinster, and it was suggested to me that my attendance for a while would be appreciated. I was delighted to do so, and was very impressed at the commitment and science involved.

That night, Mary and I met the other provincial presidents for dinner in Donnybrook. We then all went to Ciss Maddens for an extra few drinks before going back to the Four Seasons Hotel, where we stayed for the night, before the international the next day against England. It seemed a little strange to stay in a Dublin hotel when we could have got home in 30 minutes, but as all the other presidents were staying there, we decided to do the same. I also anticipated that there would be more craic later that night – and indeed I was right.

The following day had the usual pre-match reception and lunch, and then we watched Ireland defeat England, 19–9. There was a great post-match team dinner that night as we began to realise that Ireland could now win the Six Nations and even the Grand Slam. As I could invite guests – as at the previous post-international match dinner – I invited Geoff Curran, the Clontarf club chairman, and his wife, Aisling, to join Mary and me. Any time we defeat England is an occasion to celebrate, albeit it has happened more regularly in recent years than prior to 2000.

On the following Wednesday, 4 March, there was a happy occasion: eight members of the Leinster Academy graduated. The academy prepares young players who have been identified as potential elite players for life as a professional, off the field as well as on it. It includes courses on media training, basic personal financial management and basic nutrition. I was delighted to present them with their FETAC certificates. Most of the guys had their parents present, and I took the opportunity to thank them for the time that they had put into their rugby development over many years, expressing the hope that they were satisfied that we in Leinster had done our bit in their personal and professional development.

On Thursday, 5 March, there was a special general meeting of the Leinster Branch to consider – and if appropriate, adopt – revised bye-laws for the governance and management of the branch and its business. A special general meeting had a much larger entitled participation than an executive committee meeting – the same as that for an AGM – so it was held in the RDS, which had greater capacity than our usual meeting room in Newstead in Clonskeagh.

The review of the bye-laws had commenced in 2012, as it was realised that the existing bye-laws, adopted in 2009, contained a number of lacunae, inconsistencies and unclear provisions. A subcommittee, of which I was chairman, was appointed at that time to review the bye-laws; it comprised most of those involved in 2009, with a few new members, including myself. We produced a report to the management committee in early 2013, but a few issues hadn't been resolved and it was left lie without a decision.

I was determined to revive that review. I announced this determination at the first executive committee meeting in May 2014, promising that we would have a special general meeting during the season to adopt revised bye-laws. Much work, time and debate had gone into the review over a period of a few years. In January 2015, a draft was circulated to all members, with an explanatory memorandum. This resulted in a few helpful comments; we accepted any that we felt were appropriate, and a new revised version was then sent to the IRFU for approval, as was required.

The IRFU came back to me the day before our scheduled special general meeting, and only after some pushing by me. They had two issues, both of which required further discussion and negotiation with them. After these were resolved, we finally had a version that could be presented for adoption. At the meeting which I chaired, a few more suggestions for amendments were proposed – again, if I considered them appropriate and an improvement on the document presented, I allowed them. I then put the final version to a vote, after getting a seconder, and it was adopted unanimously, subject to one abstention. I was personally delighted, as it fulfilled one of my targets for the season.

I had arranged for Matt O'Connor, the Leinster head coach, to address the meeting – partly to ensure a quorum would attend, but more to allow representatives of the clubs and associations to meet and hear him. So as soon as the formal part of the meeting was finished, Matt kindly gave us his views on the season so far and how he thought the team would fare for the remainder of the season.

On the following day, I flew to Cardiff with the team again. We bussed to Swansea, where we stayed overnight. On the Saturday, after the team left for Llanelli in their team bus, I went to Swansea train station, as I had arranged to meet Mick Dawson and Ben Underwood, who had flown over that morning to Cardiff and were on a train to Llanelli. After a lunch and reception at Parc y Scarlets, the stadium, we watched Leinster losing again in the PRO12 game – despite the optimism Matt had shown two days earlier.

The pressure was building on him, and the public attitude wasn't helped by Matt's earlier verbal attack on the IRFU and Joe Schmidt in which he took umbrage with the Irish team management's lack of co-operation with the provinces, and particularly Leinster. As the Irish team were doing well and Leinster were not, Matt didn't gain much public sympathy and lost a lot of IRFU sympathy. He hadn't learned that it was unwise to criticise the IRFU in public, particularly when they were his ultimate boss.

In Clontarf, the senior team were doing reasonably well, hovering close to the top four. This was significant, as the IRFU had changed the structure again at the start of the season, reintroducing playoffs for the top four teams.

During the season, I had been asked to attend a Clontarf executive committee meeting at which the proposed new pitches were discussed. It had been suggested by me and others that rather than go with the original plan for upgrading the existing junior pitch – a grass pitch, an all-weather pitch should be considered.

The meeting was against this on the basis that when the special general meeting was held to approve the loan, there was no reference to an all-weather pitch. I pointed out that the pitch type wasn't part of the resolution passed at that meeting – that it was only part of the committee outline plans. I said that if the committee now believed that an all weather pitch was in the best interests of the club, they shouldn't be bound by their own previous plans and should be bold enough to change their minds.

It was noted that additional finance would be required, but I pointed out that by using the tax-based donation scheme, the club members were likely to support the necessary fundraising. By the end of the meeting, there was unanimity that the club should opt for an all-weather pitch. A fundraising committee was formed, and I indicated that although I didn't have time to be on the committee, I was prepared to help out with any advice that I could.

On Friday, 13 March, Mary and I flew with an IRFU party to Cardiff for the Wales international game on the following day. We stayed in the Marriott in Cardiff, which was a step up on the hotel that Leinster had stayed in recently. Again, we had a very pleasant trip, but it was spoiled slightly after Ireland lost the game by seven points – a margin that was to prove crucial. It also meant that Ireland couldn't win the Grand Slam, and that going into the last round of games, any of Ireland, Wales or England could win the Six Nations outright.

On the night of the game, while the team and IRFU executive committee members went to the team dinner hosted by the Welsh Rugby Union, the provincial presidents and our wives joined the IRFU past presidents and their wives for a dinner and drinks in the Marriott. Tom Grace, the honorary treasurer, had given the IRFU credit card to Ronnie Dawson, one of the past presidents and a trustee of the IRFU. We dined well, and after a few more drinks, Ronnie settled the bill and went to bed.

Two of the past presidents got so upset when they discovered that they would now have to pay for their own drink that I could only think of young children who discovered that the sweets and goodies at their party had all been eaten. They kicked up a stink, complaining that they were being treated like teenagers – that Ronnie should either have stayed up with them or given them the credit card. They said they would complain to Tom Grace when they saw him. I realised that they had had too much to drink, but to me it represented the ridiculous sense of entitlement – the expectation of 'freebies for life' – that some of these past presidents had. I have learned since that one of these two is a trustee now, so I hope the Finance Department of the IRFU is keeping a close eye on the budget.

We arrived back on the evening of Sunday, 15 March. The next day, I attended the Clontarf Rugby annual dinner. The day after – St Patricks Day – was, as customary, the day of the Schools Senior Cup, and this year it was between Belvedere College and Roscrea College in the RDS. This was always one of the big occasions in the Leinster Rugby calendar, and today was no exception. As I said at the pre-match lunch, this year we had probably seen the best schools cup competition for a long time, and we had ended up with an intriguing pairing. It was the first competition played on the new Donnybrook all-weather pitch, and that obviously helped the quality of the rugby. The final was a superb game, with the spectators creating an amazing atmosphere; it was climaxed with an outstanding score by Roscrea that deserved to win any final.

After the game, which Roscrea had won for the first time, I addressed the teams and the spectators from the middle of the pitch. The mother of the Roscrea captain, Tim Foley, then presented him with the cup, as is the tradition. At the post-match reception I met Willie Mullins, the horse trainer; he was a past pupil of Roscrea and had had a very successful week at Cheltenham just a few days previously, training eight winners, which was a record. I think he was more excited by Roscrea's victory than any of his Cheltenham wins, probably because it was so rare.

For me, one surprising outcome of this final is that only two of the players involved have succeeded in a professional rugby career: Hugh O'Sullivan for Belvedere, who at the time was only in fourth year, and Fineen Wycherley for Roscrea, who plays for Munster and was subsequently capped for Ireland. Nonetheless, more of those who played in earlier rounds have succeeded as professional players, which I suppose shows that rugby is very much a team game, where individual stars don't necessarily result in a star team. It is one of the many things I love about the game.

On Thursday, 19 March, I travelled to Scotland with some friends, getting the 7.30 a.m. ferry from Larne to Cairnryan and then being driven to Prestwick, where we played a very pleasant round of golf. We then travelled by car to Edinburgh – to the Bonham Hotel, a boutique hotel in Drumsheugh Gardens, close to the city centre. We were collected early the following morning for our traditional trip to Luffness New Golf Club to play our friends in the LRC, and as was the custom, we had a very liquid three-course lunch before we played. We retained the Stephenson Quaich trophy on this occasion.

Mary had arrived in Edinburgh with the IRFU party; we met up when I left my golfing friends and moved from the Bonham to the Balmoral Hotel in the city centre. The next day was the last round of the Six Nations competition. There were three successive games, each of which was critical to the eventual outcome. It was billed by the media as Super Saturday, and on this occasion it lived up to the hype.

The first game, at 12.30 p.m., resulted in Wales defeating Italy, 61–20, which gave them eight table points for four wins and a points difference of +53. It was Wales's highest victory margin against Italy – and it could have been greater, as they had a chance to score again with four minutes to go, but the ball was fumbled and Italy scored a minute later. It meant that Ireland had to defeat Scotland by at least twenty points to finish ahead of Wales.

Ireland then played Scotland at 2.30 p.m., and in a magnificent display defeated Scotland, 40–10, the captain, Paul O'Connell, scoring a try in the fourth minute and Seán O'Brien scoring two tries. It never looked as if Scotland would win, as Ireland dominated the game. It required great concentration and commitment to keep scoring and prevent Scotland from adding to their total in the second half; also needed was a heroic tackle from Jamie Heaslip on Stuart Hogg, with just a few minutes left, to prevent a likely try. This meant that the championship would depend on the result of the England and France game, which started at 4.30 p.m. England had to defeat France by more than twenty-six points to overcome Ireland.

After thirty minutes, France led England, 15–7, so as a television interviewer put it to Joe Schmidt, 'England need to win the next fifty minutes by 34 points. Do you think they can do so?' Joe replied nervously, 'I hope not.' In the end, England scored their highest ever total against France in a 55–35 victory. They scored seven converted tries, but France scored five tries themselves. England scored their last try with six minutes left to play; those final minutes were some of the most tense and exciting that I have had in sport, as England attacked brilliantly and seemed certain to score.

We were all at the post-match dinner in the hospitality area of Murrayfield, watching the game on television. When England conceded a penalty on the French line as a championship-winning try looked inevitable, some of us exploded in delight, jumping up and shouting like teenagers – an outpouring that instantaneously turned to horror when Rory Kockott, the French substitute scrum half, took a quick penalty from behind the posts and started to run with and play the ball from behind his line instead of kicking it dead. We were in a state of shock, as even if France scored, it wouldn't have won the game for them. Kockott almost gave possession back to England when he was tackled and a ruck formed, and if they scored and converted, it would have won the championship for them. Thankfully, however, France retained possession and this time kicked the ball dead. This ended the game, and we resumed our explosion.

It was described as perhaps the best day in the history of the Six Nations, going to the last play in the fifteenth game of the championship – and the third game of that day. The Irish team were dining in a different room, and suddenly everybody poured back out to the stadium for the presentation. It was an amazing evening. A huge crowd of the Irish fans had stayed back in the stadium for more than two hours after the finish of the Irish game and were rewarded by seeing the presentation to the team, who – unusually – were by this time in suits and ties.

We then went back to the Balmoral Hotel to continue the party and celebrations, and while there, three of the IRFU officers and two past presidents tried to persuade me to put my name forward in the forthcoming election for the Leinster representative to the IRFU. There wasn't an election every year, but there would be in this year. It was something that had been suggested to me previously; I had thought about it and dismissed it, but I was flattered and told these attempting persuaders that I would think about it again.

On Friday, 27 March, Leinster was due to play Glasgow in the PRO12 in the RDS. I had suggested to the management committee, and they agreed with me, that the Leinster president should host a dinner for the Leinster club presidents before one of the PRO12 games and invite them to the game afterwards – as a form of thanks for the annual club dinner invitations that were extended to the Leinster president. We had chosen this game for the event, so a new tradition was started. Unfortunately, however, it clashed with the annual dinner of Naas RFC, and some presidents had to send substitutes.

There was a large contingent from Glasgow at the dinner, as well. In my welcome address to them, I thanked Scottish Rugby for the excellent hospitality in Edinburgh on the previous weekend, saying that it wasn't easy to watch your opponents celebrate but that they were very gracious – and that their only consolation was that we had stopped England, the common enemy, from winning. We had a very pleasant evening with the Glasgow officials and then watched as Leinster produced one of their best performances of the season, coming from a 27–7 deficit at half time to tie the game, 34–34, and give us hope for the rest of the season.

On Saturday, 28 March, I watched Clontarf defeat Cork Con in the AIL in an outstanding display. I then attended the annual dinner of the ARLB, the referees association. Two of the guests at the table with me were former internationals: Mick Quinn, an outhalf, and Des Fitzgerald, a prop forward. I had a very enjoyable evening with plenty of good rugby banter and reminiscences.

On the following day, I attended the Metro Division 1 final between Lansdowne and Old Belvedere. The game was in Ballycorus, near Kilternan, which is across Dublin Bay from my home – less than 16 kilometres as the crow flies but more than 51 kilometres by road. It was one of the occasions when I thought about how much time I could have saved if Leinster had supplied me with a helicopter. Anyway, that was never an option, and after I presented the cup and medals to the winners, I drove home.

Monday, 30 March was the start of a saga that ultimately caused me a lot of angst – something I certainly didn't anticipate when, upon request, Mick Dawson and I met Finbarr Crowley and Philip Browne and the IRFU's in-house lawyer. The IRFU guys introduced the topic at hand: some amendments to the IRFU bye-laws that they wanted to have passed before the end of the season. This was outlined to us in the hope that we would get Leinster to support them on these amendments.

Apparently, the process had been going on for some time. One of the issues was whether the chief executive of the IRFU could be nominated as one of its representatives on the IRB, since renamed World Rugby. The CEOs or executive presidents of most of the other leading unions around the world had been appointed to the World Rugby council, and the IRFU officers wanted to ensure that the IRFU was not disadvantaged in any way. To achieve this objective, some rule changes were needed.

We were told that, in May 2014, the proposed rule changes were put forward to the IRFU committee. Instead of making a decision on the matter, the committee asked that senior counsel's opinion be sought as to whether the CEO, as an employee of the union, can be considered a member of the union under the then current laws – for the purposes of being nominated as a representative of the union on World Rugby. If not deemed to be a member of the union, the committee then wanted to know if the CEO could, in any event, be nominated as a representative.

Although there may have been other reasons, I was conscious that one reason for this proposed change was the solo run that one of their existing representatives on the IRB had undertaken in relation to European Rugby competition changes. Confusion under the then current laws arose from the fact that while the council – which was the supreme body of the union – is obliged to receive nominations from the committee of 'two members of the Union', Law 15(e)(xi) provides that the committee is obliged to nominate for acceptance by the council 'two representatives of the Union' to sit on World Rugby.

Previous IRFU laws provided for 'two persons' to represent the union rather than 'two members of the Union'. The term 'member' was not expressly defined under the then current laws, and although 'person' was clearly defined, it was not referred to in either Rule 14(e)(xi) or 15(e)(xi). Under the then current laws, the CEO would fall within the broad definition of a 'person' and was logically an office holder involved in the management of the union (as the senior counsel concluded) and, but for the inclusion of the undefined term 'Member of the Union', would be eligible as a representative to sit on World Rugby.

A further anomaly was that by virtue of then current Law 10(h) of the IRFU laws, a person couldn't take part in the management of the union unless he was a member of a club – exception to this could be made, however, if it was specifically authorised by the committee. If the chief executive was a member of a club, then by operation of the laws, he became a 'member' of the union.

While it was for the committee to nominate a person, it merely selected the proposed representatives. The representatives then had to be accepted by the council. It wasn't specifically set down as to whether the council could choose to refuse to accept the nominations provided by the committee; if the council had supreme authority in this regard, the laws should be clear, and currently they were not.

The IRFU committee were provided with the initial opinion of senior counsel. They agreed unanimously that clarity was needed on these issues, that flexibility was required in respect of nominations and appointments, and that it was for the IRFU committee to determine who it wished to select for nomination. A subcommittee, or laws working group, was to be set up to review the laws and recommend changes required to address the issues raised – and any other amendments deemed appropriate or consequential.

In November 2014, the subcommittee had put it to the committee as to whether the council should have the right to veto the committee's selection of the World Rugby representatives and chairman of the management committee. The committee decided unanimously that these appointments should be committee appointments and that the council shouldn't have the power to veto them.

A new expanded definition of 'Official of the Union' and of 'Person' was then included in the new revised draft version of the laws. The updated laws also provided flexibility to appoint or co-opt to the committee or a subcommittee, as deemed necessary or appropriate, a specialist in a particular field, such as finance, marketing, economics, procurement and so forth, who had no direct connection to rugby, the union or a branch. The revised version was again approved unanimously by the committee, and senior counsel confirmed it as being fit for purpose and meeting the requirements for good governance.

I didn't want to criticise the choice of senior counsel, but the person used had no particular expertise on these issues. He was a very highly regarded expert on employment law and arbitration, but – with due respect – his opinion on this matter bore no weight for me. I presume that he was retained initially because the first issue related, to some extent, to employment law issues, but it had subsequently moved well beyond that.

The IRFU guys we met asked us to deal with the matter as quickly as possible, as they wanted to then go to the other branches and get their approval so that they could convene a special meeting of the council to have the amendments adopted. Mick Dawson suggested that I would review the documents given to us and draft a response. But from the preliminary meeting that we had, Mick indicated that he was in general agreement with the proposed changes. I then spent some time reading and trying to understand all the laws and how the proposed amendments affected them.

It seemed to me from that reading that the entire governance of the IRFU needed review and change; I thought that the review of the laws should follow on from this, reflecting the new governance system. Nevertheless, I saw that they weren't yet ready for such a fundamental overhaul, even if they were vaguely considering it. For now all they wanted was a couple of changes to achieve particular objectives. I drafted a long email to each of Finbarr, Philip and Mick, unintentionally omitting the IRFU lawyer. I stated that I didn't think that I had seen any of the IRFU laws previously – and certainly hadn't given them any thought. I added that, in general, I agreed with the principle of what they were trying to achieve but that to be in a position to formally support it, I believed that I had to understand and agree the various amendments that were being proposed.

I raised queries on eight separate definitions in the Definitions section of the laws and commenced by stating that I needed to understand what the 'Union' was. The word itself implied that it was an organisation uniting other organisations or entities. I presumed that it was a union of clubs, but this presumption was challenged by the definition of 'Affiliated Club'. The definition of 'Affiliated Club' also called into question the branch bye laws – or at least those of Leinster – which I was very familiar with, and which had recently been approved by the union.

I made points on thirteen other laws, or sub paragraphs of laws, including that in Law 14(a)(viii), where there was reference to the election by council of six 'Persons to be independent members of the Committee', the introduction of the term 'independent' being new and contrasting with other members elected that didn't have that qualification I asked 'independent of what' and enquired how the branches who nominate these persons determine which of their nominees is independent and which is 'dependent'. I said that different provincial branches select their candidates for IRFU committee membership in different ways and asked whether this had been considered with other branches before its proposed introduction in the revised rules.

I asked if it was the intention that independent members couldn't be members of their branch executive committee – or, indeed, any branch committee. I added that this issue of 'independent members' was likely to cause problems in Leinster, and may result in the issues that were addressed in their explanatory memorandum, described above, not being passed if they were dependent on this also being passed.

I finished by stating that I knew that I had gone beyond what they expected, but that if I was to support the amendments that they wished to introduce, I had to be satisfied with everything else – and that as they would note, I was not so satisfied. I offered to meet again if they thought it would be of assistance.

Instead, I got a lengthy response from the IRFU lawyer. He defended the definitions and the laws, and in some cases pointed out that the Leinster representatives on the IRFU had accepted them – which, of course, was totally irrelevant to the point at hand. He seemed quite dismissive and didn't seem to understand much of what I suggested, from a drafting point of view.

Being fair, the point regarding the use of 'independent' was conceded, and was deleted in the version of the document produced later. I agreed to support the revision to the laws proposed by them on the basis that a root and branch review by an independent group would follow. At an informal meeting some weeks later, Philip Browne told me that he recognised that the IRFU laws were a bit of a mess and that inconsistencies had arisen from amendments being introduced from time to time without consideration of their knock-on effect and without a full review.

I replied that it was happening again with the then current proposal, and he confirmed that they would have to be looked at, as a whole as soon as possible. Despite my misgivings, I didn't want to hold up the adoption of the amendments and revisions that were proposed, as I thought that the principle behind them was in the best interests of rugby in Ireland and its administration. As it transpired, my support didn't save the proposals – and as I stated above, they were defeated.

The next event in Leinster was the European Champions Cup quarter-final against Bath on Saturday, 4 April. It took place in the Aviva and was preceded by a pre-match reception and lunch in the Presidents Terrace. As it was possibly the last big home game occasion of the season, I not only offered the usual welcome to guests – including Bruce Craig, the Bath Directors and the IRFU representatives – but also took the opportunity to thank a number of persons for their continuing support of European Rugby. Among those I thanked in this regard was Pat Meagher of Heineken; I added that it was testament to Heineken's support in the past that, for many of us, we believed that we were playing a Heineken Cup quarter-final that day.

I also thanked Bank of Ireland, the main sponsors of Leinster Rugby, and welcomed back their chief executive, Richie Boucher, who was recovering from a serious illness that had kept him away from rugby for a few months. Finally, I thanked the members of the Leinster management committee and their wives for their commitment and support so far in the season. I singled out Philip Brady and his wife, Mary, as when Philip wasn't organising rugby throughout the province as chairman of the rugby committee, he spent his time feeding chocolate and whiskey to his cows, which then produced the liqueur Coole Swan. They had enabled me to present a bottle of the liqueur to each visiting president during the season, and they had presented a bottle to each of the guests at the function. After all that, Leinster went out to defeat a very good Bath team, 18–15, and qualify us for a semi-final.

A few days later, at the management committee meeting, Derek McGrath – who we had retained as a project manager on the RDS development – gave a presentation. RKD Architects had been appointed by the RDS as the project architects after the competition. Derek explained to us that a major issue had arisen between the submission of the winning drawing and the point at which we signed off on the brief for the architects. The drawing indicated that the competition only covered the replacement of the Anglesea Stand and didn't deal with the corners, whereas we understood that there would be corner stands. This was essential, as the corner stands would be needed not only to achieve the capacity that we were targeting but also to prevent the creation of a wind tunnel.

We also wanted to ensure that games could continue while the development was proceeding. What's more, we wanted provision for three thousand premium grade seats, a terrace with standing room (for atmosphere reasons and to allow us to have a wider range of pricing) and facilities for corporate hospitality. It seemed to us, from Derek's briefing, that any misunderstandings had now been resolved. We were delighted that we had retained his services after his contract with the old Heineken Cup competition had terminated.

On the following Saturday, 11 April, I attended two of five girls finals at U15 and U18 level – staged consecutively between 12 p.m. and 5 p.m. – and presented trophies to the winners. I was then substituted by one of my vice presidents so that I could head off to Suttonians for the final of the Spencer Cup between Suttonians and Malahide, two local junior clubs – although Suttonians had been a senior club for a few years, until recently, and Malahide have since attained senior status.

Malahide won relatively easily at the end, but not before Malcolm O'Kelly – the former great Irish and Leinster second row – kicked the conversion of a try for Malahide. As I presented him with a Spencer Cup medal to put beside his Heineken Cup and Six Nations medals, he swore that it was his last competitive game. It wouldn't have surprised me if he continued, however, as he seemed to be enjoying himself.

I travelled to Cardiff again on the next morning, making my way to Newport for the Leinster game in the PRO12 against Dragons. To the great surprise of the home supporters, they defeated Leinster for the second time in the season – probably the one and only time that they succeeded in achieving that double.

In the meantime, I had belatedly decided to put my name forward for election as a Leinster Branch representative to the IRFU. I lodged my nomination papers at the last minute and told a few people that I had done so. There were already six other candidates for the four positions, four of whom were outgoing representatives, so I was entering a crowded arena – and well after the others had announced their candidature and had started canvassing.

It wasn't a position that I had any great ambition to attain, but a few things influenced me: firstly, the saga at the end of 2014 over the chairmanships of IRFU committees, when I felt that some of our existing representatives hadn't properly represented Leinster interests; secondly, the urging by some of the IRFU officers that I stand for election, as they thought I had something different to offer; and finally, the manner in which the IRFU were dealing with their own governance, as exemplified in their laws review – I believed that I could contribute to a thorough revision and restructuring of the IRFU by being on the inside. I was very conscious that I should not abuse my position as president in canvassing support for the IRFU position; even though I attended a number of meetings of committees in areas and sections of the branch in the following few weeks, I refused to canvas. Nonetheless, I didn't object to others doing so on their own behalf at these meetings.

We quickly came to the European Champions Cup semi-final weekend. Leinster was scheduled to play away in Marseille on the Sunday against the reigning champions, Toulon. As Toulon was seeded higher than Leinster, they were entitled to have the game in France, although not at their home ground; given this, they chose their neighbouring city, which gave them close-to-home advantage. Nevertheless, a huge crowd of Leinster supporters travelled by plane, boat, train or car – or some combination of these – and nullified the advantage that we thought that Toulon would have.

While the management committee and our respective partners wined, dined and sat out in the sun beside the pool in our Marseille hotel after arriving, Clontarf played Cork Con in the final of the Bateman Cup in Cork and were well beaten. Already disappointed by this result, I faced the Sunday game against a great Toulon team with considerable trepidation, remembering the horror of the Dragons game just a week earlier. I shouldn't have doubted the resolve and ability of the Leinster team to regroup and refocus, as they proceeded to put on their best performance of the season. It was a fantastic game that had everyone who watched it in the stadium or on TV enthralled until the very end. At the pre-match lunch, I initially addressed the attendance in French before reverting to English and supplying the usual platitudes.

The game was tied at the end of ordinary time and could have been won by either team in the last minutes. A drop goal attempt by Jimmy Gopperth missed the posts by centimetres, Rob Kearney was just short with a long-range drop kick attempt and Delon Armitage was just wide with a long-range penalty for Toulon, so extra time had to be played. Extra time in rugby is unusual, as teams have typically left every last ounce of energy on the pitch during the normal time. But in knock-out competitions like this, when there isn't sufficient flexibility in the schedule to have a replay, extra time is essential. I felt very sorry for our team, as they had given everything to win in normal time – and in hot but wet conditions, which in themselves were energy-sapping.

We had led by three points at half time of the scheduled eighty; Ian Madigan kicked three penalties, whereas Leigh Halfpenny kicked two. In a very tight and exciting second half, Ian kicked another long-range penalty, missing another – which struck the post – and Halfpenny kicked two. In extra time, they swapped penalties within two minutes, before Halfpenny edged Toulon back in front with his sixth successful penalty. Then disaster struck.

Leinster was attacking and looked to have space. Ali Williams was in the sin bin for a dangerous tackle on Devon Toner, so gaps had appeared in the otherwise excellent Toulon defence. Ian Madigan threw a long pass to the wing but hadn't seen Bryan Habana hovering and anticipating the pass. Habana intercepted the pass, sprinted fifty metres and scored a match-winning try against the run of play. Habana was the last player that one wanted to intercept a loose pass; it wasn't just his amazing speed but his reading of the play that showed why he was one of the top two or three wingers in world rugby.

Leinster didn't give up, and in the second period of extra time, Seán O'Brien scored a great try. Unfortunately, however, Ian Madigan had been substituted and Jimmy Gopperth's conversion attempt came back off the post, meaning that Leinster had to score another try in the last four minutes – and though they tried hard, Toulon held on for victory.

As usual, I went to the Leinster dressing room after the game, and the team were absolutely gutted. I tried to console Ian Madigan, who was particularly upset, and told him that Leinster wouldn't have been in that semi-final if he hadn't played so well and scored so many points in all the previous games. I also encouraged him and reminded him that he had scored fifteen points today. He thanked me, but I don't think my words were of any real consolation to him; all he could think of was the intercepted pass.

It is hard to describe how disappointed we and all the supporters were after the game. It was such a huge improvement over recent displays – and yet, cruelly, not enough. The rest of the season now looked bleak, as we had fallen behind in the PRO12 table; unless we won all our remaining games, qualification for the playoffs was out of our hands.

My attention switched back to the schools committee and schools rugby. The schools committee had two issues. The first was that their initial nomination for the junior vice presidency, to which they were entitled, was causing serious problems. I had been approached by some influential persons in Leinster Rugby; they informed me that if I didn't get the problem resolved by getting a different nominee, there would be long-term difficulties and division in Leinster.

This was awkward, as it was beyond my powers – and, indeed, those of any president – to interfere in the nomination by any club, area or section for any position. I believe that I managed to deal with the problem diplomatically. The only problem remaining was to find an alternative candidate that was willing and able to accept the nomination. I suggested Lorcan Balfe for the position, encouraging the schools section officers to pursue him; I then sat back, as they agreed with the suggestion. It was up to them to deal with the matter and approach Balfe to ascertain if he would accept the nomination. As it emerged, he did. So that problem was solved and Lorcan Balfe became the nominee of the schools section, being elected as junior vice president for the 2016/17 season and president for 2018/19.

The schools section's second issue was that it wanted to introduce restrictions in their competition regulations, preventing schools from fielding players in the Senior Cup that had recently joined the school. It was suspected that certain schools were enticing students from other schools to join them and strengthen their teams.

I was asked to consider this matter, as any changes had to be approved by the rugby committee and then by the executive committee. This was a difficult issue. Personally, I was sympathetic to the point of view of the young players, thinking of their opportunity to play on a better team with a chance of winning a schools' cup medal. It was also an avenue toward being put in a showcase for a possible professional career and toward getting a scholarship to a better-known school.

On the other hand, I knew that it distorted the competition, as it was only a limited number of schools that could afford to attract such players, and by strengthening their team they might be weakening another. What convinced me to support the schools committee proposal was the argument that by introducing a new student player for the last couple of years, another boy who had been on the team since first year would be dropped and probably lost to rugby. I told them that I could now support their proposal, and it was later incorporated in the regulations despite strong opposition from two of the three schools that were the main culprits.

On Wednesday, 22 April, there was another schools rugby event – an innovation by Tony Ward and the *Irish Independent*. It involved the selection of an elite team of the best player in each position in the Schools Senior Cup – they were to get their photograph taken, be invited to a reception with their parents and school coach and get acknowledgement of their achievement. Having seen many of the schools games, I had no quibble with most of the selections that Tony made. There was a reception for the players, their parents, their coaches, the schools committee and the sponsors in the Blue Room at the RDS, and I addressed them briefly.

Eight of the players were from Roscrea and Belvedere, as might be expected, but in some ways the day was more important for the other seven, who were from schools that had been defeated earlier. The two best players that I had seen in the schools cup competition were Jimmy O'Brien from Newbridge College, a back, and Max Deegan from St Michael's College, a forward.

The best schools player that I had seen during the year was James Ryan, but that was while he was playing for Leinster U19s; surprisingly he didn't play well in the schools cup matches. I have never since seen him giving less than an excellent performance, at any level, but for whatever reason – and it was probably because he was suffering from flu or some other seasonal bug at the time – his school games were not up to scratch. For this reason, he didn't deserve to be selected for this team, and that added to its authenticity. During my address, I wished the boys successful rugby careers, hoping that we would see all of them on Leinster teams over the next few years.

On Friday, 24 April, we travelled to Belfast for the PRO12 game against Ulster in Kingspan Park. It was too soon after the Toulon game for such an important game. Ulster had their strongest team, and Leinster couldn't afford to play too many of their second team, as they had at other times during the season. They had to select most of those who, five days earlier, had been heartbreakingly defeated in Marseille after extra time. Those players deserved a rest, but this was a must-win for Leinster: they were eight points behind Ospreys, who occupied the fourth and last qualifying position for the playoffs.

Unfortunately, Leinster couldn't re-enact the heroic Toulon performance and were well defeated, 26–10, despite having led 10–0 after seven minutes. John Kinnear, the Ulster president, and his committee entertained us very well and very late as we drowned our sorrows after the game; I had to be dragged on to the bus home, with most of the players sitting and waiting for us, half asleep already.

Nevertheless, life went on with domestic rugby as I entered the last month of my term of office. On the following day, suitably recovered, I drove to Greystones for the Women's finals in four Leinster grades. I watched the first three in appalling weather conditions, making the presentations while soaking wet. I then left to go to Lakelands Park to watch Clontarf play Terenure College in the semi-final of the AIL.

Again in horrendous conditions, Clontarf won by the unusual score of 9–0, reflecting the weather conditions rather than the quality of the play by both teams. Later that evening, I attended the Lansdowne annual dinner in their clubhouse, which resulted in good light-hearted banter, as Lansdowne had earlier defeated Young Munster in the other semi-final. They were now scheduled to play Clontarf in the final in two weeks' time.

On Sunday, 26 April, I attended the turning of the sod in Clondalkin RFC for their new development. I did so jointly with my former acquaintance Frances Fitzgerald – the Minister for Justice and the local TD – and Luke Fitzgerald, the Leinster and Ireland player. I then went to Cill Dara RFC on the Curragh for the Provincial Towns Cup final.

I was late for the scheduled start of the pre-match lunch, having got caught up in the traffic for the Kildare Shopping Village, which I wasn't used to or expecting. This wasn't helped by the fact that I didn't know exactly where Cill Dara RFC was. Those arranging the lunch did wait for me, so I addressed the large attendance once I had arrived and then went out to watch Enniscorthy defeat Kilkenny. I had never been to a Towns Cup final but had heard about previous occasions and therefore wasn't surprised by the big attendance, the side entertainment and the general atmosphere. Nonetheless, I was impressed.

There was a small, narrow rostrum for the presentation of the trophy and medals. I was lucky not to fall or at least be jostled off it on a few occasions, as the excited players jumped and danced before I could escape. It was a very well organised event, and it demonstrated to me the strength of rugby interest throughout the province.

As it was coming to the end of the season, there were a number of finals taking place and a series of AGMs of various areas and sections. I tried to attend as many as possible of these, but there were inevitable clashes, and substitutes were needed. In this regard, Paul Deering – the immediate past president – and the two vice presidents were of great assistance in trying to ensure a presence at all events.

One of the many issues that arose during the season was a breakdown of relationships between the secretary and many of the club representatives in one of the junior rugby areas. There were walk-outs and threats of boycotts, and very abusive language was used. And as always in such situations, there were two sides to the dispute – but as it threatened to disrupt the administration of rugby in an important area of Leinster, I couldn't ignore it when I was asked to find a solution.

I had decided when the issue arose to ask Des Kavanagh, a former president and honorary secretary of the Leinster Branch – and, indeed, an experienced trade union official – to mediate in the dispute. I asked him to find common ground on which both sides could proceed with the rugby business without necessarily resolving what was essentially a personal dispute. Des undertook the task, had a number of meetings with the protagonists, and reported back to me on a regular basis. We met again at the end of April, and Des informed me that a sufficient level of peace and common sense had been established, such that he felt that he could stand aside. I thanked him for his role, and we then chatted about the forthcoming election for the IRFU, in which we would be opponents. I explained why I had decided to put my name forward and assured him that I wasn't trying to take his place, as he was one of those that I believed was doing a good job in the role. I wished him well in the election, and he reciprocated.

Leinster's penultimate PRO12 game was against Treviso on Friday, 8 May, and it was an important one, as well as likely being our last home game of the season. To be sure of automatic qualification for the following season's European Champions Cup and to avoid having a playoff with Gloucester and then with the seventh-placed French team (yet to be determined), we would have to win this game – and perhaps the next one in Edinburgh, as well. In the usual presidents welcome in the match programme, I took the opportunity to thank all Leinster fans for their tremendous support during the season, even when things were not going our way.

Gordon D'Arcy had announced his retirement for the end of October 2015, after the Rugby World Cup, so on behalf of all Leinster fans, I expressed our gratitude to Gordon for all he had done for us in the previous seventeen years. Finally, I referred back to my address in the Leinster Branch Official Handbook at the commencement of the season, when I expressed the wish that a Leinster club would win the AIL again, as Leinster clubs had done in the previous four years. As the 2015 final, taking place the next day, was between Lansdowne and Clontarf, at least one of my wishes for the season would be met. Leinster did defeat Treviso 10–0 in a nervy game, but at this stage of the season, a win was more important than the quality of the play, so we accepted it.

The following day saw the final of the AIL in the Aviva Stadium, and this was an excellent game. Lansdowne had topped the league and had a tremendous team, including six who were either professional players at the time or have since made a successful professional career at fifteen- or seven-a-side rugby. Among them was Tadhg Beirne, who was on the bench that day in his last game for Lansdowne; he has now become a British and Irish Lions player. Clontarf also had four such players, who were either professional or became so soon afterwards. Clontarf had won the Leinster Senior League Cup and had been beaten finalists in the Bateman All-Ireland Cup, so the final was undoubtedly between the two best club teams in the country. Despite their best efforts and a few missed chances near the end, Clontarf lost by a point, 18–17. I was very disappointed at the result, albeit not at the performance. Nonetheless, I had to get over it quickly, as I had to be at the DoubleTree by Hilton Hotel (formerly the Burlington) that evening for 7 p.m. The occasion demanded full black-tie regalia – it was the Leinster Rugby Awards Ball.

This had become one of the big social nights of the year in Dublin. The huge hall was full to capacity with a large stage, a large screen at the front and many smaller screens around the hall. I had a number of functions to perform during the night, starting with the main address to the audience. In the course of this, I said that some people had said to me that this was a poor season in Leinster but that I disagreed with them. I referred back to my comments in the branch handbook when I pointed out that achieving success was usually the combination of hard work, talent and some good luck – when the mix is right, success follows and vice versa.

> Looking back at the season for the Leinster team, that statement is vindicated – our team always worked hard, they have incredible talent but the one element that was missing was some good luck. When we think back at drop goals at the end of games in Treviso and Marseille that missed the posts by centimetres, when we think back at the number of kicks for touch or for position that bounced the wrong way and the number of passes that were off by a fraction of a second; I'm sure that you'll agree that with just a little bit more luck we could have been going for a treble in a fortnight's time. I myself am incredibly lucky and always have been – how else could I be up here – unfortunately I don't know how to pass it on.

Many of the players thanked me that night and during the next week for standing up for them; without a doubt, the media were very tough in their assessment of the performances, and the players took a lot of criticism. I myself wasn't slow to criticise during a game, but the players came to recognise that that was down to my failure to control my excitement and commitment in the heat of the moment. They came to acknowledge that I was always supportive of them. Later that night, I made a special presentation to Gordon D'Arcy and Shane Jennings, who were retiring soon, and on behalf of everybody in Leinster Rugby, I wished them every success in their lives after rugby.

My next event was on Monday, 11 May, when I was invited to play for an IRFU team in a golf match against teams from the GAA, the FAI and the GUI in my home club, Royal Dublin. This is apparently an annual fixture, but it was my one and only time to be invited. I helped the IRFU to win the team competition; I was surprised to also win the individual competition and be presented with a fine cut-glass trophy with the logos of the four bodies inscribed on it. The teams comprised officers and former players, and some teams had former internationals. It was some consolation for the other missed trophies during the season and matched the golf victory in the Lorcan Sherlock Trophy, my first official event as president eleven months earlier.

The executive committee meeting on Tuesday, 12 May, was the last of the season. It was also the occasion for the election of the IRFU representatives. There were seven candidates, and after the voting we continued with the business of the meeting while the votes were counted. We then had an end-of-year report on rugby in the province from Philip Lawlor, the domestic rugby manager. I had dealt with Philip for the previous few years, as we were both on the rugby committee, and had always found him extremely good at his role – very much up to date with facts and figures, knowledgeable about rugby in Leinster, and very dedicated and committed to it. Again, his presentation on this occasion was superb.

The result of the voting was announced, and to my surprise, I wasn't successful – but equally to my surprise, I wasn't very disappointed. I hadn't put much effort or time into the election, and I realised that I got what I deserved. It is moot whether I would have been successful if I had decided earlier to run and put more effort into it, but thankfully it didn't upset me or spoil what had been a fantastic year. Bearing in mind that it was only the third time in my life that I had run for election for any office – despite all the various positions that I had held – and on the other two occasions I had been successful, I was comfortable with *que sera sera*.

On the following Friday, 15 May, I flew to Edinburgh for the final match of the season. There were four dinners that weekend that I had to miss, including the Clontarf Awards Dinner, which I would have liked to attend. Nevertheless, I still hadn't found out how to be in two places at the same time, and Edinburgh was the priority. The game was played in Murrayfield in front of three or four thousand people. I could vividly remember my last visit there, less than two months earlier, when Ireland won the Six Nations in front of an attendance of fifty thousand.

Leinster played really well, scored five good tries and won 36–23. After the game, I went to the Leinster dressing room, as I had after each game. This time, however, in addition to going around to each player and thanking them individually, as I normally did, I addressed them as a group. I told them that it was the thirty-second occasion that I had watched them during the season – that they had always made me very proud of them, and to be associated with them. I told them that they were always a credit to themselves, their families, their coaches and to Leinster – and I again apologised to them if I sometimes got so wound up that what I intended as encouragement sounded like criticism. I added that their efforts deserved more success but that I was sure that they would bounce back and triumph next season. I was sad that it was the last game, but I was delighted that we had done enough to ensure qualification for the European Champions Cup, which was the only target left for us after our loss to Ulster a few weeks previously.

Further dinners, AGMs and committee meetings followed in the next ten days, before the Leinster AGM and the end of my term. The only matter of significance during this time was the termination of Matt O'Connor's coaching term – or at least, its non-renewal. I was sorry to hear of it, as I had got on well with Matt during the season – and, indeed, the previous season. All the same, I wasn't surprised, as Matt had his falling out with the IRFU, and in addition – in my opinion – he didn't get the best out of his team, particularly the younger players.

That year, Leinster sorely missed the leadership on the field of Leo Cullen and Brian O'Driscoll, who had retired at the end of the previous season; Johnny Sexton, who had gone to play in Paris; and Isa Nacewa, who only came back from his retirement at the end of the year. Although Jamie Heaslip was a fantastic player for Leinster and Ireland, I believed that the captaincy role hindered his own performances – but on reflection, perhaps the coach didn't have many options.

The only matter left for me to do before the AGM was to write the presidents report for the Leinster Rugby annual report. In this, I stated that as I flew back from Edinburgh and reflected on the season, the overwhelming feeling I had was surprise – how fast the season had gone. I could honestly write that it was one of the most interesting years of my life, and I was very grateful to my club, Clontarf FC, for affording me the great honour of being nominated as president of the Leinster Branch. I hoped that I had repaid a little of that indebtedness by helping them to win the Lorcan Sherlock Trophy nearly twelve months ago and by presenting the Leinster Senior League Cup to the Clontarf president.

I thanked many people who had helped me during the season, including David Ross, the executive services manager, who had responsibility for ensuring that the new all-weather 3G pitches were delivered on time and on budget; Mick Dawson, who continued to lead the dynamic organisation that is Leinster Rugby; the Official Leinster Supporters Club, for all their tremendous support of the team, regardless of where they were playing; and all the sponsors, referees and volunteers on the myriad of committees and subcommittees. Finally, I thanked my wife Mary and my family for their unstinting support throughout the season.

At the AGM on Thursday, 28 May, in my final address, I repeated most of what I had written in the report, but I commenced by acknowledging how much a rugby fanatic like me enjoyed the whole experience – the opportunity to watch 111 games and attend 109 functions, where I enjoyed food and drink, and delivered 55 speeches. This was not to mention the articles I wrote and the meetings I attended but which I hadn't counted. I listed a number of highlights but also pointed out that I had to deal with a number of difficult situations – and in the course of that had to make a few late tackles and clear out a few rucks. I said I regretted if I had ever hurt anyone's feelings – that it was never personal and that any actions I took or decisions I made were in what I considered the best interests of Leinster Rugby. After chairing the first part of the meeting, when the various reports were presented and the accounts approved, I stood down and handed over to my successor, Robert McDermott.

I headed for our holiday home in Cap de Nice with Mary on Wednesday, 3 June, very tired and drained, and badly needing a rest from rugby and meetings. I felt a little like I had after exams in the past: I gave it all I could when I needed to, and when it was finished, I realised that I was out of adrenaline and energy. For the first few days of my holidays, I did little other than lie in the sun, swim in the pool or sea, and go to my favourite restaurants at night. I quickly recovered, played golf, went on a few walking trips and had a visit from my daughter Sinéad. I drove to Golf Club Biella Le Betulle between Turin and Milan, spending a night in Barolo, a charming but – considering the fame of its wine – surprisingly small village. I stayed in France until Tuesday, 30 June and returned refreshed, not realising that I was coming home to what transpired – later in August – to be one of the most unpleasant experiences of my life.

First though, Mary and I hosted a dinner at home for all the members of the management committee and their wives. One of the differences between Clontarf, Leinster and Ireland was that with Clontarf, wives very seldom attended games and pre-match functions, although they often came afterwards; with Leinster, it was much more common, and with Ireland it was almost *de rigueur*, so Mary met and became friendly with many of the wives of my colleagues in Leinster. We were delighted to have a good party with them, to thank them again for their support and to finish off the year.

While I was in France on holidays, the IRFU convened a special council meeting for 25 June to approve the amendments to the laws that had been an issue earlier. As I hadn't heard anything further after the exchange of emails with the IRFU lawyer a few months previously, I presumed that the IRFU had shelved their plan to propose those changes – that they were going to have a full and thorough review of the governance of the IRFU before proposing any changes to the existing laws as I had suggested.

It came as a surprise, therefore, when I received a call from my successor, Robert McDermott, to tell me that the special council meeting had been convened and that – in advance of that – one of the Leinster trustees, a past president of the IRFU, wanted a meeting with the Leinster management committee to get them to vote against the proposal. I told Robert that it was nothing to do with the trustees. I said that the trustee was acting *ultra vires* and interfering in matters that were not within the limited remit of a trustee. I told him that I had reviewed the proposal some time ago with Mick Dawson; though I acknowledged that the rules were a long way short of being perfect, I said that the changes proposed were advisable and that Leinster should support them. I added that the meeting with the trustees shouldn't be held – that he should convene a meeting of the management committee to make a decision on whether to support the IRFU proposal but that it should exclude the trustees.

I don't know what occurred then, but the meeting with the trustees did take place and that past president – probably thinking only of the limiting effect of the changes on the power and influence of the past presidents of the IRFU – persuaded the others who attended to oppose the changes. With this, a letter was drafted and sent to the IRFU. In any event, the special council meeting didn't take place on 25 June: on 24 June, it was postponed to 17 July, because there were some concerns raised in relation to the validity of the notice convening the meeting.

A Leinster management committee meeting had been scheduled for Tuesday, 14 July, by which time I had returned from holidays. The chairman of the IRFU management committee, Finbarr Crowley, the chief executive, Philip Browne, and the IRFU lawyer asked to brief the members of the Leinster management committee at this meeting in advance of the special council meeting on 17 July.

This briefing only added to the confusion, as we were told that the IRFU trustees had been consulted and had agreed with the proposal, subject to a change allowing council to veto appointments made by the IRFU committee 'in exceptional circumstances'. We were told that this change was now part of the IRFU proposal. We learned that the trustees had since changed their minds – obviously vested interests had got to them. We also learned that the Ulster Branch management committee had concerns, as well, though they were different to those expressed by Leinster in their June letter. I could see that the IRFU proposal was in trouble and that the hole they were in was getting deeper.

I and the other Leinster delegates to the IRFU special council meeting met with some of the IRFU past presidents, who had originated from Leinster, in the Sandymount Hotel an hour before the meeting on 17th July. The past presidents were entitled to attend the special council meeting and vote at it. The general attitude at this pre-meeting was that the IRFU had made a mess of their proposal: that if one agreed with one part but disagreed with others, the entire had to be opposed as the proposed changes were to be put as a single proposal. Many considered it a fiasco and thought that they should start again. I didn't disagree with that, but I argued that we should try to salvage the point of principle, as it was in the best interests of Irish rugby.

We went across to the Aviva Stadium, where the meeting was to be held, to be told that the proposal had been withdrawn by the IRFU management committee. This didn't matter too much to me, as I wasn't unduly inconvenienced; however, some people had come from various parts of the country, and even though the IRFU was putting them up in a local hotel for the night, they were very unhappy.

The IRFU committee then had its own meeting to select its representatives for World Rugby. The person who the management committee wished to have replaced, for the reason outlined earlier, failed to be elected. Another person, John O'Driscoll, a former Irish international, was elected in his place. It couldn't be the CEO, Philip Browne – as had been the intention from the beginning of the saga – so neither side could claim to have succeeded. The IRFU had arranged a drinks reception and dinner to be held after the special council meeting. Given that the food had been prepared, we sat down to dinner, but the atmosphere was very uncomfortable and hostile to those in the IRFU who were behind the proposal. I left early with Finbarr and Pat Fitzgerald, who was another IRFU past president; we had a drink elsewhere and then ended up in the bar in Clontarf.

Finbarr told me that the IRFU committee had unanimously nominated him to become the incoming junior vice president of the union at the annual council meeting, scheduled for August 14, and he asked me if I would second his nomination. It was the custom that when a person was to be proposed as vice president or president, he would be seconded by a person from his own club – if that was possible. He added that his proposer would be Martin O'Sullivan, the then current senior vice president – who would be elected president a few minutes before Finbarr's nomination. Again, this was the custom. I told Finbarr that I would be delighted to do so, and we agreed that we would see each other on that day. I knew that I would have to compose a short speech for the occasion, but as it was a month away, it wasn't anything to cause me bother.

Nonetheless, on the Monday or Tuesday of the week of the August meeting, Finbarr called me to say that he had heard that there was a movement being orchestrated behind closed doors to have Philip Orr run against him for junior vice president. This shocked me, as it was contrary to what Philip had told me, and I didn't think such a challenge to the nominee of the IRFU committee had ever occurred previously. Finbarr told me that he had been told of it by someone who had been approached to support Orr's nomination; that person was told to keep it secret, which he refused to agree to. I told Finbarr that I had discussed the matter with Philip Orr months ago – that Philip had told me that he wouldn't be running against Finbarr, and that I considered Philip to be a person of integrity and a man of his word. I tried calling Philip on his mobile to ascertain if the story was true, but I didn't get an answer or a call back from him. That per se did not make me suspicious, but perhaps it should have.

On the following day, I called Stuart Bayley, the honorary secretary of Leinster, to ascertain if he had heard anything, as I presumed that if Philip wanted to run for junior vice president, he would have the courtesy to tell Stuart. But Stuart told me that he hadn't heard a thing, which I accepted at face value. He agreed to call me if he did hear anything about it. I subsequently called Des Kavanagh, who was one of the members of the IRFU committee representing Leinster; he would have been one of those who voted unanimously for Finbarr. Des also told me that he hadn't heard anything, but he assured me when I asked him that he would continue to support Finbarr.

On the morning of the annual council meeting, I played golf in Royal Dublin and was very relaxed about the matter, based on these telephone conversations. When I finished, however, I turned on my phone and noted a few missed calls from Robert McDermott, the Leinster president, to whom I had also spoken a couple of days previously. Robert told me that a meeting of the Leinster delegates had been convened for 3.30 p.m. in the Sandymount Hotel, before the IRFU meeting in the Aviva scheduled for 5 p.m. The meeting was to discuss the junior vice presidency, as Philip Orr was running for the position and would be there himself. Robert also told me that Stuart Bayley was to second the nomination of Philip Orr.

To say that I was shocked would be a gross understatement. I had worked with these two persons for a number of years and couldn't believe that they had been so dishonest, devious and totally lacking in integrity. I called Finbarr and updated him on what I had learned; I advised him to try to salvage the position by asking Stephen Hilditch, the existing junior vice president and incoming senior vice president, to formally second him. I said I would speak in support but that Stephen's stature in the union might help in holding Finbarr's support together. He agreed, reluctantly, to call Stephen, who would already have left his home in Belfast; when he eventually contacted him, Stephen agreed.

I went to the meeting in the Sandymount Hotel, arriving a few minutes late. I quickly realised that some of the other persons in attendance had been scheming among themselves over a few days behind my back, which I deeply resented. They had decided that Leinster should support Orr. I identified the ringleaders: Bayley and Ray Ryan, the honorary treasurer. I further realised that the major weakness of the Leinster management committee – groupthink – had taken hold. I objected strongly, pointing out that there was a time and place to run against Finbarr: the IRFU committee meeting, where the matter had been decided a couple of months earlier. I said that I disliked people going back on their word, and I also disliked what I perceived as behind-the-scenes scheming and back-stabbing that had obviously been going on for the previous few weeks.

I suggested that Leinster and its delegates should be above that, as it could bring the IRFU and the game into disrepute. I added that what was proposed was more akin to behaviour at the FAI. I was then asked to leave the room, as I had indicated earlier that I would be seconding Finbarr's nomination. I hadn't heard back from Finbarr at that stage – whether Stephen had been contacted and had agreed to second the nomination – so I agreed to leave temporarily. The remainder of the Leinster delegation wanted to discuss the issue themselves, as I was now directly involved and was not impartial. I agreed to do so, but only if Philip Orr and Stuart Bayley left as well, as they couldn't be considered any less impartial than me.

This was eventually agreed to, and the three of us left. Bayley went off somewhere, and I took the opportunity to ask Philip why he was reneging on what had been agreed and on what he had said to me months ago. I asked why he couldn't be patient, as he would assuredly be elected unopposed if he waited a year – and without causing division in the union now. He acknowledged that he had gone back on his word and had given me a different answer previously, saying that his words were in line with his intentions at the time; he said that more recently, however, he had been asked to run against Finbarr, as some people didn't want Finbarr as a future president of the IRFU. When I asked who those people were, I was told that they were some of the past presidents, and that they had approached him and told him that if he agreed, they would organise a campaign on his behalf. I asked him why he didn't return my call from earlier in the week. He said that he had taken a few days to decide whether to allow his name be put forward and then gave me the lame excuse that he was in the Burren on holiday and that coverage was poor. He failed to explain how he could take other calls and work with the schemers without phone coverage, however.

We were called back into the meeting and told that if Orr was elected as junior vice president, Bayley would be nominated as a Leinster representative on the IRFU in his place. I pointed out that that was *ultra vires*, and that the vacancy, if there was one, could only be filled by the executive committee of Leinster – not on an *ad hoc* basis by the management committee. That was ignored on the grounds that they did not want Connacht to get an extra position on the IRFU committee due to a vacancy not being filled and they would worry about the validity of what they were doing at a later stage. The meeting broke up at this stage, as we had to get over to the Aviva Stadium for the council meeting. I told Finbarr on the way in that I was afraid that many of the Leinster votes would be against him; he felt, however, that because all the members of the IRFU committee had voted for him recently, they would have the integrity to be consistent. He thought that he would have enough votes overall.

The council meeting proceeded in the presence of the media with its usual business and then came the election of the new president and senior vice president. Martin O'Sullivan, the newly elected president, then proposed Finbarr and acclaimed the work that he had done in the union over many years, including his six years as chairman of the management committee. Stephen Hilditch, as arranged, seconded the proposal, endorsing what Martin had said and adding his own recommendation. I stood up before there was a counter-proposal and asked the president, Martin – who was by now in the chair – if I could address the meeting in supporting the proposal.

That was accepted, and I did so. I reminded those present that Finbarr had taken over as chairman just as the financial crisis hit in 2009 and when the finances of the union were precariously invested in the new stadium project. I added that the opening of the Aviva Stadium and the teething problems with pricing and selling tickets now seemed a long time ago – as we confidently prepared our application to host a world cup in 2023 – but that only those directly involved in the union committee with Finbarr knew how difficult the immediate future looked back in 2009. I pointed to the fact that since he became chairman, he scrupulously maintained his status as an IRFU person rather than a Leinster person – sometimes to the chagrin of his former colleagues in Leinster, but very much to the benefit of the union. On a more specific note, I mentioned that as a Clontarf member, I was particularly pleased to be able to support Finbarr, as he had done enormous work for Clontarf over many years; given that next season would be the 140th anniversary of the founding of the club. I added that it would be very fitting if Finbarr were elected to the position for that year, as he would be the first Clontarf member to have that honour. I then referred to our personal friendship, going back fifty five years: from our time in the same schools and then qualifying as solicitors together. Finally, I listed his various roles in Clontarf and Leinster, and asked that, if there were to be an election, everybody support him.

I was generously applauded, and I thought that I might have helped Finbarr's position, but on reflection I know that I should have waited to hear the proposal and seconding of his opponent. What followed was a disgusting attack on Finbarr in an almost incoherent diatribe by a past president, Billy Glynn. I had heard that he had not enjoyed his presidency a few years previously: he thought that he would be the unfettered boss of the union but found that his role was quite limited, being more of a 'meet-and-greet' responsibility – and that the real day-to-day operational power resided in the chairman and the treasurer as had been the case for a number of years previously. I had heard further that he was not highly regarded by the executive committee or the past presidents. He obviously had been waiting for an opportunity to get revenge, and when he thought that Finbarr had tried to limit the powers of the past presidents and to have one of them removed from his position in World Rugby, he found his opportunity.

I was disgusted at his speech and, indeed, learned afterwards that many of those who had decided to vote against Finbarr were equally disgusted at his lack of proper decorum and by his obnoxious behaviour. Most of his speech was an *ad hominem* attack on Finbarr rather than a support of Philip, which seemed strange. The speech was more like what I might have expected at the AGM of the Mixed Martial Arts Association rather than the IRFU. When he sat down, Stuart Bayley stood to second the proposal – and to be fair to him, he took a different approach and praised Philip instead of attacking Finbarr. I regretted that I hadn't waited to reply to the attack; if I had anticipated the vitriol, I would have done so, but it never occurred to me that anyone associated with the IRFU would behave in such a low manner.

The voting then took place. I was seated behind Stuart Bayley and Des Kavanagh, and noted – without any effort on my part, and almost as if he wanted me to see – that Des eventually voted against Finbarr, even though he was one of those on the union committee that had unanimously supported Finbarr – something he told me he would continue to do only a few days beforehand. Des seemed to hesitate before ticking the relevant box, as if he was battling with his conscience as to whether he should remain loyal and consistent to his one-time mentor or speed up his own journey to the presidency by voting against his conscience. His conscience lost. I was appalled at what I saw as a lack of integrity shown by Des on this occasion.

When the meeting adjourned to allow the counting of the vote, I went up to Finbarr, who was at the top table and still in shock at the attack on him. I told him to be ready for defeat, as even Des Kavanagh had voted against him – so at least Finbarr had a few minutes to compose himself before the result was declared. When it was announced, Finbarr addressed the meeting in a very dignified manner; he thanked everyone for assisting him during his time in the IRFU, because the result of the election meant that his time there was over, and wished Philip Orr every best wish for the future.

We all then retired for a drink and dinner. The other past president involved in the scheming campaign – the Leinster trustee – seemed to get quite inebriated and spilled at least one of his drinks across the table where some of us were sitting. I was so disgusted at the triumphalism of a few of the past presidents, which I thought was so undignified, that I left as early as I decently could. The episode added to my distaste for the IRFU's internal politics, where many committee members seemed to be scrambling for the presidency as their primary objective – over and above the good of Irish rugby – forming alliances to achieve that personal ambition, and making compromises and deals on policy issues to maintain the support of such alliances.

The presidency and its lifelong perks seemed to be a target for which some otherwise reputable members considered it worth damaging their own integrity. Taking away the lifelong perks would hopefully improve the IRFU committee members' integrity, and their work in devising and overseeing appropriate policies for the development of the game in Ireland. It had seemed to me that Finbarr was humiliated because he dared to challenge the power of the past presidents, many of whom – having wriggled their way up the ladder to presidency – developed a ridiculous sense of their own importance and ability. Undoubtedly there were exceptions to this, and some of the past presidents had made enormous contributions to Irish rugby, both as players and as administrators, and deserved the honour of presidency, but I'm sure most of these exemplary figures would accept that that shouldn't entitle them to a pension for life.

Over the next few weeks, I attended any Leinster branch meetings that I had committed to, but my attitude had changed.

I could no longer trust those that I was meeting with at the management committee; I was ashamed to have been part of the Leinster delegation because of their behaviour. Nevertheless, because I was an *ex officio* member of most committees, including the management committee, I felt that I couldn't resign. I continued to participate and contribute, but instead of enjoying the experiences – as I had for many years previously – I just did what I had to do. I guess that my colleagues in Leinster would say that I had become irritable, but it was more that the impatience I had managed to keep in check in previous years – at the groupthink and general lack of analysis – couldn't be contained further.

I continued to enjoy watching Leinster play, as I still do, and Leo Cullen had been appointed as coach, which I thought was an excellent appointment, but I was now more interested in watching Clontarf and getting on with the rest of my life after Leinster. The entire episode was still upsetting me months later – a combination of disappointment, betrayal and rage – and I knew that I had to let it go, psychologically, so I decided that as soon as I could, I would leave the Leinster Branch committees.

Louisa flew to Amsterdam from Australia in late September, with Josh and Lexi, as she was presenting to an international respiratory conference there. Mary and I, along with Sinéad, went to meet them in Amsterdam to babysit and to spend a few days sightseeing there. They then came back to Dublin with us and stayed for nearly five weeks – Lee coming a few weeks later – and they all returned to Perth on 2 November. We went to visit them in Perth on 20 December and had a great holiday in their summer, returning home to our winter on 19 January. While we were there, Louisa was offered a position as a consultant paediatrician in Sydney Children's Hospital in Randwick, so we babysat for a few days while she and Lee went to Sydney to find accommodation and make general arrangements for a move. When they got back to Perth, I flew to Melbourne to visit my brother, Gerry, for a few days. We played golf at Royal Melbourne Golf

Club, where he is a member; it is often rated in the top two or three golf courses in the world – and I would agree.

Soon after I got back to Dublin, I announced that I would be retiring as the Clontarf representative in Leinster, asking the Clontarf chairman to arrange the selection of my replacement

In the end, 2015/16 turned out to be another great season for Clontarf; in addition to the completion and opening of the new all-weather 4G pitches, we went on to reach the final of the AIL again. On this occasion, we defeated Cork Con in the final, and this was the day when the sporting public first became fully aware of the talents of Joey Carbery.

Joey starred for us in the final, which was televised nationwide, but he had starred for us all season. I had also seen him play in a schools final and then for Leinster U20s. Within six months, Joey played for Ireland in Chicago – alongside two more Clontarf players, Cian Healy and Tadhg Furlong – when Ireland defeated New Zealand for the first time. We celebrated the victory over Cork Con as if it was our first. This time it was less unexpected, so the celebrations were less spontaneous, but they were nonetheless magnificent.

During 2016, I had finally retired as a consultant for Arthur Cox and was no longer a part of any committee there. I sat on a committee that organised a fiftieth class reunion for my St Paul's College class on 13 May; soon after, on 26 May, I retired from Leinster at the AGM. When I retired from the Clontarf executive committee a few weeks after that, being replaced by my successor as Clontarf representative in Leinster, I was off all committees for the first time in more than fifty years.

I had been playing more golf since the end of my presidency in May 2015, and my handicap had come down by four shots. The only problem was that I was playing so often that I damaged my back. This required some treatment and exercises, but it didn't keep me off the course for long. I recovered and looked forward to my real retirement and a more relaxing life.

I enjoyed the vast majority of my time on committees, including in the golf club and in golf societies, but I knew that I had had enough and was ready to give it up. My younger daughter Sinéad had her first child, Charlie – another grandson for Mary and me – in early June. I could now look forward to being a granddad with three grandchildren, and to travelling even more often than I had done so far.

POLITICS AND MY INVOLVEMENT

From the time that I started debating in secondary school, I have had my opinion on most subjects and not afraid to express it. I don't ever remember being a conventional thinker or debater; I tended to come up with a different way of looking at an issue rather than the straightforward one. I don't intend to portray myself as always being an original thinker; rather, I was disinclined to follow the herd. This didn't seem to cause me any difficulties, and in third year I won the end-of-year prize for debating. I was subsequently on the school debating team in inter-school debating competitions – the principal one being sponsored by Aer Lingus. I tended to be independent in my views. Even though I don't think I was a maverick – even later in life – equally, I didn't tend to be part of any groupthink.

On one occasion in late 1965 or early 1966, I was in the audience for *Teen Talk*, which was a discussion programme on Telefís Éireann chaired by Bunny Carr in which the audience-participants were all teenagers. There were one or two regular panellists, the one panellist I remember best being Ted Bonner. A discussion was taking place on what was then Rhodesia and Ian Smith's government's announcement of the Unilateral Declaration of Independence. I spoke for a couple of minutes, making a point. I don't remember it being an issue on which I felt very strongly, but I do remember Bunny Carr commenting, 'that was a different point of view.' I didn't take that as a negative – and it would have been unlike Bunny Carr to be negative.

Although I wasn't involved in party politics as a teenager, I did take an interest in what was going on at government level, and I read the newspapers most days. I would have had an inclination towards Fianna Fáil at the time; I believe that my parents had a similar inclination, but it was never strongly held. For example, my father would have bought the *Irish Independent* every morning, which was perceived as a Fine Gael newspaper, but the *Evening Press* in the evening, which was a Fianna Fáil organ. Although I had that inclination, I always had an intense dislike of Éamon de Valera. I'm not sure how I developed that, as my mother's family would have been strong supporters of de Valera – in fact, a first cousin of my mother, who was born in 1917, was christened Thomas deV-alera Sharkey, and when he became a priest, he was always known as Fr Dev. That dislike of de Valera intensified the older I got, and I would now consider de Valera as a traitor to the country – the most disastrous leader that Ireland has ever had.

In the mid-1960s, I had become attracted to the Just Society faction of Fine Gael, led by Declan Costello and Garrett Fitzgerald. The philosophy of the Just Society, as articulated by Declan Costello, was, 'Share the resources of economic recovery fairly and when an ill wind blows, prioritise the protection of the weak and vulnerable.' Mark Fitzgerald, a son of Garrett Fitzgerald, wrote for the *Irish Times* on 25 May 2017, 'A just society should meet the needs of its population as a matter of right, not of charity.' This wasn't left wing politics, but it was left of the two major parties at the time, Fianna Fáil and Fine Gael.

That didn't stop me joining the UCD branch of Fianna Fáil at the freshers' exhibition in October 1968, but I can only explain that by the fact that the person who persuaded me to join was a very attractive blonde girl, and I couldn't say no to her. I never attended any meeting of this Fianna Fáil branch – or cumann, as it was called. The only time that I had any contact with them after that was at the end of the college year, when there was an election for the chairman for the following year and one of the candidates asked me for his vote. I had learned from the beginning that he was the boyfriend of the pretty blonde girl, so even if I had sufficient interest to vote in the election – which I hadn't – there was no chance of me voting for him.

By that time, my political allegiances had moved to the left. As I indicated, I had initially been attracted by the Just Society faction of Fine Gael, though I hadn't become involved in the party. I got caught up in UCD's Gentle Revolution of 1969 and had participated in sit-ins in Earlsfort Terrace. I was also involved in marches to the Dáil with the Dublin Housing Action Committee, which had been precipitated by the eviction of a Denis

Dennehy and his family from a tenement house that was to be demolished and redeveloped.

These marches gathered a diverse conglomeration of individuals and groups – students, political activists and different communist sects. I didn't know then what the distinction was between Maoists, Marxist–Leninists, Stalinists and Trotskyites – and I still don't – but they were all there. All I understood was that they hated each other more than they hated the right-wing students and capitalists. Anyone who didn't support one of these groups was necessarily a fascist. It seemed very exciting at the time – and in many ways was part of a worldwide student revolution, with marches and riots in France, Germany, Italy, England and the USA.

A couple of months after one of those marches, I was approached by a friend of my father's, who was a superintendent in the Garda Síochána – a man I knew myself from my involvement with Clontarf GAA Club. He explained to me that the Special Branch of the Gardaí wanted to talk to me, but as they had to go through him, he had told them that he knew me and would talk to me privately first. Apparently, photographs were taken of the marchers at this particular march – and probably at all of them – as it was suspected that the various groups involved had been infiltrated by subversive elements, and it was at a time when the IRA was splitting into the Provisionals and the Officials and becoming more volatile.

It transpired that a particular man who had been marching beside me, according to the photographs, had since been found murdered. He had been a member of the IRA, and in the investigation into his murder, the photograph of him and me, and indeed others, was being followed up. I was asked if I knew who he was, whether he had spoken to me and whether there was anyone else with him. I was able to convince the superintendent that I didn't know him or anything about him – that I didn't remember him marching beside me. In accepting what I said – and I suppose his independent acquaintance of me and my father helped to convince him – he merely told me to be careful about who I got involved with. The incident did surprise me, but it didn't sink in for a few months; in the interim, I got involved in another protest meeting in O'Connell Street in August 1969.

This was at the time of the major escalation of sectarian violence in Belfast and Derry, and the recommencement of pogroms in Belfast – the time of the famous threat by Jack Lynch, the then Taoiseach: 'The Irish government can no longer stand by and see innocent people injured and perhaps worse.' He was calling on the British government to make a request to the United Nations for a peace-keeping force to be introduced in Northern Ireland; he said that field hospitals would be established along the border with Northern Ireland to treat those who didn't want to go to a hospital in the North. There was a mass demonstration on the Saturday afternoon after the 1969 pogroms started; I can't remember which organisation convened it, but I was set on being there.

I attended with a couple of friends, partly because we anticipated some excitement. My principal reason for being there, however, was that I felt angry and helpless at what seemed to be a repeat of the pogroms in Belfast in 1914 and in the 1920s, when my grandfather was caught in them. As I have said, I didn't know much about his involvement, but I still felt it personally and thought something should be done. As the speeches continued and the crowd got more excited, someone called for a march around to Government Buildings on Kildare Street, where the government was having an emergency meeting. The intention was to call on the government to send the Irish army into the North to protect the nationalists who were being attacked. I almost felt myself losing my self control and tried to get up on the platform to call on the crowd itself to go to the North if the government didn't send the army.

Thankfully, I didn't make it to the platform, and I think the crowd, or most of them, marched to Government Buildings. I didn't go but retired to a pub to quench the thirst that had developed. That did cool me down, and after a few drinks I went home. My mother and father had just arrived home from holidays with my younger siblings, and I discussed the day with my father.

As an Ulsterman, I think he was proud about my feelings. Still, he was delighted that I hadn't taken it further. For me, it was a lesson in the dangers of large crowd demonstrations and the groupthink that can follow. I didn't learn my lesson from my experience at the Dublin Housing Action Committee march a short time previously, when I walked beside the guy who was murdered shortly afterwards, but I did this time. I was actually a little scared at how I reacted – how I nearly made a fool of myself. I had started on a career in law; it was a little early to throw the opportunities I had been given out the window. It was another example of a diverging path and being lucky enough to take the correct one.

I mentioned earlier that I had played hockey for UCD in the 1968/69 season and how this included the inter-varsity competition for the Mauritius Cup, which was held in Queen's University, Belfast in January 1969. On the penultimate evening, there was a dinner in the students' union building for all the participants and then a few drinks in the students' bar. Somehow or other, I realised that there was a lively meeting of some students in a room off the bar. I had no idea what it was or who was involved, but curiosity brought me into the room to find out. It transpired that it was the first meeting of People's Democracy after their protest march from Belfast to Derry had been attacked at Burntollet Bridge by a combination of loyalists and B-Specials, a sectarian section of the Royal Ulster Constabulary.

The march and attack had received much media attention; it had been compared to the Selma to Montgomery marches led by Martin Luther King some years previously. People's Democracy was a student organisation based in Queen's University and one of the many sections of the wider civil rights movement. The meeting was discussing the march, the public reaction to it and what they should do next in their campaign. I recognised Michael Farrell and Bernadette Devlin from earlier television coverage; they seemed to be the main speakers at the meeting.

The meeting got heated, and not everybody there agreed with the strategy of continuing the policy of peaceful protest and turning the other cheek. Although I couldn't have known it at the time, I realised some years afterwards that most of those at the meeting were interned in 1971, when the British government introduced internment as a reaction to the violence that had followed the frustration of the peaceful protests. I didn't stay long in that room, even though I was intrigued at the openness and topicality of the discussions – partly because I didn't want anybody to learn that I was a member of Fianna Fáil, as I had been since the freshers' exhibition a few months previously, and which was unlikely to make me welcome there, but mainly because I wanted to rejoin my teammates in the bar.

Later that night, at a nurses' dance at Musgrave Park Hospital, which was multi-denominational, I refused to stand for the British national anthem, which was played at the end of the night. The nurse that I had been chatting to, Kathleen, thought that it was a foolish thing to do; she said that I didn't know who might be watching me. She had sympathy with my stance but didn't join me, although she did allow me to walk her across to the nurses' home.

That was probably the limit of my bravado – probably alcohol induced – although on the following day, after playing in the last game of the tournament, I hitchhiked from Belfast back home. I had been invited to the social science students' dress dance by a friend and classmate; I wanted to get home for that rather than wait for the post-tournament dinner and coming home with the team on the following day. I'd like to think that I was sensible enough to keep my political views to myself during the few lifts it took to get me across the border, but as the Troubles had only just started and nobody knew how dangerous life in the North would become later that summer, I'm not so sure that I did.

I was a regular contributor to, and speaker at, the L&H debates in Earlsfort Terrace on a Saturday night, particularly in my first year. It was part of the Saturday night entertainment, and much cheaper than going to the cinema or staying in a pub all night. The marks awarded each night were posted on the L&H notice board in UCD's Great Hall on the following Monday or Tuesday. Towards the end of the year, an award was given to the best first year speaker – or maiden speaker, as it was called – over the course of the year, using the weekly marks to determine the winner.

I ended the year as runner-up to Patrick Honohan, who later became famous as an academic economist and as governor of the Central Bank of Ireland from 2009–15, when he assumed main responsibility for resolving the post-2008 Irish banking crisis. The auditor of the L&H that year was Dermot Gleeson, who later became a very successful senior counsel and then Attorney General, and after that chairman of Allied Irish Banks plc – one of the banks that had collapsed after 2008 and had to be rescued by the efforts of Patrick Honohan.

Although I was a regular speaker, I didn't consider myself a natural orator. And because, even then, I had a poor memory, I had to write down what I wanted to say, as otherwise I knew that I would forget it. I participated because I enjoyed the wit and repartee, the cut and thrust of debate and the exchange of ideas, which was exciting at a time when Irish society was changing very rapidly; social and religious mores were being questioned and challenged, political unrest – beginning with the civil rights movement in Northern Ireland – was moving towards outright rebellion, and of course UCD's own Gentle Revolution was beginning.

This general air of questioning the status quo and demanding change applied to women also. One of the most active leaders of the Gentle Revolution was Una Claffey; one of the leaders of the architectural students' protests at the redevelopment of Hume Street, which led to an occupation of the buildings there, was Marian Finucane. Both women became well known, as a journalist and a television presenter respectively. They were part of a movement that developed over the next few years, including – as far as I can remember – Nell McCafferty, Margaret Gaj, Mary Kenny, June Levine, Mary Maher, Nuala Fennell, Máirín de Burca and Monica Barnes. They weren't all left-wing supporters, and the women's liberation movement was radical although not socialist.

I often went to Gaj's restaurant on Lower Baggot Street for lunch with some college friends. It wasn't a conventional restaurant but it was a good and cheap alternative to the student restaurants in Earlsfort Terrace and Newman House, the latter – on St Stephen's Green – acting as the student representative council building. Gaj's attracted a liberal and radical clientele, and the conversation was usually political and intense; although I enjoyed it, it wasn't somewhere I went for light-hearted fun.

I remember one particular lunch, sometime in 1971, sitting at a table close to a group of ladies that included some of the above-mentioned. They were all very upset, and I learned from overhearing them that they, as the committee of the Irish Women's Liberation Movement, had had a meeting on the previous night in the Mansion House attended by hundreds and which was to be a fundraiser as well as a recruitment rally. Some gentlemen had offered to conduct a bucket collection among the participants. The offer was accepted, allowing the organisers to socialise, chat and recruit new members.

Nobody thought to check the credentials of the gentlemen collectors, however; they disappeared with the fairly full buckets and weren't seen again that night. One comment made by one of the ladies present at the next day's lunch was that they were never going to trust 'f—g men with our money again'. I thought it amusing at the time, and I did wonder at the naivety of the organisers. I presume that they learned their lesson, as this was a forerunner of the National Women's Council, a well-established organisation now. Despite this naivety, these ladies proceeded to try to open the eyes and minds of their peers, and society in general, and were a significant part of the social revolution that developed in the next forty years.

My interest in politics waned for a while, and my only active involvement for many years was when Feargal Quinn ran for election to Seanad Éireann in 1973 on the National University of Ireland panel. I helped his campaign by writing to graduates that I knew personally and others whom I knew sufficiently to write them a personal letter. Feargal's attempt, however, was unsuccessful. When he ran again twenty years later, I again assisted him. On this latter occasion, the campaign was operated from his business's head office – unlike in 1973, when he tried to run the campaign from his home. In 1993, it was managed like a military campaign and was successful. There weren't any particular policies that Feargal was promoting that I felt I should support; rather, I thought that he had the ability to contribute to politics, was willing to do so, and therefore was deserving of support.

He was one of the very few senators who made a useful contribution to politics and Irish life during the twenty-three years that he sat in the Senate, but that wasn't enough to justify retaining the entire Senate, and I believe it should have been abolished. He laughed when I asked him after his first election as a senator if he could now get the potholes on our road filled in. We were neighbours for many years; although never close, we were always friendly.

This assistance to Feargal in 1973 was my only involvement in politics for many years, as it took a back seat while my legal career progressed and I gave some time to my young family. But like many others, I became very disenchanted with the governing political parties from the late 1970s and could not see a future for the existing system. Fianna Fáil had never been in a coalition government and seemed to consider the possibility as being beneath their dignity. That didn't prevent their leader, Charlie Haughey, doing deals with independent deputies in return for support in the Dáil, but sharing power was not in their DNA.

There weren't sufficient ministerial candidates with appropriate ability in either of the two large parties to form a strong government on their own. Fine Gael didn't have a cultural problem with entering into a coalition government, but even when combined with the Labour Party at the time, there still weren't sufficient talented persons available. Indeed, there probably weren't sufficient suitable candidates if all three parties were combined in a national government.

The early 1980s was a difficult time in Ireland. Charles Haughey had become leader of Fianna Fáil, ousting the then leader and Taoiseach, Jack Lynch, in what was close to being a coup. Admittedly, Lynch's Fianna Fáil government had bribed its way to power in 1977 and was bankrupting the country – but Haughey was part of that government; he was as responsible as Lynch for its policies. Haughey came on TV soon after his election as Taoiseach, in a State of the Nation-style address, to tell the country to tighten their belts – that we were all living beyond our means.

Some people knew, and others suspected, that Haughey was an utter hypocrite – that he wasn't tightening his own belt, in more senses than one. He was the wrong leader at a time when good, sound leadership was required, economically and morally. Haughey – at times over the previous twenty years, as a government minister – had been responsible for introducing some good policies, but he wasn't sufficiently trustworthy to have as leader.

There was serious political instability in the early 1980s, with four changes of government in three years. The economy was in difficulty; many large companies were going into liquidation or banks were appointing receivers to try to recover monies they had lent. Personally, that was good for me. As I mentioned earlier, I had developed an expertise in corporate insolvency law, was recognised as an expert, and accordingly was involved professionally – in some capacity – in most of those cases. I wasn't entirely comfortable with this, as to some extent it was a destruction process – one that was very difficult for the many who had lost their jobs in the collapse of their employer's business – but I recognised that the process was a necessary one, not unlike pruning and clearing out deadwood in an orchard or clearing a site to allow for new, fresh buildings.

Other contemporaneous events were very damaging to spirit and morale in the country, and led to significant unemployment and renewed emigration. These were the hunger strikes in Long Kesh in Northern Ireland, which caused enormous emotional divisions in the Republic. This damaged morale was exacerbated by the war between Britain and Argentina in the Falkland or Malvinas Islands, which elicited much sympathy for Argentina among the Irish. Together with the continuing war in Northern Ireland, it brought a resurfacing of anti-British sentiment in the Republic, which was debilitating per se.

Against this background of doom and gloom, the Fine Gael–Labour coalition led by Garrett Fitzgerald, which had resumed power in late 1982, established the New Ireland Forum, strongly influenced by John Hume, 'for consultations on the manner in which lasting peace and stability can be achieved in a new Ireland through the democratic process'. This forum produced a series of reports on different aspects of the future of the island of Ireland between its first meeting in May 1983 and its conclusion in May 1984. These reports provided some very useful analyses, including *The Economic Consequences of the Division of Ireland since 1920*; *A Comparative Description of the Economic Structure and Situation, North and South*; *The Macroeconomic Consequences of Integrated Economic Policy, Planning and Co-ordination in Ireland*; and sectoral studies on *Integrated Policy and Planning for Transport in a New Ireland*; *An Analysis of Agricultural Developments in the North and South of Ireland and of the Effects of Integrated Policy and Planning*; and *Opportunities for North/South Co-Operation and Integration in Energy* (which dealt with energy production and consumption).

The final report, published on 2 May 1984, suggested three possible alternative constitutional structures: a unitary state, a federal/confederal state and a joint British–Irish authority.

This indirectly led to formal negotiations between the Irish and British governments, but only after intervention by the president of the United States, Ronald Reagan, with the British prime minister, Margaret Thatcher. The reports also provided the Irish negotiating team with very useful, up-to-date information to facilitate its negotiating position. The negotiations, which went on for some months, culminated in the signing of the Anglo-Irish Agreement in November 1985. It had the laudable aim of bringing to an end the Troubles in Northern Ireland.

This was presented to each of the three relevant parliaments for ratification. All major parties in each parliament voted in favour of its ratification, except Fianna Fáil in the Republic and the hardline unionist parties in the North. For many reasonable and progressive persons in the Republic, this repudiation by Fianna Fáil was the last straw, exacerbating the negative perceptions that followed the expulsion of Des O'Malley, one of the younger, more progressive leaders, from Fianna Fáil in February 1985 because he voted in favour of legislation introduced by the Fine Gael–Labour government to liberalise the sale of contraceptives.

The Fine Gael–Labour government, despite many good policies in other spheres, were struggling with the near bankruptcy of the state inherited from the recent Fianna Fáil governments. Even though some Fine Gael ministers may have wanted to cut government spending and borrowing, they were hampered by their government partners, while no one other than hardline Fianna Fáil supporters wanted Fianna Fáil back in power. These difficulties created something of a vacuum, which was a very dangerous situation for all. The confluence of these events and circumstances sowed the seeds of a new centrist party: the Progressive Democrats was sprouted.

More for the sake of curiosity rather than out of any intention of becoming involved, I attended the new party's first rally-style meeting, held on 8 January 1986, in the Marine Hotel in Sutton, which was very close to my home. Despite some apathy and, indeed, cynicism on my part, I was impressed by the proceedings, a very good address by Mary Harney and the emphasis being put on policy.

When a second meeting was convened shortly afterwards, on 28 January, for the Dublin North-East constituency in the Old Shieling Hotel in Raheny, this emphasis continued. Even though there were some personalities involved who were well known in politics, law or business, it seemed to me that they were there as figureheads, not policy makers. The intention espoused was to establish a series of integrated policies from the ground up on a range of topics, from education, transport, industrial development and the environment to Northern Ireland.

At the meeting in the Old Shieling Hotel, persons were asked to indicate those areas of policy in which they were particularly interested – areas that they would be prepared to get involved in, working in groups to develop more detailed policies. I indicated interest in two areas – industrial development and Northern Ireland – and at a subsequent meeting in the Old Shieling Hotel on 11 February, I was asked to chair a subcommittee that would discuss and develop a policy document on the topic of Northern Ireland. Thus began my short involvement with the PDs; I convened and held the subcommittee's first meeting a week later in my home in Offington Lawn, Sutton.

A series of meetings then ensued, most of which I hosted at home. At them, a general approach to dealing with the problems of Northern

Ireland and its relationship with the Republic was developed. We looked at the issue as one that required reconciliation as well as peace to achieve a sense of normality; then relationships could be developed from there. We started from the premise that reconciliation involves a coming together rather than a forcing together; that unionists shouldn't be considered as a homogeneous lot; that not everyone was represented by those who spoke loudest and banged the loudest drums; that we had to better understand the broader unionist population's fears of betrayal rather than constantly criticise them.

I was asked by Stephen O'Byrnes, the Progressive Democrats' recently appointed director of policy and press relations, to update him on our progress. When I did, I was asked to present a paper on Northern Ireland at the forthcoming first national conference, to be held at the end of May.

This conference was held over two days; representatives of the new party from all parts of the country were present. When the test came in an election twelve months later, however, it was discovered that the apparent strong support was limited to a few electoral areas only. There were a series of sessions over the weekend for presentations and discussions on the following topics: Changing the Structure of Government – A programme for Central and Local Government Reform; Agriculture and the Food Industry – A policy for Development; Strategies for Economic Growth – Taxation/Public Finance and Enterprise and Employment; Creating a Caring Society – Towards Equal Opportunity in Housing, Access to Education, Health and Social Welfare; Reforming the Law – Family Law, Crime and Law Reform; Working for Peace and Reconciliation in Northern Ireland. I prepared the policy discussion document for that latter topic and a separate paper setting out how our subcommittee developed that document.

The policy discussion document, which was printed in the conference documents, stated in the introduction, 'This document sets down the guidelines around which definitive party policy will be drawn up. We look forward to the critical contribution of delegates at our first national conference. That will be the substantial basis for a comprehensive policy on Northern Ireland for the Progressive Democrats.' It added:

> the Progressive Democrats believe that the reconciliation of the people of Northern Ireland, and an end to the violence and death there is the foremost priority. Until this occurs, no real progress towards unity by consent of all Irish people can be achieved. The people of the Republic have a vital role to play in the process of encouraging reconciliation of Nationalist and Unionist in Northern Ireland. As a party which was formed specifically to accommodate people who wanted to turn their back on the outmoded Civil War political divide in the south, the Progressive Democrats are uniquely placed to hold out the hand of reconciliation and understanding to communities and parties in the North who also wish to forsake past political divisions.

Among our recommendations was that studies should be initiated and continued at government level to assess partition's effect on the economy – in both macro and micro terms – of Northern Ireland and the Republic. These studies would also look into the security effects of partition and any promising areas of co-operation. We also recommended that every opportunity for co-operation between the two parts of Ireland, and private agencies in each – in particular in relation to industrial development, tourism, agriculture, roads, services and power, and exploitation of natural resources – should be sought, and that consideration should also be given to the harmonisation of Customs and Excise between the Republic and Northern Ireland with a view to facilitating greater commercial activity between the two.

In my accompanying speech, when referring to Article 2 and Article 3 of the Constitution of Ireland (which were later revised in 1999), I said that it

> was too easy to stand or sit in the Republic and shout for and demand a United Ireland; many who do that do not understand what they mean by a United Ireland, have never been to Northern Ireland, know little or nothing about its history and its people and in particular of the differences between the people of Northern Ireland and the people of the Republic. It is not necessary to over-emphasise any such differences but they are there. It was Brendan Behan who noted that while he was interned in the Curragh, 'the Northern people had a hut of their own because the Southerners couldn't stand them, there was a regional distinction there' and remember that he was talking about Northerners of the minority community.

I reminded the audience that long before the plantations of the seventeenth century, Ulster stood apart as a kingdom and a province, and didn't always readily acknowledge the right of any other king or lord in the rest of Ireland. I said that this should be borne in mind when we talked of uniting Ireland, even if the majority community in Northern Ireland were prepared to consent to this integration. I stated that a federal system of government in Ireland may have a more genuine historical pedigree than a single government operating from Dublin, calling on the audience to remember that there never was a thirty-two-county republic in the history of the island, so what right did we have to insist on it now.

All of this was leading to one of our fundamental recommendations relating to Articles 2 and 3. The policy discussion document stated:

> It is quite clear that all major constitutional parties in Ireland act, in practice, on the basis that the unity of Ireland is an aspiration rather than a legal claim. The present wording of Articles 2 and 3 give rise to considerable misunderstanding, especially in Northern Ireland. The 1937 Constitution was adopted by the people of the then Free State, nearly fifty years ago. We consider that the Articles should now be redrawn so as to express an aspiration and an invitation to unity among all the people of Ireland. The Articles should also commit the state to working towards the unity of Ireland and her people by peaceful and democratic means and should be compatible with a federal form of government.

I attended the conference on the first day and enjoyed the presentations and debates, but I planned to go out to dinner with Mary and friends that night. I was about to go out when I received a panic phone call from a senior officer of the party and one of the principal organisers of the conference, who told me that Des O'Malley – the founder of the Progressive Democrats – had just read the policy discussion document in the conference papers and was shocked at the suggestions regarding Articles 2 and 3, saying that they would have to be withdrawn.

I blankly refused and reminded the caller that the document had already been circulated to the media. He suggested that the problem could be overcome if I changed the words 'now redrawn' to 'not redrawn' so that it would read 'We consider that the Articles should not be redrawn'. The media could then be told that there was a typo. I expressed my amazement at the dishonesty of this suggestion and adamantly refused to change the wording. I told him that I would be there at the conference tomorrow and intended to speak; however, I recognised that my invitation could be withdrawn if the committee so wished. I had a high regard for that person and assumed that the suggestion was not his but that he was relaying it.

I did turn up and spoke as I had intended to do. After the presentation, I engaged in a very robust discussion with participating members of the audience, of which there were many, but only two persons there contradicted or spoke against my suggestion on the constitution. I went home vindicated, but that was the weekend that I started to leave the PDs; although I continued to work as chairman with a new committee drawn from around the country, and put quite a lot of time into it, that transpired to be the beginning of the end.

The new committee was comprised of a few very committed persons, including three successful businessmen from border counties and a former Fianna Fail TD. We decided that we should try to build a relationship with all the different political parties and groupings, with community groups – mainly led by clergymen – and with the Orange Order.

One of our committee, acting as secretary, wrote to the Official Unionist Party, the Democratic Unionist Party, the Charter Group, the Alliance Party, the SDLP and some of the community groups. One of the clergy that he was in touch with was Fr Gerry Reynolds of Clonard Monastery, who he hoped would arrange a meeting with Sinn Féin as he seemed to have a line of communication with them. We went to Belfast on two Saturdays; we met groups from the Alliance Party, the SDLP and the Official Unionists on the first day and the Charter Group and the Orange Order separately on the second day. The Charter Group was led by Harry West, an independent Unionist who had been a former Minister of Agriculture in Stormont. The DUP and Sinn Féin refused to meet us; they considered the invitation and then refused it. Michael McDowell came with us on the second occasion – presumably as a chaperone, though he did contribute to the meetings and seemed genuinely committed to the process undertaken by us.

The meetings that we did hold were very courteous, but – as we expected – barriers were not immediately taken down. It was obvious that it would take time and many meetings to make tangible progress. The Unionist Party and Orange Order representatives told us that we were the first representatives of a political party from the Republic – or the Free State, as they called us – that they had ever met in this capacity.

When we met the Unionist Party representatives at their headquarters in Glengall Street, I noted that there were British soldiers with guns along the top of the buildings overlooking the street. I knew that they hadn't just come there because we were visiting – that these headquarters were a target for destruction by extremists on both sides of the divide. It helped to make us realise the enormity of the task that faced us, or anyone who attempted to cross that divide. In subsequent years, I developed huge admiration for John Hume and Seamus Mallon, who never gave up in their efforts to do so.

Subsequent to our meetings in Belfast, two members of our committee wanted more political intervention by Des O'Malley and more immediate action; however, I felt that the best way forward was on a more personal slow-burn approach, where it might be possible to generate some confidence among the leaders of these groups.

At the request of the committee, I agreed to meet Des O'Malley to discuss the current status and our strategy; accordingly, Stephen O'Byrnes arranged a lunch for me with him. Des was against our general plan – both the idea of personally intervening to support us, which didn't surprise me, and even the continuation of meeting contacts in these groups. He told me that I was naive to think our approach would make any difference.

I tried arguing with him but quickly realised that although Des had officially left Fianna Fáil, it was a matter of personality differences rather than policy; I believed that he wouldn't allow a deviation from the Fianna Fáil position on reunification of the thirty-two counties. As Kevin Boland had said a few years earlier, in somewhat similar circumstances, 'I didn't leave Fianna Fáil, Fianna Fáil left me.' I never doubted Des's moral courage in resigning from Fianna Fáil, and later in standing up to Haughey and Reynolds in relation to the Beef Tribunal, but these actions did not reflect any change in his general political views.

I called Stephen O'Byrnes, who I greatly respected, a few days later. I told him that I was resigning as a member and as chairman of the committee, as I didn't have time to fight with the party hierarchy and was fed up with their attitude. Accordingly, I suggested that he ask someone else to take over. I didn't tell Stephen that I had just been elected managing partner of Gerrard, Scallan & O'Brien – that I knew I was going to be too busy with that and all the other things that I had going on.

When, many years later, in 1998, the Good Friday Agreement was signed, I realised that it incorporated many of the ideas that we had proposed in 1986. I could only hope that our initial contacts with the unionist representatives had at least some minute role in the evolution in thinking on both sides of the border which allowed that agreement to be finalised.

RELIGION, PHILOSOPHY AND MY INVOLVEMENT

My parents were very strong in their beliefs regarding Roman Catholicism. They inculcated in me and in my siblings very traditional beliefs and practices, such as regular Sunday Mass, personal morning and evening prayers, nightly family rosaries (with their trimmings), and regular novenas, night benedictions and devotions in the church. As I said, I made my first communion in St John's church in 1956; St Gabriel's only opened later that year and became our more regular church from then on.

We were then encouraged by teachers in Belgrove National School – which was operated on a very strict Roman Catholic ethos – to become altar boys. At some stage around the age of 8 or 9, I enrolled for classes to train as an altar boy in St Gabriel's – as did some other boys my age from Seafield Avenue. In some ways, it was an adventure to cycle or walk over to St Gabriel's in the evening with my pals; it made me feel more grown-up than my siblings.

We had weekly classes to learn the responses and procedures. The responses were in Latin at that time, and there was no indication that that might ever change, so what we learned then was used for many years. I can still recall the introductory sentences and responses: '*Introibo ad altare dei*', the priest would start, and we would reply '*Ad Deum qui laetificat juventutem meam.*' The priest continued with a series of other prayers, and we had to be ready with the answer again in Latin. The training was sometimes quite difficult; it went on for some time before we were considered ready to serve Mass as the junior servers. There were sometimes four or six servers on the altar at the same time, but everyone had some duty to perform, however trivial.

I remember in particular Fr McKernan, who was very strict and demanding, both in the training and then when actually saying the Mass.

Fr McKernan was from County Tyrone, and his uncle had been the president of St Patrick's Academy Secondary School in Dungannon when my father was a student there. Two other priests who trained us at different stages, but who were easier to please, were Fr Kennedy and Fr Baker. All three seemed very old – but of course to 8- or 9-year-old boys, all adults seemed very old. On reflection, they were probably in their late twenties or early thirties. After the initial excitement of performing as if on a stage, I got bored with the process – particularly when I was rostered to serve at the 7.30 a.m. Mass. Nevertheless, I learned that by doing those difficult shifts diligently, I was more likely to be rostered to serve at a funeral Mass – or even better, a wedding Mass – as we got paid for those duties, and sometimes very handsomely. What added even more to the attraction was that I might also get an hour off school if the funeral or wedding was on a weekday – that was considered top prize for an altar boy.

When I went to St Paul's, I joined the altar society there and was sometimes rostered to serve Mass for one or other of the priests in their residence. The main benefit of that was getting a big fry for breakfast, which was not a regular treat at home during the week; so even though I didn't like getting up early, I did feel that it was well rewarded. As I indicated earlier, I was in some other religious societies in school, and was generally considered a good practising catholic – as, indeed, I considered myself.

It wasn't until I was about 16 years old that I had any doubts about the truth of what we had learned in religion class and what I had always assumed to be immutable. I had read about Darwin and his theory of evolution and raised it in a religious knowledge class discussion; I argued that it was more credible than the Bible story of the universe being created in seven days. The priest who was taking the class recommended the book *The Phenomenon of Man* by Pierre Teilhard de Chardin, a Jesuit palaeontologist. I read it with huge interest, as it opened my eyes to the possibility that all we had learned from the Bible, both Old and New Testaments, might not have any scientific basis.

I didn't change my beliefs immediately. I thought it might be possible to reconcile Darwin's theory of evolution and palaeontological discoveries with the story of creation as described in the Book of Genesis, as de Chardin had tried to do. I didn't spend too much time thinking about it, as I had too many other things to do and think about. I did have some doubts, however, and I put them to the back of my mind, finding it easier to go along with the conventional practices of school and family without further expressing my doubts.

That remained my position until I started in UCD. Then, as often happens, the exposure to new ideas, arguments, beliefs and people – and the cross-fertilization of those with new freedom – led me and many first year students to question customs, conventions and previously unquestioned beliefs. In addition to the usual student pub and cafe discussions, the fact that I was studying philosophy lent itself to more reflection and introspection, and ultimately intellectual rebellion.

By this time, I had also tried to reconcile Catholicism with socialism. This was much easier to do in relation to their respective theories – Jesus being suggested as the first socialist. Reconciling them in relation to their practice, however, was much harder. Socialism, as practised, was exemplified by Soviet Russia and its repressive regime; Catholicism, as practised, was exemplified by pomp, ceremony and incredible wealth concentrated in the Churches and in the royalty of different countries who were professedly Christian, if not also Catholic.

In reading history, and reading in general, I learned about the persecution of the early Christians by Romans and others. But I also learned of even worse persecution – more recently – by some Christians against other Christians whom they considered heretics. Other Christians, mainly Catholics, had also committed heinous deeds against indigenous natives in South America and elsewhere. Religious practice did not live up to the theory; at the time, I didn't conclude that the theory was wrong, but I did doubt it. The rigid type of Catholic practice that I was used to didn't make sense to me, and I gradually stopped observing its rituals. Nevertheless, even though I was in my twenties, I didn't say it to my parents.

More and more of the Catholic tenets made less and less sense to me: papal infallibility, immaculate conception, transubstantiation, the Roman Catholic Church being the only true Church, confession of sins to a priest and getting forgiveness from God, and indulgences (which were to relieve time in purgatory). Soon, I didn't accept their validity. I was probably what was described as agnostic at that stage. There was a Catholic Church teaching that if one attended Mass for nine consecutive first Fridays (of the month), the indulgences earned would ensure that when you died, you would go straight to heaven, avoiding hell and bypassing purgatory. I know that at some stage in my youth I believed that, but when I later thought about it, it seemed so ridiculous that it added to the undermining of my belief in any of the teachings.

The issue for me, then, was whether it was valid to remain a general believer without accepting many of the above – and, indeed, other beliefs, such as the right of the Pope to declare contraception as unlawful. It wasn't something that I worried too much about, as these beliefs weren't of significant importance in my life. I did sometimes go to Mass, but when it came to proclaiming belief in various tenets, as required in the Credo, I was selective and opted out of many, simply omitting them while declaring others.

My first test came in 1981, when I had to undergo emergency surgery after the accident in Royal Dublin Golf Club. While lying on a trolley outside the operating theatre awaiting surgery, I was approached by the Catholic chaplain. As I said earlier that gave me a serious fright, as I didn't think that I was so seriously injured that a chaplain would need to talk to me. He asked me if I was a Catholic – the first time in many years, and maybe the first time ever, that I had been asked that. Even though fairly frightened at this stage, I said, 'Jaysus no, but I used to be; I'm not sure now, but I don't consider myself as such.' When he asked me if I wished to receive the last sacrament, I decided that I should hedge my bets. I said to him that I supposed I had nothing to lose by getting it, just in case I was wrong in my recent rationalising – that all that was told to me when I was a child was actually true.

He was happy to proceed on that basis. I knew that I wasn't a good Catholic but now realised that I wasn't a very good atheist either. I wouldn't have been a great martyr for atheism if I had lived during the Spanish Inquisition or during similar periods of religious intolerance and fanaticism.

It was either as a result of that episode or my wife Mary's influence, or maybe a combination of both, that I decided not to impose my negative views about religion as our children grew up. For this reason, I didn't stand in the way of Mary getting them to practise the Catholic religion. For me, however, it was a mild version: Mass on most Sundays, but no rosaries, benedictions or other related activities. I practised with them at least up to the stage when they could make up their own minds, but I didn't allow them to think that I accepted everything that was being preached or taught, and I largely only went along with the ceremonial aspects of the religion without trying to indoctrinate them.

When Shane was about 10 years old, we wanted to take him out of Sutton Park Junior School, as we had little regard for it by then, and he had less. We considered sending him to Belvedere College, which had a junior school at that stage; he had passed whatever tests they had set him, and we were asked to an interview as the parents. Shane wasn't admitted to Belvedere, because they weren't very impressed with my views on religion, but Mary maintains that it was because they weren't impressed with the fact that she started interviewing them as opposed to the other way around. In any event, Shane went to St Fintan's National School and then to St Michael's College; his subsequent education, up to and including PhD level, doesn't seem to have suffered by our failing the parents' interview. Shane also became an altar boy in St Fintan's church in Sutton for a couple of years. A few years later, the story of the curate, Fr Ivan Payne, and his sexual predations on altar boys became public. Many of Shane's altar boy colleagues were interviewed by the Gardaí to learn if they had experienced or seen any such behaviour. Shane wasn't asked to talk to the police, and thankfully he hadn't had any bad experience, but as he said to us, 'I'm sure you're glad now that I wasn't a nice, quiet little boy that Payne might have attacked.'

The scale and extent of abuse by individual priest predators and the level of involvement of the Church authorities – up to archbishops and even higher – in collusion and cover-up was unimaginable then, but it has obviously been highlighted since and, indeed, is still being uncovered. My poor mother, who had stuck steadfastly to her religious beliefs and practices, found it very difficult to reconcile these nefarious activities with her understanding of the Church and its teachings. Her faith was rocked to its foundations, but she stuck with her own version and was happy to continue practising in her own way. My father died a long time before these revelations, and I'm not sure how he would have reacted. For me, it was merely further proof that the Church was built on foundations of sand – that there was nothing behind it other than human greed, power and domination of innocent, uncritical people. It wasn't any different to any other secular, corrupt empire.

For many years I have realised the truth of what I had been told by some religious teachers and preachers: that without faith, you can't accept and understand the mysteries, as they were called. If you don't have faith, they don't make sense, and the entire becomes a form of primitive witchcraft and magic. Somebody, maybe Jonathan Swift, wrote at one time that you can't reason a person out of a position that they couldn't reason themselves into in the first place. That sums up my position on religious discussion now.

I avoid arguments about religion and the existence of God, because if you have faith, you accept what is taught, but if you don't have faith, you can't accept it. I haven't had faith in what the Roman Catholic Church teaches for very many years, nor do I have any faith in any other religion. I don't see any real difference between Christianity, in any of its multitude of forms, and Islam, Judaism, Buddhism, Hinduism – in my opinion, they are all merely a system of crutch to try to help humans accept the difficulties and apparent cruelties of life, and to try to understand the universe. To facilitate this crutch system, all of these religions rely on some form of God or supreme person.

My position is that I don't believe that the human being is the highest level of being that evolution will produce; rather, earth is merely one small part of the universe. Whether evolution produces a higher level of being on earth, or whether there is or will be a higher level of being elsewhere in the universe, I don't know. But when one looks at the development so far, from the single cell to the complicated being that is the human, I can't see that evolution has ceased and that we are the ultimate level of development.

Whether there is or isn't an external force, a supreme being, I can't see how it would have any similarity to any of the human-form gods that the present religions worship. It may well be that it is a natural desire for the human being to look for explanations for existence – that this desire has resulted in the development of various religions which in turn exploit this desire. But that doesn't prove anything other than that any human weakness will be exploited by some other humans. It is my firm opinion that man created God rather than, as religion teaches, that God created man.

I think that I am, and have been for many years, a real atheist. I don't deny the right of any others to have different beliefs, so long as they don't deny me my right. There are natural laws, which I believe are humanist. Religions have claimed these as part of their own; indeed, some have claimed to have found or invented them. But as the basic ones are common to all religions and indeed to primitive pre-religion societies, it indicates to me that they are part of the human condition rather than religious or God-given.

The second great commandment in Christianity, 'You should love your neighbour as yourself', is for me the number one commandment or basic law; the first commandment, 'You must love the Lord, your God', is merely self-serving and designed to continue the exploitation of humans by those who control the religions. It is akin to the secular commandment of royalty: 'to honour and obey your king'.

Humans should be courageous enough to live without the crutch of religion, but if they can't do so, they should allow those who can to do so, abiding by their second commandment. I hope that I have lived by this philosophy since the time that I first understood and accepted it, and that I can do so in future.

I have no doubt, from my understanding of history and current affairs, that my generation – that is, those born between 1945 and 1965 in Western Europe – have been the luckiest generation that have ever lived on earth. The personal freedom that we have enjoyed – benefit of property inflation, cheap travel, choice of leisure activities, availability of contraception, free or cheap education, lack of war, advances in medicine and science, and freedom of thought and expression (including with regard to religion) – have made life for most of us relatively easy, and almost incomparable with the life of the ordinary person of previous generations.

I sometimes wonder about the randomness of life: of birth, upbringing and education, and how my entire life might have been very different if some minor detail had been different in my early life. I suppose that this is an aspect of the 'butterfly effect', which effectively provides that a small change can make much bigger changes happen; one small incident can have a big impact on the future. If a butterfly flaps its wings slowly in Tokyo and a tornado occurs in Tennessee, is there a cause and effect? If the same butterfly flaps its wings fast instead of slow, might the tornado occur in Hawaii instead? The theory started with weather forecasting, but the term is now used for many things – some are scientific and some are not.

Chaos theory is part of mathematics and looks at systems that are very sensitive. It is a mathematical theory that can be used to explain complex systems, such as weather, astronomy, politics and economics. Although many complex systems appear to behave in a random manner, chaos theory holds that in reality, there is an underlying order that is merely difficult to see.

Can chaos theory explain all of life? Is what I consider to be 'luck', in my doing or not doing something, merely a good random outcome? Or in reality, is it part of a complex mathematical system that awaits explanation perhaps many millennia in the future? If so, maybe there is an external force governing everything that happens in the universe. But I still can't accept that force as any kind of deity, and definitely not as the personal God that religions claim. Indeed, such a force would be contrary to the free will that Christianity attributes to humans.

While I find the 'complex mathematical system' explanation comforting in some ways – for instance, it would mean that one cannot make a mistake; what may seem a mistake is actually compliant with the preordained complex mathematical system – I'm more inclined to accept the randomness of life, sometimes giving a good outcome and sometimes not.

One of the major global issues in recent times is climate change. All the evidence indicates that the climate on earth is changing, and changing rapidly. The extent to which such change is caused by human activity is, however, debatable. I don't deny that human activity such as the burning of fossil fuels, and the excessive use and misuse of plastics and other byproducts of fossil fuels, causes serious damage to our environment and oceans, but I believe it is arrogant of humans to believe that they can cause climate change themselves. I believe that we can do much to improve our environment but little to affect climate change.

It seems to be forgotten that climate on earth has changed radically on many occasions prior to the existence of humans – perhaps it has been continually changing since the beginning of earth's existence, and perhaps it is on a loop and we will soon revert to the climate that existed millions of years ago. I believe that climate is governed, to a greater extent, by the earth's position in the universe relative to the sun and other planets – and what is happening to these celestial bodies – rather than what we can or can't do ourselves. That is not to argue that we should be allowed to damage our immediate environment with the uncontrolled discharge and dumping of dangerous materials that we have manufactured, whether nuclear waste or asbestos or plastics or by uncontrolled destruction of forests and woodlands. Rather, that there is a greater force than human activity which will ultimately determine whether we are close to another ice age or a desertification of all continents and, consequently, the possible extinction of humans.

Is that force predetermined or is it purely random? I don't know the answer to that, but I do know that it will happen whether I or billions like me worry about it or not. So I don't worry, and therefore am happy to rely on that second commandment that I learned as a child: 'love thy neighbour as thyself.' Or as I understand it, don't do harm to others. For various reasons, whether through poverty, disability, oppression or weakness, not everybody can love others, and not everyone can do good, but for me the critical thing is not to do harm to those other humans living on earth and not to do harm to the earth on which we live. If I can pass that principle on to my descendants – Shane, Louisa, Sinéad, Josh, Lexi, Cody, Charlie and Éabha – I think my life will have had meaning.

Having written all the above, I have to qualify it by adding that they are my opinions and beliefs, and I know that I might be wrong. I'm reminded of something my eldest grandson, Josh, said to me on one occasion when he was 6 or 7. He was in Dublin, on vacation from Sydney, and I was driving him home from some event or meeting. We were having a discussion, or perhaps an argument, about what cottage pie consisted of. Neither of us gave an inch, and eventually Josh politely asked me if I knew that old people aren't always right. I don't know whether it was a moment of enlightenment on his part or perhaps an expression of his disappointment at the crumbling of his reliance on the knowledge of older people.

I disarmed him by admitting that I did know that. But before he could answer, I added that young people aren't always right either. He muttered something, but I didn't ask him to repeat what he had said. He was correct in this instance, of course, as I checked with Mary afterwards about the cottage pie. I could have continued the argument and pointed out to him that there are many situations where there isn't a simple right or wrong – that cottage pie can be made with different ingredients and that we could both be right – but I refrained from delving into that.

In fact, my belief is that there are few absolute truths in our world. Even what initially seem to be mathematical certainties and immutable laws of physics may be proved otherwise by later generations of human being, or by an advanced form of the species, whatever that may be.

So, having described my life and some of the influences on it, how do I describe myself. No doubt I have opinions on many issues and am not slow to give my point of view if I think it appropriate. I'm quiet but not shy. I'm not good at small talk, not good at sales talk, and I have a poor memory, so while I love to listen to a good raconteur, I'm very poor at remembering and retelling a story myself. I conform to social and business norms when it suits me, but when it doesn't I'm sufficiently self-confident to break with convention. I'm independent-minded and have no respect for groupthink, so I speak directly and am sometimes deliberately provocative. I'm not afraid to challenge a consensus, and I'm arrogant enough not to care whether others agree with me or not. I'm often introspective, so while I enjoy the company of others, I can survive without it. I suppose that my biggest failing or weakness is my lack of patience, particularly with those who are slower or even more incompetent at taking care of something than I am myself. I don't think that I was ever patient from the time that I was young, but hopefully, given sufficient time, I can improve that in old age.

One of my pet hates is hypocrisy, particularly by those with some level of authority, real or apparent, who advise or command something for others and at the same time ignore it for themselves. I have zero respect for those few who project themselves as good Irishmen but deliberately avoid Irish tax. They use a tax loophole that allows them to nominally reside in a jurisdiction where they pay their tax at a ridiculously low rate, but then decide themselves how much they will 'donate' to Irish charities and organisations, and thereby gain public credibility for themselves. The difference between tax evasion and tax avoidance is comparable to the difference between fraud and sharp practice, or between embezzlement and what Fr Ted described as 'the money was only resting in the account.'

Wasting time when I'm trying to do something specific is another of my pet hates, and always was; I have no difficulty with being idle or lazy – and probably only realised how lazy I inherently am after I retired from all work and committees a few years ago – but that is different. On one occasion when I was in my late fifties, I was stuck in a traffic jam while commuting to my office and worked out a calculation. I thought to myself that on average I was likely to have at best another twenty-five years of life. That amounted to 9,130 days, allowing for some leap years; that was 219,120 hours, or 13,147,200 minutes. I thought to myself, if I have only 13,147,200 minutes to live, how many of those would I be willing to waste stuck in a traffic jam going to and from the office, and going to and from meetings from the office? My answer to myself: very few. This was one of the occasions when I thought that I should retire from full-time work as early as possible, confirming what I had been considering for some time.

Covid 19 has dominated the lives of most of us since the beginning of 2020. Again, I consider myself lucky insofar as it has not had a major adverse impact on me or my family, although it may be some time before it is clear what effect it has had on young children from a social and developmental point of view. Its first immediate impact on Mary and me was our having to cancel a planned trip with two other couples to Vietnam and Cambodia, which had been scheduled for March 2020. I adapted well to the cocooning, which was imposed on my age group for the first few months of the Covid restrictions. I am very conscious, however, that not everybody had a big garden in which to isolate, and not everybody had the other facilities that I enjoyed and which made life very tolerable for me.

I did think that the cocooning and subsequent restrictions on our normal life would change the pace at which we all live our lives – and that when we resumed some level of normality, that life would be slower and not as busy or hectic as it had become prior to 2020. However, I now realise that that is very unlikely; that as soon as we can, we will live life at full pace again. In my own case, at the end of September and early October 2021, I was nearly back to, and may well have surpassed, the levels of activity that prevailed before Covid 19 struck. In one short period, I played a golf match in Dún Laoghaire Golf Club near Enniskerry, County Wicklow, then drove to Portrush in County Derry on the following morning to play a match at Royal Portrush Golf Club, driving home on the following day. Later that day I drove to Newcastle in County Down to play a match in Royal County Down Golf Club early on the following morning. I returned to Dublin later that day and got ready to travel with a friend to Killarney, County Kerry on the following day. I then played matches on successive days in Waterville Golf Club, Ballybunion Golf Club and Tralee Golf Club, before returning home on the next day; the following day, I travelled with Mary to our holiday home at Cap de Nice in the south of France. There I went back to doing nothing other than a little sea swimming and some walking trips, but I realised how easily I could be moved out of what had become my normal, slow pace of life.

What has been reinforced for me is that life is short and time is precious; perfection is the enemy of lots of things, and we rely on friends and family more than we think we do. Hopefully, we will all learn from our experiences during the Covid pandemic, and treat our doctors and frontline healthcare workers with the respect and rewards that they deserve, but which are denied them by our bureaucrats and politicians. There is nothing more certain than that we will need them again.

BIBLIOGRAPHICAL REFERENCES

PAPERS

Glackin, John A., Chestvale Properties Limited and Hoddle Investments Limited: Interim Report (Dublin: Stationery Office, 1992).

Glackin, John A., Chestvale Properties Limited and Hoddle Investments Limited: Final Report (Dublin: Stationery Office, 1993).

Progressive Democrats Policy Discussion Papers First National Conference 24–25 May 1986.

Proceedings of the New Ireland Forum, 1983–1984.

Law, Edward J., *The Enterprises of the Sharkey Sisters, Strokestown, and Their Persecution during the War of Independence* (Local History Review, 2013).

BOOKS

Currie, Austin, *All Hell Will Break Loose* (Dublin: O'Brien Press, 2004).

Gogarty, Claire, *From Village to Suburb: The Building of Clontarf since 1760* (Dublin: Clontarf Books, 2013).

Kelly, J.M., *Fundamental Rights in the Irish Law and Constitution*, 2nd ed. (Dublin: Allen Figgis & Co., 1967).

Lennon, Colm, *Clontarf – Irish Historic Towns Atlas: Dublin Suburbs, No. 1* (Dublin: Royal Irish Academy, 2018).

McBrierty, Vincent J., *The Howth Peninsula: Its History, Lore and Legend* (Dublin: North Dublin Round Table, 1981).

McCague, Eugene, *Arthur Cox 1891–1965* (Dublin: Gill and Macmillan, 1994)

Sharkey, P.A., *The Heart of Ireland* (M.J. Ward, 1927).

Short, Constance and Anthony Carroll (eds), *Eddie's Own Aquarius* (Cahermee Publications, 2005).

NEWSPAPERS

Asian Sentinel
Evening Press
Irish Times
Irish Independent
Paris Match Edition
Strokestown Democrat
Sunday Independent